Fiction/Non-Fiction

http://collections.ic.gc.ca/naismith

Dr. James Naismith

Fiction/Non-Fiction

A READER AND RHETORIC

Garry Engkent

Lucia Engkent

THOMSON

NELSON

Copyright © 2001 by Nelson, a division of Thomson Canada Limited.

For more information contact
Nelson, 1120 Birchmount Road, Scarborough, Ontario, M1K 5G4.
Or you can visit our Internet site at http://www.nelson.com

ALL RIGHTS RESERVED. No part of this work covered by the copyright hereon may be reproduced, transcribed, or used in any form or by any means—graphic, electronic, or mechanical, including photocopying, recording, taping, Web distribution or information storage and retrieval systems—without the written permission of the publisher.

For permission to use material from this text or product, contact us by
Tel 1-800-730-2214
Fax 1-800-730-2215
www.thomsonrights.com

Every effort has been made to trace ownership of all copyrighted material and to secure permission from copyright holders. In the event of any question arising as to the use of any material, we will be pleased to make the necessary corrections in future printings.

Canadian Cataloguing in Publication Data

Engkent, Garry, 1948–
Fiction/non-fiction : a reader and rhetoric

Includes index.
ISBN 0-7747-3714-X

1. College readers. 2. English language – Rhetoric. I. Engkent, Lucia Pietrusiak, 1955– . II. Title.

PE1417.E53   2001   808'.0427   C00-932261-2

Acquisitions Editor: Anne Williams
Senior Developmental Editor: Martina van de Velde
Production Editors: Linh Vu and Emily Ferguson
Production Coordinator: Cheri Westra
Copy Editor: James Leahy
Permissions Editor: Cindy Howard
Cover Design: Sonya V. Thursby, Opus House Incorporated
Interior Design: Christine Gambin
Typesetting and Assembly: Christine Gambin
Printing and Binding: Transcontinental Printing Inc.

Cover Art: *25th February* by P.J. Crook. Acrylic on canvas © 1998. Reprinted by permission of the artist and Nancy Poole's Studio Ltd.

This book was printed in Canada.

3 4 5   05 04 03 02

Preface

Fiction /Non-Fiction: A Reader and Rhetoric is designed to meet the needs of students in college-level reading and writing courses.

The text is divided into three parts: The first is a selection of short stories, the second has essays and articles, and the third is a brief overview of essay writing, with discussions of structure and language use. The two reading sections are introduced with an explanation of readings skills. Each reading is accompanied by explanatory notes, comprehension and discussion questions, explanation of literary techniques, and suggestions for writing assignments.

Including both fiction and non-fiction has many advantages. It expands the students' reading diet, opening up the world of imagination, ideas, and thought. It addresses the need of college students to explore themes in literature. It offers variety and flexibility to the instructor in theme, subject matter, and context for class discussions. For instance, the same topic can be explored in both fiction and non-fiction.

The selection of stories offers variety in length, theme, and complexity. Some stories are simple and amusing; others are thought-provoking and symbolic. Most of the selections are Canadian. Some are classic short stories that instructors will be familiar with, and some introduce relatively unknown writers. Instructors can choose stories to suit the needs, interests, and level of the class.

The essays also offer variety. Many are taken from magazines and newspapers; these include columns, op-ed (opinion-editorial) pieces, and personal essays. A few are excerpts from books. Different writing strategies, such as argumentation, process, definition, and compare/contrast, are presented. In addition, the readings explore current topics of interest, such as technology and society.

Keeping in mind that some students may have English as a second language, we have included notes to explain aspects of language and culture. For example, we explain the names of characters and what they signify. We also explain references and put articles and stories in context. However, we do not give vocabulary notes for words that are easily found in a dictionary.

Comprehension and discussion questions are grouped together in one section. They begin with content questions and move toward broader discussion questions and topics. In the content questions, we generally follow the sequence and logic of the article or the short story. The later questions open up the discussion to students' interpretations and opinions.

In the literary techniques section, we focus on the strategies used by the writers. These range from the use of symbolism to the organization of an essay.

The assignment questions are broad and open-ended so that instructors can further define what they expect the students to do, tailoring the work to course requirements. For example, a question posed in the assignment section could be written up as a short paragraph or as an essay. We have focused on academic writing, since that is what most courses require. However, instructors can easily take the suggested topics and require students to write a letter or a dialogue. A suggestion to seek further information could be followed up by a written or oral report. Instructors can also determine the length and detail of the work to be submitted. In addition, we have made links to other stories and articles so that comparisons can be made. Because some instructors like to show videos and films of stories, we have mentioned whether a film version exists. We have included only minimal biographical information about the writers; however, students could be assigned the task of researching the authors.

The writing section is a short review and reminder; it is not a comprehensive treatment of essay writing and grammar. We assume that students have learned the basics of writing five-paragraph essays and of doing research. The book has a short review of some common writing problems but does not offer grammar exercises. The students are expected to work on their writing skills as they write essays.

Because the rhetoric section is meant to be dipped into as needed, there is some overlap and repetition of points. We do not expect students to proceed through the chapters in order. Instructors can direct students to whatever sections they need.

ACKNOWLEDGEMENTS

We would like to thank the staff and students at Seneca College, especially Rob Colter, Maureen Lennon, Veronica Abbass, and Joyce Hall.

The reviewers gave helpful comments and suggestions: Jim Streeter, Seneca College; Kent Lewis, Capilano College; and Elizabeth Steig, Centennial College.

Thanks also to the hard-working and talented staff at Harcourt, especially Anne Williams, Kent Newell, Martina van de Velde, James Leahy, Susan Harrison, Linh Vu, and Emily Ferguson.

And finally, a thank-you to our children, David, Susan, and Emily, who read stories, gave their opinions, and occasionally let us use the computer.

A NOTE FROM THE PUBLISHER

Thank you for selecting *Fiction/Non-Fiction: A Reader and Rhetoric* by Garry Engkent and Lucia Engkent. The authors and publisher have devoted considerable time and care to the development of this book. We appreciate your recognition of this effort and accomplishment.

Contents

PART ONE: READING FICTION
Reading Fiction   3
The Fox and the Grapes, a fable by Aesop   19
A Girl's Story, David Arnason   22
The Fun They Had, Isaac Asimov   30
Greasy Lake, T. Coraghessan Boyle   35
All the Years of Her Life, Morley Callaghan   47
Mr. Truepenny's Book Emporium and Gallery, Charles De Lint   54
Chickens for Christmas, Garry Engkent   63
The Cowherd, a Chinese folktale, retold by Garry Engkent   73
The Immaculate Conception Photography Gallery, Katherine Govier   76
We So Seldom Look on Love, Barbara Gowdy   86
So What Are You, Anyway? Lawrence Hill   99
The Lottery, Shirley Jackson   105
The Monkey's Paw, W.W. Jacobs   116
The Loons, Margaret Laurence   128
How We Kept Mother's Day, Stephen Leacock   140
My Financial Career, Stephen Leacock   145
The Prodigal Son, Luke 15:11–32   150
An Ounce of Cure, Alice Munro   153
One Rejection Too Many, Patricia Nurse   165
The Man I Killed, Tim O'Brien   170
The Cask of Amontillado, Edgar Allan Poe   177
The Open Window, Saki (H.H. Munro)   186
Red Plaid Shirt, Diane Schoemperlen   191
Ralphie at the Races, Sam Selvon   205
The Use of Force, William Carlos Williams   216

PART TWO: READING NON-FICTION
Reading Non-Fiction   225
Grey Owl's Magnificent Masquerade, John Barber   232
Truth and Consequences, Brian Bethune   236
Toothpaste, David Bodanis   241
Junk Food Heaven, Bill Bryson   245

Growing Up on Grace, Rosie DiManno   250
The Golden Years of Electronic Helps, Fred Donnelly   258
The Patterns of Eating, Peter Farb and George Armelagos   262
Don't You Think It's Time to Start Thinking? Northrop Frye   268
The Joys of Keeping in Touch, Virtually, Charles Gordon   272
Don't Say Cheese! Shinan Govani   276
Canadian Tire Money, Wayne Grady   280
What Is an Idea? Marshall W. Gregory and Wayne C. Booth   283
Of Weirdos and Eccentrics, Pico Iyer   289
Our Father Who Art in Classrooms: No, Keith Knight   294
Our Father Who Art in Classrooms: Yes, Raheel Raza   296
The Story of Service, Jessica Mitford   301
Shooting an Elephant, George Orwell   314
Have Wheels, Will Go A-Wooing, Kurt Preinsperg   322
I'll Decide What's Broken, Spider Robinson   326
The Story of Grey Owl, Colin Ross   330
Exiled in Paradise, Ellen Singer (pseudonym)   337
Possessed by Stuff, Lynn Van der Water   345
Am I Blue? Alice Walker   349
The End of Manual Labour, Margaret Wente   355
Rediscovering Christmas, Almas Zakiuddin   359

PART THREE: WRITING ESSAYS
Chapter 1 The Writing Process   367
Chapter 2 The Principles of Good Writing   375
Chapter 3 The Essay   383
Chapter 4 Types of Essays   389
Chapter 5 Research   399
Chapter 6 Documentation   411
Chapter 7 Trouble Spots   430
Chapter 8 Common Grammar Problems   440

Credits   453
Index of Authors and Titles   457
Subject Index   459

Thematic Contents

ABORIGINAL PEOPLE
Grey Owl's Magnificent Masquerade, John Barber   232
Truth and Consequences, Brian Bethune   236
The Loons, Margaret Laurence   128
The Story of Grey Owl, Colin Ross   330

ANIMALS
The Fox and the Grapes, a fable by Aesop   19
Chickens for Christmas, Garry Engkent   63
The Cowherd, a Chinese folktale, retold by Garry Engkent   73
The Loons, Margaret Laurence   128
The Prodigal Son, Luke 15:11–32   150
Shooting an Elephant, George Orwell   314
The Open Window, Saki (H.H. Munro)   186
Ralphie at the Races, Sam Selvon   205
Am I Blue? Alice Walker   349

AUTOMOBILES
Greasy Lake, T. Coraghessan Boyle   35
How We Kept Mother's Day, Stephen Leacock   140
Have Wheels, Will Go A-Wooing, Kurt Preinsperg   322

BEHAVIOURAL STUDIES
The Fox and the Grapes, a fable by Aesop   19
The Cowherd, a Chinese folktale, retold by Garry Engkent   73
We So Seldom Look on Love, Barbara Gowdy   86
Of Weirdos and Eccentrics, Pico Iyer   289
The Lottery, Shirley Jackson   105
The Monkey's Paw, W.W. Jacobs   116
How We Kept Mother's Day, Stephen Leacock   140
My Financial Career, Stephen Leacock   145
The Prodigal Son, Luke 15:11–32   150
Shooting an Elephant, George Orwell   314

Possessed by Stuff, Lynn Van der Water   345
Am I Blue? Alice Walker   349

CHRISTMAS
Chickens for Christmas, Garry Engkent   63
Rediscovering Christmas, Almas Zakiuddin   359

CREATIVE WRITING
A Girl's Story, David Arnason   22
Mr. Truepenny's Book Emporium and Gallery, Charles De Lint   54
One Rejection Too Many, Patricia Nurse   165

DEATH
The Cowherd, a Chinese folktale, retold by Garry Engkent   73
We So Seldom Look on Love, Barbara Gowdy   86
The Lottery, Shirley Jackson   105
The Monkey's Paw, W.W. Jacobs   116
The Loons, Margaret Laurence   128
The Story of Service, Jessica Mitford   301
The Man I Killed, Tim O'Brien   170
The Cask of Amontillado, Edgar Allan Poe   177
Red Plaid Shirt, Diane Schoemperlen   191

FABLES, FOLKTALES, AND PARABLES
The Fox and the Grapes, a fable by Aesop   19
The Cowherd, a Chinese folktale, retold by Garry Engkent   73
The Prodigal Son, Luke 15:11–32   150

FAMILY
All the Years of Her Life, Morley Callaghan   47
Growing Up on Grace, Rosie DiManno   250
Chickens for Christmas, Garry Engkent   63
The Cowherd, a Chinese folktale, retold by Garry Engkent   73
The Immaculate Conception Photography Gallery, Katherine Govier   76
So What Are You, Anyway? Lawrence Hill   99
The Lottery, Shirley Jackson   105
The Loons, Margaret Laurence   128
How We Kept Mother's Day, Stephen Leacock   140
The Prodigal Son, Luke 15:11–32   150

An Ounce of Cure, Alice Munro   153
The Use of Force, William Carlos Williams   216

FOOD
Junk Food Heaven, Bill Bryson   245
Chickens for Christmas, Garry Engkent   63
The Patterns of Eating, Peter Farb and George Armelagos   262
How We Kept Mother's Day, Stephen Leacock   140
Red Plaid Shirt, Diane Schoemperlen   191

GREY OWL
Grey Owl's Magnificent Masquerade, John Barber   232
Truth and Consequences, Brian Bethune   236
The Story of Grey Owl, Colin Ross   330

GROWING UP
Greasy Lake, T. Coraghessan Boyle   35
All the Years of Her Life, Morley Callaghan   47
Growing Up on Grace, Rosie DiManno   250
The Cowherd, a Chinese folktale, retold by Garry Engkent   73
The Loons, Margaret Laurence   128
The Prodigal Son, Luke 15:11–32   150
An Ounce of Cure, Alice Munro   153

HORROR
The Lottery, Shirley Jackson   105
The Monkey's Paw, W.W. Jacobs   116
The Cask of Amontillado, Edgar Allan Poe   177
The Open Window, Saki (H.H. Munro)   186

HUMOUR
Greasy Lake, T. Coraghessan Boyle   35
Junk Food Heaven, Bill Bryson   245
Chickens for Christmas, Garry Engkent   63
How We Kept Mother's Day, Stephen Leacock   140
My Financial Career, Stephen Leacock   145
One Rejection Too Many, Patricia Nurse   165
The Open Window, Saki (H.H. Munro)   186

IDEAS
Don't You Think It's Time to Start Thinking? Northrop Frye   268
What Is an Idea? Marshall W. Gregory and Wayne C. Booth   283

IMMIGRANT EXPERIENCE
Growing Up on Grace, Rosie DiManno   250
Chickens for Christmas, Garry Engkent   63
The Immaculate Conception Photography Gallery, Katherine Govier   76
So What Are You, Anyway? Lawrence Hill   99
One Rejection Too Many, Patricia Nurse   165
Our Father Who Art in Classrooms: Yes, Raheel Raza   296
Ralphie at the Races, Sam Selvon   205
Rediscovering Christmas, Almas Zakiuddin   359

MALE-FEMALE RELATIONSHIPS
A Girl's Story, David Arnason   22
Greasy Lake, T. Coraghessan Boyle   35
The Immaculate Conception Photography Gallery, Katherine Govier   76
We So Seldom Look on Love, Barbara Gowdy   86
An Ounce of Cure, Alice Munro   153
One Rejection Too Many, Patricia Nurse   165
Have Wheels, Will Go A-Wooing, Kurt Preinsperg   322
Red Plaid Shirt, Diane Schoemperlen   191
Exiled in Paradise, Ellen Singer (pseudonym)   337

PHOTOGRAPHY
Don't Say Cheese! Shinan Govani   276
The Immaculate Conception Photography Gallery, Katherine Govier   76

RELIGION
Chickens for Christmas, Garry Engkent   63
Our Father Who Art in Classrooms: No, Keith Knight   294
Our Father Who Art in Classrooms: Yes, Raheel Raza   296
The Prodigal Son, Luke 15:11-32   150
Rediscovering Christmas, Almas Zakiuddin   359

TECHNOLOGY
The Fun They Had, Isaac Asimov   30
Toothpaste, David Bodanis   241
The Golden Years of Electronic Helps, Fred Donnelly   258
The Joys of Keeping in Touch, Virtually, Charles Gordon   272
Don't Say Cheese! Shinan Govani   276
The Immaculate Conception Photography Gallery, Katherine Govier   76
Have Wheels, Will Go A-Wooing, Kurt Preinsperg   322
I'll Decide What's Broken, Spider Robinson   326
The End of Manual Labour, Margaret Wente   355

THINGS

Toothpaste, David Bodanis   241
The Golden Years of Electronic Helps, Fred Donnelly   258
Canadian Tire Money, Wayne Grady   280
Have Wheels, Will Go A-Wooing, Kurt Preinsperg   322
Red Plaid Shirt, Diane Schoemperlen   191
Possessed by Stuff, Lynn Van der Water   345

PART ONE
READING FICTION

READING FICTION

INTRODUCTION

"Fiction" means a made-up story. Synonyms for fiction include "not true," "not real," "not existing." The characters and the action exist only in the writer's imagination. The story may be based on real events, but it is, on the whole, a fabrication. Fiction includes novels and short stories. "Literature" is a word we use to describe the best of fiction, works that display the beauty of language, that show artistry, and that engage readers' feelings. One of the main activities of English courses is reading and analyzing literature.

Some people question the value of reading fiction: Why read made-up stories? It's better to read about things that are "real." However, fiction can take us to places that we will never see and even to places that do not exist. We can visit other times and meet people who will never physically cross our paths. While the laws of physics bind reality, no such rules govern the imagination.

Reading fiction is an important intellectual activity. On one level, it is exercise for the brain. It requires readers to understand what is going on, to follow a story line, to understand what is done and why it is done, to imagine people and places, and to sympathize with characters. It draws on experience and knowledge. It makes us think.

Furthermore, reading fiction is good therapy. It can help us understand how other people feel. It can show us that we are not alone in our fears and our problems. Conversely, it brings us joy, wonder, and compassion. Made-up lives can affect us profoundly — making us cry, laugh, or sigh. Reading fiction makes us feel.

The value of literature is far-reaching. A society without its stories lacks spirit, soul, hope, because stories tell of a people: who they are, what they believe in, how they solve problems, how they live, what their dreams are. Literature then is sharing individual and collective realities, sorrows and aspirations, fears and philosophies. To the readers of these stories, literature broadens their horizons.

Sometimes, the dividing line between fiction and non-fiction is not so distinct. Some non-fiction articles step into the domain of imagination; and some fictional stories enter the realm of reality. For instance, a journalist may create a composite character to cover identities in a piece on prostitution. Docudramas on television re-create events based on what could have happened. Novels can be based on real events and can speculate on the lives of real people. However, the line between fiction and non-fiction is still valid. Just as libraries categorize their books into fiction and non-fiction, we have used this distinction in this text.

SHORT STORIES

A short story is a piece of literature that ranges from 100 to 10 000 words. It has all the elements of the novel, such as plot, character, and conflict. It tells a story. For the writer, it is a difficult art form to master. For the reader, it is a quick read, a dip into another world. However, such a general definition may do short fiction an injustice.

All short stories are imaginary. When we read a story, we enter the world created by the writer. For example, Sophie Etoile in De Lint's "Mr. Truepenny's Book Emporium and Gallery" makes up a whole world in her daydreams; so does a story writer. The setting may have some familiar basis in reality, such as the city of Winnipeg, or the same culture as the real world. However, the events and characters never existed. They have no foundation in reality. Yet we as readers are often caught up in the fictional world, and in the characters' plights and lives.

All stories tell a truth, or two. They reveal something about the human condition, the human soul, the human being. For example, "The Fox and the Grapes" shows us that people are apt to rationalize away things they cannot have, even though the story is not ostensibly about people at all. As individuals, we want to know more about other people and ourselves. We want to know what makes someone tick. In "An Ounce of Cure," we see how infatuation can lead a teenaged girl to irrational deeds. Seeing what happens to fictional people, we understand what makes us do, say, or feel certain things. We need to know we share in the well of human experience: the emotions, the passions, the thoughts, and the actions. A good story often gives us a glimpse of reality, truth, a fact of life.

All stories aim to entertain. As social beings, we need to be amused. A good story can let us live a life vicariously through the characters. We can identify with the family that tries to give the mother the best Mother's Day in Leacock's "How We Kept Mother's Day." A good story lets us escape from the drudgery of everyday routine. For when we start reading a story, we willingly suspend our disbelief that the world we enter is only a fabrication of the writer's creative mind. If the tale is well told, we have been more than entertained.

Sometimes a story also teaches us about other cultures, other races, other ways of living, other ways of thinking and believing, other times. We learn about the commonality of being human or about the differences that divide us. For example, in "The Man I Killed," Tim O'Brien not only gives life to the dead but also shows how people — cultures and distances apart — share the same goals. Often, fiction can do all this better than a text on sociology, politics, history, or anthropology. We may not know as many facts and statistics from fiction, but we comprehend facets of the human soul. And for those of us who prefer a pragmatic purpose to reading fiction, we can use both understanding and knowledge in our dealings with relatives, friends, neighbours, co-workers, and strangers.

Such is the role of fiction. Short stories entertain us, educate us, and expand our horizons and our imagination. They are, indeed, worth reading.

ELEMENTS OF FICTION

Once you have read, and hopefully enjoyed, the story, it's time to talk about it. To do this you need to know some literary terminology, the tools of the trade. If you want to discuss computers, you have to learn words such as bytes, interface, RAM, ROM, and motherboard. If you are going into nursing, you would need to know terms such as IV, CPR, and Code Blue. Similarly, then, in the study of literature, you should know the common terms used in texts and by instructors.

The elements we have defined below are not meant to be a complete listing, just commonly used terms of reference. Moreover, we lean toward giving basic meanings rather than engaging in literary theories and criticisms.

PLOT

It has been said that there are only three categories of plot: man against man, man against nature, and man against himself. And then there are stories without a plot. Dramatic situations are classified as part of plot: boy meets girl, a character makes an unpleasant choice, or a protagonist braves a storm.

Plot is conflict. Without conflict, there is no suspense. Without suspense, the reader loses interest. For example, the protagonist may struggle within herself and with her parents about her need to be an individual and to conform to parental wishes. In addition to conflict, a story has a crisis or a turning point in which the character makes a choice. The working out of the decision comes to a climax. From there, the story comes to a resolution, a logical or satisfactory ending.

Plot is cause and effect. Cause is anything that makes a character act or think in a certain way. In short, cause is the reason certain things happen. Effect is the result of an action. Often an effect can turn into a cause, similar to domino tiles tumbling one after another. In a story, a character's actions may result in something entirely different than anticipated by the character himself or by the reader.

Plot is the organized series of events. It must have a logical sequence that makes sense when we finish the story. Plot creates suspense when the anticipated outcome does not happen or is delayed. In such cases, the writer may set up new complications that the character must overcome before the resolution. Or, in other cases, the writer uses a plot twist, offering up an ending that the reader does not expect but is logically prepared for.

Traditionally, plot has a beginning, a middle, and an end — but not necessarily in that order. All stories begin in the middle of things. The opening scene of a story is usually closest to the main conflict or action, but it is not really the beginning. To have a "real beginning" the writer should start with the birth of the character or even the birth of the parents or grandparents. Since such details are not always relevant to the plot, the writer chooses an incident that engages the reader's curiosity. When and if necessary, the writer will use a flashback, that is, a scene or event in the past, to explain the current situation. In addition, the writer may hint at a possible outcome of the situation by foreshadowing. Finally, a story may have a distorted chronology. The ending may not be the real ending at all.

CHARACTER

A character is a recognizable person of any gender. There can be several characters in a short story. A protagonist is the main character in the plot. He or she moves the story to its conclusion; the protagonist has conflicts and struggles to resolve them. The protagonist is the hero or heroine, who usually has admirable traits and is the good person. An antagonist goes against the desires of the protagonist. In common parlance, the antagonist is the villain who attempts to thwart the protagonist. Sometimes the villain is not a wicked person but merely one who opposes the protagonist.

Characters make the story, for, without them, the plot does not move and becomes merely a series of events. Characters can be real human beings, animals, or abstractions. But they all must have recognizable human traits. For example, Winnie-the-Pooh looks like a stuffed teddy bear, but he acts like a small child. Human traits can be abstract qualities such as desiring love, feeling compassion, longing for recognition, struggling toward a goal, doing the wrong thing, and being sad or happy.

Many characters reveal their traits almost in the same way we judge real people—actions speak louder than words. A person who steals is seen as untrustworthy or wicked. Or, conversely, a judge dispensing justice in the courtroom suggests a person of honour and wisdom. What the characters say and how they say it reveal personality. What is said about them by other characters is equally significant.

Characters can be flat, two-dimensional, or stereotyped. In a short story, flat characters are usually supporting ones. They are not fully fleshed out. They play a specific role. For example, the sidekick helps the hero and has no other purpose in the plot. Similarly, the antagonist is often two-dimensional in that the role of the villain calls for stopping the hero from completing the task.

Often writers take shortcuts by using archetypal characters. An "archetype" is a recognizable, generic figure found in literature. Writers tap into a ready-made emotional response created by the familiar character. For example, the biblical Delilah is seen as the temptress who seduces men. In modern stories, she becomes the woman in red, the siren who leads men to their doom.

At other times, writers use "stereotypes." With minimal differences, these characters are duplicates, readily identifiable, interchangeable from one story to another. They are static quick fixes. They could be identified by physical characteristics: a small, scrawny child, for example. Names are also used as shortcuts. For example, a character named "Framton" would not be expected to be a dashing, action hero. "Ivan" or "Mei-Mei" identifies nationality and suggests racial or cultural traits in the character. Sometimes, revealing the occupation of the character is enough: she could be a lawyer or he a bus driver. These characters do not develop.

The main characters, however, are developed; that is, they are changed by the end of the story. Rarely does the protagonist remain as ignorant or unmoved as he was at the moment we first met up with him. The transformation is usually gradual: the protagonist must earn this change in character. Often, this change comes in learning a lesson, in doing the right thing, and in understanding.

Characters are us. As ungrammatical as the statement is, it holds true: we want to identify with the protagonist or with the characters in the story.

Characters provide us, the readers, with vicarious experiences. They become our surrogate selves. They do things we would like to do but dare not. They are the people we want to be or not to be. They stir our emotions and challenge our intellect. And they make us want to believe that they are not fictional but real.

Such is the power of characters in the story. We can like them, hate them, or fear them, just as real people. They remain with us long after we have finished reading the story.

SETTING

Setting is topography or place. A mere word like Toronto or Vancouver opens up the reader's imagination to a specific locale. Additional information, such as the corner of Yonge and Dundas Streets, or Pender Street, gives a clearer picture. For imaginary places, the writer may create worlds beyond our experience — a frozen planet, for example — or build on places we are already comfortable with. For example, in Charles De Lint's "Mr. Truepenny's Book Emporium and Gallery," the shop and the neighbourhood are ones we can easily imagine because we have seen such city locations.

Setting includes time. Knowing when the story takes place is important. For example, a story set in 1929 brings to mind the stock market crash and the coming of the Great Depression. The month of May suggests spring and rebirth or renewal after the dead of winter. The hour of 3 A.M. or twelve noon conjures up certain associations. Therefore, temporal information can do much to create mood, define context, and fix purpose.

Setting gives readers a grounding. While it is true that a picture is worth a thousand words, often in a short story the writer is limited in what can be detailed. She describes enough for us to fill in other pieces of information. In "The Lottery," Shirley Jackson gives this descriptive setting:

> The morning of June 27th was clear and sunny, with the fresh warmth of a full-summer day; the flowers were blossoming profusely and the grass was richly green. The people of the village began to gather in the square, between the post office and the bank, around ten o'clock. (p. 105)

We can visualize the day, the town, and the people with these words, but we also fill in with our own details. Moreover, the writer's selection of details conveys more than location or time. It helps us understand character and environment.

Setting helps to achieve focus for the plot. Satisfying the questions "where" and "when" does much to allay confusion and irritation in the reader.

THEME

Theme is the main subject matter. Around this central idea, the writer arranges the sequence of events (plot) for the characters to play out. Theme does not always moralize; rather, it dramatizes. It follows the axiom "show rather than tell." For example, in the folktale "The Cowherd," the theme is "Don't abuse your mother." However, merely stating this subject lacks punch. Having read the entire tale, we come to understand the message.

Theme is like a thesis statement. It can be the controlling device to keep the story on track. However, unlike a thesis, which is directly stated, the theme is a concept to be discovered by the reader. Other times, the subject matter does not have a moral lesson at all. Theme can be as simple as what the story is about.

POINT OF VIEW

Point of view is the approach the writer takes in telling the story. Sometimes, this term is synonymous with narration. As with all aspects of writing, the manner in which the story is told is important. Not all stories can be narrated from the first-person point of view; not all stories are suited to the third-person point of view. Many authors write their stories using different points of view until they decide on the one that tells the tale the best.

There are three "persons" in grammatical terms: first-person singular "I" and plural "we"; second-person "you"; and third-person singular "he" or "she" and plural "they." In storytelling the writer has the choice of all these "persons" to tell the story. The second-person ("you") and the plural forms are unconventional but have been used effectively. Generally speaking, the two most popular persons used in storytelling are the first-person singular and the third-person singular.

First Person

When discussing the use of first-person point of view, we must make a distinction between narrator and author. Some students may see the "I" not as a character but rather as the author. This mistake often comes about when the "I" has no identifying name in the story. Do not assume that the "I" character is the author.

There are three basic variants in the use of the first-person singular as the narrator of the story: First, the speaker is the main character. Second, the speaker is a secondary character who talks about the protagonist. And third, the narrator is the writer who slips into the story with creative asides.

The most common of the three is the narrator as the protagonist. We readers tend to identify with the narrator as the plot unfolds. Like the narrator, we know only what the narrator knows and what he or she tells us. Because of this restriction, the scope of the story may be limited to what the narrator hears, sees, does, and reports. On the other hand, the writer may solve this limiting problem by having two or more "I" narrators; this device is more often found in novels than in short stories.

Second, the narrator may be a secondary character who accompanies the protagonist (who is spoken of in the third person). For example, in Sir Arthur Conan Doyle's famous Sherlock Holmes series, the narrator is Dr. John Watson, and not the main character Sherlock Holmes. The secondary character reports the words and actions of the hero but cannot read his mind. Moreover, the speaker can make comments on the protagonist's actions or speculate on future doings.

The third variant is the writer as narrator. In humorous pieces, such as Stephen Leacock's Mariposa stories, the writer's intrusion is obvious. Leacock makes fun of his characters with his asides and comments. Similarly, in David Arnason's "A Girl's Story," the writer necessarily has to appear because he tells us how a story is written. This method tends to break the illusion of fiction and mixes fact with fiction.

On rare occasions, some writers use the first-person plural. The collective "we" does not distinguish individuals but sees from the point of view of the group. For example, Leacock's "How We Kept Mother's Day" has the "we," including father and children. By doing so, Leacock makes a distinction between them and the mother.

Second Person

The second-person point of view is infrequent in fiction. It forces the reader to become the narrator. Properly done, the technique draws the reader into the story with a certain detachment that is not found in the "I" narration. In addition, the "you" is still a distinct character. Because of the forced identification with the reader, the "you" generally has no name. A good example of this method is Diane Schoemperlen's "Red Plaid Shirt": "You eat everything and then you get the hell out of there, leaving a message for Fernando" (p. 195).

Third Person

The most common point of view in fiction is the third-person singular. It too has three branches: totally omniscient, partially omniscient, and objective.

In total omniscience, the writer tells not only the actions and words of all the characters but also their thoughts. However, total omniscience is often selective. That is, the writer chooses when to reveal the innermost thoughts of his or her characters.

In partial omniscience, only one character reveals his or her thoughts. By this device, the writer can sustain suspense and arouse curiosity. The character does not necessarily have to be the protagonist, but usually is.

In third-person objective, the writer tells the story only from the actions and words of the characters. The writer does not reveal the thoughts of any character. The reader then must anticipate future action from the information given and nothing more.

Point of view as part of narrative technique, then, is important. It creates not only reader identification with the protagonist but also suspense and curiosity.

STYLE

The way the writer chooses words and puts them down on paper is called style. Ernest Hemingway and James Joyce have distinctive, recognizable styles. Hemingway's sentences are lean and his description is minimal. Joyce's sentences are generally long and detailed with plenty of description. These are identifiable elements in their writing.

However, style is not only individual. Certain genres of stories are said to have a kind of style. For example, in the parable of "The Prodigal Son," the oral tradition is imitated with the repetition of words to begin each new thought.

Style then is difficult to define but easily recognizable if the reader has read a lot of a particular writer's works or a certain genre of story.

TONE

How the writer says something is as important as what he or she says. Tone can be serious and sombre, or humorous and light. It provides a clue as to how the writer deals with the subject matter. For example, in "The Cask of Amontillado," Edgar Allan Poe begins his tale with a serious, sinister tone: "The thousand injuries of Fortunato I had borne as I best could, but when he ventured upon insult, I vowed revenge" (p. 177). Whereas, in "My Financial Career," Stephen Leacock starts off with a light, humorous tone: "When I go into a bank I get rattled. The clerks rattle me; the wickets rattle me; the sight of the money rattles me; everything rattles me" (p. 145). Tone often helps define the story.

LITERARY TECHNIQUES

Here are some of the common techniques used by writers. This list is a quick reference to commonly used literary terminology. Although some of these terms fit drama and poetry, we have selected ones particularly relevant to short stories.

Allusion A reference to a person, event, or thing. Often writers draw relationships by making reference to something else. The reader must catch such oblique references.

Climax The maximum disturbance, or the greatest tension in the story. Often confused with crisis. Usually, the climax occurs before the conclusion or resolution.

Crisis The turning point in the story. The protagonist must make a decision that will affect the outcome. Usually, the crisis comes at the midpoint of the story.

Denouement/Conclusion/Resolution The outcome of the story.

Dramatic licence Liberties taken with accepted facts and reality to heighten the story. For example, the writer may have altered the historical sequence of events, or placed a real person in an imaginary setting.

Exposition Essential information the reader needs to know to understand the story. Usually, it is found at the beginning of the story, along with the setting.

Flashback Recalls an earlier scene to explain a dramatic point or to show cause. A flashback not only gives dramatic pause to the action but also fills in information needed to understand the action or incident. Flashbacks can be lengthy or brief.

Foreshadowing Clues given early in the story. The method creates anticipation and some suspense. Also the writer prepares the reader for the outcome.

Imagery Involves all five senses — hearing, feeling, tasting, seeing, smelling. Most often, imagery consists of pictures that the reader can visualize from the words.

In medias res In the middle of things. In this technique the story starts at the most crucial incident or scene, then uses flashbacks to fill in background information.

Irony (a) Verbal irony: what is said and done are diametrically opposite, or what is said and meant are in direct opposition; (b) Dramatic irony: the reader and a character know more than the other characters in the story and can distinguish the double meaning in the dialogue.

Juxtapositioning Putting two scenes side by side for effect. Often this shortcut brings dramatic moments together; at other times, it contrasts one scene with the next.

Metaphor A figure of speech used to make comparisons between unlike objects. For example, in the metaphor "He is a tiger in the boardroom," the person is not literally a tiger; rather, he has certain qualities of a tiger. A metaphor does not use "as" or "like."

Simile A figure of speech used to draw similarities. A simile uses "like" or "as." For example, "Like a mother hen, the residence counsellor protects her charges."

Surprise ending A conclusion that the reader is not prepared for. The surprise ending is quite popular in short stories, where the punch lines comes in the last paragraph or sentence.

Symbol Something concrete representing something abstract. For example, the concept of love may be represented by a gold ring; the belief in Christianity, by a cross. A symbol has a distinct meaning beyond the thing itself. For example, a rock can be just a rock. However, the writer may choose to add extra meaning to that rock; then it becomes a symbol. In literature, there are many symbols. Some have been standardized and are recognizable by their constant use. Other symbols are story-specific, developed for a particular story.

ANALYZING LITERATURE

When you analyze a short story, you take it apart and examine the various elements separately. Why do you do this?

Analyzing literature reinforces skills you already possess. The first skill is thinking. You engage not only your personal experience, but also what you have learned in school. You draw connections that may not always be obvious.

The second is vicarious learning. By reading, you can understand actions and emotions you may never have experienced. From fiction to real life, you begin to comprehend why people act in certain ways.

The third skill is appreciation of artistry. By taking the story apart, you come to understand how each separate item, such as plot, must be logical and compatible with the setting or the character. Or you may marvel at how the writer has manipulated your feelings with mere words. Part of artistry is making complex things seem simple.

Throughout all this analysis of a story, or a number of stories, you want to know the answers to the following questions.

"Do writers deliberately put all those details in the story?" Yes, they do. A writer makes decisions about everything that goes into a story. Whether the character is right-handed or left-handed, or has blue eyes will be integral to the plot. If something is not important or relevant, the writer does not waste time putting it in the story. David Arnason illustrates this process in "A Girl's Story" (p. 22).

"How do you see all these things in the story that I can't?" Part of the answer is that as you read more and more literature, you develop experience. Because many writers use traditional materials and time-honoured concepts and themes, you eventually discover and recognize common elements in fiction. For example, a character with a cleft foot or a limp in his left leg has been associated with the devil. Or a character with the name of Mr. Graves suggests death, cemeteries, and ominous qualities.

In addition, the cultivation of knowledge of other disciplines will help you to better understand literature. History gives you a grounding in different periods in setting and events. For example, when a writer mentions the

War Measures Act, she has set the time as 1970 and alluded to the FLQ (Front de Libération du Québec) crisis, a historic event. Psychology helps us understand human behaviour. For example, in Tim O'Brien's "The Man I Killed" (p. 170), the narrator projects his feelings and desires onto the dead man. The term is called projection. Writers draw from religious texts, especially the Bible. When a character comments, "Let's kill the fatted calf," the allusion is to the parable of "The Prodigal Son" (p. 150). Thus, a knowledge of other subjects contributes to the understanding of the short story.

"Doesn't analyzing the story kill the enjoyment in reading?" If reading is merely for entertainment, the answer would be yes. But taking a story apart and examining its separate parts gives greater appreciation of the story. There is joy in such discoveries.

In addition, analysis gives you more practice in examining objectively the society or world you live in. If you can pick a story apart, you can use the same skill to solve or attack problems. Practice makes things easier as you go on. In short, analyzing a story has practical as well as academic applications.

Several popular methods of analyzing fiction exist, including checklist, context, and interpretation.

THE CHECKLIST

Using Poe's "The Cask of Amontillado" (p. 177), we can draw up a series of questions and answers to examine each of the elements of fiction described above and see how they work in context with the theme:

What is the title of the story?	"The Cask of Amontillado"
Why is it so titled?	Bait to lure Fortunato, the victim; Amontillado is an expensive wine
Who wrote it?	Edgar Allan Poe, a 19th century American writer
What kind of story is this (genre)?	Horror
What is the point of the story (theme)?	Getting away with murder
Who are the main characters?	Montresor and Fortunato

Who is the "hero" (protagonist)? Describe him or her briefly.	None —
Who is the "villain" (antagonist)? Describe him or her briefly.	Montresor, the narrator Vengeful, careful, intelligent, knows human nature
Who are the secondary characters, if any? Name them and give a sketch.	Fortunato, the victim A gullible drunkard
How is the story told?	First-person narration by Montresor
What happens in the story (plot summary)?	Montresor avenges Fortunato's insult by walling him alive in the catacombs
What is the conflict?	How to lure Fortunato to his death
How does the story end?	With a surprise; Montresor gets away with murder for 50 years; he confesses to a priest
What is (are) the setting(s)?	Italy, during carnival time with people in masquerade; could be 19th century or Renaissance
How do the other elements support the plot, characterization, and theme?	Going downwards to the catacombs, Montresor's trowel, clown clothing for Fortunato, alcohol, nitre
How does the author create mood and atmosphere?	Description of the dampness, evening, isolation
Is there irony?	Fortunato doesn't realize his situation until the end,

	and there is no cask of Amontillado
Is there humour?	Macabre humour
Are there any obvious symbols?	Montresor's trowel, the catacombs (graves), going downward as to hell or the grave
Is this story effectively written?	Yes
How?	We cheer for Montresor
Why?	He gets away with murder and wants to do so in heaven. That's why he confesses to a priest.
Is there something more to the story?	The nature of evil is deceptive; beware of treachery

Of course, we can keep on asking more detailed questions. This method certainly covers all aspects of the story, but it can be tedious to go through such detail.

CONTEXT

In this type of analysis, the story is seen in relation to social, historical, autobiographical factors. This method requires not only a good understanding of the story but also information not included in the telling. You may need to research a number of peripheral areas, including the following:

Author's other works Writers tend to return to favourite themes, concepts, or symbols. For example, James Joyce wrote mainly about Dublin, Ireland, and his basic theme is spiritual dryness.

Biography Knowing something about the author's life may help you understand and appreciate the story. What were her inspirations and influences? Whose work did she read?

History An author living in one century can certainly write convincingly about other epochs, but that writer is still influenced by his own period.

Setting Where did the author write? A Canadian author would certainly see patriotism quite differently than an American writer.

Social context What were some of the main preoccupations of the people in that place and at that time? For example, in the mid-thirties in Canada, what did people think about immigration or homosexuality?

Time When did the author write? That is, was the author writing in the 20th century? 18th century? Each period has certain recognizable, collective patterns in theme and technique.

INTERPRETATION

You can try to understand the story or the characters according to what teachers, scholars, and literary critics say on this subject, or you can delve into your own experience.

First, let others explain what they see in the story. Their insights may help you appreciate the subtext or the significance of symbols.

Second, draw from your own experience and test the validity of feelings and actions of the characters. You may want to discuss the story's ending with other students in the class or with the instructor.

MIXED TECHNIQUES

Most of the time you will analyze the story using a bit of all the techniques discussed here. First, read the story entirely and ask yourself, "Do I like this story or not?" If your answer is "yes," a second and more important question is "Why?" What you have done is to engage both emotion and intellect. You move from feeling to thinking; you shift from subjectivity to objectivity in your analysis of the piece.

If your answer is "no," then you must find reasons for not liking the story. Is it due to the writing? The characters? The theme?

There are other ways to analyze a literary piece. Your instructor may want to share one or two with you. Or he may dictate a certain methodology to follow. If you are left to your own designs, we suggest you try one of the procedures described above.

The Fox and the Grapes
a fable by Aesop

Once there was a hungry fox walking through an orchard. He spied a bunch of grapes hanging overhead on a trellis. The fox looked up at the grapes dangling there and thought, "Some juicy grapes would be good to eat right now." He stretched up to get at the grapes, but they were too far out of reach. He tried to leap in the air, but he fell short. Then he used a running start and jumped as high into the air as he possibly could go. But still he could not get at the fruit. The fox gave the grapes a rueful glance. Then he walked away with an air of dignity, saying, "I don't really want those grapes. I'm sure they are sour."

Moral: It is easy to despise what you cannot have.

about 600 B.C.

NOTES

According to the ancient Greek historian Herodotus, Aesop (600 B.C.) was a Greek slave and a famed storyteller. His beast fables have been handed down through the generations, first as part of the oral tradition and later in the written tradition. Collections of the fables are often printed as children's books. Other famous Aesop's fables include "The Tortoise and the Hare," "The North Wind and the Sun," "The Crow and the Pitcher," "The Town Mouse and the Country Mouse," and "The Grasshopper and the Ants."

You can find versions of "The Fox and the Grapes" with slightly different English wording, since many words in the Greek language have different possible translations. This is our retelling of the story.

In literature, animals represent certain abstract traits. For example, the fox is associated with cunning, the owl with wisdom, and the lion with dignity. We still use expressions such as "sly as a fox," "wise as an owl," "timid as a mouse," or "busy as a bee." These associations may be quite different in other cultures.

The English expression "sour grapes" comes from this story. It is used to describe the attitude of a person who is bitter about not getting something and therefore denigrates it. For example, if someone said negative things about a promotion that she or he failed to attain, we would call her or his attitude "sour grapes."

COMPREHENSION AND DISCUSSION

1. Is the specific place and time setting for this story important?
2. Would you have figured out the moral of this story if it had not been included at the end?
3. Would the moral work if the story had another animal instead of the fox in it? Would the fable be as effective, say, with a young child in the fox's role?
4. Why is there a lesson or moral to every story?
5. What examples of "sour grapes" behaviour have you observed? Have you ever felt that way?

LITERARY TECHNIQUES

Fable A short narrative with a message or a moral attached. It makes a point about an aspect of human behaviour. Often in a fable, animals act and speak like human beings although they retain their animal form. The term "beast fable" is also used.

The beast fable has the same opening as the fairy tale. Here is a short list of opening expressions: "Once upon a time...," "There was a...," "Once there was...," "Once...," "There was a...." The opening promptly establishes the fantastic or imaginary world, into which the reader enters.

Personification A literary technique in which animals, inanimate objects, imaginary characters, even abstractions appear in human form or have human traits. The term personification means to make into a person or human.

ASSIGNMENTS

1. Read other Aesop's fables. You can find them in children's books in the public library or on the Internet. Explain why the fables are so enduring. Or, write a comparison essay discussing two or three of the fables.

2. Decide on a simple moral lesson and write a fable illustrating this message.
3. Watch some cartoons with animal characters such as Bugs Bunny, Mickey Mouse, Donald Duck, the Road Runner, and Woody Woodpecker. Discuss how the animals are personified (given human characteristics).
4. What are some differences between a fable and a fairy tale? Or between a fable and a folktale such as "The Cowherd"?
5. Research Native Canadian myths, such as Sedna, Nanabush, Glooscap, the Petrel, and Raven. Retell one of the stories and explain its significance.

A Girl's Story

David Arnason

1   You've wondered what it would be like to be a character in a story, to sort of slip out of your ordinary self and into some other character. Well, I'm offering you the opportunity. I've been trying to think of a heroine for this story, and frankly, it hasn't been going too well. A writer's life isn't easy, especially if, like me, he's got a tendency sometimes to drink a little bit too much. Yesterday, I went for a beer with Dennis and Ken (they're real-life friends of mine) and we stayed a little longer than we should have. Then I came home and quickly mixed a drink and started drinking it so my wife would think the liquor on my breath came from the drink I was drinking and not from the drinks I had had earlier. I wasn't going to tell her about those drinks. Anyway, Wayne dropped over in the evening and I had some more drinks, and this morning my head isn't working very well.

2   To be absolutely frank about it, I always have trouble getting characters, even when I'm stone cold sober. I can think of plots; plots are really easy. If you can't think of one, you just pick up a book, and sure enough, there's a plot. You just move a few things around and nobody knows you stole the idea. Characters are the problem. It doesn't matter how good the plot is if your characters are dull. You can steal characters too, and put them into different plots. I've done that. I stole Eustacia Vye from Hardy and gave her another name. The problem was that she turned out a lot sulkier than I remembered and the plot I put her in was a light comedy. Now nobody wants to publish the story. I'm still sending it out, though. If you send a story to enough publishers, no matter how bad it is, somebody will ultimately publish it.

3   For this story I need a beautiful girl. You probably don't think you're beautiful enough, but I can fix that. I can do all kinds of retouching once I've got the basic material, and if I miss anything, Karl (he's my editor) will find it. So I'm going to make you fairly tall, about five-foot-eight and a quarter in your stocking feet. I'm going to give you long blonde hair because long blonde hair is sexy and virtuous. Black hair can be sexy too, but it doesn't go with virtue. I've got to deal with a whole literary tradition where black-haired women are basically evil. If I were feeling better I might be able to do it in an ironic way, then black hair would be OK, but I don't think I'm up to it this morning. If you're going to use irony, then you've got to be really careful about tone. I could make you a redhead, but

redheads have a way of turning out pixie-ish, and that would wreck my plot.

So you've got long blonde hair and you're this tall slender girl with amazingly blue eyes. Your face is narrow and your nose is straight and thin. I could have turned up the nose a little, but that would have made you cute, and I really need a beautiful girl. I'm going to put a tiny black mole on your cheek. It's traditional. If you want your character to be really beautiful there has to be some minor defect.

Now, I'm going to sit you on the bank of a river. I'm not much for setting. I've read so many things where you get great long descriptions of the setting, and mostly it's just boring. When my last book came out, one of the reviewers suggested that the reason I don't do settings is that I'm not very good at them. That's just silly. I'm writing a different kind of story, not that old realist stuff. If you think I can't do setting, just watch.

There's a curl in the river just below the old dam where the water seems to make a broad sweep. That flatness is deceptive, though. Under the innocent sheen of the mirroring surface, the current is treacherous. The water swirls, stabs, takes sharp angles and dangerous vectors. The trees that lean from the bank shimmer with the multi-hued greenness of elm, oak, maple and aspen. The leaves turn in the gentle breeze, showing their paler green undersides. The undergrowth, too, is thick and green, hiding the poison ivy, the poison sumac and the thorns. On a patch of grass that slopes gently to the water, the only clear part of the bank on that side of the river, a girl sits, a girl with long blonde hair. She has slipped a ring from her finger and seems to be holding it toward the light.

You see? I could do a lot more of that, but you wouldn't like it. I slipped a lot of details in there and provided all those hints about strange and dangerous things under the surface. That's called foreshadowing. I put in the ring at the end there so that you'd wonder what was going to happen. That's to create suspense. You're supposed to ask yourself what the ring means. Obviously it has something to do with love, rings always do, and since she's taken it off, obviously something has gone wrong in the love relationship. Now I just have to hold off answering that question for as long as I can, and I've got my story. I've got a friend who's also a writer who says never tell the buggers anything until they absolutely have to know.

I'm going to have trouble with the feminists about this story. I can see that already. I've got that river that's calm on the surface and boiling underneath, and I've got those trees that are gentle and beautiful with poisonous and dangerous undergrowth. Obviously, the girl is going to be like that, calm on the surface but passionate underneath. The feminists are going to say that I'm perpetuating stereotypes, that by giving the impression the girl is full of hidden passion I'm encouraging rapists. That's crazy. I'm just using a literary convention. Most of the world's great books are about the conflict between reason and passion. If you take that away, what's left to write about?

9   So I've got you sitting on the riverbank, twirling your ring. I forgot the birds. The trees are full of singing birds. There are meadowlarks and vireos and even Blackburnian warblers. I know a lot about birds but I'm not going to put in too many. You've got to be careful not to overdo things. In a minute I'm going to enter your mind and reveal what you're thinking. I'm going to do this in the third person. Using the first person is sometimes more effective, but I'm always afraid to do a female character in the first person. It seems wrong to me, like putting on a woman's dress.

10   Your name is Linda. I had to be careful not to give you a biblical name like Judith or Rachel. I don't want any symbolism in this story. Symbolism makes me sick, especially biblical symbolism. You always end up with some crazy moral argument that you don't believe and none of the readers believe. Then you lose control of your characters, because they've got to be like the biblical characters. You've got this terrific episode you'd like to use, but you can't because Rachel or Judith or whoever wouldn't do it. I think of stories with a lot of symbolism in them as sticky.

11   Here goes.

12   Linda held the ring up toward the light. The diamond flashed rainbow colours. It was a small diamond, and Linda reflected that it was probably a perfect symbol of her relationship with Gregg. Everything Gregg did was on a small scale. He was careful with his money and just as careful with his emotions. In one week they would have a small wedding and then move into a small apartment. She supposed that she ought to be happy. Gregg was very handsome, and she did love him. Why did it seem that she was walking into a trap?

13   That sounds kind of distant, but it's supposed to be distant. I'm using indirect quotation because the reader has just met Linda, and we don't want to get too intimate right away. Besides, I've got to get a lot of explaining done quickly, and if you can do it with the character's thoughts, then that's best.

14   Linda twirled the ring again, then with a suddenness that surprised her, she stood up and threw it into the river. She was immediately struck by a feeling of panic. For a moment she almost decided to dive into the river to try to recover it. Then, suddenly, she felt free. It was now impossible to marry Gregg. He would not forgive her for throwing the ring away. Gregg would say he'd had enough of her theatrics for one lifetime. He always

accused her of being a romantic. She'd never had the courage to admit that he was correct, and that she intended to continue being a romantic. She was sitting alone by the river in a long blue dress because it was a romantic pose. Anyway, she thought a little wryly, you're only likely to find romance if you look for it in romantic places and dress for the occasion.

Suddenly, she heard a rustling in the bush, the sound of someone coming down the narrow path from the road above.

I had to do that, you see. I'd used up all the potential in the relationship with Gregg, and the plot would have started to flag if I hadn't introduced a new character. The man who is coming down the path is tall and athletic with wavy brown hair. He has dark brown eyes that crinkle when he smiles, and he looks kind. His skin is tanned, as if he spends a lot of time outdoors, and he moves gracefully. He is smoking a pipe. I don't want to give too many details. I'm not absolutely sure what features women find attractive in men these days, but what I've described seems safe enough. I got all of it from stories written by women, and I assume they must know. I could give him a chiselled jaw, but that's about as far as I'll go.

The man stepped into the clearing. He carried an old-fashioned wicker fishing creel and a telescoped fishing rod. Linda remained sitting on the grass, her blue dress spread out around her. The man noticed her and apologized.

"I'm sorry, I always come here to fish on Saturday afternoons and I've never encountered anyone here before." His voice was low with something of an amused tone in it.

"Don't worry," Linda replied. "I'll only be here for a little while. Go ahead and fish. I won't make any noise." In some way she couldn't understand, the man looked familiar to her. She felt she knew him. She thought she might have seen him on television or in a movie, but of course she knew that movie and television stars do not spend every Saturday afternoon fishing on the banks of small, muddy rivers.

"You can make all the noise you want," he told her. "The fish in this river are almost entirely deaf. Besides, I don't care if I catch any. I only like the act of fishing. If I catch them, then I have to take them home and clean them. Then I've got to cook them and eat them. I don't even like fish that much, and the fish you catch here all taste of mud."

"Why do you bother fishing then?" Linda asked him. "Why don't you just come and sit on the riverbank?"

"It's not that easy," he told her. "A beautiful girl in a blue dress may go and sit on a riverbank any time she wants. But a man can only sit on a riverbank if he has a very good reason. Because I fish, I am a man with a hobby. After a hard week of work, I deserve some relaxation. But if I just came and sat on the riverbank, I would be a romantic fool. People would make fun of me. They would think I was irresponsible, and before long I would be a failure." As he spoke, he attached a lure to his line, untelescoped his fishing pole and cast his line into the water.

23 You may object that this would not have happened in real life, that the conversation would have been awkward, that Linda would have been a bit frightened by the man. Well, why don't you just run out to the grocery store and buy a bottle of milk and a loaf of bread? The grocer will give you your change without even looking at you. That's what happens in real life, and if that's what you're after, why are you reading a book?

24 I'm sorry. I shouldn't have got upset. But it's not easy you know. Dialogue is about the hardest stuff to write. You've got all those "he saids" and "she saids" and "he replieds." And you've got to remember the quotation marks and whether the comma is inside or outside the quotation marks. Sometimes you can leave out the "he saids" and the "she saids" but then the reader gets confused and can't figure out who's talking. Hemingway is bad for that. Sometimes you can read an entire chapter without figuring out who is on what side.

25 Anyway, something must have been in the air that afternoon. Linda felt free and open.

26 Did I mention that it was warm and the sun was shining?

27 She chattered away, telling the stranger all about her life, what she had done when she was a little girl, the time her dad had taken the whole family to Hawaii and she got such a bad sunburn that she was peeling in February, how she was a better water skier than Gregg and how mad he got when she beat him at tennis. The man, whose name was Michael (you can use biblical names for men as long as you avoid Joshua or Isaac), told her he was a doctor, but had always wanted to be cowboy. He told her about the time he skinned his knee when he fell off his bicycle and had to spend two weeks in the hospital because of infection. In short, they did what people who are falling in love always do. They unfolded their brightest and happiest memories and gave them to each other as gifts.

28 Then Michael took a bottle of wine and a Klik sandwich out of his wicker creel and invited Linda to join him in a picnic. He had forgotten his corkscrew and he had to push the cork down into the bottle with his filletting knife. They drank wine and laughed and spat out little pieces of cork. Michael reeled in his line, and to his amazement discovered a diamond ring on his hook. Linda didn't dare tell him where the ring had come from. Then Michael took Linda's hand, and slipped the ring onto her finger. In a comic-solemn voice, he asked her to marry him. With the same kind of

comic solemnity, she agreed. Then they kissed, a first gentle kiss with their lips barely brushing and without touching each other.

Now I've got to bring this to some kind of ending. You think writers know how stories end before they write them, but that's not true. We're wracked with confusion and guilt about how things are going to end. And just as you're playing the role of Linda in this story, Michael is my alter ego. He even looks a little like me and he smokes the same kind of pipe. We all want this to end happily. If I were going to be realistic about this, I suppose I'd have to let them make love. Then, shaken with guilt and horror, Linda would go back and marry Gregg, and the doctor would go back to his practice. But I'm not going to do that. In the story from which I stole the plot, Michael turned out not to be a doctor at all, but a returned soldier who had always been in love with Linda. She recognized him as they kissed, because they had kissed as children, and even though they had grown up and changed, she recognized the flavour of wintergreen on his breath. That's no good. It brings in too many unexplained facts at the last minute.

I'm going to end it right here at the moment of the kiss. You can do what you want with the rest of it, except you can't make him a returned soldier, and you can't have them make love then separate forever. I've eliminated those options. In fact, I think I'll eliminate all options. This is where the story ends, at the moment of the kiss. It goes on and on forever while cities burn, nations rise and fall, galaxies are born and die, and the universe snuffs out the stars one by one. It goes on, the story, the brush of a kiss.

1989

NOTES

Arnason makes fun of the stereotype of an alcoholic writer who works with a hangover in the morning. Since he refers to himself, he is self-mocking.

Eustacia Vye A character in Thomas Hardy's *The Return of the Native* (1878). She is a beautiful but tragic figure who uses her feminine wiles to escape her environment. Note the irony in Arnason's makeover of the character.

Arnason alludes to a famous poem in *The Rubaiyat of Omar Khayyam* (via Edward Fitzgerald, 1859) when he has Michael taking out a sandwich and a bottle of wine:

> Here with a Loaf of Bread beneath the Bough,
> A Flask of Wine, a Book of Verse — and Thou
> Beside me singing in the Wilderness —
> And Wilderness is Paradise enow.

This verse is generally simplified to "a loaf of bread, a jug of wine, and thou," a romantic expression of a person's basic needs.

Klik A canned sandwich meat, like Spam.

COMPREHENSION AND DISCUSSION

1. What is the main story? What kind of story is it?
2. How does Arnason draw you into his story?
3. Does it matter that Arnason assumes the reader to be female? Why does he make the heroine a beautiful, blonde, blue-eyed girl named Linda, with a minor defect?
4. How does Arnason differentiate between the story and the process of creating and commenting on the story?
5. Does Arnason's story follow his observation about the "conflict between reason and passion"? Is it true that "most of the world's great books" are about this conflict (p. 24)?
6. To what literary traditions and stereotypes does Arnason refer? Do you think they are valid? For example, are black-haired women "basically evil" (p. 22)?
7. Why is this a fun story to read? What makes it so?
8. What point does Arnason make when he ends the story with the two people kissing?
9. Is this story romantic? Does Arnason explain love well when he says, "In short, they did what people who are falling in love always do. They unfolded their brightest and happiest memories and gave them to each other as gifts" (p. 26)?

LITERARY TECHNIQUES

Arnason is doing two things simultaneously: telling a story and showing the steps in creating a story. This technique is called metafiction. Note how he invites the female reader to become a character in his story. Then he explains all the ingredients necessary in writing a tale: plot, character, names. As Arnason contrives the episode between Linda and Michael, he intrudes on the action to explain the techniques he is using. Finally, he tells the reader that out of the many possible endings he chooses the one he wants. In short, as creative writer, Arnason determines what goes in and what does not.

This story answers the common question, "Does the writer deliberately put all those details in the story?" Part of writing, especially in fiction, is decision making. Every detail in the story must be relevant to the whole. Arnason shows how much control he has over the basic elements of storytelling.

This story also responds to the next question, "How much does the writer put himself into his story?" All writing has an element of autobiography. In this story, Arnason makes the point that the character, Michael, is similar to his own personality.

Reader participation is more than just passive reading here. Arnason engages the reader by inviting you to become a character in his story. The technique is the direct address to the reader. Arnason creates the illusion that you have a part to play and that he is speaking only to you, and not just anybody.

ASSIGNMENTS

1. Look up the meanings of the names of characters that the writer mentions, such as Joshua, Isaac, Michael, Gregg, and Linda. You can find this information in a baby name book or on the Internet.
2. Arnason has given you the process analysis of short story writing. Write a set of instructions on how to write a story.
3. Arnason mentions brunettes, blondes, and redheads and discusses colour imagery. List the primary colours and explain what they represent. For another story using colour imagery, read Schoemperlen's "Red Plaid Shirt" (p. 191) or Alice Walker's "Am I Blue?" (p. 349).
4. If you wish to read more stories with elements of metafiction, see O'Brien's "The Man I Killed" (p. 170) and De Lint's "Mr. Truepenny's Book Emporium and Gallery" (p. 54). How are they the same; how do they differ?

The Fun They Had

Isaac Asimov

Margie even wrote about it that night in her diary. On the page headed May 17, 2157, she wrote, "Today Tommy found a real book!"

It was a very old book. Margie's grandfather once said that when he was a little boy *his* grandfather told him that there was a time when all stories were printed on paper.

They turned the pages, which were yellow and crinkly, and it was awfully funny to read words that stood still instead of moving the way they were supposed to — on a screen, you know. And then, when they turned back to the page before, it had the same words on it that it had had when they read it the first time.

"Gee," said Tommy, "what a waste. When you're through with the book, you just throw it away, I guess. Our television screen must have had a million books on it and it's good for plenty more. I wouldn't throw *it* away."

"Same with mine," said Margie. She was eleven and hadn't seen as many telebooks as Tommy had. He was thirteen.

She said, "Where did you find it?"

"In my house." He pointed without looking, because he was busy reading. "In the attic."

"What's it about?"

"School."

Margie was scornful. "School? What's there to write about school? I hate school."

Margie always hated school, but now she hated it more than ever. The mechanical teacher had been giving her test after test in geography and she had been doing worse and worse until her mother had shaken her head sorrowfully and sent for the County Inspector.

He was a round little man with a red face and a whole box of tools with dials and wires. He smiled at Margie and gave her an apple, then took the teacher apart. Margie had hoped he wouldn't know how to put it together again, but he knew how all right, and, after an hour or so, there it was again, large and black and ugly, with a big screen on which all the lessons were shown and the questions were asked. That wasn't so bad. The part Margie hated most was the slot where she had to put homework and test papers. She always had to write them out in a punch code they made her learn when she was six years old, and the mechanical teacher calculated the mark in no time.

The Inspector had smiled after he was finished and patted Margie's head. He said to her mother, "It's not the little girl's fault, Mrs. Jones. I think the geography sector was geared a little too quick. Those things happen sometimes. I've slowed it up to an average ten-year level. Actually, the over-all pattern of her progress is quite satisfactory." And he patted Margie's head again.

Margie was disappointed. She had been hoping they would take the teacher away altogether. They had once taken Tommy's teacher away for nearly a month because the history sector had blanked out completely.

So she said to Tommy, "Why would anyone write about school?"

Tommy looked at her with very superior eyes. "Because it's not our kind of school, stupid. This is the old kind of school that they had hundreds and hundreds of years ago." He added loftily, pronouncing the word carefully, "*Centuries* ago."

Margie was hurt. "Well, I don't know what kind of school they had all that time ago." She read the book over his shoulder for a while, then said, "Anyway, they had a teacher."

"Sure they had a teacher, but it wasn't a *regular* teacher. It was a man."

"A man? How could a man be a teacher?"

"Well, he just told the boys and girls things and gave them homework and asked them questions."

"A man isn't smart enough."

"Sure he is. My father knows as much as my teacher."

"He can't. A man can't know as much as a teacher."

"He knows almost as much, I betcha."

Margie wasn't prepared to dispute that. She said, "I wouldn't want a strange man in my house to teach me."

Tommy screamed with laughter. "You don't know much, Margie. The teachers didn't live in the house. They had a special building and all the kids went there."

"And all the kids learned the same thing?"

"Sure, if they were the same age."

"But my mother says a teacher has to be adjusted to fit the mind of each boy and girl it teaches and that each kid has to be taught differently."

"Just the same they didn't do it that way then. If you don't like it, you don't have to read the book."

"I didn't say I didn't like it," Margie said quickly. She wanted to read about those funny schools.

32   They weren't even half-finished when Margie's mother called, "Margie! School!"

33   Margie looked up. "Not yet, Mamma."

34   "Now!" said Mrs. Jones. "And it's probably time for Tommy, too."

35   Margie said to Tommy, "Can I read the book some more with you after school?"

36   "Maybe," he said nonchalantly. He walked away whistling, the dusty old book tucked beneath his arm.

37   Margie went into the schoolroom. It was right next to her bedroom, and the mechanical teacher was on and waiting for her. It was always on at the same time every day except Saturday and Sunday, because her mother said little girls learned better if they learned at regular hours.

38   The screen was lit up, and it said: "Today's arithmetic lesson is on the addition of proper fractions. Please insert yesterday's homework in the proper slot."

39   Margie did so with a sigh. She was thinking about the old schools they had when her grandfather's grandfather was a little boy. All the kids from the whole neighbourhood came, laughing and shouting in the schoolyard, sitting together in the schoolroom, going home together at the end of the day. They learned the same things, so they could help one another on the homework and talk about it.

40   And the teachers were people....

41   The mechanical teacher was flashing on the screen: "When we add the fractions $1/2$ and $1/4$—"

42   Margie was thinking about how the kids must have loved it in the old days. She was thinking about the fun they had.

1957

NOTES

Isaac Asimov (1920–1992) is one of the most famous and prolific science fiction writers ever, completing about 500 books in his lifetime. He was a scientist, with a doctorate in biochemistry.

In the 1950s, when this story was written, computers were huge, room-sized machines that weighed several tons, ran on vacuum tubes, and read punch cards. Although Asimov's description of the technology is dated, the issues are the same as the ones we deal with today.

When this story was written, the term "computer," meaning an electronic machine, was not common parlance. Note how Asimov calls it a "mechanical" teacher.

Punch code A method of storing information that consisted of punching holes into cards and feeding them into a computer for processing. From this action, the words "input" and "output" have entered our everyday vocabulary.

COMPREHENSION AND DISCUSSION

1. What image do Margie and Tommy have about books?
2. Describe Margie's schooling in your own words.
3. Why does Margie yearn for the school days of her great-great-grandparents? Why isn't Margie's schooling as fun as in the olden days?
4. Besides information, what else do you acquire as you go to school with other students?
5. Would you learn faster or better if you learned at home using the computer and the Internet? Explain your answer.
6. How do you know that this story is dated? What clues do you have to support your view?

LITERARY TECHNIQUES

The names of characters are an important part of the story. "Margie" and "Tommy" are both children's names. Often, names that end in an "ee" sound are children's nicknames. As adults, the characters would more likely be "Marge" or "Margaret," "Tom" or "Thomas." These names were also more common in the 1950s and 1960s than today.

Science fiction is a literary genre that places science and technology in the forefront with humanity and speculates what may happen in some near or distant future. While highly imaginative, it still adheres to a sense of logic and reasonableness in speculating on things to come.

Asimov depends on the reader's experience with traditional schooling in which the pupil goes to school and reads from a printed book. In order to heighten the irony, he also speculates that the reader may not have enjoyed traditional education and may not consider school to be much fun. (In this story, irony is the contrast or contradiction between what is perceived and what is actual.)

ASSIGNMENTS

1. Discuss the advantages or disadvantages of distance education through the Internet. Would you prefer home schooling to regular schooling?
2. Write a paragraph comparing classroom learning and individual learning.
3. Will the book and the printed page be totally obsolete within the next 50 or 100 years? Use research on the electronic book to support your arguments.
4. Speculate on the educational system twenty years from now.
5. A major problem with books printed in the 20th century is the use of acid paper. Because acid paper deteriorates quickly, many of the books from this time are ruined, whereas older books remain in relatively good condition. Write a report on the current use of acid-free paper.
6. What is the most significant development in the evolution of computer technology? Research the history of computers to supplement what you already know.
7. Some predictions of future technological advancements have proved to be spectacularly inaccurate. For example, in 1943, Thomas Watson, the chairman of IBM said, "I think there is a world market for maybe five computers." It was also predicted that with advances in technology, we would have trouble looking for ways to fill our ample leisure time; instead, we are working more hours than ever. Choose a prediction for the future, either in fiction or non-fiction, that was proved wrong and explain why it did not come to fruition.
8. Isaac Asimov is a character in the story "One Rejection Too Many" (p. 165). What image do you get of him from these two readings?

Greasy Lake
T. Coraghessan Boyle

It's about a mile down on the dark side of Route 8.
— Bruce Springsteen

There was a time when courtesy and winning ways went out of style, when it was good to be bad, when you cultivated decadence like a taste. We were all dangerous characters then. We wore torn-up leather jackets, slouched around with toothpicks in our mouths, sniffed glue and ether and what somebody claimed was cocaine. When we wheeled our parents' whining station wagons out onto the street we left a patch of rubber half a block long. We drank gin and grape juice, Tango, Thunderbird, and Bali Hai. We were nineteen. We were bad. We read André Gide and struck elaborate poses to show that we didn't give a shit about anything. At night, we went up to Greasy Lake.

Through the centre of town, up the strip, past the housing developments and shopping malls, street lights giving way to the thin streaming illumination of the headlights, trees crowding the asphalt in a black unbroken wall: that was the way out to Greasy Lake. The Indians had called it Wakan, a reference to the clarity of its waters. Now it was fetid and murky, the mud banks glittering with broken glass and strewn with beer cans and the charred remains of bonfires. There was a single ravaged island a hundred yards from shore, so stripped of vegetation it looked as if the air force had strafed it. We went up to the lake because everyone went there, because we wanted to snuff the rich scent of possibility on the breeze, watch a girl take off her clothes and plunge into the festering murk, drink beer, smoke pot, howl at the stars, savour the incongruous full-throated roar of rock and roll against the primeval susurrus of frogs and crickets. This was nature.

I was there one night, late, in the company of two dangerous characters. Digby wore a gold star in his right ear and allowed his father to pay his tuition at Cornell; Jeff was thinking of quitting school to become a painter/musician/headshop proprietor. They were both expert in the social graces, quick with a sneer, able to manage a Ford with lousy shocks over a rutted and gutted blacktop road at eighty-five while rolling a joint as compact as a Tootsie Roll Pop stick. They could lounge against a bank of booming speakers and trade "man"s with the best of them or roll out across the dance floor as if their joints worked on bearings. They were slick and quick and they wore their mirror shades at breakfast and dinner, in the shower, in closets and caves. In short, they were bad.

4   I drove. Digby pounded the dashboard and shouted along with Toots & the Maytals while Jeff hung his head out the window and streaked the side of my mother's Bel Air with vomit. It was early June, the air soft as a hand on your cheek, the third night of summer vacation. The first two nights we'd been out till dawn, looking for something we never found. On this, the third night, we'd cruised the strip sixty-seven times, been in and out of every bar and club we could think of in a twenty-mile radius, stopped twice for bucket chicken and forty-cent hamburgers, debated going to a party at the house of a girl Jeff's sister knew, and chucked two dozen raw eggs at mailboxes and hitchhikers. It was 2:00 A.M.; the bars were closing. There was nothing to do but take a bottle of lemon-flavoured gin up to Greasy Lake.

5   The taillights of a single car winked at us as we swung into the dirt lot with its tufts of weed and washboard corrugations; '57 Chevy, mint, metallic blue. On the far side of the lot, like the exoskeleton of some gaunt chrome insect, a chopper leaned against its kickstand. And that was it for excitement: some junkie halfwit biker and a car freak pumping his girlfriend. Whatever it was we were looking for, we weren't about to find it at Greasy Lake. Not that night.

6   But then all of a sudden Digby was fighting for the wheel. "Hey, that's Tony Lovett's car! Hey!" he shouted, while I stabbed at the brake pedal and the Bel Air nosed up to the gleaming bumper of the parked Chevy. Digby leaned on the horn, laughing, and instructed me to put my brights on. I flicked on the brights. This was hilarious. A joke. Tony would experience premature withdrawal and expect to be confronted by grim-looking state troopers with flashlights. We hit the horn, strobed the lights, and then jumped out of the car to press our witty faces to Tony's windows; for all we knew we might even catch a glimpse of some little fox's tit, and then we could slap backs with red-faced Tony, roughhouse a little, and go on to new heights of adventure and daring.

7   The first mistake, the one that opened the whole floodgate, was losing my grip on the keys. In the excitement, leaping from the car with the gin in one hand and a roach clip in the other, I spilled them in the grass — in the dark, rank, mysterious nighttime grass of Greasy Lake. This was a tactical error, as damaging and irreversible in its way as Westmoreland's decision to dig in at Khe Sanh. I felt it like a jab of intuition, and I stopped there by the open door, peering vaguely into the night that puddled up round my feet.

8   The second mistake — and this was inextricably bound up with the first — was identifying the car as Tony Lovett's. Even before the very bad

character in greasy jeans and engineer boots ripped out of the driver's door, I began to realize that this chrome blue was much lighter than the robin's-egg of Tony's car, and that Tony's car didn't have rear-mounted speakers. Judging from their expressions, Digby and Jeff were privately groping toward the same inevitable and unsettling conclusion as I was.

In any case, there was no reasoning with this bad greasy character — clearly he was a man of action. The first lusty Rockette kick of his steel-toed boot caught me under the chin, chipped my favourite tooth, and left me sprawled in the dirt. Like a fool, I'd gone down on one knee to comb the stiff hacked grass for the keys, my mind making connections in the most dragged-out, testudineous way, knowing that things had gone wrong, that I was in a lot of trouble, and that the lost ignition key was my grail and my salvation. The three or four succeeding blows were mainly absorbed by my right buttock and the tough piece of bone at the base of my spine.

Meanwhile, Digby vaulted the kissing bumpers and delivered a savage kung-fu blow to the greasy character's collarbone. Digby had just finished a course in martial arts for phys-ed credit and had spend the better part of the past two nights telling us apocryphal tales of Bruce Lee types and of the raw power invested in lightning blows shot from coiled wrists, ankles, and elbows. The greasy character was unimpressed. He merely backed off a step, his face like a Toltec mask, and laid Digby out with a single whistling roundhouse blow... but by now Jeff had got into the act, and I was beginning to extricate myself from the dirt, a tinny compound of shock, rage, and impotence wadded in my throat.

Jeff was on the guy's back, biting at his ear. Digby was on the ground, cursing. I went for the tire iron I kept under the driver's seat. I kept it there because bad characters always keep tire irons under the driver's seat, for just such an occasion as this. Never mind that I hadn't been involved in a fight since sixth grade, when a kid with a sleepy eye and two streams of mucus depending from his nostrils hit me in the knee with a Louisville slugger, never mind that I'd touched the tire iron exactly twice before, to change tires: it was there. And I went for it.

I was terrified. Blood was beating in my ears, my hands were shaking, my heart turning over like a dirtbike in the wrong gear. My antagonist was shirtless, and a single cord of muscle flashed across his chest as he bent forward to peel Jeff from his back like a wet overcoat. "Motherfucker," he spat, over and over, and I was aware in that instant that all four of us — Digby, Jeff, and myself included — were chanting "motherfucker, motherfucker," as if it were a battle cry. (What happened next? the detective asks the murderer from beneath the turned-down brim of his porkpie hat. I don't know, the murderer says, something came over me. Exactly.)

13   Digby poked the flat of his hand in the bad character's face and I came at him like a kamikaze, mindless, raging, stung with humiliation—the whole thing, from the initial boot in the chin to this murderous primal instinct involving no more than sixty hyperventilating, gland-flooding seconds—I came at him and brought the tire iron down across his ear. The effect was instantaneous, astonishing. He was a stunt man and this was Hollywood, he was a big grimacing toothy balloon and I was a man with a straight pin. He collapsed. Wet his pants. Went loose in his boots.

14   A single second, big as a zeppelin, floated by. We were standing over him in a circle, gritting our teeth, jerking our necks, our limbs and hands and feet twitching with glandular discharges. No one said anything. We just stared down at the guy, the car freak, the lover, the bad greasy character laid low. Digby looked at me; so did Jeff. I was still holding the tire iron, a tuft of hair clinging to the crook like dandelion fluff, like down. Rattled, I dropped it in the dirt, already envisioning the headlines, the pitted faces of the police inquisitors, the gleam of handcuffs, clank of bars, the big black shadows rising from the back of the cell... when suddenly a raw torn shriek cut through me like all the juice in all the electric chairs in the country.

15   It was the fox. She was short, barefoot, dressed in panties and a man's shirt. "Animals!" she screamed, running at us with her fists clenched and wisps of blow-dried hair in her face. There was a silver chain round her ankle, and her toenails flashed in the glare of the headlights. I think it was the toenails that did it. Sure, the gin and cannibis and even the Kentucky Fried may have had a hand in it, but it was the sight of those flaming toes that set us off—the toad emerging from the loaf in *Virgin Spring,* lipstick smeared on a child; she was already tainted. We were on her like Bergman's deranged brothers—see no evil, hear none, speak none—panting, wheezing, tearing at her clothes, grabbing for flesh. We were bad characters, and we were scared and hot and three steps over the line—anything could have happened.

16   It didn't.

17   Before we could pin her to the hood of the car, our eyes masked with lust and greed and the purest primal badness, a pair of headlights swung into the lot. There we were, dirty, bloody, guilty, dissociated from humanity and civilization, the first of the Ur-crimes behind us, the second in progress, shreds of nylon panty and spandex brassiere dangling from our fingers, our flies open, lips licked—there we were, caught in the spotlight. Nailed.

We bolted. First for the car, and then, realizing we had no way of starting it, for the woods. I thought nothing. I thought escape. The headlights came at me like accusing fingers. I was gone.

Ram-bam-bam, across the parking lot, past the chopper and into the feculent undergrowth at the lake's edge, insects flying up in my face, weeds whipping, frogs and snakes and red-eyed turtles splashing off into the night: I was already ankle-deep in muck and tepid water and still going strong. Behind me, the girl's screams rose in intensity, disconsolate, incriminating, the screams of the Sabine women, the Christian martyrs, Anne Frank dragged from the garret. I kept going, pursued by those cries, imagining cops and bloodhounds. The water was up to my knees when I realized what I was doing: I was going to swim for it. Swim the breadth of Greasy Lake and hide myself in the thick clot of woods on the far side. They'd never find me there.

I was breathing in sobs, in gasps. The water lapped at my waist as I looked out over the moon-burnished ripples, the mats of algae that clung to the surface like scabs. Digby and Jeff had vanished. I paused. Listened. The girl was quieter now, screams tapering to sobs, but there were male voices, angry, excited, and the high-pitched ticking of the second car's engine. I waded deeper, stealthy, hunted, the ooze sucking at my sneakers. As I was about to take the plunge — at the very instant I dropped my shoulder for the first slashing stroke — I blundered into something. Something unspeakable, obscene, something soft, wet, moss-grown. A patch of weed? A log? When I reached out to touch it, it gave like a rubber duck, it gave like flesh.

In one of those nasty little epiphanies for which we are prepared by films and TV and childhood visits to the funeral home to ponder the shrunken painted forms of dead grandparents, I understood what it was that bobbed there so inadmissibly in the dark. Understood, and stumbled back in horror and revulsion, my mind yanked in six different directions (I was nineteen, a mere child, an infant, and here in the space of five minutes I'd struck down one greasy character and blundered into the waterlogged carcass of a second), thinking, The keys, the keys, why did I have to go and lose the keys? I stumbled back, but the muck took hold of my feet — a sneaker snagged, balance lost — and suddenly I was pitching face forward into the buoyant black mass, throwing out my hands in desperation while simultaneously conjuring the image of reeking frogs and muskrats revolving in slicks of their own deliquescing juices. AAAAArrrgh! I shot from the water like a torpedo, the dead man rotating to expose a mossy beard and eyes cold as the moon. I must have shouted out, thrashing around in the weeds, because the voices behind me suddenly became animated.

22 "What was that?"

23 "It's them, it's them: they tried to, tried to... *rape* me!" Sobs.

24 A man's voice, flat Midwestern accent. "You sons a bitches, we'll kill you!"

25 Frogs, crickets.

26 Then another voice, harsh, *r*-less, Lower East Side: "Motherfucker!" I recognized the verbal virtuosity of the bad greasy character in the engineer boots. Tooth chipped, sneakers gone, coated in mud and slime and worse, crouching breathless in the weeds waiting to have my ass thoroughly and definitively kicked and fresh from the hideous stinking embrace of a three-days-dead-corpse, I suddenly felt a rush of joy and vindication: the son of a bitch was alive! Just as quickly, my bowels turned to ice. "Come on out of there, you pansy mothers!" the bad greasy character was screaming. He shouted curses till he was out of breath.

27 The crickets started up again, then the frogs. I held my breath. All at once was a sound in the reeds, a swishing, a splash: thunk-a-thunk. They were throwing rocks. The frogs fell silent. I cradled my head. Swish, swish, thunk-a-thunk. A wedge of feldspar the size of a cue ball glanced off my knee. I bit my finger.

28 It was then that they turned to the car. I heard a door slam, a curse, and then the sound of the headlights shattering — almost a good-natured sound, celebratory, like corks popping from the necks of bottles. This was succeeded by the dull booming of fenders, metal on metal, and then the icy crash of the windshield. I inched forward, elbows and knees, my belly pressed to the muck, thinking of guerrillas and commandos and *The Naked and the Dead*. I parted the weeds and squinted the length of the parking lot.

29 The second car — it was a Trans-Am — was still running, its high beams washing the scene in a lurid stagy light. Tire iron flailing, the greasy bad character was laying into the side of my mother's Bel Air like an avenging demon, his shadow riding up the trunks of the trees. Whomp. Whomp. Whomp-whomp. The other two guys — blond types, in fraternity jackets — were helping out with tree branches and skull-sized boulders. One of them was gathering up bottles, rocks, muck, candy wrappers, used condoms, poptops, and other refuse and pitching it through the window on the driver's side. I could see the fox, a white bulb behind the windshield of the '57 Chevy. "Bobbie," she wined over the thumping, "come on." The greasy character paused a moment, took one good swipe at the left taillight, and then heaved the tire iron halfway across the lake. Then he fired up the '57 and was gone.

Blond head nodded at blond head. One said something to the other, too low for me to catch. They were no doubt thinking that in helping to annihilate my mother's car they'd committed a fairly rash act, and thinking too that there were three bad characters connected with that very car watching them from the woods. Perhaps other possibilities occurred to them as well — police, jail cells, justices of the peace, reparations, lawyers, irate parents, fraternal censure. Whatever they were thinking, they suddenly dropped branches, bottles, and rocks and sprang for their car in unison, as if they'd choreographed it. Five seconds. That's all it took. The engine shrieked, the tires squealed, a cloud of dust rose from the rutted lot and then settled back on darkness.

I don't know how long I lay there, the bad breath of decay all around me, my jacket heavy as a bear, the primordial ooze subtly reconstituting itself to accommodate my upper thighs and testicles. My jaws ached, my knee throbbed, my coccyx was on fire. I contemplated suicide, wondered if I'd need bridgework, scraped the recesses of my brain for some sort of excuse to give my parents — a tree had fallen on the car, I was blinded by a bread truck, hit and run, vandals had got to it while we were playing chess at Digby's. Then I thought of the dead man. He was probably the only person on the planet worse off than I was. I thought about him, fog on the lake, insects chirring eerily, and felt the tug of fear, felt the darkness opening up inside me like a set of jaws. Who was he, I wondered, this victim of time and circumstance bobbing sorrowfully in the lake at my back. The owner of the chopper, no doubt, a bad older character come to this. Shot during a murky drug deal, drowned while drunkenly frolicking in the lake. Another headline. My car was wrecked; he was dead.

When the eastern half of the sky went from black to cobalt and the trees began to separate themselves from the shadows, I pushed myself up from the mud and stepped out into the open. By now the birds had begun to take over for the crickets, and dew lay slick on the leaves. There was a smell in the air, raw and sweet at the same time, the smell of the sun firing buds and opening blossoms. I contemplated the car. It lay there like a wreck along the highway, like a steel sculpture left over from a vanished civilization. Everything was still. This was nature.

I was circling the car, as dazed and bedraggled as the sole survivor of an air blitz, when Digby and Jeff emerged from the trees behind me. Digby's face was crosshatched with smears of dirt; Jeff's jacket was gone and his shirt was torn across the shoulder. They slouched across the lot, looking sheepish, and silently came up beside me to gape at the ravaged automobile. No one said a word. After a while Jeff swung open the driver's door and began to scoop the broken glass and garbage off the seat. I looked at Digby. He shrugged. "At least they didn't slash the tires," he said.

34   It was true: the tires were intact. There was no windshield, the headlights were staved in, and the body looked as if it had been sledge-hammered for a quarter a shot at the county fair, but the tires were inflated to regulation pressure. The car was drivable. In silence, all three of us bent to scrape the mud and shattered glass from the interior. I said nothing about the biker. When we were finished, I reached in my pocket for the keys, experienced a nasty stab of recollection, cursed myself, and turned to search the grass. I spotted them almost immediately, no more than five feet from the open door, glinting like jewels in the first tapering shaft of sunlight. There was no reason to get philosophical about it: I eased into the seat and turned the engine over.

35   It was at that precise moment that the silver Mustang with the flame decals rumbled into the lot. All three of us froze; then Digby and Jeff slid into the car and slammed the door. We watched as the Mustang rocked and bobbed across the ruts and finally jerked to a halt beside the forlorn chopper at the far end of the lot. "Let's go," Digby said. I hesitated, the Bel Air wheezing beneath me.

36   Two girls emerged from the Mustang. Tight jeans, stiletto heels, hair like frozen fur. They bent over the motorcycle, paced back and forth aimlessly, glanced once or twice at us, and then ambled over to where the reeds sprang up in a green fence round the perimeter of the lake. One of them cupped her hands to her mouth. "Al," she called. "Hey, Al!"

37   "Come on," Digby hissed. "Let's get out of here."

38   But it was too late. The second girl was picking her way across the lot, unsteady on her heels, looking up at us and then away. She was older — twenty-five or -six — and as she came closer we could see there was something wrong with her: she was stoned or drunk, lurching now and waving her arms for balance. I gripped the steering wheel as if it were the ejection lever of a flaming jet, and Digby spat out my name, twice, terse and impatient.

39   "Hi," the girl said.

40   We looked at her like zombies, like war veterans, like deaf-and-dumb pencil peddlars.

41   She smiled, her lips cracked and dry. "Listen," she said, bending from the waist to look in the window, "you guys seen Al?" Her pupils were pinpoints, her eyes glass. She jerked her neck. "That's his bike over there — Al's. You seen him?"

42   Al. I didn't know what to say. I wanted to get out of the car and retch, I wanted to go home to my parents' house and crawl into bed. Digby poked me in the ribs. "We haven't seen anybody," I said.

The girl seemed to consider this, reaching out a slim veiny arm to brace herself against the car. "No matter," she said, slurring the *t*'s, "he'll turn up." And then, as if she'd just taken stock of the whole scene — the ravaged car and our battered faces, the desolation of the place — she said: "Hey, you guys look like some pretty bad characters — been fightin', huh?" We stared straight ahead, rigid as catatonics. She was fumbling in her pocket and muttering something. Finally she held out a handful of tablets in glassine wrappers: "Hey, you want to party, you want to do some of these with me and Sarah?"

I just looked at her. I thought I was going to cry. Digby broke the silence. "No thanks," he said, leaning over me. "Some other time."

I put the car in gear and it inched forward with a groan, shaking off pellets of glass like an old dog shedding water after a bath, heaving over the ruts on its worn springs, creeping toward the highway. There was a sheen of sun on the lake. I looked back. The girl was still standing there, watching us, her shoulders slumped, hand outstretched.

1979

NOTES

The quotation at the beginning of the story is from Bruce Springsteen's song "Spirit in the Night," which talks about Greasy Lake.

Gin and grape juice, Tango, Thunderbird and Bali Hai Names of popular alcoholic beverages.

André Gide (1869–1951) A French writer, won a Nobel Prize for Literature (1947). In his works, he expressed ideas on liberating feelings and hedonistic living. His writings influenced a generation of young rebels.

Toots & the Maytals A ska and reggae music band that lasted from 1962 to 1981 and reformed in the '90s.

Khe Sanh During the Vietnam War, the American soldiers were attacked by the Viet Cong and North Vietnamese soldiers at Khe Sanh (1967). In the beginning, this site had little strategic value. In short, what started as a minor incident suddenly became a major issue. General Westmoreland was the commander-in-chief of the American armed forces.

Rockettes A famous troupe of dancing girls at New York's Radio City Music Hall. They are renowned for their precision high kicks.

Bruce Lee (1940–1973) A Chinese American actor and legendary kung-fu master who died in the prime of his life. His most famous movie is *Enter the Dragon;* his renowned TV role is Kato in the series *The Green Hornet.* He still has a cult following.

Toltec mask Mask made by people who lived in Mexico before the Aztecs, characteristically rigid.

Louisville slugger A brand of baseball bat.

Fox Slang term meaning a girl.

Ingmar Bergman A Swedish filmmaker. His movies have a strong philosophical bent. His work, *Virgin Spring* (1960), won an Oscar for Best Foreign Film.

Ur-crimes Archetypal or primal wrongdoings, dating back to the early civilization of Ur, in Mesopotamia. The narrator refers to violent crimes, like murder, and sexual acts, like rape.

Sabine women Women who inhabited villages near Rome who were kidnapped by early Romans and taken as wives. This mythological story has been adapted into a musical, *Seven Brides for Seven Brothers,* and depicted in *The Rape of the Sabine Women,* a painting by Nicolas Poussin.

Anne Frank (1929–1945) A Jewish adolescent who wrote about her wartime experiences hiding from the Nazis during WWII. She was later captured and taken to a concentration camp, where she died. Her diary is now a famous book.

The Naked and the Dead (1948) A book by Norman Mailer, one of the definitive WWII novels about American soldiers in the Pacific theatre.

COMPREHENSION AND DISCUSSION

1. Describe the three main characters.
2. Explain the boys' actions in the story.

3. How do these boys define "bad"? What do you think of the values they hold?
4. Should the "greasy" character have beaten up on the three boys?
5. Who is Al? Why is he important to the rehabilitation of the narrator?
6. At what point do the boys learn from their mistakes? Or, do they learn anything at all?
7. Why is the setting of Greasy Lake important? Why do teenagers go there?
8. When do you think this story took place?
9. How is this story about youth culture? Has anything really changed for teenagers?
10. What makes this story funny rather than tragic? Can you identify the elements used to lighten the story?
11. Why is the following statement humorous and truthful: "Understood and stumbled back in horror and revulsion, my mind yanked in six different directions (I was nineteen, a mere child, an infant, and here in the space of five minutes I'd struck down one greasy character and blundered into the waterlogged carcass of a second), thinking, The keys, the keys, why did I have to go and lose the keys?" (p. 39).

LITERARY TECHNIQUES

Boyle's narrator remains nameless or anonymous throughout. The merit of this technique is that the "I" represents all young adults who must perform certain immature deeds before they learn restraint and wisdom. Do not conclude that the "I" narrator is the writer, Boyle. The "I" is a character in the story.

Boyle makes a number of allusions in this story. Allusion is a figure of speech that draws a quick reference to persons (historical or living), events, literature, and such. It taps into common knowledge, experience, or memory mutual to both reader and writer. Its purpose is to elicit recognition, comparison, and response. See the Notes section for the explanation of some allusions and references.

Note the repetition of the phrase "bad, greasy character" and its variations. The context of the word "bad" changes meaning. When the narrator refers to himself and his friends, the word has positive connotations; when he says it about others, it has negative meanings.

Humour is defined as something that causes laughter. Often in literature, humour helps lighten certain serious situations. For example, Digby's use of kung-fu is ineffectual against the "greasy" opponent. The fighting is serious, but the way it is described is funny: Upon being struck by Digby, "[t]he greasy character was unimpressed. He merely backed off a step, his face like a Toltec mask, and laid Digby out with a single whistling round-house blow..." (p. 37).

Many times, humour comes out of irony. (Here, irony may be defined as unexpected twists in the story.) For example, the girl in the Chevy resists the three boys' advances, whereas later, after their harrowing experience, the two girls in "[t]ight jeans, stiletto heels, hair like frozen fur" (p. 42) are quite available. By this time, however, the boys are no longer interested in the invitation.

ASSIGNMENTS

1. Write a short dialogue in which the narrator explains to his mother how her Bel Air station wagon was damaged.
2. What would have happened had the boys taken up the two girls' offer at the end? Would this action confirm that they were "bad" — that they found available women and that the night was not entirely wasted? In short, imagine an alternate ending.
3. There is a short film of "Greasy Lake," but it may be hard to find. Compare it with the story.
4. Listen to the Bruce Springsteen song "Spirit in the Night" in which the lake is mentioned. Compare Springsteen's idea of Greasy Lake with Boyle's.
5. Watch George Lucas's 1973 film *American Graffiti,* and compare the shenanigans of the main characters in the movie to those in Boyle's short story.
6. Read Alice Munro's "An Ounce of Cure" (p. 153). Both stories deal with teenagers getting into trouble. Explain the differences.
7. Write an essay on teenage drinking. Discuss the causes and effects.

All the Years of Her Life
Morley Callaghan

They were closing the drugstore, and Alfred Higgins, who had just taken off his white jacket, was putting on his coat and getting ready to go home. The little grey-haired man, Sam Carr, who owned the drugstore, was bending down behind the cash register, and when Alfred Higgins passed him, he looked up and said softly, "Just a moment, Alfred. One moment before you go."

The soft, confident, quiet way in which Sam Carr spoke made Alfred start to button his coat nervously. He felt sure his face was white. Sam Carr usually said, "Good night," brusquely, without looking up. In the six months he had been working in the drugstore Alfred had never heard his employer speak softly like that. His heart began to beat so loud it was hard for him to get his breath. "What is it, Mr. Carr?" he asked.

"Maybe you'd be good enough to take a few things out of your pocket and leave them here before you go," Sam Carr said.

"What things? What are you talking about?"

"You've got a compact and a lipstick and at least two tubes of toothpaste in your pockets, Alfred."

"What do you mean? Do you think I'm crazy?" Alfred blustered. His face got red and he knew he looked fierce with indignation. But Sam Carr, standing by the door with his blue eyes shining brightly behind his glasses and his lips moving underneath his grey mustache, only nodded his head a few times, and then Alfred grew very frightened and he didn't know what to say. Slowly he raised his hand and dipped it into his pocket, and with his eyes never meeting Sam Carr's eyes, he took out a blue compact and two tubes of toothpaste and a lipstick, and he laid them one by one on the counter.

"Petty thieving, eh, Alfred?" Sam Carr said. "And maybe you'd be good enough to tell me how long this has been going on."

"This is the first time I ever took anything."

"So now you think you'll tell me a lie, eh? What kind of a sap do I look like, huh? I don't know what goes on in my own store, eh? I tell you you've been doing this pretty steady," Sam Carr said as he went over and stood behind the cash register.

Ever since Alfred had left school he had been getting into trouble wherever he worked. He lived at home with his mother and his father, who was a printer. His two older brothers were married and his sister had got married last year, and it would have been all right for his parents now if Alfred had only been able to keep a job.

11 While Sam Carr smiled and stroked the side of his face very delicately with the tips of his fingers, Alfred began to feel that familiar terror growing in him that had been in him every time he had got into such trouble.

12 "I liked you," Sam Carr was saying. "I liked you and would have trusted you, and now look what I got to do." While Alfred watched with his alert, frightened blue eyes, Sam Carr drummed with his fingers on the counter. "I don't like to call a cop in point-blank," he was saying as he looked very worried. "You're a fool, and maybe I should call your father and tell him you're a fool. Maybe I should let them know I'm going to have you locked up."

13 "My father's not at home. He's a printer. He works nights," Alfred said.

14 "Who's at home?"

15 "My mother, I guess."

16 "Then we'll see what she says." Sam Carr went to the phone and dialled the number. Alfred was not so much ashamed, but there was that deep fright growing in him, and he blurted out arrogantly, like a strong, full-grown man, "Just a minute. You don't need to draw anybody else in. You don't need to tell her." He wanted to sound like a swaggering, big guy who could look after himself, yet the old, childish hope was in him, the longing that someone at home would come and help him. "Yeah, that's right, he's in trouble," Mr. Carr was saying. "Yeah, your boy works for me. You'd better come down in a hurry." And when he was finished Mr. Carr went over to the door and looked out at the street and watched the people passing in the late summer night. "I'll keep my eye out for a cop," was all he said.

17 Alfred knew how his mother would come rushing in; she would rush in with her eyes blazing, or maybe she would be crying, and she would push him away when he tried to talk to her, and make him feel her dreadful contempt; yet he longed that she might come before Mr. Carr saw the cop on the beat passing the door.

18 While they waited — and it seemed a long time — they did not speak, and when at last they heard someone tapping on the closed door, Mr. Carr, turning the latch, said crisply, "Come in, Mrs. Higgins." He looked hard-faced and stern.

19 Mrs. Higgins must have been going to bed when he telephoned, for her hair was tucked in loosely under her hat, and her hand at her throat held her light coat tight across her chest so her dress would not show. She came in, large and plump, with a little smile on her friendly face. Most of the store

lights had been turned out and at first she did not see Alfred, who was standing in the shadow at the end of the counter. Yet as soon as she saw him she did not look as Alfred thought she would look: she smiled, her blue eyes never wavered, and with a calmness and dignity that made them forget that her clothes seemed to have been thrown on her, she put out her hand to Mr. Carr and said politely, "I'm Mrs. Higgins. I'm Alfred's mother."

Mr. Carr was a bit embarrassed by her lack of terror and her simplicity, and he hardly knew what to say to her, so she asked, "Is Alfred in trouble?"

"He is. He's been taking things from the store. I caught him red-handed. Little things like compacts and toothpaste and lipsticks. Stuff he can sell easily," the proprietor said.

As she listened Mrs. Higgins looked at Alfred sometimes and nodded her head sadly, and when Sam Carr had finished she said gravely, "Is it so, Alfred?"

"Yes."

"Why have you been doing it?"

"I been spending money, I guess."

"On what?"

"Going around with the guys, I guess," Alfred said.

Mrs. Higgins put out her hand and touched Sam Carr's arms with an understanding gentleness, and speaking as though afraid of disturbing him, she said, "If you would only listen to me before doing anything." Her simple earnestness made her shy; her humility made her falter and look away, but in a moment she was smiling gravely again, and she said with a kind of patient dignity, "What did you intend to do, Mr. Carr?"

"I was going to get a cop. That's what I ought to do."

"Yes, I suppose so. It's not for me to say, because he's my son. Yet I sometimes think a little good advice is the best thing for a boy when he's at a certain period in his life," she said.

Alfred couldn't understand his mother's quiet composure, for if they had been at home and someone had suggested that he was going to be arrested, he knew she would be in a rage and would cry out against him. Yet now she was standing there with that gentle, pleading smile on her face, saying, "I wonder if you don't think it would be better just to let him come home with me. He looks a big fellow, doesn't he? It takes some of them a long time to get any sense," and they both stared at Alfred, who shifted away with a bit of light shining for a moment on his thin face and the tiny pimples over his cheekbone.

But even while he was turning away uneasily Alfred was realizing that Mr. Carr had become aware that his mother was really a fine woman; he knew that Sam Carr was puzzled by his mother, as if he had expected her to come in and plead with him tearfully, and instead he was being made to feel a bit ashamed by her vast tolerance. While there was only the sound of the mother's soft, assured voice in the store, Mr. Carr began to nod his head encouragingly at her. Without being alarmed, while being just large and still and simple and hopeful, she was becoming dominant there in the dimly lit store. "Of course, I don't want to be harsh," Mr. Carr was saying, "I'll tell you what I'll do. I'll just fire him and let it go at that. How's that?" and he got up and shook hands with Mrs. Higgins, bowing low to her in deep respect.

33 There was such warmth and gratitude in the way she said, "I'll never forget your kindness," that Mr. Carr began to feel warm and genial himself.

34 "Sorry we had to meet this way," he said. "But I'm glad I got in touch with you. Just wanted to do the right thing, that's all," he said.

35 "It's better to meet like this than never, isn't it?" she said. Suddenly they clasped hands as if they liked each other, as if they had known each other a long time. "Good night, sir," she said.

36 "Good night, Mrs. Higgins. I'm truly sorry," he said.

37 The mother and son walked along the street together, and the mother was taking a long, firm stride as she looked ahead with her stern face full of worry. Alfred was afraid to speak to her, he was afraid of the silence that was between them, so he only looked ahead too, for the excitement and relief was still pretty strong in him; but in a little while, going along like that in silence made him terribly aware of the strength and the sternness in her; he began to wonder what she was thinking of as she stared ahead so grimly; she seemed to have forgotten that he walked beside her; so when they were passing under the Sixth Avenue elevated and the rumble of the train seemed to break the silence, he said in his old, blustering way, "Thank God it turned out like that. I certainly won't get in a jam like that again."

38 "Be quiet. Don't speak to me. You've disgraced me again and again," she said bitterly.

39 "That's the last time. That's all I'm saying."

40 "Have the decency to be quiet," she snapped. They kept on their way, looking straight ahead.

41 When they were at home and his mother took off her coat, Alfred saw that she was really only half-dressed, and she made him feel afraid again when she said, without even looking at him, "You're a bad lot. God forgive you. It's one thing after another and always has been. Why do you stand there stupidly? Go to bed, why don't you?" When he was going, she said,

"I'm going to make myself a cup of tea. Mind, now, not a word about tonight to your father."

While Alfred was undressing in his bedroom, he heard his mother moving around in the kitchen. She filled the kettle and put it on the stove. She moved a chair. And as he listened there was no shame in him, just wonder and a kind of admiration of her strength and repose. He could still see Sam Carr nodding his head encouragingly at her; he could hear her talking simply and earnestly, and as he sat on his bed he felt a pride in her strength. "She certainly was smooth," he thought. "Gee, I'd like to tell her she sounded swell."

And at last he got up and went along to the kitchen, and when he was at the door he saw his mother pouring herself a cup of tea. He watched and he didn't move. Her face, as she sat there, was a frightened, broken face utterly unlike the face of the woman who had been so assured a little while ago in the drugstore. When she reached out and lifted the kettle to pour hot water in her cup, her hand trembled and the water splashed on the stove. Leaning back in the chair, she sighed and lifted the cup to her lips, and her lips were groping loosely as if they would never reach the cup. She swallowed the hot tea eagerly, and then she straightened up in relief, though her hand holding the cup still trembled. She looked very old.

It seemed to Alfred that this was the way it had been every time he had been in trouble before, that his trembling had really been in her as she hurried out half-dressed to the drugstore. He understood why she had sat alone in the kitchen the night his young sister had kept repeating doggedly that she was getting married. Now he felt all that his mother had been thinking of as they walked along the street together a little while ago. He watched his mother, and he never spoke, but at that moment his youth seemed to be over; he knew all the years of her life by the way her hand trembled as she raised the cup to her lips. It seemed to him that this was the first time he had ever looked upon his mother.

1959

NOTES

Morley Callaghan (1903–1990) is a well-known Canadian writer. His novel *More Joy in Heaven* is one of his best-known works.

Sap A slang term meaning a stupid person or one easily fooled.

COMPREHENSION AND DISCUSSION

1. What kind of person is Alfred Higgins? Why does he steal? How old do you think he is?
2. Should Sam Carr have insisted on having Alfred arrested for shoplifting? What would that have solved?
3. Why didn't Alfred's father come instead? What does this suggest about the Higgins household?
4. Why is Alfred surprised at his mother's behaviour? How is Sam Carr affected by Mrs. Higgins?
5. How does Callaghan gain your interest in the first few paragraphs?
6. What does Alfred Higgins learn upon observing his mother in the kitchen? Do you think he will become a better person for having had this insight?

LITERARY TECHNIQUES

Callaghan uses the third-person limited point of view. We learn the thoughts of only Alfred Higgins, and of no other character. This particular restriction is important to show how the young man comes to understand what he has observed but missed in his previous scraps in which his mother bailed him out. Notice how the story follows Alfred, not his mother, and we see everything from his point of view.

Epiphany A sudden insight. James Joyce (1882–1941) coined this term for his collection of short stories, *The Dubliners*. Borrowed from a religious context, the literary meaning of epiphany is the sudden enlightenment of a character about himself or his surroundings. In the last paragraph, Alfred Higgins has an epiphany. Whether he becomes a better person for it is left to the reader's speculation.

ASSIGNMENTS

1. Compare this story with Boyle's "Greasy Lake" (p. 35) or Munro's "An Ounce of Cure" (p. 153). What lessons are learned, and are they the same lessons?
2. What is the difference between shoplifting and stealing? Is there a difference? Write a short piece on employee pilferage, or on the cost of shoplifting to the economy.

3. Watch the video adaptation of Callaghan's story. (It may be available at your public library.) Note the changes from print to screen. Which do you prefer, the story or the video? Explain in an essay.
4. Can a person learn the right way without first making mistakes? Is experience the best teacher?
5. Recount a moment in your experience when you have had a sudden insight into your life or your soul.

Mr. Truepenny's Book Emporium and Gallery

Charles De Lint

The constellations were consulted for advice, but no one understood them.
—attributed to Elias Canetti

1. My name's Sophie and my friend Jilly says I have faerie blood. Maybe she's right.

2. Faeries are supposed to have problems dealing with modern technology and I certainly have trouble with anything technological. The simplest appliances develop horrendous problems when I'm around. I can't wear a watch because they start to run backwards, unless they're digital; then they just flash random numbers as though the watch's inner workings have taken to measuring fractals instead of time. If I take a subway or bus, it's sure to be late. Or it'll have a new driver who takes a wrong turn and we all get lost.

3. This actually happened to me once. I got on the number 3 at the Kelly Street Bridge and somehow, instead of going downtown on Lee, we ended up heading north into Foxville.

4. I also have strange dreams.

5. I used to think they were the place that my art came from, that my subconscious was playing around with images, tossing them up in my sleep before I put them down on canvas or paper. But then a few months ago I had this serial dream that ran on for a half dozen nights in a row, a kind of fairy tale that was either me stepping into faerie, and therefore real within its own parameters—which is what Jilly would like me to believe—or it was just my subconscious making another attempt to deal with the way my mother abandoned my father and me when I was a kid. I don't really know which I believe anymore, because I still find myself going back to that dream world from time to time and meeting the people I first met there.

6. I even have a boyfriend in that place, which probably tells you more about my usual ongoing social status than it does my state of mind.

7. Rationally, I know it's just a continuation of that serial dream. And I'd let it go at that, except if feels so damn real. Every morning when I wake up from the latest installment, my head's filled with memories of what I've done that seem as real as anything I do during the day—sometimes more so.

But I'm getting off on a tangent. I started off meaning just to introduce myself, and here I am, giving you my life story. What I really wanted to tell you about was Mr. Truepenny.

The thing you have to understand is that I made him up. He was like one of those invisible childhood friends, except I deliberately created him.

We weren't exactly well-off when I was growing up. When my mother left us, I ended up being one of those latchkey kids. We didn't live in the best part of town; Upper Foxville is a rough part of the city and it could be a scary place for a little girl who loved art and books and got teased for that love by the other neighbourhood kids, who couldn't even be bothered to learn how to read. When I got home from school, I went straight in and locked the door.

I'd get supper ready for my dad, but there were always a couple of hours to kill in between my arriving home and when he finished work — longer if he had to work late. We didn't have a TV, so I read a lot, but we couldn't afford to buy books. On Saturday mornings, we'd go to the library and I'd take out my limit — five books — which I'd finish by Tuesday, even if I tried to stretch them out.

To fill the rest of the time, I'd draw on shopping bags or the pads of paper that dad brought me home from work, but that never seemed to occupy enough hours. So one day I made up Mr. Truepenny.

I'd daydream about going to his shop. It was the most perfect place that I could imagine: all dark wood and leaded glass, thick carpets and club chairs with carved wooden-based reading lamps strategically placed throughout. The shelves were filled with leather-bound books and folios, and there was a small art gallery in the back.

The special thing about Mr. Truepenny's shop was that all of its contents existed only within its walls. Shakespeare's *The Storm of Winter*. *The Chapman's Tale* by Chaucer. *The Blissful Stream* by William Morris. Steinbeck's companion collection to *The Long Valley, Salinas*. *North Country Stoic* by Emily Brontë.

None of these books existed, of course, but being the dreamy sort of kid that I was, not only could I daydream of visiting Mr. Truepenny's shop, but I could actually read these unwritten stories. The gallery in the back of the shop was much the same. There hung works by the masters that saw the light of day only in my imagination. Van Goghs and Monets and da Vincis. Rossettis and Homers and Cézannes.

Mr. Truepenny himself was a wonderfully eccentric individual who never once chased me out for being unable to make a purchase. He had a Don Quixote air about him, a sense that he was forever tilting at windmills.

He was tall and thin with a thatch of mouse-brown hair and round spectacles, a rumpled tweed suit and a huge briar pipe that he continually fussed with but never actually lit. He always greeted me with genuine affection and seemed disappointed when it was time for me to go.

17   My imagination was so vivid that my daydream visits to his shop were as real to me as when my dad took me to the library or the Newford Gallery of Fine Art. But it didn't last. I grew up, went to Butler University on student loans and the money from far too many menial jobs — "got a life," as the old saying goes. I made friends, I was so busy, there was no time, no *need* to visit the shop anymore. Eventually I simply forgot all about it.

18   Until I met Janice Petrie.

19   Wendy and I were in the Market after a late night at her place the previous evening. I was on my way home, but we'd decided to shop for groceries together before I left. Trying to make up my mind between green beans and a head of broccoli, my gaze lifted above the vegetable stand and met that of a little girl standing nearby with her parents. Her eyes widened with recognition though I'd never seen her before.

20   "You're the woman!" she cried. "You're the woman who's evicting Mr. Truepenny. I think it's a horrible thing to do. You're a horrible woman!"

21   And then she started to cry. Her mother shushed her and apologized to me for the outburst before bustling the little girl away.

22   "What was all *that* about, Sophie?" Wendy asked me.

23   "I have no idea," I said.

24   But of course I did. I was just so astonished by the encounter that I didn't know what to say. I changed the subject and that was the end of it until I got home. I dug out an old cardboard box from the back of my hall closet and rooted about in it until I came up with a folder of drawings I'd done when I still lived with my dad. Near the back I found the ones I was looking for.

25   They were studies of Mr. Truepenny and his amazing shop.

26   God, I thought, looking at these awkward drawings, pencil on brown grocery-bag paper, ballpoint on foolscap. The things we forget.

27   I took the drawings out onto my balcony and lay down on the old sofa I kept out there, studying them, one by one. There was Mr. Truepenny, writing something in his big leather-bound ledger. Here was another of him, holding his cat, Dodger, the two of them looking out the leaded glass windows of the shop. There was a view of the main aisle of the shop, leading down to the gallery, the perspective slightly askew, but not half bad considering I was no older when I did them than was the little girl in the Market today.

How could she have *known*? I found myself thinking. Mr. Truepenny and his shop were something I'd made up. I couldn't remember ever telling anyone else about them — not even Jilly. And what did she mean about my evicting him from the shop?

I could think of no rational response. After a while, I just set the drawings aside and tried to forget about it. Exhaustion from the late night before soon had me nodding off, and I fell asleep only to find myself, not in my boyfriend's faerie dream world, but on the streets of Mabon, the made-up city in which I'd put Mr. Truepenny's Book Emporium and Gallery.

I'm half a block from the shop. The area's changed. The once-neat cobblestones are thick with grime. Refuse lies everywhere. Most of the storefronts are boarded up, their walls festooned with graffiti. When I reach Mr. Truepenny's shop, I see a sign in the window that reads, CLOSING SOON DUE TO LEASE EXPIRATION.

Half-dreading what I'll find, I open the door and hear the familiar little bell tinkle as I step inside. The shop's dusty and dim, and much smaller than I remember it. The shelves are almost bare. The door leading to the gallery is shut and has a CLOSED sign tacked onto it.

"Ah, Miss Etoile. It's been so very long."

I turn to find Mr. Truepenny at his usual station behind the front counter. He's smaller than I remember as well, and looks a little shabby now. Hair thinning, tweed suit threadbare and more shapeless than ever.

"What... what's happened to the shop?" I ask.

I've forgotten that I'm asleep on the sofa out on my balcony. All I know is this awful feeling I have inside as I look at what's become of my old childhood haunt.

"Well, times change," he says. "The world moves on."

"This — is this my doing?"

His eyebrows rise quizzically.

"I met this little girl and she said I was evicting you."

"I don't blame you," Mr. Truepenny says, and I can see in his sad eyes that it's true. "You've no more need for me or my wares, so it's only fair that you let us fade."

"But you... that is... well, you're not real."

I feel weird saying this, because while I remember now that I'm dreaming, this place is like one of my faerie dreams that feel as real as the waking world.

"That's not strictly true," he tells me. "You did conceive of the city and this shop, but we were drawn to fit the blueprint of your plan from... elsewhere."

"What elsewhere?"

He frowns, brow furrowing as he thinks.

"I'm not really sure myself," he tells me.

"You're saying I didn't make you up, I just drew you here from somewhere else?"

He nods.

"And now you have to go back?"

"So it would seem."

"And this little girl — how can she know about you?"

"Once a reputable establishment is open for business, it really can't deny any customer access, regardless of their age or station in life."

"She's visiting my daydream?" I ask. This is too much to accept, even for a dream.

Mr. Truepenny shakes his head. "You brought this world into being through your single-minded desire, but now it has a life of its own."

"Until I forgot about it."

"You had a very strong will," he says. "You made us so real that we've been able to hang on for decades. But now we really have to go."

There's a very twisty sort of logic involved here, I can see. It doesn't make sense by way of the waking world's logic, but I think there are different rules in a dreamscape. After all, my faerie boyfriend can turn into a crow.

"Do you have more customers, other than that little girl?" I ask.

"Oh yes. Or at least, we did." He waves a hand to encompass the shop. "Not much stock left, I'm afraid. That was the first to go."

"Why doesn't *their* desire keep things running?"

"Well, they don't have faerie blood, now do they? They can visit, but they haven't the magic to bring us across or keep us here."

It figures. I think. We're back to that faerie-blood thing again. Jilly would love this.

I'm about to ask him to explain it all a little more clearly when I get this odd jangling sound in my ears and wake up back on the sofa. My doorbell's ringing. I go inside the apartment to accept what turns out to be a FedEx package.

"Can dreams be real?" I ask the courier. "Can we invent something in a dream and have it turn out to be a real place?"

"Beats me, lady," he replies, never blinking an eye. "Just sign here."

I guess he gets all kinds.

So now I visit Mr. Truepenny's shop on a regular basis again. The area's vastly improved. There's a café nearby where Jeck — that's my boyfriend that I've been telling you about—and I go for tea after we've browsed through Mr. Truepenny's latest wares. Jeck likes this part of Mabon so much that he's now got an apartment on the same street as the shop. I think I might set up a studio nearby.

I've even run into Janice—the little girl who brought me back here in the first place. She's forgiven me, of course, now that she knows it was all a misunderstanding, and lets me buy her an ice cream from the soda fountain sometimes before she goes home.

I'm very accepting of it all—you get that way after a while. The thing that worries me now is, what happens to Mabon when I die? Will the city get run down again and eventually disappear? And what about its residents? There's all these people here; they've got family, friends, lives. I get the feeling it wouldn't be the same for them if they have to go back to that elsewhere place Mr. Truepenny was so vague about.

So that's the reason I've written all this down and had it printed up into a little folio by one of Mr. Truepenny's friends in the waking world. I'm hoping somebody out there's like me. Someone's got enough faerie blood not only to visit, but to keep the place going. Naturally, not just anyone will do. It has to be the right sort of person, a book lover, a lover of old places and tradition, as well as the new.

If you think you're the person for the position, please send a résumé to me care of Mr. Truepenny's Book Emporium and Gallery, Mabon. I'll get back to you as soon as I can.

1995

NOTES

Latchkey kid A young child with a key to the house. This term refers to children who go home to an empty house after school.

Chaucer, Geoffrey (1343–1400) A 14th-century English poet, known for *The Canterbury Tales*.

Morris, William (1834–1896) A 19th-century English poet who lived during Queen Victoria's reign.

Steinbeck, John (1902–1968) A 20th-century American writer. His best-known work is *The Grapes of Wrath*.

Brontë, Emily (1818–1848) A 19th-century English novelist. Her only novel is *Wuthering Heights*, a Gothic romance. Her two sisters, Charlotte and Anne, also wrote and published.

Van Gogh, Vincent (1853–1890) A Dutch Post-Impressionist painter of the 19th century.

Monet, Claude (1840–1926) A French Impressionist painter of the 19th century.

da Vinci, Leonardo (1452–1519) An Italian Renaissance painter, sculptor, and architect.

Rossetti, Dante Gabriel (1828–1882) A Victorian painter and poet who, along with his sister Christina, was one of the founders of the Pre-Raphaelite movement.

Homer, Winslow (1836–1910) A 19th-century American painter well known for his interpretative watercolours and oils.

Cézanne, Paul (1839–1906) A French Impressionist painter of the 19th century who influenced the Cubist movement in art.

Don Quixote The title character in the Spanish epic by Miguel de Cervantes (1547–1616). Don Quixote thought that he was a knight in armour, and attacked windmills that he believed were giants. The phrase "tilting at windmills" is used to express the idea of fighting imaginary enemies.

Sophie Etoile The character's name is significant. In Greek, *sophia* means wisdom; in French, *étoile* means star.

COMPREHENSION AND DISCUSSION

1. What relevance does faerie blood have to this story?
2. What has Sophie the narrator created in her imagination?
3. Who is Janice Petrie?
4. What has happened to Mr. Truepenny and the neighbourhood since Sophie stopped visiting?
5. Why does Sophie, as an adult, rebuild her imagined world?

6. When you are immersed in a novel, short story, or movie, are you not like Janice, who enters Sophie's created world? Has this story succeeded in transporting you into Charles De Lint's imagination about a faerie girl who creates a world where others may enter? Discuss the similarity between a writer's work and what Sophie does when she daydreams.
7. Do you create worlds in your daydreams? Do you revisit daydreams you enjoy?
8. What is reality? What is imagination? Can the distinction be blurred?

LITERARY TECHNIQUES

De Lint uses an epigraph, a quotation from Elias Canetti, a Bulgarian writer who won the Nobel Prize for Literature in 1981. An epigraph is a short quotation from another source, relevant to the story that follows it.

Note how this story is similar to "A Girl's Story" (p. 22) and "The Man I Killed" (p. 170); as the plot unfolds, the writer is also telling you how the story is created. This technique is called metafiction.

Fantasy is an offshoot of fiction. Readers know beforehand that the element of unreality and imagination is in effect. They participate by willingly suspending their disbelief, and letting the story progress without objecting to the lack of logic in the plot or characters.

Mentioning historical and renowned writers and artists brings about an authentication. It makes the story sound more realistic. In this case, De Lint shows Sophie's taste in literature and art. Note that some of the titles of works by these famous artists are made up from Sophie's imagination.

ASSIGNMENTS

1. Imagination plays an important part in reading, but less so in videos and computer games. Explain why we need imagination in our lives.
2. When we read a novel, we enter the world the author created. Sometimes when we finish the book, we don't want it to be over. We want to read more about the people's lives, or see more of the place. Choose a book you've read that had this effect on you and explain why the work was so effective.

3. Compare this story with Arnason's "A Girl's Story" (p. 22). How are they similar on the topics of imagination and creative writing?
4. "When I was a child, I spake as a child, I understood as a child, I thought as a child, but when I became a man, I put away childish things" (1 Corinthians 13:11). Explain how this quotation is relevant to the story. Consider what "childish things" people should put away as they age.
5. Listen to the popular 1960s song "Puff the Magic Dragon" by Peter, Paul, and Mary. Explain similarities in themes to De Lint's story.
6. Writers often toy with the idea that imaginary characters can interact with real people. Woody Allen has used this situation in his movie *The Purple Rose of Cairo* (1985). Watch the film, and compare it with De Lint's story.

Chickens for Christmas

Garry Engkent

My father wanted us to adapt to the new country, and one of his many schemes was to embrace the Christmas spirit. My mother thought this idea was too *fan gwei*. She was Buddhist and had some success in not celebrating the holiday in *gum san*, Canada. My father, however, had recently been made a member of two service clubs in Thibeault Falls, and admittance had fired his zeal to be Canadian.

"What do you know about this white devil commotion?" my mother questioned. "What is Christmas?"

My father was taken aback. He had been in Canada much longer than my mother and I, but when asked so straightforwardly he couldn't come up with anything more than I could. I was in grade 4, and I knew about the Nativity, the baby in the manger, the shepherds and the three wise men, Santa Claus and presents, and a lot of carols. Even though he didn't know all the words, my father liked humming *Good King Wenceslaus* off-key.

"Christmas is a good time for business," he said. "Make a lot of money."

My father owned a half-interest in the Panama Cafe, a share he'd bought from Great Uncle Liu who had founded the establishment in the early 1920s. We all toiled in the restaurant, and we slept upstairs in a cramped two-bedroom apartment. My father had liked the closeness to his work until recently. The fervour for the Canadian way got hold of him, and without my mother's consent he bought a two-storey house some distance from the restaurant, but not too far that he couldn't walk should the car not turn over in winter.

"In a new house, we start a new tradition," he announced. "We honour the Christmas season!"

"How?" my mother asked. "Chop down an evergreen and decorate it? Hang coloured lights around the veranda? We are Chinese, not *fan gwei*."

My mother believed she had won the argument. There would be no Christmas tradition in the Ko family. Then my father brightened. "We make Christmas, Chinese-style!"

My father's vision involved me. Two Saturdays before the big event he and I drove past Powassan and down snowy country roads. The farmer who supplied the restaurant with fresh eggs had some year-old chickens for sale. My father made a deal with him, and before noon we had five sacks of clucking Rhode Island Reds, three in a sack.

"Why didn't we buy the big white Leghorns?" I asked.

"Red is the colour of good luck."

Well, good luck wasn't quite with us. A sudden snow squall hit, and we returned home, eight hours later, to a worried wife and mother at midnight.

"So where are you going to put the hens?" my mother asked. "You can't leave them in the sacks. They'll suffocate. You can't release them in our basement, husband!"

My father thought of leaving them in one of the storage rooms in the Panama Cafe, but he quickly turned the idea down. The unsacked hens would make a mess, and someone might inform the health department. These live chickens were meant to be a surprise Christmas gift for the Chinese cooks, waiters, and relatives with families.

Fortunately, our back porch had an enclosed storage area under the floor where we kept the storm windows. Now this space became a temporary roost. At two in the morning, we went to bed, thinking the problem solved.

Until the chickens started crowing at first light.

"Aiyee, that damn farmer!" my father cursed. "Sold me a rooster! Two! No, three! They'll wake up the whole neighbourhood."

My poor father saw his Christmas Chinese-style crashing with each distinct cock-a-doodle-doo. If we could hear the sound inside the house, how much louder would it be outside? Canadians keep dogs and cats as domestic pets, and, yes, dogs bark and cats meow — but fifteen chickens, flapping about and crowing underneath the back porch?

"Find those noisy birds," my mother advised, "and — " She made a swift downward motion with her open hand. "Fresh steamed chicken for supper."

"You are small enough, Hardy," my father said. "You go inside and grab those damn roosters."

"Which ones are roosters?"

"The ones that crow!" he shouted, exasperated.

"Roosters won't crow, they'll just cluck loudly if they're frightened," my mother pointed out. "Look for a flappy red cockscomb."

Catching three roosters in a confined space wasn't easy. My father blocked the opening, in case the hens got out. The compartment was dark, and the only light came from the tiny door. I held a flashlight in one hand and with the other I snatched at cockscombs. All the birds began squawking and flapping their wings as they evaded capture. I started coughing, and got mouthfuls of dust and feathers. I grabbed a rooster and it pecked at me. Finally, after what seemed a long time (because my father kept telling me to hurry up every five seconds), I handed him two roosters. As he was passing them to my mother in an unguarded moment, two birds slipped out. One was a hen; the other — the third rooster!

"Get those chickens!" my father cried. He ran after them. I stumbled out of the compartment, and my mother slammed the door shut.

I would never have imagined how quickly scared fowl could dash over knee-deep snow. My legs sank into it, slowing me down. As the rooster paused momentarily on top of a snowdrift, I threw myself in a desperate lunge, arms outstretched and hands poised to snatch. But I got only a handful of tail feathers. The bird squawked and escaped down the road to an uncertain freedom.

I spent the next few hours shivering in the December cold, walking around the neighbourhood searching for chicken tracks. When some neighbours asked what I was doing, I didn't dare tell them the embarrassing truth. I returned home, defeated. For the next few mornings, I swore I could hear the faint cock-a-doodle-doo of a Rhode Island rooster mocking me.

The only consolation was that my mother caught the hen. The silly bird backtracked right (well, almost) into her waiting hands.

"We can't give these hens as gifts," my mother said. She lifted one and weighed it by bouncing it up and down. "So scrawny! That farmer didn't fatten them. By Christmas, these birds won't be worth eating."

For once my father had to agree. But he wasn't stymied. We spent the afternoon scouring Thibeault Falls for poultry-fattening mash. My father sent me into the stores, figuring it was less embarrassing for a kid to ask for chicken feed, than an adult. I would get amused smirks from clerks. ("A hundred-pound bag! Starting your own poultry farm, eh?") Finally, we trekked to a feed store in Powassan and loaded the trunk of my father's Oldsmobile with four fifty-pound bags of chicken feed.

When we returned home, a curious neighbour asked my father, "What have you got in there, Joe? There's city ordinances against keeping farm animals, you know. Chickens, eh? I thought I heard a cock crowing this morning." He chuckled and went away, shaking his head.

My father's demeanour soured. His shoulders slumped and he let out a resigned sigh. This Christmas Chinese-style thing was getting out of hand. The birds were making a ruckus. And just tossing in handfuls of chicken feed wasn't going to work. You can't keep twelve hens in the dark, in a confined area, in the cold, for two weeks. As we unloaded the chicken feed, my father could see the problems multiplying. But he brightened by the time we lugged the bags down to the basement.

We went to the local lumber mill and loaded up with top-quality materials. Normally, my father never rushed into such projects. My mother had been after him to fix some ill-fitting bedroom doors and that task was yet to be done. But for the chicken coop he had in mind, he took the day off work.

34   When my mother came home from the Panama Cafe, the chicken coop was almost done. It was eight feet by four by five. It had a feeding trough and watering cans, and a hinged, slatted lid, with a smaller built-in drop-latched door. It was raised six inches above the ground. "We can slip in cardboard to catch the droppings," he said.

35   My father had even used screws instead of nails. Before he went to bed that night, he put a coat of varnish on. He would apply three more coats before he deemed it worthy of housing the hens. His chicken coop was a labour of love, and he'd built it to last. It would remain in the basement, under the stairwell nook, until the house was finally sold decades later.

36   We rounded up the hens and put them in their new home. My job was to keep the troughs well supplied with fattening mash and the tin cans filled with fresh water. Every alternate day, I would replace the flattened cardboard sheets splattered with chicken droppings. One of the fringe benefits of having the hens was that some were still laying eggs, and we ended up with a generous supply, which we turned over to the restaurant. We got used to the fowl smell in the basement.

37   The hens started plumping up satisfactorily. My father would grab one or two, weigh them and nod approvingly. He would say, more to himself than to me, "Next year, we'll fatten the chickens earlier." My mother showed her disapproval with silence.

38   My father wanted to wait until Christmas Eve before distributing the live hens. He had this idea, probably from the Santa Claus stories, that gifts had to be delivered that evening. I could have told him that the three wise men didn't give the baby Jesus gold, frankincense and myrrh until twelve days after the Nativity.

39   He made a list and checked it more than twice. There weren't that many Chinese families in Thibeault Falls, maybe ten in all. My father did not include the bachelor employees. "Where would they keep a live hen? Under their beds?"

40   The Christmas Chinese-style package included a Christmas card in a red envelope with a token silver dollar, a bottle of Johnny Walker Black Label, and of course a live chicken in a cardboard box tied with red ribbon. He wrote in Chinese the name of the head of the household on the envelope, and taped the envelope to the box. Then we loaded the fussing hens, liquor, and all into the Oldsmobile, both back seat and trunk. My father planned the route carefully.

"You are Santa's helper," my father said. He gave me a fluorescent-red elongated toque with a white pompom. I looked in the mirror and made a face. I didn't want to be Santa's elf. Anyway, Santa's elves wore green tights, but I didn't tell my father that.

"I drive up, you take the presents to the door. If I do it, they might make a fuss because they won't have a return present. But you so young, you can be excused for lack of good Chinese manners. Just hand over the stuff, say Merry Christmas, and leave. Understand?"

I didn't, but nodded anyway. I knew enough to understand that reciprocal gifts were deemed necessary. I could see that my father was becoming *fan gwei* in that 'tis better to give than to receive. My mother would surely disapprove, because this white devil concept made the other person lose face.

Our first stop was the Hong family residence on the third floor of a five-storey apartment house. Mr. Hong worked as a cook for another restaurant, but he was on the list because he was my father's clan-cousin. I had to climb all those stairs with Johnny Walker tucked under one arm and both hands holding the boxed hen. I knocked on the door, and someone yelled out in broken English: "Who there?"

"Santa Claus!" I just couldn't resist.

"What you say?"

"Santa Claus. Ho-ho-ho!"

"Go away. I call police now!"

I mustered up some halting Chinese, and it came out something like: "My father says to give you this." The Chinese words did the trick, and a woman opened the door a crack. Satisfied that I was too young to do her harm, she stepped out. I quickly handed her the Johnny Walker and the hen. Bewildered, she held onto the box with the agitated chicken. I dashed down the stairs, shouting loudly: "*Gong hai sing dan!*" — Merry Christmas to you.

My father looked at me expectantly as I panted. "Well? Did you give it to Hong?"

"I don't think he was in. An old woman came to the door."

"Old woman? Apartment 306, yes?"

"No. 303."

"Aiyyeee! That's the wrong one. Can't you read what I wrote?" My father slammed his hand on the steering wheel and the car horn blasted.

I broke out in a sob. "I can't read Chinese!"

We couldn't just go to apartment 303 and ask for the presents back. That would mean a loss of face for the old woman and for us. My father hoped that she couldn't make out his Chinese scrawls. Fortunately, he'd had the foresight to prepare an extra package. This time we both climbed to apartment 306, and Hong was pleased no end, although he kept apologizing for having nothing to reciprocate.

57 As we rode to our next destination, my father said, "Don't tell your mother about this. I'll never hear the end of it."

58 The next Christmas, my father had fine tuned his plan. We bought the chickens in late October so they could be fattened longer. Business improved, so instead of Johnny Walker he decided on Haig Pinch, and he wrote in English right under the Chinese. We still delivered on Christmas Eve, and like Good King Wenceslaus and his faithful page, we trekked in the snow.

59 This time, however, the recipients were ready for Santa and his helper. Even before the boxed hen left my hands, they would be full of return gifts. A box of Tuero cigars, or a fine bottle of expensive liquor, or packaged Chinese cookies from Hong Kong. We were piling up the car as much as we were unloading it. My father had started something grand in the Chinese community.

60 "So Christmas is nothing more than giving and receiving gifts," my mother commented afterwards. "We Chinese do that all the time anyway. Even when it isn't Christmas."

61 "It's the thought," my father quoted from something he had heard.

62 "It seems to me," my mother observed critically, "that we are doing too much. Every year now, you and Hardy start Christmas shopping for hens. They smell up the house for three months. It takes another six months to get rid of the stink and disinfect the basement. We spend money on feed. Then when the chickens are nice and plump, you give them away to someone else's dinner table. And what do you get? Bottles of liquor and cigars, Chinatown tins of dried-out cookies. Why can't we give store-bought things?"

63 "*Lai! Lai!* Tradition!" my father answered loudly. "I have started a tradition. It has been going on for six years. We will lose face if we stop."

64 By the look on my mother's face, I knew she wasn't convinced. She dropped the subject with her characteristic tightly pursed lips, but I knew what was in her heart.

65 My father was pleased when I got my driver's licence. Now I could play Santa Claus all by myself. By this time, my father's Christmas Chinese-style was an accepted fact in Thibeault Falls' Chinese community. His list had changed as families moved away and new ones came. Still, some names and addresses remained constant. Mr. Hong was still in apartment 306.

One year, Mr. Hong's Christmas package was my last delivery. The temperature had fallen into a deep freeze; not even the highest setting on the car heater was enough to ward off the bone-chilling cold. The boxed hen was in the trunk the whole time. While I was climbing the stairs, the hen flapped lamely and gurgled, sounding like a death rattle.

Mr. Hong's wife came to the door and we exchanged gifts. Her small children, curious about the hen, started opening the box under the mild protest of Mrs. Hong. They wanted to see a live chicken. She expected the bird to entertain and occupy the two unruly eight-year-olds, but the Rhode Island Red lay in a corner of the cardboard box, unmoving. I knew it wouldn't live through the hour.

I saw the panic in Mrs. Hong's eyes and paling face. It was a bad omen to have a live gift die, especially near a holy day. This incident would be gossiped about for years.

"Maybe I should prepare the chicken for you," I blurted.

Mrs. Hong didn't know what to do. She gave me a faint nod, and I took the bird to the tiny kitchen. I slaughtered it, draining the blood into a bowl with a mixture of salt and water. Then I plucked the feathers and dressed it in the Chinese style: a thick salt rubdown, then rinse and dry. Throughout this procedure, Mrs. Hong and her children watched, fascinated.

"So that's how you do it, *Amah!*" one of the kids said.

Later, I heard that the hen was the best poultry the Hongs had ever eaten. I earned a place in the anecdotes of the Hong family, a saga embellished with each successive telling. My mother was pleased with the way I'd salvaged the situation.

Even when I went to university, my father's tradition continued. When I'd return for Thanksgiving weekend, before I could even unload my bags, my father would hurry me into the car and off we would go to Powassan for the Rhode Island Reds. By Christmastime the hens were all fattened, and I was Santa's helper once more. But then my father's Christmas Chinese-style faced another obstacle.

My father died.

His Christmas tradition had had its run. Even when my father sold his interest in the Panama Cafe and promptly bought himself a Mom-Pop-and-Son diner, he argued for his little piece of Christmas. Throughout the tempestuous years of the tradition, my mother often grumbled, "We are not Christian, we Chinese!"

Now he was gone, and we sold the diner to a cousin. In September, I returned to university and my mother secluded herself in the house that she'd toiled for twenty years to pay off. The chicken coop had served its purpose. I marvelled at how it had survived the scratches and constant peckings over the years. My father had built it to last. The coop would now sit idle, to gather dust and memories.

77 As the only son, I returned home during the university break to look after my mother's finances and utility payments, and to keep her company.

78 "We go to Powassan," she declared that Thanksgiving weekend.

79 "Why?"

80 Normally, I would drive her to all the plazas in Thibeault Falls where we would spend hours shopping for household necessities. She looked at me disapprovingly. I had not read her mind.

81 "Chickens, my son, chickens!"

82 "Why? You've got a freezer full."

83 "Christmas Chinese-style!" she explained. "Your father's tradition must carry on."

84 So that Christmas Eve, I wore my ratty red Santa toque with pompom still intact and drove to all the destinations. My last stop was the Hong family.

85 "You know, Hardy," he said, "your family doesn't need to do this after..." He paused; it was not proper in Chinese to remind me of our recent loss. "This tradition is good—after all these years, I must confess."

86 "Confess?"

87 "All those years, all those hens," Mr. Hong said slowly.

88 "Yes?" I prompted.

89 "That Christmas Eve when you prepared the bird was the only time we ate farm-fresh chicken."

90 "The other years?"

91 "I—we gave the hens away. I can't prepare live chicken."

92 "And you a chef!"

93 "My wife and I just can't do the—" His index finger slashed across his throat.

94 I laughed. The irony of it all! My father had assumed that any cook from China knew how to slaughter a chicken. I wondered what he would say if he knew. Twenty some years of giving a Christmas gift that the recipient didn't know what to do with! If and when I'd tell my mother, I wondered what kind of laughter she would have.

95 "Well, Mr. Hong," I said as I carried the Christmas hen into the kitchen. I sharpened the cleaver. "Maybe I should add something new to my father's tradition of Christmas Chinese-style."

2000

NOTES

Fan gwei A Chinese term for white Canadians; literally, it means "return demon, ghost, or devil." It is a word from one of the many Cantonese dialects. Other phrases are *fan gwei lo*, *lo fan*, and *gwei lo*.

Gum san A Chinese term for Canada; literally, it means "gold mountain."

Giving a live chicken on special occasions is traditional in Chinese culture.

The red envelope with lucky money, or *lai shi*, is another Chinese tradition. Usually it is given to children, especially at Chinese New Year.

Tueros Expensive cigars, packaged in boxes of 25.

Amah A Chinese word for "mother" or "mom." Sometimes it is transliterated as "Ah-mah."

COMPREHENSION AND DISCUSSION

1. Why does the father want to start a Christmas tradition in his household?
2. Why does the mother object to a Christmas tradition? (Note: there are different reasons at different times in the story.)
3. Briefly explain the father's scheme for Christmas Chinese-style.
4. What relevance has the Christmas carol "Good King Wenceslaus" to the story?
5. Why does the mother continue the tradition after the father's death?
6. What does the son discover at the Hong apartment?
7. Will he tell his mother what he has learned? Why or why not?
8. Which phrases indicate that time has passed between scenes?
9. What are some gift-giving traditions that you follow?
10. What do you do with gifts that you don't want but must accept, or gifts that you don't know how to use?

LITERARY TECHNIQUES

A story that stretches over time requires the writer to give clues to each period so that the reader will not be lost or confused. The writer here cues the reader in different ways: the mention of years, the growth of the narrator at different stages of his life, and the passing of the father.

Writers often use words and expressions from other languages even though readers may not be familiar with the terms. These phrases give colour and authenticity to the story. The term is either immediately translated in an appositive form or left for the reader to catch in context. Longer passages are usually translated. Look at the clues Engkent gives to help readers understand the Chinese phrases.

Autobiographical fiction Writers write what they know, and often in fiction they incorporate personal experiences and observations in the story. (See Arnason's "A Girl's Story" [p. 22] and O'Brien's "The Man I Killed" [p. 170] for examples of autobiographical fiction.) However, not every element of a story is always personal or based on real life. Things may be added to enhance the literary and artistic quality of the story. Reality is much more complex than the ordered and simplified arrangement of incidents in fiction. In short, literature is art; life is chaos.

Irony A literary device that reveals absolute contrast or contradiction, and often the unexpected. For example, in the story, the father assumes that a chef would know how to slaughter a chicken and, for twenty years, he gives a live bird to the Hongs. Only much later does the son discover the truth.

ASSIGNMENTS

1. Compare this story with Leacock's "How We Kept Mother's Day" (p. 140). You can examine the irony or the humour.
2. How should immigrants adapt traditions from their new homeland? What makes a tradition important to keep or to discard? Suggest guidelines.
3. Compare this short story with "Growing Up on Grace" (p. 250), a non-fiction account of an immigrant family in Canada. Discuss the common experiences of both narrators. Or contrast the fictional treatment and the non-fictional.
4. Read "Rediscovering Christmas" (p. 359) by Almas Zakiuddin. Write an essay describing the universality of the Christmas celebration with references to Zakiuddin's article and Engkent's story.
5. Read "Ralphie at the Races" (p. 205). Compare the different attitudes toward Canada and Canadian culture exhibited by the characters in the two stories.

The Cowherd

a Chinese folktale, retold by Garry Engkent

1. Once upon a time there was a poor cowherd. His father died, and he had to work to support himself and his widowed mother.

2. He tended cows several leagues away from his home. Everyday, rain or shine, his mother would bring him a hot midday meal. She would travel across the rugged fields, over a bridge where the deep river swiftly flowed, and to the spot under the tree where he would eat.

3. Now this cowherd was a peevish lad. Whenever his mother came early with his lunch, he would scold her for being so early. Whenever she came late, he would beat her with the long switch he used to train wayward calves. Whenever she came on time, he would say how cold or hot his lunch was.

4. This went on for a long time. The cowherd's widowed mother never complained, and bore her pains to herself.

5. One day the heavens opened up, and rain poured all morning.

6. The cowherd took shelter under his favourite tree. By chance, he heard the sound of chirping. He spotted a mother bird feeding her babies. She would fly out into the slashing rain again and again, and bring back food to her hungry brood.

7. Suddenly it dawned on him. This was exactly what his widowed mother was doing for him day in and day out. Remorse engulfed him.

8. That day, he vowed to change his ways. When his mother brought him his meal, he would fall upon her feet and beg forgiveness. He would become a good son.

9. Then in the distance he saw his mother. Almost bent double from the pounding rain, she trudged on, sheltering his lunch.

10. The cowherd cried out, "Mother!" He dashed from his dry shelter into the rain. His arms flayed as he ran to meet her.

11. As she reached the middle of the bridge, the cowherd's mother saw her son running madly towards her. She could hear his loud voice above the crackling thunder. She could see in his hand the stick.

12. At another time she might have bore it. But today she was tired of another scolding and of another beating.

13. She put his lunch down, and jumped into the swift flowing river. And perished.

Date unknown

NOTES

Many Western folktales or fairy tales have changed to suit the tastes of a contemporary audience; however, the Chinese folktale retains its harsh bite. For example, in "Little Red Riding Hood," the original ending, in which the wolf wins, has been changed so that the girl and grandmother are rescued. Chinese folktales lack such sentimentality. Their driving force is to reiterate a basic lesson about life.

Stories translated from one language to another often lose the texture and subtlety of the originals. A translation can never hope to duplicate everything.

COMPREHENSION AND DISCUSSION

1. What makes the cowherd angry?
2. What incident changed him? How? Why?
3. How do you know that this story is not real?
4. How has the storyteller prepared you for the ending?
5. What is the lesson in this folktale?
6. Why do you like or dislike this story?
7. Would this story be as effective if it had a happy ending? Does it need an uplifting conclusion?
8. What is the difference between a folktale and a parable? Are urban legends just updated folktales?

LITERARY TECHNIQUES

A folktale is a story that originates in the oral tradition. Its authorship is unknown as the tale is handed down through the generations. The narrative is simple in construction and contains little detail. Description is kept to a minimum. The starkness of its telling becomes part of its charm and power. Often the purpose is not so much to entertain as it is to give a moral lesson.

Didactic stories Literary works that provide a lesson or instruction. One theory is that all literature has an implicit or explicit lesson to impart. The intent of the author determines whether the didactic quality is strong or mild. Most Chinese tales are didactic.

Like the fairy tale, the folktale is told simply. Note the similarity in the opening: "Once upon a time...," "Once there was...," "There was a...," or "A long time ago...." The setting is stark, and the characters are generically named for universal appeal.

ASSIGNMENTS

1. Retell a favourite folktale or fairy tale in your own words with a specific audience in mind.
2. How does this story compare with Hans Christian Andersen's original "Little Mermaid" or "The Little Match Girl"?
3. Compare the Disney version of "Cinderella" with the version by the Brothers Grimm.
4. Which is more important in storytelling — entertainment value or moral lesson? Write a persuasive paper discussing this question.
5. How are the folktale and the beast fable, for example, Aesop's "The Fox and the Grapes" (p. 19) similar? How are they different?
6. Compare the insight and the ending of this story with Callaghan's "All the Years of Her Life" (p. 47).

The Immaculate Conception Photography Gallery

Katherine Govier

1 Sandro named the little photography shop on St. Clair Avenue West, between Lord's Shoes and Bargain Jimmies, after the parish church in the village where he was born. He had hankered after wider horizons, the rippled brown prairies, the hard-edged mountains. But when he reached Toronto he met necessity in the form of a wife and babies, and, never having seen a western sunset, he settled down in Little Italy. He photographed the brides in their fat lacquered curls and imported lace and their quick babies in christening gowns brought over from home. Blown up to near life size on cardboard cutouts, their pictures filled the windows of his little shop.

2 Sandro had been there ten years already when he first really saw his sign and the window. He stood still in front of it and looked. A particularly buxom bride with a lace bodice and cap sleeves cut in little scallops shimmered in a haze of concupiscence under the sign reading Immaculate Conception Photography Gallery. Sandro was not like his neighbours any more, he was modern, a Canadian. He no longer went to church. As he stared, one of the street drunks shuffled into place beside him. Sandro knew them all, they came into the shop in winter. (No one ought to have to stay outside in that cold, Sandro believed.) But he especially knew Becker. Becker was a smart man; he used to be a philosopher at a university.

3 "Immaculate conception," said Sandro to Becker. "What do you think?"

4 Becker lifted his eyes to the window. He made a squeezing gesture at the breasts. "I never could buy that story," he said.

5 Sandro laughed, but he didn't change the sign that year or the next, and he got to be forty-five and then fifty and it didn't seem worth it. The Immaculate Conception Photography Gallery had a reputation. Business came in from as far away as Rosedale and North Toronto, because Sandro was a magician with a camera. He also had skill with brushes and lights and paint, he reshot his negatives, he lined them with silver, he had tricks even new graduates of photography school couldn't (or wouldn't) copy.

6 Sandro was not proud of his tricks. They began in a gradual way, fixing stray hairs and taking wrinkles out of dresses. He did it once, then twice, then people came in asking for it. Perhaps he'd have gone on this

way, with small lies, but he met with a situation that was larger than most; it would have started a feud in the old country. During a very large and very expensive wedding party, Tony the bridegroom seduced Alicia the bridesmaid in the basketball storage room under the floor of the parish hall. Six months later, Tony confessed, hoping perhaps to be released from his vows. But the parents judged it was too late to dissolve the union: Diora was used, she was no longer a virgin, there was a child coming. Tony was reprimanded, Diora consoled, the mothers became enemies, the newlyweds made up. Only Alicia remained to be dealt with. The offence became hers.

In Italy, community ostracism would have been the punishment of choice. But this was Canada, and if no one acknowledged Alicia on the street, if no one visited her mother, who was heavy on her feet and forced to sit on the sofa protesting her daughter's innocence, if no one invited her father out behind to drink home-made wine, Alicia didn't care. She went off to her job behind the till in a drugstore with her chin thrust out much as before. The in-laws perceived that the young woman could not be subdued by the old methods. This being the case, it was better she did not exist at all.

Which was why Diora's mother turned up at Sandro's counter with the wedding photos. The pain Alicia had caused! she began. Diora's mother's very own miserable wages, saved these eighteen years, had paid for these photographs! She wept. The money was spent, but the joy was spoiled. When she and Diora's father looked at the row of faces flanking the bride and groom there she was — Alicia, the whore! She wiped her tears and made her pitch.

"You can solve our problem, Sandro. I will get a new cake, we will all come to the parish hall. You will take the photographs again. Of course," she added, "we can't pay you again."

Sandro smiled, it was so preposterous. "Even if I could afford to do all that work for nothing, I hate to say it, but Diora's out to here."

"Don't argue with me."

"I wouldn't be so bold," said Sandro. "But I will not take the photographs over."

The woman slapped the photographs where they lay on the counter. "You will! I don't care how you do it!" And she left.

Sandro went to the back and put his negatives on the light box. He brought out his magic solution and his razor blades and his brushes. He circled Alicia's head and shoulders in the first row and went to work. He felt a little badly, watching the bright circle of her face fade and swim, darken down to nothing. But how easily she vanished! He filled in the white spot with a bit of velvet curtain trimmed from the side.

15 "I'm like a plastic surgeon," he told his wife. "Take that patch of skin from the inner thigh and put it over the scar on the face. Then sand the edges. Isn't that what they do? Only it isn't a face I'm fixing, it's a memory."

16 His wife stood on two flat feet beside the sink. She shook the carrot she was peeling. "I don't care about Alicia," she said, "but Diora's mother is making a mistake. She is starting them off with a lie in their marriage. And why is she doing it? For her pride! I don't like this, Sandro."

17 "You're missing the point," said Sandro.

18 The next day he had another look at his work. Alicia's shoulders and the bodice of her dress were still there, in front of the chest of the uncle of the bride. He couldn't remove them; it would leave a hole in Uncle. Sandro had nothing to fill the hole, no spare male torsos in black tie. He considered putting a head on top, but whose head? There was no such thing as a free face. A stranger would be questioned, a friend would have an alibi. Perhaps Diora's mother would not notice the black velvet space, as where a tooth had been knocked out, between the smiling faces.

19 Indeed she didn't but kissed his hand fervently and thanked him with tears in her eyes. "Twenty-five thousand that wedding cost me. Twenty-five thousand to get this photograph, and you have rescued it."

20 "Surely you got dinner and a dance, too?" said Sandro.

21 "The wedding was one day. This is forever," said Diora's mother.

22 "I won't do that again," said Sandro, putting the cloth over his head and looking into his camera lens to do a passport photo. In the community the doctored photograph had been examined and re-examined. Alicia's detractors enjoyed the headless shoulders as evidence of a violent punishment. "No, I won't do that again at all," said Sandro to himself, turning aside compliments with a shake of his head. But there was another wedding. After the prosciutto e melone, the veal picata, the many-tiered cake topped with swans, the father of the bride drew Sandro aside and asked for a set of prints with the groom's parents removed.

23 "My God, why?" said Sandro.

24 "He's a bastard. A bad man."

25 "Shouldn't have let her marry his son, then," said Sandro, pulling a cigarette out of the pack in his pocket. These conversations made him nervous.

26 The father's weathered face was dark, his dinner jacket did not button around his chest. He moaned and ground his lower teeth against his uppers.

"You know how they are, these girls in Canada. I am ashamed to say it, but I couldn't stop her."

Sandro said nothing.

"Look, I sat here all night long, said nothing, did nothing. I don't wanna look at him for the next twenty years."

Sandro drew in a long tube of smoke.

"I paid a bundle for this night. I wanna remember it nice-like."

The smoke made Sandro nauseous. He dropped his cigarette and ground it into the floor with his toe, damning his own weakness. "So what am I going to do with the table?"

The father put out a hand like a tool, narrowed his eyes, and began to saw where the other man sat.

"And leave it dangling, no legs?"

"So make new legs."

"I'm a photographer, not a carpenter," said Sandro. "I don't make table legs."

"Where you get legs is your problem," said the father. "I'm doing well here. I've got ten guys working for me. You look like you could use some new equipment."

And what harm was it after all, it was only a photograph, said Sandro to himself. Then, too, there was the technical challenge. Waiting until they all got up to get their bonbonnière, he took a shot of the head table empty. Working neatly with his scalpel, he cut the table from this second negative, removed the in-laws and their chairs from the first one, stuck the empty table-end onto the table in the first picture, blended over the join neatly, and printed it. Presto! Only one set of in-laws.

"I don't mind telling you, it gives me a sick feeling," said Sandro to his wife. "I was there. I saw them. We had a conversation. They smiled for me. Now..." He shrugged. "An empty table. Lucky I don't go to church any more."

"Let the man who paid good money to have you do it confess, not you," she said. "A photograph is a photograph."

"That's what I thought, too," said Sandro.

The next morning Sandro went to the Donut House, got himself a take-out coffee and stood on the street beside his window.

"Why do people care about photographs so much?" he asked Becker. Becker had newspaper stuffed in the soles of his shoes. He had on a pair of stained brown pants tied up at the waist with a paisley necktie. His bottle was clutched in a paper bag gathered around the neck.

"You can put them on your mantel," said Becker. "They don't talk back."

44 "Don't people prefer life?" said Sandro.
45 "People prefer things," said Becker.
46 "Don't they want their memories to be true?"
47 "No," said Becker.
48 "Another thing. Are we here just to get our photograph taken? Do we have a higher purpose?"
49 Becker pulled one of the newspapers out of his shoe. There were Brian and Mila Mulroney having a gloaty kiss. They were smeared by muddy water and depressed by the joint in the ball of Becker's foot.
50 "I mean real people," said Sandro. "Have we no loyalty to the natural?"
51 "These are existential questions, Sandro," said Becker. "Too many more of them and you'll be out here on the street with the rest of us."
52 Sandro drained the coffee from his cup, pitched it in the bin painted "Keep Toronto Clean" and went back into his gallery. The existential questions nagged. But he did go out and get the motor drive for the camera. In the next few months he eradicated a pregnancy from a wedding photo, added a daughter-in-law who complained of being left out of the Christmas shots, and made a groom taller. Working in the dark-room, he was hit by vertigo. He was on a slide, beginning a descent. He wanted to know what the bottom felt like.
53 After a year of such operations a man from the Beaches came in with a tiny black and white photo of a long-lost brother. He wanted it coloured and fitted into a family shot around a picnic table on Centre Island.
54 "Is this some kind of joke?" said Sandro. It was the only discretion he practised now: he wanted to talk about it before he did it.
55 "No. I'm going to send it to Mother. She thinks Christopher wrote us all off."
56 "Did he?" said Sandro.
57 "Better she should not know."

58 Sandro neglected to ask if Christopher was fat or thin. He ended up taking a medium-sized pair of shoulders from his own cousin and propping them up behind a bush, with Christopher's head on top. Afterward, Sandro lay sleepless in his bed. Suppose that in the next few months Christopher should turn up dead, say, murdered. Then Mother would produce the photograph stamped Immaculate Conception Photography Gallery, 1816 St. Clair Avenue West. Sandro would be implicated. The police might come.
59 "I believe adding people is worse than taking them away," he said to his wife.
60 "You say yes to do it, then you do it. You think it's wrong, you say no."

"Let me try this on you, Becker," said Sandro the next morning. "To take a person out is only half a lie. It proves nothing except that he was not in that shot. To add a person is a whole lie: it proves that he was there, when he was not."

"You haven't proven a thing, you're just fooling around with celluloid. Have you got a buck?" said Becker.

"It is better to be a murderer than a creator. I am playing God, outplaying God at His own game." He was smarter than Becker now. He knew it was the photographs that lasted, not the people. In the end the proof was in the proof. Though he hadn't prayed in thirty years, Sandro began to pray. It was like riding a bicycle: he got the hang of it again instantly. "Make me strong," he prayed, "strong enough to resist the new equipment that I might buy, strong enough to resist the temptation to expand the gallery, to buy a house in the suburbs. Make me say no to people who want alterations."

But Sandro's prayers were not answered. When people offered him money to dissolve an errant relative, he said yes. He said yes out of curiosity. He said yes out of a desire to test his skills. He said yes out of greed. He said yes out of compassion. "What is the cost of a little happiness?" he said. "Perhaps God doesn't count photographs. After all, they're not one of a kind."

Sandro began to be haunted, in slow moments behind the counter in the Immaculate Conception, by the faces of those whose presence he had tampered with. He kept a file — Alicia the lusty bridesmaid, Antonia and Marco, the undesired in-laws. Their heads, their shoes and their hands, removed from the scene with surgical precision, he saved for the moment when, God willing, a forgiving relative would ask him to replace them. But the day did not come. Sandro was not happy.

"Becker," he said, for he had a habit now of buying Becker a coffee first thing in the morning and standing out if it was warm, or in if it was cold, for a chat. "Becker, let's say it's a good service I'm doing. It makes people happy, even if it tells lies."

"Sandro," said Becker, who enjoyed his coffee, "these photographs, doctored by request of the subjects, reflect back the lives they wish to have. The unpleasant bits were removed, the wishes are added. If you didn't do it, someone else would. Memory would. It's a service."

"It's also money," said Sandro. He found Becker too eager to make excuses now. He liked him better before.

"You're like Tintoretto, painting in his patron, softening his greedy profile, lifting the chin of his fat wife. It pays for the part that's true art."

"Which part is that?" said Sandro, but Becker didn't answer. He was still standing there when Diora came in. She'd matured, she'd gained weight, and her twins, now six years old, were handsome and strong. Sandro's heart flew up in his breast. Perhaps she had made friends with Alicia, perhaps Diora had come to have her bridesmaid re-instated.

71 "The long nightmare is over," said Diora. "I've left him."

72 The boys were running from shelf to shelf lifting up the photographs with their glass frames and putting them down again. Sandro watched them with one eye. He knew what she was going to say.

73 "I want you to take him out of those pictures," she said.

74 "You'd look very foolish as a bride with no groom," he said severely.

75 "No, no, not those," she said. "I mean the kids' birthday shots."

76 They had been particularly fine, those shots, taken only two weeks ago, Tony tall and dark, Diora and the children radiant and blond.

77 "Be reasonable, Diora," he said. "I never liked him myself. But he balances the portrait. Besides, he was there."

78 "He was not there!" cried Diora. Her sons went on turning all the pictures to face the walls. "He was never there. He was running around, in his heart he was not with me. I was alone with my children."

79 "I'll take another one," said Sandro. "Of you and the boys. Whenever you like. This one stays like it is."

80 "We won't pay."

81 "But Diora," said Sandro, "everyone knows he's their father."

82 "They have no father," said Diora flatly.

83 "It's immaculate conception," said Becker gleefully.

84 But Diora did not hear. "It's our photograph, and we want him out. You do your job. The rest of it's none of your business." She put one hand on the back of the head of each of her twins and marched them out the door.

85 Sandro leaned on his counter idly flipping the pages of a wedding album. He had a vision of a great decorated room with a cake on the table. Everyone had had his way, the husband had removed the wife, the wife the husband, the bridesmaid her parents, and so forth. There was no one there.

86 "We make up our lives out of the people around us," he said to Becker. "When they don't live up to standard, we can't just wipe them out."

87 "Don't ask me," said Becker. "I just lit out for the streets. Couldn't live up to a damn thing." Then he, too, went out the door.

88 "Lucky bugger," said Sandro.

89 Alone, he went to his darkroom. He opened the drawer of bits and pieces. His disappeared ones, the inconvenient people. His body parts, his halves of torsos, tips of shiny black shoes. Each face, each item of clothing punctured him a little. He looked at his negatives stored in drawers.

They were scarred, pathetic things. I haven't the stomach for it, not any more, thought Sandro.

As he walked home, St. Clair Avenue seemed very fine. The best part was, he thought, there were no relationships. Neither this leaning drunk nor that window-shopper was so connected to any other as to endanger his or her existence. The tolerance of indifference, said Sandro to himself, trying to remember it so that he could tell Becker.

But Sandro felt ill at ease in his own home, by its very definition a dangerous and unreliable setting. His wife was stirring something, with her lips tight together. His children, almost grown up now, bred secrets as they looked at television. He himself only posed in the doorway, looking for hidden seams and the faint hair-lines of an airbrush.

That night he stood exhausted by his bed. His wife lay on her side with one round shoulder above the sheet. Behind her on the wall was the photo he'd taken of their village before he left Italy. He ought to reshoot it, take out that gas station and clean up the square a little. His pillow had an indentation, as if a head had been erased. He slept in a chair.

In the morning he went down to the shop. He got his best camera and set up a tripod on the sidewalk directly across the street. He took several shots in the solid bright morning light. He locked the door and placed the CLOSED sign in the window. In the darkroom he developed the film, floating the negatives in the pungent fluid until the row of shop fronts came through clearly, the flat brick faces, the curving concrete trim, the two balls on the crowns. Deftly he dissolved each brick of his store, the window and the sign. Deftly he reattached each brick of the store on the west side to the bricks of the store to the east.

I have been many things in my life, thought Sandro, a presser of shutters, a confessor, a false prophet. Now I am a bricklayer, and a good one. He taped the negatives together and developed them. He touched up the join and then photographed it again. He developed this second negative and it was perfect. Number 1812, Lord's Shoes, joined directly to 1820, Bargain Jimmies: the Immaculate Conception Photography Gallery at 1816 no longer existed. Working quickly, because he wanted to finish before the day was over, he blew it up to two feet by three feet. He cleared out his window display of brides and babies and stood up this new photograph — one of the finest he'd ever taken, he thought. Then he took a couple of cameras and a bag with the tripod and some lenses. He turned out the light, pulling the door shut behind him, and began to walk west.

1988

NOTES

In Christian belief, the Immaculate Conception refers to Mary, the mother of Jesus. According to religious dogma, she was born without original sin. (Some people erroneously believe that the reference is to Jesus's birth.) Becker, Sandro's mentor and friend, uses this term mockingly (paragraphs 81–83, p. 82). Note also the irony in the title of this story.

Prosciutto e melone Italian ham with melon, a traditional appetizer.

Bonbonniere Sugared almond wrapped in netting, given as wedding favours.

Brian and Mila Mulroney Brian Mulroney was the prime minister of Canada (1984–1993); his wife is Mila. Sandro dismisses them as not being "real people" (p. 80).

Tintoretto (1518–1594) An Italian painter of the mannerist style. The suggestion here is that Tintoretto deliberately falsified his portraits of his wealthy patrons, as Sandro does with his photographs.

COMPREHENSION AND DISCUSSION

1. How old is Sandro? How long has he had the store when the story begins? Why is his Italian heritage important to the story?
2. Why did the community want to punish Alicia? What do you think of the way she was treated? Was it fair?
3. What is Becker's role in this story?
4. Why does Sandro doctor the photographs despite his objections?
5. What finally makes Sandro quit his profession? Why does he tamper with his last photograph in which he removes his own place of business?
6. Explain this statement that Sandro makes: "It is better to be a murderer than a creator. I am playing God, outplaying God at His own game" (paragraph 63, p. 81).
7. Explain the religious subtext in this story. In short, why are the store and the story called "The Immaculate Conception Photography Gallery"? What purpose do the religious references serve, for example, the references to weddings and Lord's Shoes?
8. Explain the comments on human relationships in this story. Are they too cynical?

LITERARY TECHNIQUES

Confidant Usually, a secondary character to whom the protagonist reveals inner thoughts and confidences. Sandro pitches his questions to Becker, who gives back philosophical answers.

Foil A contrasting character who helps show up opposite traits or actions of the main character. Again, Becker is a foil to Sandro and to other affluent people in Canadian society.

Ironic juxtapositioning Irony is the sense of contrast or contradiction, and juxtapositioning is the deliberate placing of ideas, scenes, and such to create an effect. Govier subtly employs this device by having Sandro's shop sandwiched between Lord's Shoes and Bargain Jimmie's. The focus of attention is on the two words and ideas "Lord" and "Bargain." Throughout the story, Sandro is forever caught between taking wedding pictures ("Lord" because of the sanctity of marriage) and removing people from the originals as requested by family members ("Bargain" because of Sandro's complicity and the fact that they try to negotiate a lower fee).

ASSIGNMENTS

1. Computers have made it much easier to change photographs. Write an essay on the repercussions or ethics of digital photography. You could write about the use of photographs as evidence in a criminal trial. Or, you could detail guidelines to be used in the media and advertising for altering such images. For example, is it ethical to alter a view of scenery to be more picturesque for a travel brochure?
2. In the story, Diora's mother says "The wedding was one day. This is forever." Read Shinan Govani's article "Don't Say Cheese!" (p. 276). What would Govani say to the people in Govier's story?
3. Can memory be as easily altered as Sandro's photographs? (If you can no longer trust a photograph, can you still trust your memory?)
4. Why do people take photographs or have their picture taken? What does a photograph represent?

We So Seldom Look on Love

Barbara Gowdy

1. When you die, and your earthly self begins turning into your disintegrated self, you radiate an intense current of energy. There is always energy given off when a thing turns into its opposite, when love, for instance, turns into hate. There are always sparks at those extreme points. But life turning into death is the most extreme of extreme points. So just after you die, the sparks are really stupendous. Really magical and explosive.

2. I've seen cadavers shining like stars. I'm the only person I've ever heard of who has. Almost everyone senses something, though, some vitality. That's why you get resistance to the idea of cremation or organ donation. "I want to be in one piece," people say. Even Matt, who claimed there was no soul and no afterlife, wrote a P.S. in his suicide note that he be buried intact.

3. As if it would have made any difference to his energy emission. No matter what you do — slice open the flesh, dissect everything, burn everything — you're in the path of a power way beyond your little interferences.

4. I grew up in a nice, normal, happy family outside a small town in New Jersey. My parents and my brother are still living there. My dad owned a flower store. Now my brother owns it. My brother is three years older than I am, a serious, remote man. But loyal. When I made the headlines he phoned to say that if I needed money for a lawyer, he would give it to me. I was really touched. Especially as he was standing up to Carol, his wife. She got on the extension and screamed, "You're sick! You should be put away!"

5. She'd been wanting to tell me that since we were thirteen years old.

6. I had an animal cemetery back then. Our house was beside a woods and we had three outdoor cats, great hunters who tended to leave their kills in one piece. Whenever I found a body, usually a mouse or a bird, I took it into my bedroom and hid it until midnight. I didn't know anything about the ritual significance of the midnight hour. My burials took place then because that's when I woke up. It no longer happens, but I was such a sensitive child that I think I must have been aroused by the energy given off as day clicked over into the dead of night and, simultaneously, as the dead of night clicked over into the next day.

7. In any case, I'd be wide awake. I'd get up and go to the bathroom to wrap the body in toilet paper. I felt compelled to be so careful, so respectful. I whispered a chant. At each step of the burial I chanted. "I shroud the

body, shroud the body, shroud little sparrow with broken wing." Or "I lower the body, lower the body..." And so on.

Climbing out of the bathroom window was accompanied by: "I enter the night, enter the night..." At my cemetery I set the body down on a special flat rock and took my pyjamas off. I was behaving out of pure inclination. I dug up four or five graves and unwrapped the animals from their shrouds. The rotting smell was crucial. So was the cool air. Normally I'd be so keyed up at this point that I'd burst into a dance.

I used to dance for dead men, too. Before I climbed on top of them, I'd dance all around my prep room. When I told Matt about this he said that I was shaking my personality out of my body so that the sensation of participating in the cadaver's energy eruption would be intensified. "You're trying to imitate the disintegration process," he said.

Maybe — on an unconscious level. But what I was aware of was the heat, the heat of my danced-out body, which I cooled by lying on top of the cadaver. As a child I'd gently wipe my skin with two of the animals I'd just unwrapped. When I was covered all over with their scent, I put them aside, unwrapped the new corpse and did the same with it. I called this the Anointment. I can't describe how it felt. The high, high rapture. The electricity that shot through me.

The rest, wrapping the bodies back up and burying them, was pretty much what you'd expect.

It astonishes me now to think how naive I was. I thought I had discovered something that certain other people, if they weren't afraid to give it a try, would find just as fantastic as I did. It was a dark and forbidden thing, yes, but so was sex. I really had no idea that I was jumping across a vast behavioural gulf. In fact, I couldn't see that I was doing anything wrong. I still can't, and I'm including what happened with Matt. Carol said I should have been put away, but I'm not bad-looking, so if offering my body to dead men is a crime, I'd like to know who the victim is.

Carol has always been jealous of me. She's fat and has a wandering eye. Her eye gives her a dreamy, distracted quality that I fell for (as I suppose my brother would eventually do) one day at a friend's thirteenth birthday party. It was the beginning of the summer holidays, and I was yearning for a kindred spirit, someone to share my secret life with. I saw Carol standing alone, looking everywhere at once, and I chose her.

I knew to take it easy, though. I knew not to push anything. We'd search for dead animals and birds, we'd chant and swaddle the bodies, dig graves, make popsicle-stick crosses. All by daylight. At midnight I'd go out and dig up the grave and conduct a proper burial.

15 There must have been some chipmunk sickness that summer. Carol and I found an incredible number of chipmunks, and a lot of them had no blood on them, no sign of cat. One day we found a chipmunk that evacuated a string of fetuses when I picked it up. The fetuses were still alive, but there was no saving them, so I took them into the house and flushed them down the toilet.

16 A mighty force was coming from the mother chipmunk. It was as if, along with her own energy, she was discharging all the energy of her dead brood. When Carol and I began to dance for her, we both went a little crazy. We stripped down to our underwear, screamed, spun in circles, threw dirt up into the air. Carol has always denied it, but she took off her bra and began whipping trees with it. I'm sure the sight of her doing this is what inspired me to take off my undershirt and underpants and to perform the Anointment.

17 Carol stopped dancing. I looked at her, and the expression on her face stopped me dancing, too. I looked down at the chipmunk in my hand. It was bloody. There were streaks of blood all over my body. I was horrified. I thought I'd squeezed the chipmunk too hard.

18 But what had happened was, I'd begun my period. I figured this out a few minutes after Carol ran off. I wrapped the chipmunk in its shroud and buried it. Then I got dressed and lay down on the grass. A little while later my mother appeared over me.

19 "Carol's mother phoned," she said. "Carol is very upset. She says you made her perform some disgusting witchcraft dance. You made her take her clothes off, and you attacked her with a bloody chipmunk."

20 "That's a lie," I said. "I'm menstruating."

21 After my mother had fixed me up with a sanitary napkin, she told me she didn't think I should play with Carol any more. "There's a screw loose in there somewhere," she said.

22 I had no intention of playing with Carol any more, but I cried at what seemed like a cruel loss. I think I knew that it was all loneliness from that moment on. Even though I was only thirteen, I was cutting any lines that still drifted out toward normal eroticism. Bosom friends, crushes, pyjama-party intimacy, I was cutting all those lines off.

23 A month or so after becoming a woman I developed a craving to perform autopsies. I resisted doing it for almost a year, though. I was frightened. Violating the intactness of the animal seemed sacrilegious and dangerous. Also unimaginable — I couldn't imagine what would happen.

24 Nothing. Nothing would happen, as I found out. I've read that necrophiles are frightened of getting hurt by normal sexual relationships,

and maybe there's some truth in that (although my heart's been broken plenty of times by cadavers, and not once by a live man), but I think that my attraction to cadavers isn't driven by fear, it's driven by excitement, and that one of the most exciting things about a cadaver is how dedicated it is to dying. Its will is all directed to a single intention, like a huge wave heading for shore, and you can ride along on the wave if you want to, because no matter what you do, because with you or without you, that wave is going to hit the beach.

I felt this impetus the first time I worked up enough nerve to cut open a mouse. Like anyone else, I balked a little at slicing into the flesh, and I was repelled for a few seconds when I saw the insides. But something drove me to go through these compunctions. It was as if I were acting solely on instinct and curiosity, and anything I did was all right, provided it didn't kill me.

After the first few times, I started sticking my tongue into the incision. I don't know why. I thought about it, I did it, and I kept on doing it. One day I removed the organs and cleaned them with water, then put them back in, and I kept on doing that, too. Again, I couldn't tell you why except to say that any provocative thought, if you act upon it, seems to set you on a trajectory.

By the time I was sixteen I wanted human corpses. Men. (That way I'm straight.) I got my chauffeur's licence, but I had to wait until I was finished high school before Mr. Wallis would hire me as a hearse driver at the funeral home.

Mr. Wallis knew me because he bought bereavement flowers at my father's store. Now *there* was a weird man. He would take a trocar, which is the big needle you use to draw out a cadaver's fluids, and he would push it up the penises of dead men to make them look semi-erect, and then he'd sodomize them. I caught him at it once, and he tried to tell me that he'd been urinating in the hopper. I pretended to believe him. I was upset though, because I knew that dead men were just dead flesh to him. One minute he'd be locked up with a young male corpse, having his way with him, and the next minute he'd be embalming him as if nothing had happened, and making sick jokes about him, pretending to find evidence of rampant homosexuality — colons stalagmited with dried semen, and so on.

None of this joking ever happened in front of me. I heard about it from the crazy old man who did the mopping up. He was also a necrophile, I'm almost certain, but no longer active. He called dead women Madonnas. He rhapsodized about the beautiful Madonnas he'd had the privilege of seeing in the 1940s, about how much more womanly and feminine the Madonnas were twenty years before.

30   I just listened. I never let on what I was feeling, and I don't think anyone suspected. Necrophiles aren't supposed to be blond and pretty, let alone female. When I'd been working at the funeral home for about a year, a committee from the town council tried to get me to enter the Milk Marketer's Beauty Pageant. They knew about my job, and they knew I was studying embalming at night, but I had told people I was preparing myself for medical school, and I guess the council believed me.

31   For fifteen years, ever since Matt died, people have been asking me how a woman makes love to a corpse.

32   Matt was the only person who figured it out. He was a medical student, so he knew that if you apply pressure to the chest of certain fresh corpses, they purge blood out of their mouths.

33   Matt was smart. I wish I could have loved him with more than sisterly love. He was tall and thin. My type. We met at the doughnut shop across from the medical library, got to talking, and liked each other immediately, an unusual experience for both of us. After about an hour I knew that he loved me and that his love was unconditional. When I told him where I worked and what I was studying, he asked why.

34   "Because I'm a necrophile," I said.

35   He lifted his head and stared at me. He had eyes like high-resolution monitors. Almost too vivid. Normally I don't like looking people in the eye, but I found myself staring back. I could see that he believed me.

36   "I've never told anyone else," I said.

37   "With men or women?" he asked.

38   "Men. Young men."

39   "How?"

40   "Cunnilingus,"

41   "Fresh corpses?"

42   "If I can get them."

43   "What do you do, climb on top of them?"

44   "Yes."

45   "You're turned on by blood."

46   "It's a lubricant," I said. "It's colourful. Stimulating. It's the ultimate bodily fluid."

47   "Yes," he said, nodding. "When you think about it. Sperm propagates life. But blood sustains it. Blood is primary."

48   He kept asking questions, and I answered them as truthfully as I could. Having confessed what I was, I felt myself driven to testing his intellectual rigour and the strength of his love at first sight. Throwing rocks at him

without any expectation that he'd stay standing. He did, though. He caught the whole arsenal and asked for more. It began to excite me.

We went back to his place. He had a basement apartment in an old run-down building. There were books in orange-crate shelves, in piles on the floor, all over the bed. On the wall above his desk was a poster of Doris Day in the movie *Tea for Two*. Matt said she looked like me.

"Do you want to dance first?" he asked, heading for his record player. I'd told him about how I danced before climbing on corpses.

"No."

He swept the books off the bed. Then he undressed me. He had an erection until I told him I was a virgin. "Don't worry," he said, sliding his head down my stomach. "Lie still."

The next morning he phoned me at work. I was hungover and blue from the night before. After leaving his place I'd gone straight to the funeral home and made love to an autopsy case. Then I'd got drunk in a seedy country-and-western bar and debated going back to the funeral home and suctioning out my own blood until I lost consciousness.

It had finally hit me that I was incapable of falling in love with a man who wasn't dead. I kept thinking, "I'm not normal." I'd never faced this before. Obviously, making love to corpses isn't normal, but while I was still a virgin I must have been assuming that I could give it up any time I liked. Get married, have babies. I must have been banking on a future that I didn't even want let alone have access to.

Matt was phoning to get me to come around again after work.

"I don't know," I said.

"You had a good time. Didn't you?"

"Sure, I guess."

"I think you're fascinating," he said.

I sighed.

"Please," he said. "Please."

A few nights later I went to his apartment. From then on we started to meet every Tuesday and Thursday evening after my embalming class, and as soon as I left his place, if I knew there was a corpse at the mortuary — any male corpse, young or old — I went straight there and climbed in a basement window.

Entering the prep room, especially at night when there was nobody else around, was like diving into a lake. Sudden cold and silence, and the sensation of penetrating a new element where the rules of other elements don't apply. Being with Matt was like lying on the beach of the lake. Matt had warm, dry skin. His apartment was overheated and noisy. I lay on

Matt's bed and soaked him up, but only to make the moment when I entered the prep room even more overpowering.

64   If the cadaver was freshly embalmed, I could usually smell him from the basement. The smell is like a hospital and old cheese. For me, it's the smell of danger and permission, it used to key me up like amphetamine, so that by the time I reached the prep room, tremors were running up and down my legs. I locked the door behind me and broke into a wild dance, tearing my clothes off, spinning around, pulling at my hair. I'm not sure what this was all about, whether or not I was trying to take part in the chaos of the corpse's disintegration, as Matt suggested. Maybe I was prostrating myself, I don't know.

65   Once the dancing was over I was always very calm, almost entranced. I drew back the sheet. This was the most exquisite moment. I felt as if I were being blasted by white light. Almost blinded, I climbed onto the table and straddled the corpse. I ran my hands over his skin. My hands and the insides of my thighs burned as if I were touching dry ice. After a few minutes I lay down and pulled the sheet up over my head. I began to kiss his mouth. By now he might be drooling blood. A corpse's blood is thick, cool, and sweet. My head roared.

66   I was no longer depressed. Far from it, I felt better, more confident, than I had ever felt in my life. I had discovered myself to be irredeemably abnormal. I could either slit my throat or surrender—wholeheartedly now—to my obsession. I surrendered. And what happened was that obsession began to storm through me, as if I were a tunnel. I became the medium of obsession as well as both ends of it. With Matt, when we made love, I was the receiving end, I was the cadaver. When I left him and went to the funeral home, I was the lover. Through me Matt's love poured into the cadavers at the funeral home, and through me the cadavers filled Matt with explosive energy.

67   He quickly got addicted to this energy. The minute I arrived at his apartment, he had to hear every detail about the last corpse I'd been with. For a month or so I had him pegged as a latent homosexual necrophile voyeur, but then I began to see that it wasn't the corpses themselves that excited him, it was my passion for them. It was the power that went into that passion and that came back, doubled, for his pleasure. He kept asking, "How did you feel? Why do you think you felt that way?" And then, because the source of all this power disturbed him, he'd try to prove that my feelings were delusory.

68   "A corpse shows simultaneous extremes of character," I told him. "Wisdom and innocence, happiness and grief, and so on."

"Therefore all corpses are alike," he said. "Once you've had one you've had them all."

"No, no. They're all different. Each corpse contains his own extremes. Each corpse is only as wise and as innocent as the living person could have been."

He said, "You're drafting personalities onto corpses in order to have power over them."

"In that case," I said, "I'm pretty imaginative, since I've never met two corpses who were alike."

"You *could* be that imaginative," he argued. "Schizophrenics are capable of manufacturing dozens of complex personalities."

I didn't mind these attacks. There was no malice in them, and there was no way they could touch me, either. It was as if I were luxuriously pouring my heart out to a very clever, very concerned, very tormented analyst. I felt sorry for him. I understood his twisted desire to turn me into somebody else (somebody who might love him). I used to fall madly in love with cadavers and then cry because they were dead. The difference between Matt and me was that I had become philosophical. I was all right.

I thought that he was, too. He was in pain, yes, but he seemed confident that what he was going through was temporary and not unnatural. "I am excessively curious," he said. "My fascination is any curious man's fascination with the unusual." He said that by feeding his lust through mine, he would eventually saturate it, then turn it to disgust.

I told him to go ahead, give it a try. So he began to scour the newspapers for my cadavers' obituaries and to go to their funerals and memorial services. He made charts of my preferences and the frequency of my morgue encounters. He followed me to the morgue at night and waited outside so that he could get a replay while I was still in an erotic haze. He sniffed my skin. He pulled me over to streetlights and examined the blood on my face and hands.

I suppose I shouldn't have encouraged him. I can't really say why I did, except that in the beginning I saw his obsession as the outer edge of my own obsession, a place I didn't have to visit as long as he was there. And then later, and despite his increasingly erratic behaviour, I started to have doubts about an obsession that could come on so suddenly and that could come through me.

One night he announced that he might as well face it, he was going to have to make love to corpses, male corpses. The idea nauseated him, he said, but he said that secretly, deep down, unknown even to himself, making love to male corpses was clearly the target of his desire. I blew up. I told him that necrophilia wasn't something you forced yourself to do. You longed to do it, you needed to do it. You were born to do it.

He wasn't listening. He was glued to the dresser mirror. In the last weeks of his life he stared at himself in the mirror without the least self-consciousness. He focused on his face, even though what was going on from the neck down was the arresting part. He had begun to wear incredibly weird outfits. Velvet capes, pantaloons, high-heeled red boots. When we made love, he kept these outfits on. He stared into my eyes, riveted (it later occurred to me) by his own reflection.

Matt committed suicide, there was never any doubt about that. As for the necrophilia, it wasn't a crime, not fifteen years ago. So even though I was caught in the act, naked and straddling an unmistakably dead body, even though the newspapers found out about it and made it front-page news, there was nothing the police could charge me with.

In spite of which I made a full confession. It was crucial to me that the official report contain more than one detective's bleak observations. I wanted two things on record: one, that Matt was ravished by a reverential expert; two, that his cadaver blasted the energy of a star.

"Did this energy blast happen before or after he died?" the detective asked.

"After," I said, adding quickly that I couldn't have foreseen such a blast. The one tricky area is why I hadn't stopped the suicide. Why I hadn't talked, or cut, Matt down.

I lied. I said that as soon as I entered Matt's room, he kicked away the ladder. Nobody could prove otherwise. But I've often wondered how much time actually passed between when I opened the door and when his neck broke. In crises, a minute isn't a minute. There's the same chaos you get at the instant of death, with time and form breaking free, and everything magnifying and coming apart.

Matt must have been in a state of crisis for days, maybe weeks before he died. All that staring in mirrors, thinking, "Is this my face?" Watching as his face separated into its infinitesimal particles and reassembled into a strange new face. The night before he died, he had a mask on. A Dracula mask, but he wasn't joking. He wanted to wear the mask while I made love to him as if he were a cadaver. No way, I said. The whole point, I reminded him, was that *I* played the cadaver. He begged me, and I laughed because of the mask and with relief. If he wanted to turn the game around, then it was over between us, and I was suddenly aware of how much I liked that idea.

The next night he phoned me at my parents' and said, "I love you," then hung up.

I don't know how I knew, but I did. A gun, I thought. Men always use guns. And then I thought, no, poison, cyanide. He was a medical student and had access to drugs. When I arrived at his apartment, the door was open. Across from the door, taped to the wall, was a note: "DEAD PERSON IN BEDROOM."

But he wasn't dead. He was standing on a step-ladder. He was naked. An impressively knotted noose, attached to a pipe that ran across the ceiling, was looped around his neck.

He smiled tenderly. "I knew you'd come," he said.

"So why the note?" I demanded.

"Pull away the ladder," he crooned. "My beloved."

"Come on. This is stupid. Get down." I went up to him and punched his leg.

"All you have to do," he said, "is pull away the ladder."

His eyes were even darker and more expressive than usual. His cheekbones appeared to be highlighted. (I discovered minutes later he had makeup on.) I glanced around the room for a chair or a table that I could bring over and stand on. I was going to take the noose off him myself.

"If you leave," he said, "if you take a step back, if you do anything other than pull away the ladder, I'll kick it away."

"I love you," I said. "Okay?"

"No, you don't," he said.

"I do!" To sound like I meant it I stared at his legs and imagined them lifeless. "I do!"

"No, you don't," he said softly. "But," he said, "you will."

I was gripping the ladder. I remember thinking that if I held tight to the ladder, he wouldn't be able to kick it away. I was gripping the ladder, and then it was by the wall, tipped over. I have no memory of transition between these two events. There was a loud crack, and gushing water. Matt dropped gracefully, like a girl fainting. Water poured on him from the broken pipe. There was a smell of excrement. I dragged him by the noose.

In the living room I pulled him onto the green shag carpet. I took my clothes off. I knelt over him. I kissed the blood at the corner of his mouth.

True obsession depends on the object's absolute unresponsiveness. When I used to fall for a particular cadaver, I would feel as if I were a hollow instrument, a bell or a flute. I'd empty out. *I* would clear out (it was involuntary) until I was an instrument for the cadaver to swell into and be amplified. As the object of Matt's obsession how could I be other than impassive, while he was alive?

He was playing with fire, playing with me. Not just because I couldn't love him, but because I was irradiated. The whole time that I was involved with Matt, I was making love to corpses, absorbing their energy, blazing it back out. Since that energy came from the act of life alchemizing into death, there's a possibility that it was alchemical itself. Even if I wasn't, I'm sure it gave Matt the impression that I had the power to change him in some huge and dangerous way.

I now believe that his addiction to my energy was really a craving for such a transformation. In fact, I think that all desire is desire for transformation, and that all transformation — all movement, all process — happens because life turns into death.

I am still a necrophile, occasionally, and recklessly. I have found no replacement for the torrid serenity of a cadaver.

1992

NOTES

Necrophile A person obsessed with the dead, usually with a sexual attraction to corpses. The two roots of these words are found in other words. *Necro* is from the Greek word for corpse, as in necropolis and necromancy. *Phile* is from the Greek word for love, as in philosophy (the love of wisdom), bibliophile (a lover of books), Sinophile (the love of Chinese culture).

Madonna Literally "my lady." It is a term for the Virgin Mary. Here, the janitor uses "Madonnas" to refer to young, virginal, good-looking women.

Doris Day A popular, blonde Hollywood actress in the 1950s and 1960s, known for her portrayal of sweet and wholesome love interests in light, romantic comedies.

Tea for Two (1950) A musical in which Doris Day plays a girl who wants to be in a Broadway show.

Dracula Synonym for vampire. Bram Stoker's novel *Dracula* (1897) inspired an interest in bloodsucking, undead creatures who prey on the living.

COMPREHENSION AND DISCUSSION

1. When does the narrator discover her true attraction to dead things?
2. What does she do about it?
3. Why is Carol so abusive to the narrator? How did Carol's rejection affect the narrator?
4. Why does the protagonist find Matt attractive?
5. Who is stranger: Matt or the narrator? Why?
6. Can you understand (at least intellectually) a person like this girl? Do you feel sorry for her? Why or why not?
7. What do you think the narrator did with her life after the events of the story?
8. Would this story be as effective in the third person?

LITERARY TECHNIQUES

Gowdy uses the first-person narrative technique. This method reveals the thoughts of the narrator. For this story, it is essential to have her explain her fascination with dead things, especially dead young men. Note how matter-of-factly she speaks, as if these actions are quite normal (for her).

Liebestod or love-death is a popular theme in literature. Eroticism of some form, usually the bizarre, plays a role in the plot and structure of the story. (The currently popular genre of vampires is an offshoot, such as in Anne Rice's novels and the TV series *Buffy the Vampire Slayer*.) Both love (or sex) and death are mysteries that must be fathomed by the main character, and through her, by the reader. Such obsession comes from the desire to know and often to experience vicariously.

Dying for a loved one is another theme found in many tragic-romance tales. Gowdy's short story follows this particular tradition, with a new twist. Usually the male character sacrifices himself nobly for his beloved; in this case, Matt commits suicide to win her love.

Uncompromising endings: many contemporary writers do not adhere to comfortable, feel-good, moralistic conclusions. For example, Gowdy's necrophilic narrator does not change her ways even though Matt dies. A total change in her behaviour would be illogical and untrue to the spirit of the story. It would also deny nearly a lifetime of her pathological needs.

ASSIGNMENTS

1. Compare this treatment of death with Jessica Mitford's "The Story of Service" (p. 301).
2. Why is necrophilia a taboo subject? What makes people uncomfortable with this topic? What are some other taboo subjects that you would prefer not to talk about? Why?
3. Explain the title in relation to the theme and plot.
4. Read Pico Iyer's "Of Weirdos and Eccentrics" (p. 289). Is Gowdy's narrator a weirdo or an eccentric, according to Iyer's definition?
5. This story has been made into a movie called *Kissed* (1996), which is available on video. Compare the movie and the short story. Or, write a critique of the movie.

So What Are You, Anyway?
Lawrence Hill

Carole settles in Seat 12A, beside the window, puts her doll on a vacant seat and snaps open her purse. She holds up a mirror. She looks into her own dark eyes. She examines her handful of freckles, which are tiny ink spots dotting her cheeks. She checks for pimples, but finds none. Only the clear complexion that her father sometimes calls "milk milk milk milk chocolate" as he burrows into her neck with kisses.

"This is yours, I believe." A big man with a sunburnt face is holding her doll upside down.

"May I have her, please?" Carole says.

He turns the doll right side up. "A black doll! I never saw such a thing!"

"Her name's Amy. May I have her, please?"

"Henry Norton!" cries the man's wife. "Give that doll back this instant!"

Carole tucks the doll close to the window.

The man sits beside Carole. The woman takes the aisle seat.

"Don't mind him," the woman says, leaning towards Carole. "By the way, I'm Betty Norton, and he's my husband, Henry."

The man next to Carole hogs the armrest. His feet sprawl onto her side. And he keeps looking at her.

The stewardess passes by, checking seat belts. "Everything okay?"

"May I go to the bathroom?" Carole asks.

"Do you think you could wait? We're about to take off."

"Okay."

Carole looks out the window, sees the Toronto airport buildings fall behind and wonders if her parents are watching. Say goodbye, she instructs Amy, waving the doll's hand, say goodbye to Mom and Dad. The engines charge to life. Her seat hums. They taxi down the runway. She feels a hollowness in her stomach when they lift into the air. Her ears plug and stay that way until the plane levels out over pillows of cotton. They burn as bright as the sun. So that is what the other side of clouds look like!

"Excuse me. *Excuse me!*" The man is talking to her. "You can go to the bathroom now, you know."

"No, that's all right," Carole says.

"Travelling all alone, are you?"

Carole swallows with difficulty.

20 "Where do you live?" he asks.
21 "Don Mills."
22 "Oh, really?" he says. "Were you born there?"
23 "Yes."
24 "And your parents?"
25 "My mother was born in Chicago and my father was born in Tucson."
26 "And you're going to visit your grandparents?"
27 She nods.
28 "And you parents let you travel alone!"
29 "It's only an airplane! And I'm a big girl."
30 The man lowers the back of his seat, chuckling. He whispers to his wife. "No!" Carole hears her whisper back, "*You* ask her!"
31 Carole yawns, holds Amy's hand and goes to sleep. The clinking of silverware wakens her, but she hears the man and woman talking about her, so she keeps her eyes shut.
32 "I don't know, Henry," says the woman. "Don't ask me. Ask *her*."
33 "I'm kind of curious," he says. "Aren't you?"
34 Carole can't make out the woman's answer. But then she hears her say:
35 "I just can't see it. It's not fair to children. I don't mind them mixed, but the world isn't ready for it. They're neither one thing nor the other. Henry, wake that child and see if she wants to eat."
36 When the man taps her shoulder, Carole opens her eyes. "I have to go to the bathroom," she says.
37 "But they're going to serve the meal," the man says.
38 "Henry! If she wants out, let her out. She's only a child."
39 Carole grimaces. She is definitely not a child. She is a young lady! She can identify Drambuie, Kahlua, and Grand Marnier by smell!
40 Once in the aisle, Carole realizes she has forgotten Amy.
41 Henry Norton hands her the doll. "There you go. And don't fall out of the plane, now. There's a big hole down by the toilet."
42 "There is not!" Carole says. "There isn't any such thing!" She heads down the aisle with an eye out just in case there is a hole, after all.
43 Coming out of the toilet, Carole finds the stewardess. "Excuse me, miss. Could I sit somewhere else?"
44 The woman frowns. "Why?"
45 "I don't like the window."
46 "Is that it? Is that the only reason?"
47 "Well...yes."
48 "I'm sorry, but we don't have time to move you now. We're serving a meal. Ask me later, if you like."

After Carole had eaten and had her tray taken and been served a hot face towel, the man says: "What *are* you, anyway? My wife and I were wondering."

Carole blinks, sees the man's clear blue eyes and drops her head.

"What do you mean?" she says.

"You know, what are you? What race?"

Carole's mouth drops. Race? What is that? She doesn't understand. Yet she senses that the man is asking a bad question. It is as if he is asking her something dirty, or touching her in a bad place. She wishes her Mom and Dad were there. They could tell her what "race" meant.

"That doll of yours is black," Henry Norton says. "That's a Negro doll. That's race. Negro. What's your race?"

The question still confuses her.

"Put it this way," the man says. "What is your father?"

The question baffles her. What is her father? He is her Dad! He is her Dad and every Sunday morning he makes pancakes for the whole family and lets Carole pour hot syrup on them and afterwards he sits her on his lap and tells stories.

Mrs. Norton leans toward Carole. "Say you had a colouring book. What colour would you make your Dad?"

"I never use just one colour."

"Okay. What colour would you make his face?"

"Brown."

"And your mother?"

Carole imagines a blank page. What would she put in her mother's face? She has to put something in there. She can't just leave it blank. "I don't know."

"Sure you do," Mrs. Norton says. "How would you colour your mother's face?"

"Yellow."

Carole sees Mr. and Mrs. Norton look at each other.

"Is your mother Chinese?" Mrs. Norton asks.

"No."

"Are you sure you'd colour her yellow?"

"No."

"What else might you colour her?"

What else? Carole feels ashamed at her stupidity. A tear races down her cheek. "Red," she says, finally.

"Red! You can't colour a face red! Is your mother white? Is she like me? Her face! Is it the same colour as mine?"

74 "Yes."

75 "And your father's brown?"

76 Carole nods.

77 "When you say brown, do you mean he is a Negro?"

78 "Yes." Of course her father is a Negro. If Mrs. Norton wanted to know all along if her Dad was a Negro, why didn't she just ask?

79 "So you're mixed?" Mrs. Norton says. "You're a mulatto!"

80 Carole's lip quivers. What is mulatto? Why do they keep asking her what she is? She isn't anything!

81 "So is that it? You're a mulatto? You know what a mulatto is, don't you? Haven't your parents taught you that word?"

82 Approaching with a cart of juice, the stewardess looks up and smiles at Carole. That gives her a rush of courage.

83 "Leave me alone!" she screams at Mrs. Norton.

84 Passengers stare. The stewardess spills a drink. Mrs. Norton sits back hard in her seat, her hands raised, fingers spread. Carole sees people watching.

85 "Why do you keep asking me if my Dad is Negro? Yes, he's a Negro! Okay? OKAY? Negro Negro Negro!"

86 "Calm down," Mrs. Norton says, reaching over.

87 "Don't touch her," the stewardess says.

88 "Who are these people?" someone says from across the aisle. "Imagine, talking to a child like that, and in 1970!"

89 One woman sitting in front of Carole stands up and turns around.

90 "Would you like to come and sit with me, little girl?"

91 "No!" Carole shouts. "I don't like all these questions. She keeps asking me how I would colour my parents in a colouring book! Why do you keep asking me that?"

92 Mrs. Norton pleads with Carole to stop.

93 "How would you like it if that happened to you?" Carole says. "So what are you, anyway? What are your parents? How would you colour them? Well, I don't care! I don't even care!"

94 "How would you like to come and sit with me?" the stewardess says, smiling. "I'll make you a special drink. Have you ever had a Shirley Temple?"

95 Carole nods enthusiastically. Already she feels better. Clutching Amy, she passes by the Nortons, who swing their legs to let her out.

96 "My God," Carole hears Mrs. Norton tell her husband, "talk about sensitive."

1992

NOTES

Don Mills A suburb of Toronto.

Negro A term that was once considered a euphemism and is now considered a racial slur. Accepted terms have changed from "coloured," to "Negro," to "black," to "Afro-American."

Shirley Temple A nonalcoholic drink served in a cocktail glass, named after a child actress.

COMPREHENSION AND DISCUSSION

1. How old do you think Carole is? How does the writer provide you with this information?
2. Who are the Nortons? Describe them.
3. How do you know the Nortons are imposing on Carole? Why do they persist on asking her personal questions when they realize she is uncomfortable talking to them?
4. Are the Nortons racist, just curious, or adult bullies?
5. Explain Mrs. Norton's statement: "It's not fair to children. I don't mind them mixed, but the world isn't ready for it. They're neither one thing nor the other" (p. 100).
6. What is proper etiquette in such encounters? How would you have handled the situation? What do you think Carole should have done?
7. Explain how Hill sets up the situation. How does he lead up to the Norton's questioning?
8. Why does Hill set the story in 1970? Have racial attitudes changed in the last 30 years? Do you think racially mixed children are more accepted now?

LITERARY TECHNIQUES

Point of view The story is told in third person; however, the focus stays on Carole, not the Nortons. Thus, the reader is able to sense that the old couple are intruders into Carole's life and privacy.

Present tense The writer uses the present tense rather than the simple past. This technique simulates immediacy as if the action is happening now and the reader is right there with Carole and the Nortons.

Foreshadowing An arrangement of clues to prepare for later action or events. This technique works twofold: the author plays fair with the reader and the reader can anticipate the outcome. For example, Hill informs the reader about Carole's racial heritage when he refers to her complexion as "milk chocolate" in the opening paragraph (p. 99). He also reveals Henry Norton's character by describing him as redfaced ("sunburnt") to suggest "redneck" or bigot, and by having him hold the doll upside down (p. 99).

Dialogue Much of the story is carried by dialogue rather than by description and extended narration. In general, dialogue gives the story a rapid movement because the speeches of the characters are usually kept short. Second, it shows character traits: how a person says something defines that person. In this case, Carole sounds like a small, vulnerable young child in the way she responds to the Nortons. Third, dialogue draws readers into the story as if we were overhearing a conversation.

ASSIGNMENTS

1. What questions do you consider improper to ask a stranger? Explain why.
2. Define the following words: racism, bigotry, discrimination, prejudice, stereotype. First use the dictionary meanings; then add your own in the form of observation, anecdote, or feelings.
3. Can anyone ever be totally free of prejudice? Can a society be free of discrimination? What are some causes of racial prejudice?
4. Compare Carole to Piquette in Margaret Laurence's "The Loons" (p. 128). How do they handle their respective problems with a prejudiced society? How are their situations similar?
5. While talking about breeding in animals is acceptable, it is a controversial subject when applied to human beings. Eugenics (the study of controlled breeding in the human race to improve certain hereditary traits), for example, is associated with the Nazis and with forced sterilization. Some people argue for racial purity, while others say that mixing races is an important step to eliminating prejudice. Research one of the issues in this topic, and write an explanation of the controversy.

The Lottery
Shirley Jackson

The morning of June 27th was clear and sunny, with the fresh warmth of a full-summer day; the flowers were blossoming profusely and the grass was richly green. The people of the village began to gather in the square, between the post office and the bank, around ten o'clock; in some towns there were so many people that the lottery took two days and had to be started on June 26th, but in this village, where there were only about three hundred people, the whole lottery took less than two hours, so it could begin at ten o'clock in the morning and still be through in time to allow the villagers to get home for noon dinner.

The children assembled first, of course. School was recently over for the summer, and the feeling of liberty sat uneasily on most of them; they tended to gather together quietly for a while before they broke into boisterous play, and their talk was still of the classroom and the teacher, of books and reprimands. Bobby Martin had already stuffed his pockets full of stones, and the other boys soon followed his example, selecting the smoothest and roundest stones; Bobby and Harry Jones and Dickie Delacroix — the villagers pronounced this name "Dellacroy" — eventually made a great pile of stones in one corner of the square and guarded it against the raids of the other boys. The girls stood aside, talking among themselves, looking over their shoulders at the boys, and the very small children rolled in the dust or clung to the hands of their older brothers or sisters.

Soon the men began to gather, surveying their own children, speaking of planting and rain, tractors and taxes. They stood together, away from the pile of stones in the corner, and their jokes were quiet and they smiled rather than laughed. The women, wearing faded house dresses and sweaters, came shortly after their menfolk. They greeted one another and exchanged bits of gossip as they went to join their husbands. Soon the women, standing by their husbands, began to call to their children, and the children came reluctantly, having to be called four or five times. Bobby Martin ducked under his mother's grasping hand and ran, laughing, back to the pile of stones. His father spoke up sharply, and Bobby came quickly and took his place between his father and his oldest brother.

The lottery was conducted — as were the square dances, the teen club, the Halloween program — by Mr. Summers, who had time and energy to devote to civic activities. He was a round-faced, jovial man and he ran the coal business, and people were sorry for him, because he had no children and his wife was a scold. When he arrived in the square, carrying the black wooden box, there was a murmur of conversation among the villagers, and he waved and called, "Little late today, folks." The postmaster, Mr. Graves, followed him, carrying a three-legged stool, and the stool was put in the centre of the square and Mr. Summers set the black box down on it. The villagers kept their distance, leaving a space between themselves and the stool, and when Mr. Summers said, "Some of you fellows want to give me a hand?" there was a hesitation before two men, Mr. Martin and his oldest son, Baxter, came forward to hold the box steady on the stool while Mr. Summers stirred up the papers inside it.

5   The original paraphernalia for the lottery had been lost long ago, and the black box now resting on the stool had been put into use even before Old Man Warner, the oldest man in town, was born. Mr. Summers spoke frequently to the villagers about making a new box, but no one liked to upset even as much tradition as was represented by the black box. There was a story that the present box had been made with some pieces of the box that had preceded it, the one that had been constructed when the first people settled down to make a village here. Every year, after the lottery, Mr. Summers began talking again about a new box, but every year the subject was allowed to fade off without anything's being done. The black box grew shabbier each year; by now it was no longer completely black but splintered badly along one side to show the original wood colour, and in some places faded or stained.

6   Mr. Martin and his oldest son, Baxter, held the black box securely on the stool until Mr. Summers had stirred the papers thoroughly with his hand. Because so much of the ritual had been forgotten or discarded, Mr. Summers had been successful in having slips of paper substituted for the chips of wood that had been used for generations. Chips of wood, Mr. Summers had argued, had been all very well when the village was tiny, but now that the population was more than three hundred and likely to keep on growing, it was necessary to use something that would fit more easily into the black box. The night before the lottery, Mr. Summers and Mr. Graves made up the slips of paper and put them in the box, and it was then taken to the safe of Mr. Summers' coal company and locked up until Mr. Summers was ready to take it to the square next morning. The rest of the year, the box was put way, sometimes one place, sometimes another; it had spent one year in Mr. Graves's barn and another year underfoot in the post office, and sometimes it was set on a shelf in the Martin grocery and left there.

There was a great deal of fussing to be done before Mr. Summers declared the lottery open. There were the lists to make up—of heads of families, heads of households in each family, members of each household in each family. There was the proper swearing-in of Mr. Summers by the postmaster, as the official of the lottery; at one time, some people remembered, there had been a recital of some sort, performed by the official of the lottery, a perfunctory, tuneless chant that had been rattled off duly each year; some people believed that the official of the lottery used to stand just so when he said or sang it, others believed that he was supposed to walk among the people, but years and years ago this part of the ritual had been allowed to lapse. There had been, also, a ritual salute, which the official of the lottery had had to use in addressing each person who came up to draw from the box, but this also had changed with time, until now it was felt necessary only for the official to speak to each person approaching. Mr. Summers was very good at all this; in his clean white shirt and blue jeans, with one hand resting carelessly on the black box, he seemed very proper and important as he talked interminably to Mr. Graves and the Martins.

Just as Mr. Summers finally left off talking and turned to the assembled villagers, Mrs. Hutchinson came hurriedly along the path to the square, her sweater thrown over her shoulders, and slid into place in the back of the crowd. "Clean forgot what day it was," she said to Mrs. Delacroix, who stood next to her, and they both laughed softly. "Thought my old man was out back stacking wood," Mrs. Hutchinson went on, "and then I looked out the window and the kids was gone, and then I remembered it was the twenty-seventh and came a-running." She dried her hands on her apron, and Mrs. Delacroix said, "You're in time, though. They're still talking away up there."

Mrs. Hutchinson craned her neck to see through the crowd and found her husband and children standing near the front. She tapped Mrs. Delacroix on the arm as a farewell and began to make her way through the crowd. The people separated good-humouredly to let her through; two or three people said, in voices just loud enough to be heard across the crowd, "Here comes your Missus, Hutchinson," and "Bill, she made it after all." Mrs. Hutchinson reached her husband, and Mr. Summers, who had been waiting, said cheerfully, "Thought we were going to have to get on without you, Tessie." Mrs. Hutchinson said, grinning, "Wouldn't have me leave m'dishes in the sink, now, would you, Joe?" and soft laughter ran through the crowd as the people stirred back into position after Mrs. Hutchinson's arrival.

"Well, now," Mr. Summers said soberly, "guess we better get started, get this over with, so's we can go back to work. Anybody ain't here?"

11   "Dunbar," several people said. "Dunbar, Dunbar."

12   Mr. Summers consulted his list. "Clyde Dunbar," he said. "That's right. He's broke his leg, hasn't he? Who's drawing for him?"

13   "Me. I guess," a woman said, and Mr. Summers turned to look at her. "Wife draws for her husband," Mr. Summers said. "Don't you have a grown boy to do it for you, Janey?" Although Mr. Summers and everyone else in the village knew the answer perfectly well, it was the business of the official of the lottery to ask such questions formally. Mr. Summers waited with an expression of polite interest while Mrs. Dunbar answered.

14   "Horace's not but sixteen yet," Mrs. Dunbar said regretfully. "Guess I gotta fill in for the old man this year."

15   "Right," Mr. Summers said. He made a note on the list he was holding. Then he asked, "Watson boy drawing this year?"

16   A tall boy in the crowd raised his hand. "Here," he said. "I'm drawing for m'mother and me." He blinked his eyes nervously and ducked his head as several voices in the crowd said things like "Good fellow, Jack," and "Glad to see your mother's got a man to do it."

17   "Well," Mr. Summers said, "guess that's everyone. Old Man Warner make it?"

18   "Here," a voice said, and Mr. Summers nodded.

19   A sudden hush fell on the crowd as Mr. Summers cleared his throat and looked at the list. "All ready?" he called. "Now, I'll read the names — heads of families first — and the men come up and take a paper out of the box. Keep the paper folded in your hand without looking at it until everyone has had a turn. Everything clear?"

20   The people had done it so many times that they only half listened to the directions; most of them were quiet, wetting their lips, not looking around. Then Mr. Summers raised one hand high and said, "Adams." A man disengaged himself from the crowd and came forward. "Hi, Steve," Mr. Summers said, and Mr. Adams said, "Hi, Joe." They grinned at one another humourlessly and nervously. Then Mr. Adams reached into the black box and took out a folded paper. He held it firmly by one corner as he turned and went hastily back to his place in the crowd, where he stood a little apart from his family, not looking down at his hand.

21   "Allen," Mr. Summers said. "Anderson...Bentham."

22   "Seems like there's no time at all between lotteries any more," Mrs. Delacroix said to Mrs. Graves in the back row. "Seems like we got through with the last one only last week."

23   "Time sure goes fast," Mrs. Graves said.

24   "Clark...Delacroix."

"There goes my old man," Mrs. Delacroix said. She held her breath while her husband went forward.

"Dunbar," Mr. Summers said, and Mrs. Dunbar went steadily to the box while one of the women said. "Go on, Janey," and another said, "There she goes."

"We're next," Mrs. Graves said. She watched while Mr. Graves came around from the side of the box, greeted Mr. Summers gravely, and selected a slip of paper from the box. By now, all through the crowd there were men holding the small folded papers in their large hands, turning them over and over nervously. Mrs. Dunbar and her two sons stood together, Mrs. Dunbar holding the slip of paper.

"Harburt... Hutchinson."

"Get up there, Bill," Mrs. Hutchinson said, and the people near her laughed.

"Jones."

"They do say," Mr. Adams said to Old Man Warner, who stood next to him, "that over in the north village they're talking of giving up the lottery."

Old Man Warner snorted. "Pack of crazy fools," he said. "Listening to the young folks, nothing's good enough for *them*. Next thing you know, they'll be wanting to go back to living in caves, nobody work any more, live *that* way for a while. Used to be a saying about 'Lottery in June, corn be heavy soon.' First thing you know, we'd all be eating stewed chickweed and acorns. There's *always* been a lottery," he added petulantly. "Bad enough to see young Joe Summers up there joking with everybody."

"Some places have already quit lotteries," Mrs. Adams said.

"Nothing but trouble in *that*," Old Man Warner said stoutly. "Pack of young fools."

"Martin." And Bobby Martin watched his father go forward. "Overdyke... Percy."

"I wish they'd hurry," Mrs. Dunbar said to her older son. "I wish they'd hurry."

"They're almost through," her son said.

"You get ready to run tell Dad," Mrs. Dunbar said.

Mr. Summers called his own name and then stepped forward precisely and selected a slip from the box. Then he called, "Warner."

"Seventy-seventh year I been in the lottery," Old Man Warner said as he went through the crowd. "Seventy-seventh time."

"Watson." The tall boy came awkwardly through the crowd. Someone said, "Don't be nervous, Jack," and Mr. Summers said, "Take your time, son."

"Zanini."

43   After that, there was a long pause, a breathless pause, until Mr. Summers, holding his slip of paper in the air, said, "All right, fellows." For a minute, no one moved, and then all the slips of paper were opened. Suddenly, all the women began to speak at once, saying, "Who is it?," "Who's got it?," "Is it the Dunbars?," "Is it the Watsons?" Then the voices began to say, "It's Hutchinson. It's Bill," "Bill Hutchinson's got it."

44   "Go tell your father," Mrs. Dunbar said to her older son.

45   People began to look around to see the Hutchinsons. Bill Hutchinson was standing quiet, staring down at the paper in his hand. Suddenly, Tessie Hutchinson shouted to Mr. Summers, "You didn't give him time enough to take any paper he wanted. I saw you. It wasn't fair!"

46   "Be a good sport, Tessie," Mrs. Delacroix called, and Mrs. Graves said, "All of us took the same chance."

47   "Shut up, Tessie," Bill Hutchinson said.

48   "Well, everyone," Mr. Summers said, "that was done pretty fast, and now we've got to be hurrying a little more to get done in time." He consulted his next list. "Bill," he said, "you draw for the Hutchinson family. You got any other households in the Hutchinsons?"

49   "There's Don and Eva," Mrs. Hutchinson yelled, "Make *them* take their chance!"

50   "Daughters draw with their husbands' families, Tessie," Mr. Summers said gently. "You know that as well as anyone else."

51   "It wasn't *fair*," Tessie said.

52   "I guess not, Joe," Bill Hutchinson said regretfully. "My daughter draws with her husband's family, that's only fair. And I've got no other family except the kids."

53   "Then, as far as drawing for families is concerned, it's you," Mr. Summers said in explanation, "and as far as drawing for households is concerned, that's you, too. Right?"

54   "Right," Bill Hutchinson said.

55   "How many kids, Bill?" Mr. Summers asked formally.

56   "Three," Bill Hutchinson said. "There's Bill, Jr., and Nancy, and little Dave. And Tessie and me."

57   "All right, then," Mr. Summers said. "Harry, you got their tickets back?"

58   Mr. Graves nodded and held up the slips of paper. "Put them in the box, then," Mr. Summers directed. "Take Bill's and put it in."

59   "I think we ought to start over," Mrs. Hutchinson said, as quietly as she could. "I tell you it wasn't *fair*. You didn't give him time enough to choose. *Every*body saw that."

Mr. Graves had selected the five slips and put them in the box, and he dropped all the papers but those onto the ground, where the breeze caught them and lifted them off.

"Listen, everybody," Mrs. Hutchinson was saying to the people around her.

"Ready, Bill?" Mr. Summers asked, and Bill Hutchinson, with one quick glance around at his wife and children, nodded.

"Remember," Mr. Summers said, "take the slips and keep them folded until each person has taken one. Harry, you help little Dave." Mr. Graves took the hand of the little boy, who came willingly with him up to the box. "Take a paper out of the box, Davy," Mr. Summers said. Davy put his hand into the box and laughed. "Take just *one* paper," Mr. Summers said. "Harry, you hold it for him." Mr. Graves took the child's hand and removed the folded paper from the tight fist and held it while little Dave stood next to him and looked at him wonderingly.

"Nancy next," Mr. Summers said. Nancy was twelve, and her school friends breathed heavily as she went forward, switching her skirt, and took a slip daintily from the box "Bill, Jr.," Mr. Summers said, and Billy, his face red and his feet overlarge, near knocked the box over as he got a paper out. "Tessie," Mr. Summers said. She hesitated for a minute, looking around defiantly, and then set her lips and went up to the box. She snatched a paper out and held it behind her.

"Bill," Mr. Summers said, and Bill Hutchinson reached into the box and felt around, bringing his hand out at last with the slip of paper in it.

The crowd was quiet. A girl whispered, "I hope it's not Nancy," and the sound of the whisper reached the edges of the crowd.

"It's not the way it used to be," Old Man Warner said clearly. "People ain't the way they used to be."

"All right," Mr. Summers said. "Open the papers. Harry, you open little Dave's."

Mr. Graves opened the slip of paper and there was a general sigh through the crowd as he held it up and everyone could see that it was blank. Nancy and Bill, Jr., opened theirs at the same time, and both beamed and laughed, turning around to the crowd and holding their slips of paper above their heads.

"Tessie," Mr. Summers said. There was a pause, and then Mr. Summers looked at Bill Hutchinson, and Bill unfolded his paper and showed it. It was blank.

"It's Tessie," Mr. Summers said, and his voice was hushed. "Show us her paper, Bill."

72   Bill Hutchinson went over to his wife and forced the slip of paper out of her hand. It had a black spot on it, the black spot Mr. Summers had made the night before with the heavy pencil in the coal-company office. Bill Hutchinson held it up, and there was a stir in the crowd.

73   "All right, folks," Mr. Summers said. "Let's finish quickly."

74   Although the villagers had forgotten the ritual and lost the original black box, they still remembered to use stones. The pile of stones the boys had made earlier was ready; there were stones on the ground with the blowing scraps of paper that had come out of the box. Mrs. Delacroix selected a stone so large she had to pick it up with both hands and turned to Mrs. Dunbar. "Come on," she said. "Hurry up."

75   Mrs. Dunbar had small stones in both hands, and she said, gasping for breath, "I can't run at all. You'll have to go ahead and I'll catch up with you."

76   The children had stones already, and someone gave little Davy Hutchinson a few pebbles.

77   Tessie Hutchinson was in the centre of a cleared space by now, and she held her hands out desperately as the villagers moved in on her. "It isn't fair," she said. A stone hit her on the side of the head.

78   Old Man Warner was saying, "Come on, come on, everyone." Steve Adams was in the front of the crowd of villagers, with Mrs. Graves beside him.

79   "It isn't fair, it isn't right," Mrs. Hutchinson screamed, and then they were upon her.

1948

NOTES

"The Lottery" is a classic and is considered one of the most famous short stories in English. Shirley Jackson (1919–1965) is also known for the book *The Haunting of Hill House*, which has been made into two films, both called *The Haunting* (1963, 1999).

The word "lottery" comes from the drawing of lots. A "lot" is an object, a chit, or a piece of paper used to make a choice, often about a person's fortune or fate. The verb form is "allot."

Stoning is an ancient and inexpensive method of punishment. Death resulting from it is quite agonizing and protracted. Often the act is a communal one in which all members participate in the condemning of the victim. One of the first martyred saints was St. Stephen, who was stoned to death for his beliefs.

Fertility rituals, including those asking for a bountiful harvest from the land, can be found in all cultures and societies, particularly in earlier times. Often these rites involve human sacrifice. The purpose of a ritual is to appease forces greater than humanity in the hope that these powers may help the tribe to survive (or, at least, refrain them from hindering the tribe's survival). Later, many fertility rituals were transformed into religious rituals.

There have been many kinds of lotteries throughout history. For example, the ancient Athenians used a lottery system to banish undesirable citizens. From this practice, we have the words "ostracize" and "ostracism."

COMPREHENSION AND DISCUSSION

1. What is so special about June 27?
2. What is the importance of the black box? Why does the box have to be black? Why old?
3. How do you know that this ceremony or ritual is in decline?
4. Explain how the lottery is conducted.
5. Is the process democratic and fair? What is Tessie Hutchinson's objection to the lottery?
6. Why are there so many names in this story? What is the symbolic importance of names like Mr. Graves, Mr. Summers, Old Man Warner, Dickie Delacroix, and Tessie Hutchinson?
7. What are Old Man Warner's reasons for continuing the lottery? Why does he disparage the young joking about the lottery, and other communities for abandoning the tradition?
8. Will this lottery really help the village to harvest a bumper crop? Why would the villagers continue with this practice if they are so impatient to have the process concluded?
9. Were you surprised at the ending? How did Jackson prepare you for it?

LITERARY TECHNIQUES

The surprise ending is a popular strategy in writing short stories. It makes the reader go through the story again just to see what clues he or she may have missed. Surprise endings require the writer to use foreshadowing and to drop clues for the astute reader. Note how Jackson innocently mentions the piles of stones in the beginning.

Jackson uses the third-person objective point of view. She does not reveal the thoughts of the characters, but reports only what they say and what they do. In a sense, the strategy is crucial to the surprise ending.

A symbol represents meanings greater than and outside of the object itself. It is something concrete that represents something abstract. For example, although a flag is just a piece of cloth with a colourful design, it also represents a country. In this inanimate object, recognition of state, love of country, respect for its existence, and other ideals are all woven. Symbols are important to Jackson's story, especially the stones, the old box, and the colour black. On the surface, Old Man Warner is just another long survivor of the lottery in this community, but symbolically, he represents the unchanging tradition to which others also adhere.

Microcosmic view Writers often use a smaller unit or number of characters in a story to give focus and suggest a larger picture. An example of a small unit is a village; an even smaller unit is the family. As the story progresses we see what happens to the Hutchinson family in particular. In theory, the microcosm reflects the macrocosm, or the larger unit. Therefore, if this type of ritual occurs in the Hutchinsons' neighbourhood, then it may also be performed across the state, the country, and the world.

ASSIGNMENTS

1. Research the concept of "scapegoating" as a religious or social practice and write a short explanation.
2. Read the story of Abraham and Isaac (Genesis 22:1–19). How is this story the same as or different from Jackson's?
3. Define the terms "sacrifice" and "lottery."
4. Write an essay explaining why rituals are important in a society. You may wish to examine the following: the marriage ceremony, graduations, courtship rituals in different cultures, handshakes, burial services, and baptisms.
5. Speculate on the aftermath of Tessie Hutchinson's death. You can focus on the entire town or just on the Hutchinson family at the dinner table that evening.

6. Violence and brutality are within each human soul. We like to hurt people; hurting others gives us pleasure, satisfaction, and entertainment. Is this statement valid? Explain.
7. "The Lottery" has been turned into a play and several films. The 1996 TV movie expands on the story and takes liberties with the plot. Write a critique of the film.

The Monkey's Paw
W.W. Jacobs

I

1. Without, the night was cold and wet, but in the small parlour of Laburnam Villa the blinds were drawn and the fire burned brightly. Father and son were at chess, the former, who possessed ideas about the game involving radical changes, putting his king into such sharp and unnecessary perils that it even provoked comment from the white-haired old lady knitting placidly by the fire.

2. "Hark at the wind," said Mr. White, who, having seen a fatal mistake after it was too late, was amiably desirous of preventing his son from seeing it.

3. "I'm listening," said the latter, grimly surveying the board as he stretched out his hand. "Check."

4. "I should hardly think that he'd come tonight," said his father, with his hand poised over the board.

5. "Mate," replied the son.

6. "That's the worst of living so far out," bawled Mr. White, with sudden and unlooked-for violence; "of all the beastly, slushy, out-of-the-way places to live in, this is the worst. Pathway's a bog, and the road's a torrent. I don't know what people are thinking about. I suppose because only two houses on the road are let, they think it doesn't matter."

7. "Never mind, dear," said his wife soothingly; "perhaps you'll win the next one."

8. Mr. White looked up sharply, just in time to intercept a knowing glance between mother and son. The words died away on his lips, and he hid a guilty grin in his thin grey beard.

9. "There he is," said Herbert White, as the gate banged to loudly and heavy footsteps came toward the door.

10. The old man rose with hospitable haste, and opening the door, was heard condoling with the new arrival. The new arrival also condoled with himself, so that Mrs. White said, "Tut, tut!" and coughed gently as her husband entered the room, followed by a tall, burly man, beady of eye and rubicund of visage.

11. "Sergeant-Major Morris," he said, introducing him.

12. The sergeant-major shook hands, and taking the proffered seat by the fire, watched contentedly while his host got out whisky and tumblers and stood a small copper kettle on the fire.

At the third glass his eyes got brighter, and he began to talk, the little family circle regarding with eager interest this visitor from distant parts, as he squared his broad shoulders in the chair and spoke of strange scenes and doughty deeds, of wars and plagues and strange peoples.

"Twenty-one years of it," said Mr. White, nodding at his wife and son. "When he went away he was a slip of a youth in the warehouse. Now look at him."

"He don't look to have taken much harm," said Mrs. White politely.

"I'd like to go to India myself," said the old man, "just to look round a bit, you know."

"Better where you are," said the sergeant-major, shaking his head. He put down the empty glass, and sighing softly, shook it again.

"I should like to see those old temples and fakirs and jugglers," said the old man. "What was that you started telling me the other day about a monkey's paw or something, Morris?"

"Nothing," said the soldier hastily. "Leastways, nothing worth hearing."

"Monkey's paw?" said Mrs. White curiously.

"Well, it's just a bit of what you might call magic, perhaps," said the sergeant-major offhandedly.

His three listeners leaned forward eagerly. The visitor absent-mindedly put his empty glass to his lips and then set it down again. His host filled it for him.

"To look at," said the sergeant-major, fumbling in his pocket, "it's just an ordinary little paw, dried to a mummy."

He took something out of his pocket and proffered it. Mrs. White drew back with a grimace, but her son, taking it, examined it curiously.

"And what is there special about it?" inquired Mr. White, as he took it from his son, and having examined it, placed it upon the table.

"It had a spell put on it by an old fakir," said the sergeant-major, "a very holy man. He wanted to show that fate ruled people's lives, and that those who interfered with it did so to their sorrow. He put a spell on it so that three separate men could each have three wishes from it."

His manner was so impressive that his hearers were conscious that their light laughter jarred somewhat.

"Well, why don't you have three, sir?" said Herbert White cleverly.

The soldier regarded him in the way that middle age is wont to regard presumptuous youth. "I have," he said quietly, and his blotchy face whitened.

"And did you really have the three wishes granted?" asked Mrs. White.

"I did," said the sergeant-major, and his glass tapped against his strong teeth.

32   "And has anybody else wished?" inquired the old lady.

33   "The first man had his three wishes, yes," was the reply. "I don't know what the first two were, but the third was for death. That's how I got the paw."

34   His tones were so grave that a hush fell upon the group.

35   "If you've had your three wishes, it's no good to you now, then, Morris," said the old man at last. "What do you keep it for?"

36   The soldier shook his head. "Fancy, I suppose," he said slowly. "I did have some idea of selling it, but I don't think I will. It has caused enough mischief already. Besides, people won't buy. They think it's a fairy tale, some of them, and those who do think anything of it want to try it first and pay me afterward."

37   "If you could have another three wishes," said the old man, eyeing him keenly, "would you have them?"

38   "I don't know," said the other. "I don't know."

39   He took the paw, and dangling it between his front finger and thumb, suddenly threw it upon the fire. White, with a slight cry, stooped down and snatched it off.

40   "Better let it burn," said the soldier solemnly.

41   "If you don't want it, Morris," said the old man, "give it to me."

42   "I won't," said his friend doggedly. "I threw it on the fire. If you keep it, don't blame me for what happens. Pitch it on the fire again, like a sensible man."

43   The other shook his head and examined his new possession closely. "How do you do it?" he inquired.

44   "Hold it up in your right hand and wish aloud," said the sergeant-major, "but I warn you of the consequences."

45   "Sounds like the *Arabian Nights*," said Mrs. White, as she rose and began to set the supper. "Don't you think you might wish for four pairs of hands for me?"

46   Her husband drew the talisman from his pocket and then all three burst into laughter as the sergeant-major, with a look of alarm on his face, caught him by the arm.

47   "If you must wish," he said gruffly, "wish for something sensible."

48   Mr. White dropped it back into his pocket, and placing chairs, motioned his friend to the table. In the business of supper the talisman was partly forgotten, and afterward the three sat listening in an enthralled fashion to a second installment of the soldier's adventures in India.

49   "If the tale about the monkey's paw is not more truthful than those he has been telling us," said Herbert, as the door closed behind their guest, just in time for him to catch the last train, "we shan't make much out of it."

"Did you give him anything for it, Father?" inquired Mrs. White, regarding her husband closely.

"A trifle," said he, colouring slightly. "He didn't want it, but I made him take it. And he pressed me again to throw it away."

"Likely," said Herbert, with pretended horror. "Why, we're going to be rich, and famous, and happy. Wish to be an emperor, Father, to begin with; then you can't be henpecked."

He darted around the table, pursued by the maligned Mrs. White armed with an antimacassar.

Mr. White took the paw from his pocket and eyed it dubiously. "I don't know what to wish for, and that's a fact," he said slowly. "It seems to me I've got all I want."

"If you only cleared the house, you'd be quite happy, wouldn't you?" said Herbert, with his hand on his shoulder. "Well, wish for two hundred pounds, then; that'll just do it."

His father, smiling shamefacedly at his own credulity, held up the talisman, as his son, with a solemn face somewhat marred by a wink at his mother, sat down at the piano and struck a few impressive chords.

"I wish for two hundred pounds," said the old man distinctly.

A fine crash from the piano greeted the words, interrupted by a shuddering cry from the old man. His wife and son ran toward him.

"It moved," he cried, with a glance of disgust at the object as it lay on the floor. "As I wished, it twisted in my hand like a snake."

"Well, I don't see the money," said his son, as he picked it up and placed it on the table, "and I bet I never shall."

"It must have been your fancy, Father," said his wife, regarding him anxiously.

He shook his head. "Never mind, though; there's no harm done, but it gave me a shock all the same."

They sat down by the fire again while the two men finished their pipes. Outside, the wind was higher than ever, and the old man started nervously at the sound of a door banging upstairs. A silence unusual and depressing settled upon all three, which lasted until the old couple rose to retire for the night.

"I expect you'll find the cash tied up in a big bag in the middle of your bed," said Herbert, as he bade them good-night, "and something horrible squatting up on top of the wardrobe watching you as you pocket your ill-gotten gains."

He sat alone in the darkness, gazing at the dying fire, and seeing faces in it. The last face was so horrible and so simian that he gazed at it in amazement. It got so vivid that, with a little uneasy laugh, he felt on the table for a glass containing a little water to throw over it. His hand grasped the monkey's paw, and with a little shiver he wiped his hand on his coat and went up to bed.

II

66 In the brightness of the wintry sun next morning as it streamed over the breakfast table Herbert laughed at his fears. There was an air of prosaic wholesomeness about the room which it had lacked on the previous night, and the dirty, shrivelled little paw was pitched on the sideboard with a carelessness which betokened no great belief in its virtues.

67 "I suppose all old soldiers are the same," said Mrs. White. "The idea of our listening to such nonsense! How could wishes be granted in these days? And if they could, how could two hundred pounds hurt you, Father?"

68 "Might drop on his head from the sky," said the frivolous Herbert.

69 "Morris said the things happened so naturally," said his father, "that you might, if you so wished, attribute it to coincidence."

70 "Well, don't break into the money before I come back," said Herbert, as he rose from the table. "I'm afraid it'll turn you into a mean, avaricious man, and we shall have to disown you."

71 His mother laughed, and following him to the door, watched him down the road, and returning to the breakfast table, was very happy at the expense of her husband's credulity. All of which did not prevent her from scurrying to the door at the postman's knock, nor prevent her from referring somewhat shortly to retired sergeant-majors of bibulous habits, when she found that the post brought a tailor's bill.

72 "Herbert will have some more of his funny remarks, I expect, when he comes home," she said, as they sat at dinner.

73 "I daresay," said Mr. White, pouring himself out some beer; "but for all that, the thing moved in my hand; that I'll swear to."

74 "You thought it did," said the old lady soothingly.

75 "I say it did," replied the other. "There was no thought about it; I had just — What's the matter?"

76 His wife made no reply. She was watching the mysterious movements of a man outside, who, peering in an undecided fashion at the house, appeared to be trying to make up his mind to enter. In mental connection with the two hundred pounds, she noticed that the stranger was well dressed and wore a silk hat of glossy newness. Three times he paused at the gate, and then walked on again. The fourth time he stood with his hand

upon it, and then with sudden resolution flung it open and walked up the path. Mrs. White at the same moment placed her hands behind her, and hurriedly unfastening the strings of her apron, put that useful article of apparel beneath the cushion of her chair.

She brought the stranger, who seemed ill at ease, into the room. He gazed furtively at Mrs. White, and listened in a preoccupied fashion as the old lady apologized for the appearance of the room, and her husband's coat, a garment which he usually reserved for the garden. She then waited as patiently as her sex would permit for him to broach his business, but he was at first strangely silent.

"I — was asked to call," he said at last, and stooped and picked a piece of cotton from his trousers. "I come from Maw and Meggins."

The old lady started. "Is anything the matter?" she asked breathlessly. "Has anything happened to Herbert? What is it? What is it?"

Her husband interposed. "There, there, Mother," he said hastily. "Sit down, and don't jump to conclusions. You've not brought bad news, I'm sure, sir," and he eyed the other wistfully.

"I'm sorry — " began the visitor.

"Is he hurt?" demanded the mother.

The visitor bowed in assent. "Badly hurt," he said quietly, "but he is not in any pain."

"Oh, thank God!" said the old woman, clasping her hands. "Thank God for that! Thank — "

She broke off suddenly as the sinister meaning of the assurance dawned upon her and she saw the awful confirmation of her fears in the other's averted face. She caught her breath, and turning to her slower-witted husband, laid her trembling old hand upon his. There was a long silence.

"He was caught in the machinery," said the visitor at length, in a low voice.

"Caught in the machinery," repeated Mr. White, in a dazed fashion, "yes."

He sat staring blankly out at the window, and taking his wife's hand between his own, pressed it as he had been wont to do in their old courting days nearly forty years before.

"He was the only one left to us," he said, turning gently to the visitor. "It is hard."

The other coughed, and rising, walked slowly to the window. "The firm wished me to convey their sincere sympathy with you in your great loss," he said, without looking around. "I beg that you will understand I am only their servant and merely obeying orders."

There was no reply; the old woman's face was white, her eyes staring, and her breath inaudible; on the husband's face was a look such as his friend the sergeant might have carried into his first action.

"I was to say that Maw and Meggins disclaim all responsibility," continued the other. "They admit no liability at all, but in consideration of your son's services they wish to present you with a certain sum as compensation."

Mr. White dropped his wife's hand, and rising to his feet, gazed with a look of horror at his visitor. His dry lips shaped the words, "How much?"

"Two hundred pounds," was the answer.

Unconscious of his wife's shriek, the old man smiled faintly, put out his hands like a sightless man, and dropped, a senseless heap, to the floor.

III

In the huge new cemetery, some two miles distant, the old people buried their dead, and came back to a house steeped in shadow and silence. It was all over so quickly that at first they could hardly realize it, and remained in a state of expectation, as though of something else to happen — something else which was to lighten this load, too heavy for old hearts to bear.

But the days passed, and expectation gave place to resignation — the hopeless resignation of the old, sometimes miscalled apathy. Sometimes they hardly exchanged a word, for now they had nothing to talk about, and their days were long to weariness.

It was about a week after that that the old man, waking suddenly in the night, stretched out his hand and found himself alone. The room was in darkness, and the sound of subdued weeping came from the window. He raised himself in bed and listened.

"Come back," he said tenderly. "You will be cold."

"It is colder for my son," said the old woman, and wept afresh.

The sound of her sobs died away on his ears. The bed was warm, and his eyes heavy with sleep. He dozed fitfully, and then slept until a sudden wild cry from his wife awoke him with a start.

"*The paw!*" she cried wildly. "The monkey's paw!"

He started up in alarm. "Where? Where is it? What's the matter?"

She came stumbling across the room toward him. "I want it," she said quietly. "You've not destroyed it?"

"It's in the parlour, on the bracket," he replied, marvelling. "Why?"

She cried and laughed together, and bending over, kissed his cheek.

"I only just thought of it," she said hysterically. "Why didn't I think of it before? Why didn't *you* think of it?"

"Think of what?" he questioned.

"The other two wishes," she replied rapidly. "We've only had one."

"Was not that enough?" he demanded fiercely.

"No," she cried triumphantly; "we'll have one more. Go down and get it quickly, and wish our boy alive again."

The man sat up in bed and flung the bedclothes from his quaking limbs. "Good God, you are mad!" he cried, aghast.

"Get it," she panted; "get it quickly, and wish — Oh, my boy, my boy!"

Her husband struck a match and lit the candle. "Get back to bed," he said unsteadily. "You don't know what you are saying."

"We had the first wish granted," said the old woman feverishly; "why not the second?"

"A coincidence," stammered the old man.

"Go and get it and wish," cried the old woman, quivering with excitement.

The old man turned and regarded her, and his voice shook. "He has been dead ten days, and besides he — I would not tell you else, but — I could only recognize him by his clothing. If he was too terrible for you to see then, how now?"

"Bring him back," cried the old woman, and dragged him toward the door. "Do you think I fear the child I have nursed?"

He went down in the darkness, and felt his way to the parlour, and then to the mantelpiece. The talisman was in its place, and a horrible fear that the unspoken wish might bring his mutilated son before him ere he could escape from the room seized upon him, and he caught his breath as he found that he had lost the direction of the door. His brow cold with sweat, he felt his way around the table, and groped along the wall until he found himself in the small passage with the unwholesome thing in his hand.

Even his wife's face seemed changed as he entered the room. It was white and expectant, and to his fears seemed to have an unnatural look upon it. He was afraid of her.

"*Wish!*" she cried, in a strong voice.

"It is foolish and wicked," he faltered.

"*Wish!*" repeated his wife.

He raised his hand. "I wish my son alive again."

The talisman fell to the floor, and he regarded it fearfully. Then he sank trembling into a chair as the old woman, with burning eyes, walked to the window and raised the blind.

He sat until he was chilled with the cold, glancing occasionally at the figure of the old woman peering through the window. The candle end, which had burned below the rim of the china candlestick, was throwing pulsating shadows on the ceiling and walls, until, with a flicker larger than the rest, it expired. The old man, with an unspeakable sense of relief at the failure of the talisman, crept back to his bed, and a minute or two afterward the old woman came silently and apathetically beside him.

128   Neither spoke, but both lay silently listening to the ticking of the clock. A stair creaked, and a squeaky mouse scurried noisily through the wall. The darkness was oppressive, and after lying for some time screwing up his courage, the husband took the box of matches, and striking one, went downstairs for a candle.

129   At the foot of the stairs the match went out, and he paused to strike another, and at the same moment a knock, so quiet and stealthy as to be scarcely audible, sounded on the front door.

130   The matches fell from his hand. He stood motionless, his breath suspended until the knock was repeated. Then he turned and fled swiftly back to his room, and closed the door behind him. A third knock sounded through the house.

131   "*What's that?*" cried the old woman, starting up.

132   "A rat," said the old man, in shaking tones—"a rat. It passed me on the stairs."

133   His wife sat up in bed listening. A loud knock resounded through the house.

134   "It's Herbert!" she screamed. "It's Herbert!"

135   She ran to the door, but her husband was before her, and catching her by the arm, held her tightly.

136   "What are you going to do?" he whispered hoarsely.

137   "It's my boy; it's Herbert!" she cried, struggling mechanically. "I forgot it was two miles away. What are you holding me for? Let go. I must open the door."

138   "For God's sake don't let it in," cried the old man, trembling.

139   "You're afraid of your own son," she cried, struggling. "Let me go. I'm coming, Herbert; I'm coming."

140   There was another knock, and another. The old woman with a sudden wrench broke free and ran from the room. Her husband followed to the landing, and called after her appealingly as she hurried downstairs. He heard the chain rattle back and the bottom bolt drawn slowly and stiffly from the socket. Then the old woman's voice, strained and panting.

141   "The bolt," she cried loudly. "Come down. I can't reach it."

142   But her husband was on his hands and knees groping wildly on the floor in search of the paw. If he could only find it before the thing outside got in. A perfect fusillade of knocks reverberated through the house, and he

heard the scraping of a chair as his wife put it down in the passage against the door. He heard the creaking of the bolt as it came slowly back, and at the same moment, he found the monkey's paw, and frantically breathed his third and last wish.

The knocking ceased suddenly, although the echoes of it were still in the house. He heard the chair drawn back and the door opened. A cold wind rushed up the staircase, and a long, loud wail of disappointment and misery from his wife gave him courage to run down to her side, and then to the gate beyond. The street lamp flickering opposite shone on a quiet and deserted road.

1902

NOTES

W.W. Jacobs (1863–1943) was a British writer. "The Monkey's Paw" is a classic horror story.

The monkey has always been a symbol of mischief, particularly in Oriental literature. See the legend of the Monkey King in traditional Chinese literature. Note that this monkey's paw has travelled all the way from India.

Chess A popular board game of strategy rather than of chance. One form of chess has its origins in India. The term "check" means that the king is in jeopardy; the term "mate" means that the king has no means of escape and is captured by the opponent's pieces.

Arabian Nights A collection of fantasy stories supposedly told by Scheherazade, the bride of a sultan, to postpone her execution. Sir Richard Burton's translation (1888) was very popular in 19th-century England.

COMPREHENSION AND DISCUSSION

1. How is the chess game that Mr. White loses to his son Herbert important to the ending of the story?
2. How does the weather foreshadow the atmosphere and tone of the story?
3. Why is Mr. White so impatient to see his friend? Why does this impatience become ironic?

4. What indications are there that Mr. White's friend is different or strange? Is Morris a bad person who tempts the Whites with the paw? What is Morris's role in this story?
5. Explain the first wish and how it comes true.
6. What would Herbert be like if he came back?
7. Earlier in the story, Sergeant-Major Morris said that a fakir wanted to demonstrate a lesson. What is the original intent, and what lesson has Mr. White learned that his wife has not?
8. Speculate on the wishes made by the other owners of the paw and how they may have come true.
9. Do you believe in the supernatural? Why or why not?
10. Why does Jacobs follow the literary tradition of "three" as in three wishes, three strikes at bat, three tries at something, or the trinity? Is three a magic number?

LITERARY TECHNIQUES

The horror story is a subgenre of fantasy. Cryptic or mysterious actions or sayings are standard fare in creating uneasiness and dread. Note how tone and atmosphere contribute to these feelings. Often supernatural elements such as ghosts, goblins, and fairies play a dominant role. A surprise ending is crucial. Readers of this genre want to be scared.

Atmosphere The mood of the story, often established by the setting (physical landscape or environment) in the story. Atmosphere also incorporates emotional states generated by the setting. For example, the opening lines of the story, "Without, the night was cold and wet, but in the small parlour of Laburnam Villa the blinds were drawn and the fire burned brightly" (p. 116), draw a sharp contrast between the coldness outside and the warmth inside. However, in the second half of the sentence there is a suggestion that the fire is the only thing keeping out the cold and the dark, which surround the Whites' household. And it is to the fire that Morris wishes to consign the paw.

A cautionary tale emphasizes a lesson in life for the reader but not for the characters, who must suffer through the experience. Mr. White has, for example, learned a lesson after his first wish turned out poorly. Many fairy tales have explicit or implicit cautions for young readers. For example, "Little Red Riding Hood" warns children not to talk to strangers.

ASSIGNMENTS

1. Recount other stories that depend on wishes: King Midas, Aladdin, the Magic Fish. Compare the outcomes.
2. Explain why wishes come in threes in literature. Or, research the belief in (or use of) numerology, especially the number three.
3. Compare this ending with those in other stories in this text: "The Cowherd" (p. 73), "The Lottery" (p. 105), and "The Cask of Amontillado" (p. 177).
4. Explain the use of lucky charms and other superstitions.
5. What makes horror stories so popular? Books by such writers as Stephen King and Anne Rice are bestsellers. Movies such as *Halloween* and *Scream* have multiple sequels. Explain the attraction.

The Loons

Margaret Laurence

1   Just below Manawaka, where the Wachakwa River ran brown and noisy over the pebbles, the scrub oak and grey-green willow and chokecherry bushes grew in a dense thicket. In a clearing at the centre of the thicket stood the Tonnerre family's shack. The basis of this dwelling was a small square cabin made of poplar poles and chinked with mud, which had been built by Jules Tonnerre some fifty years before, when he came back from the Batoche with a bullet in his thigh, the year that Riel was hung and the voices of the Métis entered their long silence. Jules had only intended to stay the winter in the Wachakwa Valley, but the family was still there in the thirties, when I was a child. As the Tonnerres had increased, their settlement had been added to, until the clearing at the foot of the town hill was a chaos of lean-tos, wooden packing cases, warped lumber, discarded car tires, ramshackle chicken coops, tangled strands of barbed wire and rusty tin cans.

2   The Tonnerres were French halfbreeds, and among themselves they spoke a *patois* that was neither Cree nor French. Their English was broken and full of obscenities. They did not belong among the Cree of the Galloping Mountain reservation, further north, and they did not belong among the Scots-Irish and Ukrainians of Manawaka, either. They were, as my Grandmother MacLeod would have put it, neither flesh, fowl, nor good salt herring. When their men were not working at odd jobs or as section hands on the C.P.R., they lived on relief. In the summers, one of the Tonnerre youngsters, with a face that seemed totally unfamiliar with laughter, would knock at the doors of the town's brick houses and offer for sale a lard-pail full of bruised wild strawberries, and if he got as much as a quarter he would grab the coin and run before the customer had time to change her mind. Sometimes old Jules, or his son Lazarus, would get mixed up in a Saturday-night brawl, and would hit out at whoever was nearest, or howl drunkenly among the offended shoppers on Main Street, and then the Mountie would put them for the night in the barred cell underneath the Court House, and the next morning they would be quiet again.

3   Piquette Tonnerre, the daughter of Lazarus, was in my class at school. She was older than I, but she had failed several grades, perhaps because her attendance had always been sporadic and her interest in schoolwork negligible. Part of the reason she had missed a lot of school was that she had had

tuberculosis of the bone, and had once spent many months in hospital. I knew this because my father was the doctor who had looked after her. Her sickness was almost the only thing I knew about her, however. Otherwise, she existed for me only as a vaguely embarrassing presence, with her hoarse voice and her clumsy limping walk and her grimy cotton dresses that were always miles too long. I was neither friendly nor unfriendly towards her. She dwelt and moved somewhere within my scope of vision, but I did not actually notice her very much until that peculiar summer when I was eleven.

"I don't know what to do about that kid," my father said at dinner one evening. "Piquette Tonnerre, I mean. The damn bone's flared up again. I've had her in hospital for quite a while now, and it's under control all right, but I hate like the dickens to send her home again."

"Couldn't you explain to her mother that she has to rest a lot?" my mother said.

"The mother's not there," my father replied. "She took off a few years back. Can't say I blame her. Piquette cooks for them, and she says Lazarus would never do anything for himself as long as she's there. Anyway, I don't think she'd take much care of herself, once she got back. She's only thirteen, after all. Beth, I was thinking — what about taking her up to Diamond Lake with us for the summer? A couple of months rest would give that bone a much better chance."

My mother looked stunned.

"But Ewen – what about Roddie and Vanessa?"

"She's not contagious," my father said. "And it would be company for Vanessa."

"Oh dear," my mother said in distress, "I'll bet anything she has nits in her hair."

"For Pete's sake," my father said crossly, "do you think Matron would let her stay in the hospital for all this time like that? Don't be silly, Beth."

Grandmother MacLeod, her delicately featured face as rigid as a cameo, now brought her mauve-veined hands together as though she were about to begin a prayer.

"Ewen, if that half-breed youngster comes along to Diamond Lake, I'm not going," she announced. "I'll go to Morag's for the summer."

I had trouble in stifling my urge to laugh, for my mother brightened visibly and quickly tried to hide it. If it came to a choice between Grandmother MacLeod and Piquette, Piquette would win hands down, nits or not.

"It might be quite nice for you, at that," she mused. "You haven't seen Morag for over a year, and you might enjoy being in the city for a while.

Well, Ewen dear, you do what you think best. If you think it would do Piquette some good, then we'll be glad to have her, as long as she behaves herself."

16   So it happened that several weeks later, when we all piled into my father's old Nash, surrounded by suitcases and boxes of provisions and toys for my ten-month-old brother, Piquette was with us and Grandmother MacLeod, miraculously, was not. My father would only be staying at the cottage for a couple of weeks, for he had to get back to his practice, but the rest of us would stay at Diamond Lake until the end of August.

17   Our cottage was not named, as many were, "Dew Drop Inn" or "Bide-a-Wee," or "Bonnie Doon." The sign on the roadway bore in austere letters only our name, MacLeod. It was not a large cottage, but it was on the lakefront. You could look out the windows and see, through the filigree of the spruce trees, the water glistening greenly as the sun caught it. All around the cottage were ferns, and sharp-branched raspberry bushes, and moss that had grown over fallen tree trunks. If you looked carefully among the weeds and grass, you could find wild strawberry plants which were in white flower now and in another month would bear fruit, the fragrant globes hanging like miniature scarlet lanterns on the thin hairy stems. The two grey squirrels were still there, gossiping at us from the tall spruce beside the cottage, and by the end of the summer they would again be tame enough to take pieces of crust from my hands. The broad moose antlers that hung above the back door were a little more bleached and fissured after the winter, but otherwise everything was the same. I raced joyfully around my kingdom, greeting all the places I had not seen for a year. My brother, Roderick, who had not been born when we were here last summer, sat on the car rug in the sunshine and examined a brown spruce cone, meticulously turning it round and round in his small and curious hands. My mother and father toted the luggage from car to cottage, exclaiming over how well the place had wintered, no broken windows, thank goodness, no apparent damage from storm-felled branches or snow.

18   Only after I had finished looking around did I notice Piquette. She was sitting on the swing, her lame leg held stiffly out, and her other foot scuffling the ground as she swung slowly back and forth. Her long hair hung black and straight around her shoulders, and her broad coarse-featured face bore no expression—it was blank, as though she no longer dwelt within her own skull, as though she had gone elsewhere. I approached her very hesitantly.

19   "Want to come and play?"

20   Piquette looked at me with a sudden flash of scorn.

21   "I ain't a kid," she said.

Wounded, I stamped angrily away, swearing I would not speak to her for the rest of the summer. In the days that followed, however, Piquette began to interest me, and I began to want to interest her. My reasons did not appear bizarre to me. Unlikely as it may seem, I had only just realized that the Tonnerre family, whom I had always heard called half-breeds, were actually Indians, or as near as made no difference. My acquaintance with Indians was not extensive. I did not remember ever having seen a real Indian, and my new awareness that Piquette sprang from the people of Big Bear and Poundmaker, of Tecumseh, of the Iroquois who had eaten Father Brebeuf's heart—all this gave her an instant attraction in my eyes. I was a devoted reader of Pauline Johnson at this age, and sometimes would orate aloud in an exalted voice, *West Wind, blow from your prairie nest; Blow from the mountains, blow from the west*—and so on. It seemed to me that Piquette must be in some way a daughter of the forest, a kind of junior prophetess of the wilds, who might impart to me, if I took the right approach, some of the secrets which she undoubtedly knew—where the whippoorwill made her nest, how the coyote reared her young, or whatever it was that it said in *Hiawatha*.

I set about gaining Piquette's trust. She was not allowed to go swimming, with her bad leg, but I managed to lure her down to the beach—or rather, she came because there was nothing else to do. The water was always icy, for the lake was fed by springs, but I swam like a dog, thrashing my arms and legs around at such a speed and with such an output of energy that I never grew cold. Finally, when I had had enough, I came out and sat beside Piquette on the sand. When she saw me approaching, her hand squashed flat the sand castle she had been building, and she looked at me sullenly, without speaking.

"Do you like this place?" I asked, after a while, intending to lead on from there into the question of forest lore.

Piquette shrugged. "It's okay. Good as anywhere."

"I love it," I said. "We come here every summer."

"So what?" Her voice was distant, and I glanced at her uncertainly, wondering what I could have said wrong.

"Do you want to come for a walk?" I asked her. "We wouldn't need to go far. If you just walk around the point there, you come to a bay where great big reeds grow in the water, and all kinds of fish hang around there. Want to? Come on."

She shook her head.

"Your dad said I ain't supposed to do no more walking that I got to."

I tried another line.

32   "I bet you know a lot about the woods and all that, eh?" I began respectfully.

33   Piquette looked at me from her large dark unsmiling eyes.

34   "I don't know what in hell you're talkin' about," she replied. "You nuts or somethin'? If you mean where my old man, and me, and all them live, you better shut up, by Jesus, you hear?"

35   I was startled and my feelings were hurt, but I had a kind of dogged perseverance. I ignored her rebuff.

36   "You know something, Piquette? There's loons here, on this lake. You can see their nests just up the shore there, behind those logs. At night, you can hear them even from the cottage, but it's better to listen from the beach. My dad says we should listen and try to remember how they sound because in a few years when more cottages are built at Diamond Lake and more people come in, the loons will go away."

37   Piquette was picking up stones and snail shells and then dropping them again.

38   "Who gives a good goddamn?" she said.

39   It became increasingly obvious that, as an Indian, Piquette was a dead loss. That evening I went out by myself, scrambling through the bushes that overhung the steep path, my feet slipping on the fallen spruce needles that covered the ground. When I reached the shore, I walked along the firm damp sand to the small pier that my father had built, and sat down there. I heard someone else crashing through the undergrowth and the bracken, and for a moment I thought Piquette had changed her mind, but it turned out to be my father. He sat beside me on the pier and we waited, without speaking.

40   At night the lake was like black glass with a streak of amber which was the path of the moon. All around, the spruce trees grew tall and close-set, branches blackly sharp against the sky, which was lightened by a cold flickering of stars. Then the loons began their calling. They rose like phantom birds from the nests on the shore, and flew out onto the dark still surface of the water.

41   No one can ever describe that ululating sound, the crying of the loons, and no one who has heard it can ever forget it. Plaintive, and yet with a quality of chilling mockery, those voices belonged to a world separated by eons from our neat world of summer cottages and the lighted lamps of home.

42   "They must have sounded just like that," my father remarked, "before any person ever set foot here."

43   Then he laughed. "You could say the same, of course, about sparrows, or chipmunks, but somehow it only strikes you that way with the loons."

44   "I know," I said.

Neither of us suspected that this would be the last time we would ever sit here together on the shore, listening. We stayed for perhaps half an hour, and then we went back to the cottage. My mother was reading beside the fireplace. Piquette was looking at the burning birch log, and not doing anything.

"You should have come along," I said, although in fact I was glad she had not.

"Not me," Piquette said. "You wouldn' catch me walkin' way down there jus' for a bunch of squawkin' birds."

Piquette and I remained ill at ease with one another. I felt I had somehow failed my father, but I did not know what was the matter, nor why she would not or could not respond when I suggested exploring the woods or playing house. I thought it was probably her slow and difficult walking that held her back. She stayed most of the time in the cottage with my mother, helping her with the dishes or with Roddie, but hardly ever talking. Then the Duncans arrived at their cottage, and I spend my days with Mavis, who was my best friend. I could not reach Piquette at all, and I soon lost interest in trying. But all that summer she remained as both a reproach and a mystery to me.

That winter, my father died of pneumonia, after less than a week's illness. For some time I saw nothing around me, being completely immersed in my own pain and my mother's. When I looked outward once more, I scarcely noticed that Piquette Tonnerre was no longer at school. I do not remember seeing her at all until four years later, one Saturday night when Mavis and I were having Cokes in the Regal Café. The jukebox was booming like tuneful thunder, and beside it, leaning lightly on its chrome and its rainbow glass, was a girl.

Piquette must have been seventeen then, although she looked about twenty. I stared at her, astounded that anyone could have changed so much. Her face, so stolid and expressionless before, was animated now with a gaiety that was almost violent. She laughed and talked very loudly with the boys around her. Her lipstick was bright carmine, and her hair was cut short and frizzily permed. She had not been pretty as a child, and she was not pretty now, for her features were still heavy and blunt. But her dark and slightly slanted eyes were beautiful, and her skin-tight skirt and orange sweater displayed to enviable advantage a soft and slender body.

She saw me, and walked over. She teetered a little, but it was not due to her once-tubercular leg, for her limp was almost gone.

"Hi, Vanessa." Her voice still had the same hoarseness. "Long time no see, eh?"

"Hi," I said. "Where've you been keeping yourself, Piquette?"

54   "Oh, I been around," she said. "I been away almost two years now. Been all over the place — Winnipeg, Regina, Saskatoon. Jesus, what I could tell you! I come back this summer, but I ain't stayin'. You kids goin' to the dance?"

55   "No," I said abruptly, for this was a sore point with me. I was fifteen, and thought I was old enough to go to the Saturday-night dances at the Flamingo. My mother, however, thought otherwise.

56   "Y'oughta come," Piquette said. "I never miss one. It's just about the on'y thing in this jerkwater town that's any fun. Boy, you couldn' catch me stayin' here. I don' give a shit about this place. It stinks."

57   She sat down beside me, and I caught the harsh over-sweetness of her perfume.

58   "Listen, you wanna know something, Vanessa?" she confided, her voice only slightly blurred. "Your dad was the only person in Manawaka that ever done anything good to me."

59   I nodded speechlessly. I was certain she was speaking the truth. I knew a little more than I had that summer at Diamond Lake, but I could not reach her now any more than I had then. I was ashamed, ashamed of my own timidity, the frightened tendency to look the other way. Yet I felt no real warmth towards her — I only felt that I ought to, because of that distant summer and because my father had hoped she would be company for me, or perhaps that I would be for her, but it had not happened that way. At this moment, meeting her again, I had to admit that she repelled and embarrassed me, and I could not help despising the self-pity in her voice. I wished she would go away. I did not want to see her. I did not know what to say to her. It seemed that we had nothing to say to one another.

60   "I'll tell you something else," Piquette went on. "All the old bitches an' biddies in this town will sure be surprised. I'm gettin' married this fall — my boyfriend, he's an English fella, works in the stockyards in the city there, a very tall guy, got blond wavy hair. Gee, is he ever handsome. Got this real classy name. Alvin Gerald Cummings — some handle, eh? They call him Al."

61   For the merest instant, then, I saw her. I really did see her, for the first and only time in all the years we had both lived in the same town. Her defiant face, momentarily, became unguarded and unmasked, and in her eyes there was a terrifying hope.

62   "Gee, Piquette — " I burst out awkwardly, "that's swell. That's really wonderful. Congratulations — good luck — I hope you'll be happy — "

63   As I mouthed the conventional phrases, I could only guess how great her need must have been, that she had been forced to seek the very things she so bitterly rejected.

When I was eighteen, I left Manawaka and went away to college. At the end of my first year, I came back home for the summer. I spent the first few days in talking non-stop with my mother, as we exchanged all the news that somehow had not found its way into letters — what had happened in my life and what had happened here in Manawaka while I was away. My mother searched her memory for events that concerned people I knew.

"Did I ever write to you about Piquette Tonnerre, Vanessa?" she asked one morning.

"No, I don't think so," I replied. "Last I heard of her, she was going to marry some guy in the city. Is she still there?"

My mother looked perturbed, and it was a moment before she spoke, as though she did not know how to express what she had to tell and wished she did not need to try.

"She's dead," she said at last. Then, as I stared at her, "Oh, Vanessa, when it happened, I couldn't help thinking of her as she was that summer — so sullen and gauche and badly dressed. I couldn't help wondering if we could have done something more at that time — but what could we do? She used to be around in the cottage there with me all day, and honestly, it was all I could do to get a word out of her. She didn't even talk to your father very much, although I think she liked him, in her way."

"What happened?" I asked.

"Either her husband left her, or she left him," my mother said. "I don't know which. Anyway, she came back here with two youngsters, both only babies — they must have been born very close together. She kept house, I guess, for Lazarus and her brothers, down the valley there, in the old Tonnerre place. I used to see her on the street sometimes, but she never spoke to me. She'd put on an awful lot of weight, and she looked a mess, to tell you the truth, a real slattern, dressed any old how. She was up in court a couple of times — drunk and disorderly, of course. One Saturday night last winter, during the coldest weather, Piquette was alone in the shack with the children. The Tonnerres made home brew all the time, so I've heard, and Lazarus said later she'd been drinking most of the day when he and the boys went out that evening. They had an old woodstove there — you know the kind, with exposed pipes. The shack caught fire. Piquette didn't get out, and neither did the children."

I did not say anything. As so often with Piquette, there did not seem to be anything to say. There was a kind of silence around the image in my mind of the fire and the snow, and I wished I could put from my memory the look that I had seen once in Piquette's eyes.

72   I went up to Diamond Lake for a few days that summer, with Mavis and her family. The MacLeod cottage had been sold after my father's death, and I did not even go to look at it, not wanting to witness my long-ago kingdom possessed now by strangers. But one evening I went down to the shore by myself.

73   The small pier which my father had built was gone, and in its place there was a large and solid pier built by the government, for Galloping Mountain was now a national park, and Diamond Lake had been re-named Lake Wapakata, for it was felt that an Indian name would have a greater appeal to tourists. The one store had become several dozen, and the settlement had all the attributes of a flourishing resort—hotels, a dance-hall, cafés with neon signs, the penetrating odours of potato chips and hot dogs.

74   I sat on the government pier and looked out across the water. At night the lake at least was the same as it had always been, darkly shining and bearing within its black glass the streak of amber that was the path of the moon. There was no wind that evening, and everything was quiet all around me. It seemed too quiet, and then I realized that the loons were no longer here. I listened for some time, to make sure, but never once did I hear that long-drawn call, half mocking and half plaintive, spearing through the stillness across the lake.

75   I did not know what happened to the birds. Perhaps they had gone away to some far place of belonging. Perhaps they had been unable to find such a place, and had simply died out, having ceased to care any longer whether they lived or not.

76   I remembered how Piquette had scorned to come along, when my father and I sat there and listened to the lake birds. It seemed to me now that in some unconscious and totally unrecognized way, Piquette might have been the only one, after all, who had heard the crying of the loons.

1974

NOTES

Margaret Laurence (1926–1987) is one of Canada's most famous writers. This story is part of the Manawaka series of short stories and novels and may be found in the Vanessa MacLeod collection of stories *A Bird in the House*.

Piquette and the Tonnerre family play prominent roles in the Manawaka stories. Piquette's tragic life is recounted in Laurence's novels *The Stone Angel* and *The Diviners*.

Louis Riel (1844–1885) A Métis leader who formed a provisional government in Manitoba, led two rebellions, and was executed for treason. The Métis were people of mixed Native and European parentage.

Batoche, Saskatchewan The capital of Louis Riel's provisional government for the Northwest.

C.P.R. Canadian Pacific Railway. The railway that joins Canada from east coast to west coast.

Nash The make of a car that is no longer manufactured.

Big Bear (1825–1888) Cree leader in the North-West Rebellion of 1885. He was tried for treason and imprisoned.

Poundmaker (1842–1886) Cree chief who also participated in the North-West Rebellion.

Tecumseh (1768–1813) Shawnee chief who fought beside the British in the War of 1812 against the Americans. He died in battle.

Father Brebeuf (1593–1649) A Jesuit missionary to the Hurons. He was tortured and killed by the Iroquois near what is now Midland, Ontario. This martyr was made a saint in 1930.

Pauline Johnson (1861–1913) Born Tekahionwake, this Mohawk poet's work celebrated her Native heritage.

Hiawatha An epic poem, *The Song of Hiawatha*, written by Henry Wadsworth Longfellow in 1885.

COMPREHENSION AND DISCUSSION

1. Why doesn't Grandmother MacLeod go to Diamond Lake with the family?
2. What sort of person is Ewen MacLeod?
3. Why is Piquette's sickness, tuberculosis of the bone, important to the story? How is this disease significant symbolically about the girl herself?

4. What does Vanessa first believe Piquette possesses? How is she disappointed? What lesson does Vanessa learn?
5. Recount at least three ways in which Piquette tries to fit into white Anglo-Saxon society.
6. What does Vanessa learn about her mother from the way she talks about Piquette?
7. What makes Piquette a stereotype? What makes her an individual?
8. Is Piquette's life tragic, especially in the manner of her death? Would her life have improved had she lived longer?
9. Explain the last line in the story.

LITERARY TECHNIQUES

Although Laurence uses the first-person point of view, the narrator, Vanessa MacLeod, is not actually the main character. The story is really about Piquette Tonnerre. By using this particular technique, we see the episodes unfold from Vanessa's perspective, and we learn about Piquette only through Vanessa.

Symbol Something concrete that represents something abstract. To illustrate, a ring is just a small, round ornament that a person wears on a finger; however, worn in marriage, a ring represents the love two people have for each other. In this story, the loons represent the wilderness, which is fast disappearing with white society's progress.

ASSIGNMENTS

1. In this story, the Tonnerres are called "half-breeds": "neither flesh, fowl, nor good salt herring" (p. 128). In "So What Are You, Anyway?", Mrs. Norton says, "I don't mind them mixed, but the world isn't ready for it. They're neither one thing nor the other" (p. 100). Explain these attitudes about mixed-raced children and discuss how relevant these views are in today's world.
2. Vanessa thinks that "Piquette must be in some way a daughter of the forest, a kind of junior prophetess of the wilds." Read the three articles about Grey Owl (pp. 232, 236, and 330). Discuss this view of Native people and its implications.
3. Research one of the historical figures mentioned in the story. Write a short biography.

4. In a short essay, explain the attraction of summer cottages.
5. In the last paragraphs of the story, Vanessa describes the changes to the lake area where her family had a cottage. Should such development be restricted? For example, should national and provincial parks remain undeveloped? What kind of restrictions, if any, should be imposed?
6. Look up *The Song of Hiawatha* or the poems of Pauline Johnson. Choose an excerpt and write a literary analysis of it.

How We Kept Mother's Day

Stephen Leacock

1. Of all the different ideas that have been started lately, I think that the very best is the notion of celebrating once a year "Mother's Day." I don't wonder that May the eleventh is becoming such a popular date all over America and I am sure the idea will spread to England too.

2. It is especially in a big family like ours that such an idea takes hold. So we decided to have a special celebration of Mother's Day. We thought it a fine idea. It made us all realize how much Mother had done for us for years, and all the efforts and sacrifice that she had made for our sake.

3. So we decided that we'd make it a great day, a holiday for all the family, and do everything we could to make Mother happy. Father decided to take a holiday from his office, so as to help in celebrating the day, and my sister Anne and I stayed home from college classes, and Mary and my brother Will stayed home from high school.

4. It was our plan to make it a day just like Xmas or any big holiday, and so we decided to decorate the house with flowers and with mottoes over the mantelpieces, and all that kind of thing. We got Mother to make mottoes and arrange the decorations, because she always does it at Xmas.

5. The two girls thought it would be a nice thing to dress in our very best for such a big occasion, and so they both got new hats. Mother trimmed both the hats, and they looked fine, and Father had bought four-in-hand silk ties for himself and us boys as a souvenir of the day to remember Mother by. We were going to get Mother a new hat too, but it turned out that she seemed to really like her old grey bonnet better than a new one, and both the girls said that it was awfully becoming to her.

6. Well, after breakfast we had it arranged as a surprise for Mother that we would hire a motor car and take her for a beautiful drive away into the country. Mother is hardly ever able to have a treat like that, because we can only afford to keep one maid, and so Mother is busy in the house nearly all the time. And of course the country is so lovely now that it would be just grand for her to have a lovely morning, driving for miles and miles.

7. But on the very morning of the day we changed the plan a little bit, because it occurred to Father that a thing it would be better to do even than to take Mother for a motor drive would be to take her fishing. Father said that as the car was hired and paid for, we might just as well use it for a drive up into hills where the streams are. As Father said, if you just go out driv-

ing without any object, you have a sense of aimlessness, but if you are going to fish, there is a definite purpose in front of you to heighten the enjoyment.

So we all felt that it would be nicer for Mother to have a definite purpose; and anyway, it turned out that Father had just got a new rod the day before, which made the idea of fishing all the more appropriate, and he said that Mother could use it if she wanted to; in fact, he said it was practically for her, only Mother said she would much rather watch him fish and not try to fish herself.

So we got everything arranged for the trip, and we got Mother to cut up some sandwiches and make up a sort of lunch in case we got hungry, though of course we were to come back home again to a big dinner in the middle of the day, just like Xmas or New Year's Day. Mother packed it all up in a basket for us ready to go in the motor.

Well, when the car came to the door, it turned out that there hardly seemed as much room in it as we had supposed, because we hadn't reckoned on Father's fishing basket and the rods and the lunch, and it was plain enough that we couldn't all get in.

Father said not to mind him, he said that he could just as well stay home, and that he was sure that he could put in the time working in the garden; he said that there was a lot of rough dirty work that he could do, like digging a trench for the garbage, that would save hiring a man, and so he said that he'd stay home; he said that we were not to let the fact of his not having had a real holiday for three years stand in our way; he wanted us to go right ahead and be happy and have a big day, and not to mind him. He said that he could plug away all day, and in fact he said he'd been a fool to think there'd be any holiday for him.

But of course we all felt that it would never do to let Father stay home, especially as we knew he would make trouble if he did. The two girls, Anne and Mary, would gladly have stayed and helped the maid get dinner, only it seemed such a pity to, on a lovely day like this, having their new hats. But they both said that Mother had only to say the word, and they'd gladly stay home and work. Will and I would have dropped out, but unfortunately we wouldn't have been any use in getting the dinner.

So in the end it was decided that Mother would stay home and just have a lovely restful day round the house, and get the dinner. It turned out anyway that Mother doesn't care for fishing, and also it was just a little bit cold and fresh out of doors, though it was lovely and sunny, and Father was rather afraid that Mother might take cold if she came.

He said he would never forgive himself if he dragged Mother round the country and let her take a severe cold at a time when she might be having a beautiful rest. He said it was our duty to try and let Mother get all the rest and quiet that she could, after all that she had done for all of us, and he said that that was principally why he had fallen in with this idea of a fishing trip, so as to give Mother a little quiet. He said that young people seldom realize how much quiet means to people who are getting old. As to himself, he could still stand the racket, but he was glad to shelter Mother from it.

So we all drove away with three cheers for Mother, and Mother stood and watched us from the verandah for as long as she could see us, and Father waved his hand back to her every few minutes till he hit his hand on the back edge of the car, and then said that he didn't think Mother could see us any longer.

Well, we had the loveliest day up among the hills that you could possibly imagine, and Father caught such big specimens that he felt sure that Mother couldn't have landed them anyway, if she had been fishing for them, and Will and I fished too, though we didn't get so many as Father, and the two girls met quite a lot of people that they knew as we drove along, and there were some young men friends of theirs that they met along the stream and talked to, and so we all had a splendid time.

It was quite late when we got back, nearly seven o'clock in the evening, but Mother had guessed that we would be late, so she had kept back the dinner so as to have it just nicely ready and hot for us. Only first she had to get towels and soap for Father and clean things for him to put on, because he always gets so messed up with fishing, and that kept Mother busy for a little while, that and helping the girls get ready.

But at last everything was ready, and we sat down to the grandest kind of dinner — roast turkey and all sorts of things like on Xmas Day. Mother had to get up and down a good bit during the meal fetching things back and forward, but at the end Father noticed it and said she simply mustn't do it, that he wanted her to spare herself, and he got up and fetched the walnuts over from the sideboard himself.

The dinner lasted a long while, and was great fun, and when it was over all of us wanted to help clear the things up and wash the dishes, only Mother said that she would really much rather do it, and so we let her, because we wanted just for once to humour her.

It was quite late when it was all over, and when we all kissed Mother before going to bed, she said it had been the most wonderful day in her life, and I think there were tears in her eyes. So we all felt awfully repaid for all that we had done.

1926

NOTES

Stephen Leacock (1869–1944) is one of Canada's most famous writers. He has an award for humorous writing named after him.

The observance of Mother's Day has been standardized as the second Sunday in May. However, when the holiday first originated, in about 1910, the day was set and moved accordingly with each year. For example, in Leacock's story, the set date is May 11, so if Mother's Day occurs on Tuesday one year, the next year it would fall on Wednesday.

Note the word "kept" in the story title. It means observed, celebrated, or paid close attention to.

COMPREHENSION AND DISCUSSION

1. The family members have good intentions of making the day easier for Mother. What do they do? Then what really happens?
2. What evidence in the story tells you that the setting and time are in the early 20th century?
3. Are the father and children selfish in their celebration or are they just unaware of what they do?
4. Recount the various changes in the plan which cause the mother to end up staying at home.
5. List all the extra work, beyond the normal running of the house, that the family members make for the mother.
6. How does the mother take all this?
7. Explain the concluding paragraph to the story: "It was quite late when it was all over, and when we all kissed Mother before going to bed, she said it had been the most wonderful day in her life, and I think there were tears in her eyes. So we all felt awfully repaid for all that we had done" (p. 142).
8. What would you do for your mother to celebrate Mother's Day?

LITERARY TECHNIQUES

Note how this story lacks dialogue; there is no direct speech from any of the characters. There is, however, indirect speech. With this strategy, Leacock blurs the distinction between a fictional story and a remembrance of the past. Unless the reader is aware of the writer's biography, he or she could take this piece as an article, a non-fiction account.

Leacock uses irony to create humour. Irony may be defined in several ways. First, what is said and done is diametrically opposite; for example, the sisters in the story want their mother to rest, but she ends up mending the girls' newly bought hats. Second, irony has the element of the unexpected; for instance, the father's fishing tackle takes up so much space in the car that the family decides to leave Mother at home.

Humour depends on recognition. A situation is funny only if the reader understands what is going on or has had a similar experience. Leacock relies on common experiences that most readers have had sometime in their lives. For example, most of us can identify with the father in this story, who offers to sacrifice his chance to go fishing and offers to stay at home and do work around the house while at the same time drawing attention to his sad plight.

This story is unusual in that it is told from a first-person-plural point of view.

ASSIGNMENTS

1. How should family roles and responsibilities be divided? Write a persuasive essay.
2. Write a dialogue based on one of the conversational exchanges in the story.
3. Describe a holiday, such as Father's Day, Halloween, or Canada Day, and explain how it is celebrated. Research the background.
4. Compare this story with Leacock's "My Financial Career" (p. 145).
5. In 1994, the National Film Board of Canada (NFB) produced a ten-minute animated film of this story. Watch the film and compare it with the written version.

My Financial Career
Stephen Leacock

When I go into a bank I get rattled. The clerks rattle me; the wickets rattle me; the sight of the money rattles me; everything rattles me.

The moment I cross the threshold of a bank and attempt to transact business there, I become an irresponsible idiot.

I knew this beforehand, but my salary had been raised to fifty dollars a month and I felt that the bank was the only place for it.

So I shambled in and looked timidly round at the clerks. I had an idea that a person about to open an account must needs consult the manager.

I went up to a wicket marked "Accountant." The accountant was a tall, cool devil. The very sight of him rattled me. My voice was sepulchral.

"Can I see the manager?" I said, and added solemnly, "alone." I don't know why I said "alone."

"Certainly," said the accountant, and fetched him.

The manager was a grave, calm man. I held my fifty-six dollars clutched in a crumpled ball in my pocket.

"Are you the manager?" I said. God knows I didn't doubt it.

"Yes," he said.

"Can I see you," I asked, "alone?" I didn't want to say "alone" again, but without it the thing seemed self-evident.

The manager looked at me in some alarm. He felt that I had an awful secret to reveal.

"Come in here," he said, and led the way to a private room. He turned the key in the lock.

"We are safe from interruption here," he said; "sit down."

We both sat down and looked at each other. I found no voice to speak.

"You are one of Pinkerton's men, I presume," he said.

He had gathered from my mysterious manner that I was a detective. I knew what he was thinking, and it made me worse.

"No, not from Pinkerton's," I said, seeming to imply that I came from a rival agency.

"To tell the truth," I went on, as if I had been prompted to lie about it, "I am not a detective at all. I have come to open an account. I intend to keep all my money in this bank."

The manager looked relieved but still serious; he concluded now that I was a son of Baron Rothschild or a young Gould.

21   "A large account, I suppose," he said.
22   "Fairly large," I whispered. "I propose to deposit fifty-six dollars now and fifty dollars a month regularly."
23   The manager got up and opened the door. He called to the accountant.
24   "Mr. Montgomery," he said unkindly loud, "this gentleman is opening an account, he will deposit fifty-six dollars. Good morning."
25   I rose.
26   A big iron door stood open at the side of the room.
27   "Good morning," I said, and stepped into the safe.
28   "Come out," said the manager coldly, and showed me the other way.
29   I went up to the accountant's wicket and poked the ball of money at him with a quick convulsive movement as if I were doing a conjuring trick.
30   My face was ghastly pale.
31   "Here," I said, "deposit it." The tone of the words seemed to mean, "Let us do this painful thing while the fit is on us."
32   He took the money and gave it to another clerk.
33   He made me write the sum on a slip and sign my name in a book. I no longer knew what I was doing. The bank swam before my eyes.
34   "Is it deposited?" I asked in a hollow, vibrating voice.
35   "It is," said the accountant.
36   "Then I want to draw a cheque."
37   My idea was to draw out six dollars of it for present use. Someone gave me a cheque-book through a wicket and someone else began telling me how to write it out. The people in the bank had the impression that I was an invalid millionaire. I wrote something on the cheque and thrust it in at the clerk. He looked at it.
38   "What! are you drawing it all out again?" he asked in surprise. Then I realized that I had written fifty-six instead of six. I was too far gone to reason now. I had a feeling that it was impossible to explain the thing. All the clerks had stopped writing to look at me.
39   Reckless with misery, I made a plunge.
40   "Yes, the whole thing."
41   "You withdraw your money from the bank?"
42   "Every cent of it."
43   "Are you not going to deposit any more?" said the clerk, astonished.
44   "Never."
45   An idiot hope struck me that they might think something had insulted me while I was writing the cheque and that I had changed my mind. I made a wretched attempt to look like a man with a fearfully quick temper.
46   The clerk prepared to pay the money.

"How will you have it?" he said.

"What?"

"How will you have it?"

"Oh"—I caught his meaning and answered without even trying to think—"in fifties."

He gave me a fifty-dollar bill.

"And the six?" he asked dryly.

"In sixes," I said.

He gave it me and I rushed out.

As the big door swung behind me I caught the echo of a roar of laughter that went up to the ceiling of the bank. Since then I bank no more. I keep my money in cash in my trousers pocket and my savings in silver dollars in a sock.

1910

NOTES

Stephen Leacock (1869–1944) is one of Canada's most famous writers. He has an award for humorous writing named after him.

Pinkerton Detective Agency A well-known private investigation and security company in the United States, with branches in Canada.

Baron Rothschild (1808–1879) A wealthy banker from the United Kingdom.

Gould, Jay (1836–1892) A railroad tycoon from the United States. His sons succeeded him in his business.

COMPREHENSION AND DISCUSSION

1. What makes the narrator nervous?
2. How do others interpret his nervousness and silence at first?
3. Even without knowing who "young Gould" (p. 145) is, can you surmise his importance from the context of the sentence?
4. How do the manager and the teller treat him once they realize he is merely opening an account?
5. Explain the process of opening an account at this bank.
6. Why doesn't the narrator admit his error when the teller points it out?

7. Do you feel sorry for the narrator? Does he deserve to be laughed at?
8. How might this story have been told in today's situation of electronic banking?
9. Explain the title. Why is it a "career"?

LITERARY TECHNIQUES

Compare this story with Leacock's "How We Kept Mother's Day" (p. 140). Notice that one story is told with direct dialogue, and the other is told with indirect speech. Direct speech not only reveals a great deal about the character but also propels the action of the story forward.

Much of the story's humour comes from the context in which things are said. The direct speeches are, in themselves, bland and mundane but given the situation that the reader knows what the other characters do not, the context changes. We are aware that everything the narrator says will be misinterpreted and misunderstood by the others.

Leacock uses word play to create humour. Note how he repeats the verb "rattle" in different ways.

Mistaken identity is a staple of comedy that results in dramatic irony. In this story, the narrator and the reader know what is truly happening whereas the other characters do not. Because of this discrepancy, actions and words have double and different meanings. For example, the reader knows the narrator only wishes to open a bank account, but from the narrator's demeanour, the teller and manager draw different conclusions.

ASSIGNMENTS

1. What makes us laugh? Write an analytical essay on this topic. Provide examples and illustrations from this story and/or from "How We Kept Mother's Day" (p. 140).
2. Describe a situation in which you felt out of your depth.
3. Explain how banking has changed since the time of this story. Has the situation improved?
4. What are the advantages and/or disadvantages of electronic banking and a cashless society?

5. In 1962, the National Film Board of Canada (NFB) released a six-minute animated film of this story. Watch the film version and compare it with the original story.
6. Research Stephen Leacock and write a short biographical essay about him.

The Prodigal Son
Luke 15:11–32

from The King James Authorized Version of the Holy Bible

11 And he said, A certain man had two sons:
12 And the younger of them said to *his* father, Father, give me the portion of goods that falleth *to me*. And he divided unto them *his* living.
13 And not many days after the younger son gathered all together, and took his journey into a far country, and there wasted his substance with riotous living.
14 And when he had spent all, there arose a mighty famine in that land; and he began to be in want.
15 And he went and joined himself to a citizen of that country; and he sent him into his fields to feed swine.
16 And he would fain have filled his belly with the husks that the swine did eat: and no man gave unto him.
17 And when he came to himself, he said, How many hired servants of my father's have bread enough and to spare, and I perish with hunger!
18 I will arise and go to my father, and will say unto him, Father, I have sinned against heaven, and before thee,
19 And am no more worthy to be called thy son: make me as one of thy hired servants.
20 And he arose, and came to his father. But when he was yet a great way off, his father saw him, and had compassion, and ran, and fell on his neck, and kissed him.
21 And the son said unto him, Father, I have sinned against heaven, and in thy sight, and am no more worthy to be called thy son.
22 But the father said to his servants, Bring forth the best robe, and put it on him; and put this ring on his hand, and shoes on *his* feet:
23 And bring hither the fatted calf, and kill *it*; and let us eat, and be merry:
24 For this my son was dead, and is alive again; he was lost, and is found. And they began to be merry.
25 Now his elder son was in the field: and as he came and drew nigh to the house, he heard musick and dancing.
26 And he called one of the servants, and asked what these things meant.
27 And he said unto him, Thy brother is come; and thy father had killed the fatted calf, because he hath received him safe and sound.

And he was angry, and would not go in: therefore came his father out, and intreated him. 28

And he answering said to *his* father, Lo, these many years do I serve thee, neither transgressed I at any time thy commandment: and yet thou never gavest me a kid, that I might make merry with my friends: 29

But as soon as this thy son was come, which hath devoured thy living with harlots, thou hast killed for him this fatted calf. 30

And he said unto him, Son, thou art ever with me, and all that I have is thine. 31

It was meet that we should make merry, and be glad: for this thy brother was dead, and is alive again; and was lost, and is found. 32

around 30 A.D., translated 1611

NOTES

A parable is a story that illustrates a moral lesson. Often a parable has more than just surface meaning. It resonates with spiritual teachings. In the West, the most famous and memorable parables are those told by Jesus. In his short ministry, Jesus was often asked questions, and he would reply by telling a parable. Thus, this story begins, "And he said" (p. 150). Other famous parables are "The Good Samaritan" and "The Lost Lamb."

People often refer to the ideas of the prodigal son and the fatted calf and use these expressions in their writing.

To tend swine is an insulting and humiliating task, especially for a Jew. The young man has fallen quite low socially, financially, and spiritually. According to the dietary and divine laws in the Bible, the pig is a prohibited animal: "And the swine, though he divide the hoof, and be clovenfooted, yet he cheweth not the cud; he is unclean to you. Of their flesh shall ye not eat, and their carcase shall ye not touch; they *are* unclean to you" (Leviticus 11:7–8).

A fattened animal is kept for special occasions. The father has deemed the return of his son a time to celebrate.

COMPREHENSION AND DISCUSSION

1. What does the word "prodigal" mean?
2. Why does the son want his inheritance?

3. At what point does the young man realize his mistake?
4. What is the moral of this story? Or, what is the point that Jesus makes in telling this story to the Pharisees and scribes?
5. Does an adult child have the right to demand a share of the inheritance from parents who are still living?
6. How do you know whether your friends are true or merely fair-weather ones?
7. Does the other son have legitimate reason to complain? Should people who break the rules be given greater consideration than those who are "good"?

LITERARY TECHNIQUES

This well-known parable was translated from the original Greek during the reign of King James I of England, 1603–1625. The translators attempted to preserve not only the veracity of the message but also the simple style of the original.

The parable is meant to be spoken rather than read. It imitates speech, albeit an archaic 17th-century pattern of speaking. The constant use of "and" to begin the verses suggests a chaining of ideas.

This parable has stark sentences that move the story along. In each verse or paragraph, there are no more than two sentences. There is little description, and there are no quotation marks to distinguish speech from narration.

Note that the moral lesson is not explicit. Unlike Aesop's fables, in which the moral is reiterated, the parable lets the listener or reader come to realize the point.

ASSIGNMENTS

1. How does this parable differ from the folktale, "The Cowherd" (p. 73)?
2. Read the other well-known parable, "The Good Samaritan" (Luke 10:25–37). Which one do you prefer and why?
3. Rewrite the story in modern English. You can write it from the same point of view, or that of the parent or the brother who remains at home.
4. Compare the son in this parable and the son in "All the Years of Her Life" (p. 47) or the son in "The Cowherd" (p. 73).

An Ounce of Cure

Alice Munro

My parents didn't drink. They weren't rabid about it, and in fact I remember that when I signed a pledge in grade seven, with the rest of that superbly if impermanently indoctrinated class, my mother said, "It's just nonsense and fanaticism, children of that age." My father would drink a beer on a hot day, but my mother did not join him, and — whether accidentally or symbolically — this drink was always consumed *outside* the house. Most of the people we knew were the same way, in the small town where we lived. I ought not to say that it was this which got me into difficulties, because the difficulties I got into were a faithful expression of my own incommodious nature — the same nature that caused my mother to look at me, on any occasion which traditionally calls for feelings of pride and maternal accomplishment (my departure for my first formal dance, I mean, or my hellbent preparations for a descent on college) with an expression of brooding and fascinated despair, as if she could not possibly expect, did not ask, that it should go with me as it did with other girls; the dreamed-of spoils of daughters — orchids, nice boys, diamond rings — would be borne home in due course by the daughters of her friends, but not by me; all she could do was hope for a lesser rather than a greater disaster — an elopement, say, with a boy who could never earn his living, rather than an abduction into the White Slave trade.

But ignorance, my mother said, ignorance, or innocence if you like, is not always such a fine thing as people think and I am not sure it may not be dangerous for a girl like you; then she emphasized her point, as she had a habit of doing, with some quotation which had an innocent pomposity and odour of mothballs. I didn't even wince at it, knowing full well how it must have worked wonders with Mr. Berryman.

The evening I baby-sat for the Berrymans must have been in April. I had been in love all year, or at least since the first week in September, when a boy named Martin Collingwood had given me a surprised, appreciative, and rather ominously complacent smile in the school assembly. I never knew what surprised him; I was not looking like anybody but me; I had an old blouse on and my home-permanent had turned out badly. A few weeks after that he took me out for the first time, and kissed me on the dark side of the porch — also, I ought to say, on the mouth; I am sure it was the first time anybody had ever kissed me effectively, and I know that I did not wash my face that night or the next morning, in order to keep the imprint of those kisses intact. (I showed the most painful banality in the conduct of this whole affair, as you will see.) Two months, and a few amatory stages later, he dropped me. He had fallen for the girl who played opposite him in the Christmas production of *Pride and Prejudice*.

4   I said I was not going to have anything to do with that play, and I got another girl to work on Makeup in my place, but of course I went to it after all, and sat down in front with my girl friend Joyce, who pressed my hand when I was overcome with pain and delight at the sight of Mr. Darcy in white breeches, silk waistcoat, and sideburns. It was surely seeing Martin as Darcy that did for me; every girl is in love with Darcy anyway, and the part gave Martin an arrogance and male splendour in my eyes which made it impossible to remember that he was simply a high-school senior, passably good-looking and of medium intelligence (and with a reputation slightly tainted, at that, by such preferences as the Drama Club and the Cadet Band) who appeared to be the first boy, the first really presentable boy, to take an interest in me. In the last act they gave him a chance to embrace Elizabeth (Mary Bishop, with a sallow complexion and no figure, but big vivacious eyes) and during this realistic encounter I dug my nails bitterly into Joyce's sympathetic palm.

5   That night was the beginning of months of real, if more or less self-inflicted, misery for me. Why is it a temptation to refer to this sort of thing lightly, with irony, with amazement even, at finding oneself involved with such preposterous emotions in the unaccountable past? That is what we are apt to do, speaking of love; with adolescent love, of course, it's practically obligatory; you would think we sat around, dull afternoons, amusing ourselves with these tidbit recollections of pain. But it really doesn't make me feel very gay — worse still, it doesn't really surprise me — to remember all the stupid, sad, half-ashamed things I did, that people in love always do. I hung around the places where he might be seen, and then pretended not to see him; I made absurdly roundabout approaches, in conversation, to the bitter pleasure of casually mentioning his name. I daydreamed endlessly; in fact if you want to put it mathematically, I spent perhaps ten times as many hours thinking about Martin Collingwood — yes, pining and weeping for him — as I ever spent with him; the idea of him dominated my mind relentlessly and, after a while, against my will. For if at first I had dramatized my feelings, the time came when I would have been glad to escape them; my well-worn daydreams had become depressing and not even temporarily consoling. As I worked my math problems I would torture myself, quite mechanically and helplessly, with an exact recollection

of Martin kissing my throat. I had an exact recollection of *everything*. One night I had an impulse to swallow all the aspirins in the bathroom cabinet, but stopped after I had taken six.

My mother noticed that something was wrong and got me some iron pills. She said, "Are you sure everything is going all right at school?" *School!* When I told her that Martin and I had broken up all she said was, "Well so much the better for that. I never saw a boy so stuck on himself." "Martin has enough conceit to sink a battleship," I said morosely and went upstairs and cried.

    The night I went to the Berrymans was a Saturday night. I baby-sat for them quite often on Saturday nights because they liked to drive over to Baileyville, a much bigger, livelier town about twenty miles away, and perhaps have supper and go to a show. They had been living in our town only two or three years — Mr. Berryman had been brought in as plant manager of the new door-factory — and they remained, I suppose by choice, on the fringes of its society; most of their friends were youngish couples like themselves, born in other places, who lived in new ranch-style houses on a hill outside town where we used to go tobogganing. This Saturday night they had two other couples in for drinks before they all drove over to Baileyville for the opening of a new supper-club; they were all rather festive. I sat in the kitchen and pretended to do Latin. Last night had been the Spring Dance at the High School. I had not gone, since the only boy who had asked me was Millerd Crompton, who asked so many girls that he was suspected of working his way through the whole class alphabetically. But the dance was held in the Armouries, which was only half a block away from our house; I had been able to see the boys in dark suits, the girls in long pale formals under their coats, passing gravely under the street-lights, stepping around the last patches of snow. I could even hear the music and I have not forgotten to this day that they played "Ballerina," and — oh, song of my aching heart — "Slow Boat to China." Joyce had phoned me up this morning and told me in her hushed way (we might have been discussing an incurable disease I had) that yes, M.C. *had* been there with M.B., and she had on a formal that must have been made out of somebody's old lace tablecloth, it just *hung*.

    When the Berrymans and their friends had gone I went into the living room and read a magazine. I was mortally depressed. The big softly lit room, with its green and leaf-brown colours, made an uncluttered setting for the development of the emotions, such as you would get on a stage. At home the life of the emotions went on all right, but it always seemed to get buried under the piles of mending to be done, the ironing, the children's jigsaw puzzles and rock collections. It was the sort of house where people were always colliding with one another on the stairs and listening to hockey games and Superman on the radio.

9   I got up and found the Berrymans' "Danse Macabre" and put it on the record player and turned out the living-room lights. The curtains were only partly drawn. A street light shone obliquely on the windowpane, making a rectangle of thin dusty gold, in which the shadows of bare branches moved, caught in the huge sweet winds of spring. It was a mild black night when the last snow was melting. A year ago all this—the music, the wind and darkness, the shadows of the branches—would have given me tremendous happiness; when they did not do so now, but only called up tediously familiar, somehow humiliatingly personal thoughts, I gave up my soul for dead and walked into the kitchen and decided to get drunk.

10   No, it was not like that. I walked into the kitchen to look for a coke or something in the refrigerator, and there on the front of the counter were three tall beautiful bottles, all about half full of gold. But even after I had looked at them and lifted them to feel their weight I had not decided to get drunk; I had decided to have a drink.

11   Now here is where my ignorance, my disastrous innocence, comes in. It is true that I had seen the Berrymans and their friends drinking their highballs as casually as I could drink a coke, but I did not apply this attitude to myself. No; I thought of hard liquor as something to be taken in extremities, and relied upon for extravagant results, one way or another. My approach could not have been less casual if I had been the Little Mermaid drinking the witch's crystal potion. Gravely, with a glance at my set face in the black window above the sink, I poured a little whisky from each of the bottles (I think now there were two brands of rye and an expensive Scotch) until I had my glass full. For I had never in my life seen anyone pour a drink and I had no idea that people frequently diluted their liquor with water, soda, et cetera, and I had seen that the glasses the Berrymans' guests were holding when I came through the living room were nearly full.

12   I drank it off as quickly as possible. I set the glass down and stood looking at my face in the window, half expecting to see it altered. My throat was burning, but I felt nothing else. It was very disappointing, when I had worked myself up to it. But I was not going to let it go at that. I poured another full glass, then filled each of the bottles with water to approximately the level I had seen when I came in. I drank the second glass only a little more slowly than the first. I put the empty glass down on the

counter with care, perhaps feeling in my head a rustle of things to come, and went and sat down on a chair in the living room. I reached up and turned on a floor lamp beside the chair, and the room jumped on me.

When I say that I was expecting extravagant results I do not mean that I was expecting this. I had thought of some sweeping emotional change, an upsurge of gaiety and irresponsibility, a feeling of lawlessness and escape, accompanied by a little dizziness and perhaps a tendency to giggle out loud. I did not have in mind the ceiling spinning like a great plate somebody had thrown at me, nor the pale green blobs of the chairs swelling, converging, disintegrating, playing with me a game full of enormous senseless inanimate malice. My head sank back; I closed my eyes. And at once opened them, opened them wide, threw myself out of the chair and down the hall and reached—thank God, thank God!—the Berrymans' bathroom, where I was sick everywhere, everywhere, and dropped like a stone.

From this point on I have no continuous picture of what happened; my memories of the next hour or two are split into vivid and improbable segments, with nothing but murk and uncertainty between. I do remember lying on the bathroom floor looking sideways at the little six-sided white tiles, which lay together in such an admirable and logical pattern, seeing them with the brief broken gratitude and sanity of one who has just been torn to pieces with vomiting. Then I remember sitting on the stool in front of the hall phone, asking weakly for Joyce's number. Joyce was not home. I was told by her mother (a rather rattlebrained woman, who didn't seem to notice a thing the matter—for which I felt weakly, mechanically grateful) that she was at Kay Stringer's house. I didn't know Kay's number so I just asked the operator; I felt I couldn't risk looking down at the telephone book.

Kay Stringer was not a friend of mine but a new friend of Joyce's. She had a vague reputation for wildness and a long switch of hair, very oddly, though naturally, coloured—from soap-yellow to caramel-brown. She knew a lot of boys more exciting than Martin Collingwood, boys who had quit school or been imported into town to play on the hockey team. She and Joyce rode around in these boys' cars, and sometimes went with them— having lied of course to their mothers—to the Gay-la dance hall on the highway north of town.

I got Joyce on the phone. She was very keyed-up, as she always was with boys around, and she hardly seemed to hear what I was saying.

"Oh, I can't tonight," she said. "Some kids are here. We're going to play cards. You know Bill Kline? He's here. Ross Armour—"

18   "I'm *sick*," I said trying to speak distinctly; it came out an inhuman croak. "I'm *drunk*. Joyce!" Then I fell off the stool and the receiver dropped out of my hand and banged for a while dismally against the wall.

19   I had not told Joyce where I was, so after thinking about it for a moment she phoned my mother, and using the elaborate and unnecessary subterfuge that young girls delight in, she found out. She and Kay and the boys — there were three of them — told some story about where they were going to Kay's mother, and got into the car and drove out. They found me still lying on the broadloom carpet in the hall; I had been sick again, and this time I had not made it to the bathroom.

20   It turned out that Kay Stringer, who arrived on this scene only by accident, was exactly the person I needed. She loved a crisis, particularly one like this, which had a shady and scandalous aspect and which must be kept secret from the adult world. She became excited, aggressive, efficient; that energy which was termed wildness was simply the overflow of a great female instinct to manage, comfort and control. I could hear her voice coming at me from all directions, telling me not to worry, telling Joyce to find the biggest coffeepot they had and make it full of coffee (*strong* coffee, she said), telling the boys to pick me up and carry me to the sofa. Later, in the fog beyond my reach, she was calling for a scrub-brush.

21   Then I was lying on the sofa, covered with some kind of crocheted throw they had found in the bedroom. I didn't want to lift my head. The house was full of the smell of coffee. Joyce came in, looking very pale; she said that the Berryman kids had wakened up but she had given them a cookie and told them to go back to bed, it was all right; she hadn't let them out of their room and she didn't believe they'd remember. She said that she and Kay had cleaned up the bathroom and the hall though she was afraid there was still a spot on the rug. The coffee was ready. I didn't understand anything very well. The boys had turned on the radio and were going through the Berrymans' record collection; they had it out on the floor. I felt there was something odd about this but I could not think what it was.

22   Kay brought me a huge breakfast mug full of coffee.

23   "I don't know if I can," I said. "Thanks."

24   "Sit up," she said briskly, as if dealing with drunks was an everyday business for her, I had no need to feel myself important. (I met, and recognized, that tone of voice years later, in the maternity ward.) "Now drink," she said. I drank, and at the same time realized that I was wearing only my slip. Joyce and Kay had taken off my blouse and skirt. They had brushed off the skirt and washed out the blouse, since it was nylon; it was hanging

in the bathroom. I pulled the throw up under my arms and Kay laughed. She got everybody coffee. Joyce brought in the coffeepot and on Kay's instructions she kept filling my cup whenever I drank from it. Somebody said to me with interest, "You must have really wanted to tie one on."

"No," I said rather sulkily, obediently drinking my coffee. "I only had two drinks."

Kay laughed, "Well it certainly gets to you, I'll say that. What time do you expect *they'll* be back?" she said.

"Late. After one, I think."

"You should be all right by that time. Have some more coffee."

Kay and one of the boys began dancing to the radio. Kay danced very sexily, but her face had the gently superior and indulgent, rather cold look it had when she was lifting me up to drink the coffee. The boy was whispering to her and she was smiling, shaking her head. Joyce said she was hungry, and she went out to the kitchen to see what there was — potato chips or crackers, or something like that, that you could eat without making too noticeable a dint. Bill Kline came over and sat on the sofa beside me and patted my legs through the crocheted throw. He didn't say anything to me, just patted my legs and looked at me with what seemed to me a very stupid, half-sick, absurd and alarming expression. I felt very uncomfortable; I wondered how it had ever got around that Bill Kline was so good looking, with an expression like that. I moved my legs nervously and he gave me a look of contempt, not ceasing to pat me. Then I scrambled off the sofa, pulling the throw around me, with the idea of going to the bathroom to see if my blouse was dry. I lurched a little when I started to walk, and for some reason — probably to show Bill Kline that he had not panicked me — I immediately exaggerated this, and calling out, "Watch me walk a straight line!" I lurched and stumbled, to the accompaniment of everybody's laughter, towards the hall. I was standing in the archway between the hall and the living room when the knob of the front door turned with a small matter-of-fact click and everything became silent behind me except the radio of course and the crocheted throw inspired by some delicate malice of its own slithered down around my feet and there — oh, delicious moment in a well-organized farce! — there stood the Berrymans, Mr. and Mrs., with expressions on their faces as appropriate to the occasion as any old-fashioned director of farces could wish. They must have been preparing those expressions, of course; they could not have produced them in the first moment of shock; with the noise we were making, they had no doubt heard us as soon as they got out of the car; for the same reason, we had not heard them. I don't think I ever knew what brought them home so early—a headache, an argument—and I was not really in a position to ask.

30   Mr. Berryman drove me home. I don't remember how I got into that car, or how I found my clothes and put them on, or what kind of a good-night, if any, I said to Mrs. Berryman. I don't remember what happened to my friends, though I imagine they gathered up their coats and fled, covering up the ignominy of their departure with a mechanical roar of defiance. I remember Joyce with a box of crackers in her hand, saying that I had become terribly sick from eating—I think she said *sauerkraut*—for supper, and that I had called them for help. (When I asked her later what they made of this she said, "It wasn't any use. You *reeked*.") I remember also her saying, "Oh, no, Mr. Berryman I beg of you, my mother is a terribly nervous person I don't know what the shock might do to her. I will go down on my knees to you if you like but *you must not phone my mother*." I have no picture of her down on her knees—and she would have done it in a minute—so it seems this threat was not carried out.

31   Mr. Berryman said to me, "Well, I guess you know your behaviour tonight is a pretty serious thing." He made it sound as if I might be charged with criminal negligence or something worse. "It would be very wrong of me to overlook it," he said. I suppose that besides being angry and disgusted with *me*, he was worried about taking me home in this condition to my strait-laced parents, who could always say I got the liquor in his house. Plenty of Temperance people would think that enough to hold him responsible, and the town was full of Temperance people. Good relations with the town were very important to him from a business point of view.

32   "I have an idea it wasn't the first time," he said. "If it was the first time, would a girl be smart enough to fill three bottles up with water? No. Well in this case, she *was* smart enough, but not smart enough to know I could spot it. What do you say to that?" I opened my mouth to answer and although I was feeling quite sober the only sound that came out was a loud, desolate-sounding giggle. He stopped in front of our house. "Light's on," he said. "Now go in and tell your parents the straight truth. And if you don't, remember I will." He did not mention paying me for my babysitting services of the evening and the subject did not occur to me either.

33   I went into the house and tried to go straight upstairs but my mother called to me. She came into the front hall, where I had not turned on the light, and she must have smelled me at once for she ran forward with a cry of pure amazement, as if she had seen somebody falling, and caught me by the shoulders as I did indeed fall down against the bannister, overwhelmed

by my fantastic lucklessness, and I told her everything from the start, not omitting even the name of Martin Collingwood and my flirtation with the aspirin bottle, which was a mistake.

On Monday morning my mother took the bus over to Baileyville and found the liquor store and bought a bottle of Scotch whisky. Then she had to wait for a bus back, and she met some people she knew and was not quite able to hide the bottle in her bag; she was furious with herself for not bringing a proper shopping-bag. As soon as she got back she walked out to the Berrymans'; she had not even had lunch. Mr. Berryman had not gone back to the factory. My mother went in and had a talk with both of them and made an excellent impression and then Mr. Berryman drove her home. She talked to them in the forthright and unemotional way she had, which was always agreeably surprising to people prepared to deal with a mother, and she told them that although I seemed to do well enough at school I was extremely backward — or perhaps eccentric — in my emotional development. I imagine that this analysis of my behaviour was especially effective with Mrs. Berryman, a great reader of Child Guidance books. Relations between them warmed to the point where my mother brought up a specific instance of my difficulties, and disarmingly related the whole story of Martin Collingwood.

Within a few days it was all over town and the school that I had tried to commit suicide over Martin Collingwood. But it was already all over school and the town that the Berrymans had come home on Saturday night to find me drunk, staggering, wearing nothing but my slip, in a room with three boys, one of whom was Bill Kline. My mother had said that I was to pay for the bottle she had taken the Berrymans out of my baby-sitting earnings, but my clients melted away like the last April snow, and it would not be paid for yet if newcomers to town had not moved in across the street in July, and needed a baby-sitter before they talked to any of their neighbours.

My mother also said that it had been a great mistake to let me go out with boys and that I would not be going out again until well after my sixteenth birthday, if then. This did not prove to be a concrete hardship at all, because it was at least that long before anybody asked me. If you think that news of the Berrymans' adventure would put me in demand for whatever gambols and orgies were going on in and around that town, you could not be more mistaken. The extraordinary publicity which attended my first debauch may have made me seemed marked for a special kind of ill luck, like the girl whose illegitimate baby turns out to be triplets: nobody wants to have anything to do with her. At any rate I had at the same time one of the most silent telephones and positively the most sinful reputation in the whole High School. I had to put up with this until the next fall, when a fat blonde girl in Grade Ten ran away with a married man and was picked up two months later, living in sin—though not with the same man—in the city of Sault Ste. Marie. Then everybody forgot about me.

37   But there was a positive, a splendidly unexpected, result of this affair: I got completely over Martin Collingwood. It was not only that he at once said, publicly, that he had always thought I was a nut; where he was concerned I had no pride, and my tender fancy could have found a way around that, a month, a week, before. What was it that brought me back into the world again? It was the terrible and fascinating reality of my disaster; it was *the way things happened*. Not that I enjoyed it; I was a self-conscious girl and I suffered a good deal from all this exposure. But the development of events on that Saturday night—that fascinated me; I felt that I had had a glimpse of the shameless, marvellous, shattering absurdity with which the plots of life, though not of fiction, are improvised. I could not take my eyes off it.

38   And of course Martin Collingwood wrote his Senior Matric that June, and went away to the city to take a course at a school for Morticians, as I think it is called, and when he came back he went into his uncle's undertaking business. We lived in the same town and we would hear most things that happened to each other but I do not think we met face to face or saw one another, except at a distance, for years. I went to a shower for the girl he married, but then everybody went to everybody else's showers. No, I do not think I really saw him again until I came home after I had been married several years, to attend a relative's funeral. Then I saw him; not quite Mr. Darcy but still very nice-looking in those black clothes. And I saw him looking over at me with an expression as close to a reminiscent smile as the occasion would permit, and I knew that he had been surprised by a memory either of my devotion or my little buried catastrophe. I gave him a gentle uncomprehending look in return. I am a grown-up woman now; let him unbury his own catastrophes.

1968

NOTES

White Slave trade   The kidnapping of young, white girls for the purpose of prostitution and slavery.

Pride and Prejudice   A romantic novel written by Jane Austen (1775–1817). It is a story about young women trying to find wealthy husbands. Mr. Darcy is the main male character and Elizabeth Bennett is the protagonist who is pursued by Mr. Darcy.

Danse Macabre Literally, "dance of death" (French). The recording of the same title is probably that of Saint-Saëns (1835–1921).

The Little Mermaid A fairy tale written by Hans Christian Andersen (1805–1875). A young mermaid who falls in love with a mortal prince and trades her soul to be human and secure his love. She sacrifices her own happiness for the prince's. (Note that the Disney version changes the story to include a happy ending.)

Temperance Avoidance of alcohol.

COMPREHENSION AND DISCUSSION

1. What is the significance of the first sentence? Why does the narrative begin that way?
2. For whom does the narrator babysit? How is this family different from the other neighbours?
3. Why is the narrator infatuated with Martin Collingwood?
4. What happens when Joyce and her friends come to rescue the narrator? Are they helpful?
5. What does the mother do to make amends to the Berrymans? What does she do to her daughter, the narrator? How would you have handled the situation?
6. What rumours begin to circulate about this incident? What are the results?
7. Has she learned anything from the experience at the Berrymans and its aftermath? How do you know?
8. Why does Munro have Martin Collingwood become a mortician? Is this significant to the story?
9. Is Munro's portrayal of teenage love realistic?
10. A proverb says, "An ounce of prevention is worth a pound of cure." Discuss the meaning of the title of the story.

LITERARY TECHNIQUES

The "I" narrator remains unnamed throughout the story. The narrator is not the author. Often writers prefer an anonymous narrator in order to make her "everywoman," in this case the generic teenager who has had experiences with infatuation and drunkenness similar to those of many teenagers. In addition, the first-person point of view restricts the perspective to the unnamed narrator.

In the first paragraph, Munro writes a very long sentence beginning with "I ought not to say..." and ending with "...into the White Slave trade" (p. 153). In this instance, the rambling quality of the sentence shows the narrator's state of mind, her views on life, and her relationship with her family all at once. The sentence employs, in a minor way, the stream-of-consciousness method in which the writer attempts to show the progress of a character's thoughts.

Time shifts One of Munro's favourite techniques is to jump ahead several years after the events narrated in the story. The ending then gives a different perspective: the narrator can evaluate her youthful follies and comment on her maturity. Note that Martin Collingwood has become an undertaker. His occupation allows for a play on the words "unbury" and "catastrophe" (p. 162).

ASSIGNMENTS

1. Compare this story with Boyle's "Greasy Lake" (p. 35). You can examine the themes of maturity, adolescent angst, teenage rites of passage, influence of alcohol, or lessons.
2. The narrator says that Martin Collingwood has "a reputation slightly tainted, at that, by such preferences as the Drama Club and the Cadet Band" (p. 154). Discuss the qualities teenagers value in their peers. What makes a person "cool," for example? You can also consider the characters in "Greasy Lake" (p. 35) to answer this question.
3. How are the problems of teenage boys different from those of teenage girls? What problems do both share? Write an expository paper.
4. Write a set of guidelines for babysitters.
5. What immature acts have you done that you later regretted? What were the consequences?
6. Atlantis Television made a 1983 film based on this story. Compare the film with the original story.

One Rejection Too Many
Patricia Nurse

Dear Dr. Asimov:

    Imagine my delight when I spotted your new science fiction magazine on the newsstands. I have been a fan of yours for many, many years, and I naturally wasted no time in buying a copy. I wish you every success in this new venture.

    In your second issue I read with interest your plea for stories from new authors. While no writer myself, I have had a time traveller living with me for the past two weeks (he materialized in the bathtub without clothes or money, so I felt obliged to offer him shelter), and he has written a story of life on earth as it will be in the year 5000.

    Before he leaves this time frame, it would give him great pleasure to see his story in print — I hope you will feel able to make this wish come true.

                      Yours sincerely,
                      Nancy Morrison (Miss)

Dear Miss Morrison:

    Thank you for your kind letter and good wishes.

    It is always refreshing to hear from a new author. You have included some most imaginative material in your story; however, it is a little short on plot and human interest — perhaps you could rewrite it with this thought in mind.

                      Yours sincerely,
                      Isaac Asimov

Dear Dr. Asimov:

    I was sorry that you were unable to print the story I sent you. Vahl (the time traveller who wrote it) was quite hurt as he tells me he is an author of some note in his own time. He has, however, rewritten the story and this time has included plenty of plot and some rather interesting mating rituals which he has borrowed from the year 3000. In his own time (the year 5015) sex is no longer practised, so you can see that it is perfectly respectable having him in my house. I do wish, though, that he could adapt himself to our custom of wearing clothes — my neighbours are starting to talk!

12   Anything that you can do to expedite the publishing of Vahl's story would be most appreciated, so that he will feel free to return to his own time.
13   Yours sincerely,
                        Nancy Morrison (Miss)

14   Dear Miss Morrison:
15   Thank you for your rewritten short story.
16   I don't want to discourage you but I'm afraid you followed my suggestions with a little too much enthusiasm — however, I can understand that having an imaginary nude visitor from another time is a rather heady experience. I'm afraid that your story now rather resembles a far-future episode of "Mary Hartman, Mary Hartman" or "Soap."
17   Could you tone it down a bit and omit the more bizarre sex rituals of the year 3000 — we must remember that *Isaac Asimov's Science Fiction Magazine* is intended to be a family publication.
18   Perhaps a little humour would improve the tale too.
19   Yours sincerely,
                        Isaac Asimov

20   Dear Dr. Asimov:
21   Vahl was extremely offended by your second rejection — he said he has never received a rejection slip before, and your referring to him as "imaginary" didn't help matters at all. I'm afraid he rather lost his temper and stormed out into the garden — it was at this unfortunate moment that the vicar happened to pass by.
22   Anyway, I managed to get Vahl calmed down and he has rewritten the story and added plenty of humour. I'm afraid my subsequent meeting with the vicar was not blessed with such success! I'm quite sure Vahl would not understand another rejection.
23   Yours truly,
                        Nancy Morrison (Miss)

24   Dear Miss Morrison:
25   I really admire your persistence in rewriting your story yet another time. Please don't give up hope — you can become a fairly competent writer in time, I feel sure.
26   I'm afraid the humour you added was not the kind of thing I had in mind at all — you're not collaborating with Henny Youngman by any

chance are you? I really had a more sophisticated type of humour in mind.
Yours truly,
Isaac Asimov
P.S. Have you considered reading your story, as it is, on "The Gong Show"?

Dear Dr. Asimov:

It really was very distressing to receive the return of my manuscript once again—Vahl was quite speechless with anger.

It was only with the greatest difficulty that I prevailed upon him to refine the humour you found so distasteful, and I am submitting his latest rewrite herewith.

In his disappointment, Vahl has decided to return to his own time right away. I shall be sorry to see him leave as I was getting very fond of him—a pity he wasn't from the year 3000 though. Still, he wouldn't have made a very satisfactory husband; I'd have never known where (or when) he was. It rather looks as though my plans to marry the vicar have suffered a severe setback too. Are you married, Dr. Asimov?

I must close this letter now as I have to say good-bye to Vahl. He says he has just finished making some long overdue improvements to our time frame as a parting gift—isn't that kind of him?
Yours sincerely,
Nancy Morrison (Miss)

Dear Miss Morrison:

I am very confused by your letter. Who is Isaac Asimov? I have checked with several publishers and none of them has heard of *Isaac Asimov's Science Fiction Magazine*, although the address on the envelope was correct for *this* magazine.

However, I was very impressed with your story and will be pleased to accept it for our next issue. Seldom do we receive a story combining such virtues as a well-conceived plot, plenty of human interest, and a delightfully subtle brand of humour.
Yours truly,
George H. Scithers,
Editor,
Arthur C. Clarke's Science Fiction Magazine

1978

NOTES

Isaac Asimov (1920–1992) A prolific writer of science fiction and other genres, and biochemistry professor at Boston University. He is the author of "The Fun They Had" (p. 30). *Isaac Asimov's Science Fiction Magazine* is a real publication, not a fictional creation.

Mary Hartman, Mary Hartman (1976–1977) A TV comedy show mocking soap operas (overly dramatic continuing television series, usually shown in the afternoon).

Soap (1977–1981) A popular TV series, also spoofing soap operas.

Henny Youngman (1960–1998) An American comedian known for such one-liners as "Take my wife...please!"

The Gong Show A 1970s TV series in which contestants displayed their various and often limited talents until they were stopped by the sound of a gong.

George H. Scithers A real-life editor of *Isaac Asimov's Science Fiction Magazine*.

Arthur C. Clarke A renowned writer of science and science fiction. His best-known work is a collaboration with director Stanley Kubrick on *2001: A Space Odyssey* (1968). He does not have a science fiction magazine in his name.

COMPREHENSION AND DISCUSSION

1. Explain what happens in this story.
2. What are some of Miss Morrison's hopes and dreams?
3. What year does Vahl come from? How do you picture him?
4. How does Isaac Asimov keep offending Miss Morrison more unkindly with each reply?
5. How does Vahl get his revenge? What clues does the writer give to foreshadow this conclusion?
6. Explain how Patricia Nurse creates humour in this story.
7. This was Nurse's first published story. Do you think she made several attempts to be published before? How can you tell?

8. Discuss the letter technique used here. How else could this story have been told? Why is the use of letters effective?

LITERARY TECHNIQUES

Letter form Using a series of letters, the writer concocts a story line or plot, often with parts left out to be filled in by the reader's imagination. For example, the letters hint at Vahl's subject matter but never completely tell of it; Miss Morrison includes asides about her desire for marriage and companionship ("Are you married, Dr. Asimov?" (p. 167)).

Time-travel One of the most popular themes in science fiction, it offers not only adventurous and imaginative story lines but also social commentary. Here, the time traveller Vahl becomes vital to the conclusion of the story.

Plausibility By using real names and transforming these people into fictional story characters (such as Isaac Asimov and Arthur C. Clarke), the writer lends a credible note to the story. In short, the letters seem like real correspondence. The content (although outrageous) is delivered matter-of-factly and in all seriousness.

Surprise ending A conclusion to a story that the reader is not expecting. Often the ending has a twist. When the reader re-reads the story, he or she discovers that the writer has inserted clues throughout to play fair with the astute reader.

ASSIGNMENTS

1. Read "The Fun They Had" by Isaac Asimov (p. 30). What do you think Asimov's opinion was of Nurse's story?
2. What is the difference between science fiction and fantasy? Read Charles De Lint's story (p. 54) and compare the two works.
3. If time travel were possible, which time period would you visit? Why?
4. Explain the benefits and/or problems of time travel.
5. Read "A Girl's Story" (p. 22) and "Mr. Truepenny's Book Emporium and Gallery" (p. 54). Explain what these two stories, and "One Rejection Too Many," tell about being a writer.

The Man I Killed

Tim O'Brien

1. His jaw was in his throat, his upper lip and teeth were gone, his one eye was shut, his other eye was a star-shaped hole, his eyebrows were thin and arched like a woman's, his nose was undamaged, there was a slight tear at the lobe of one ear, his clean black hair was swept upward into a cowlick at the rear of the skull, his forehead was lightly freckled, his fingernails were clean, the skin at his left cheek was peeled back in three ragged strips, his right cheek was smooth and hairless, there was a butterfly on his chin, his neck was open to the spinal cord and the blood there was thick and shiny and it was this wound that had killed him. He lay face-up in the centre of the trail, a slim, dead, almost dainty young man. He had bony legs, a narrow waist, long shapely fingers. His chest was sunken and poorly muscled — a scholar, maybe. His wrists were the wrists of a child. He wore a black shirt, black pajama pants, a grey ammunition belt, a gold ring on the third finger of his right hand. His rubber sandals had been blown off. One lay beside him, the other a few metres up the trail. He had been born, maybe, in 1946 in the village of My Khe near the central coastline of Quang Ngai Province, where his parents farmed, and where his family had lived for several centuries, and where, during the time of the French, his father and two uncles and many neighbours had joined in the struggle for independence. He was not a Communist. He was a citizen and a soldier. In the village of My Khe, as in all of Quang Ngai, patriotic resistance had the force of tradition, which was partly the force of legend, and from his earliest boyhood the man I killed had listened to stories about the heroic Trung sisters and Tran Hung Dao's famous rout of the Mongols and Le Loi's final victory against the Chinese at Tot Dong. He had been taught that to defend the land was a man's highest duty and highest privilege. He accepted this. It was never open to question. Secretly, though, it also frightened him. He was not a fighter. His health was poor, his body small and frail. He liked books. He wanted someday to be a teacher of mathematics. At night, lying on his mat, he could not picture himself doing the brave things his father had done, or his uncles, or the heroes of other stories. He hoped in his heart that he would never be tested. He hoped the Americans would go away. Soon, he hoped. He kept hoping and hoping, always, even when he was asleep.

"Oh, man, you fuckin' trashed the fucker," Azar said. "You scrambled his sorry self, look at that, you *did*, you laid him out like Shredded fuckin' Wheat."

"Go away," Kiowa said.

"I'm just saying the truth. Like oatmeal."

"Go," Kiowa said.

"Okay, then, I take it back," Azar said. He started to move away, then stopped and said, "Rice Krispies, you know? On the dead test, this particular individual gets A-plus."

Smiling at this, he shrugged and walked up the trail toward the village behind the trees.

Kiowa kneeled down.

"Just forget that crud," he said. He opened up his canteen and held it out for a while and then sighed and pulled it away. "No sweat, man. What else could you do?"

Later, Kiowa said, "I'm serious. Nothing *anybody* could do. Come on, Tim, stop staring."

The trail junction was shaded by a row of trees and tall brush. The slim young man lay with his legs in the shade. His jaw was in his throat. His one eye was shut and the other was a star-shaped hole.

Kiowa glanced at the body.

"All right, let me ask a question," he said. "You want to trade places with him? Turn it all upside down — you *want* that? I mean, be honest."

The star-shaped hole was red and yellow. The yellow part seemed to be getting wider, spreading out at the centre of the star. The upper lip and gum and teeth were gone. The man's head was cocked at a wrong angle, as if loose at the neck, and the neck was wet with blood.

"Think it over," Kiowa said.

Then later he said, "Tim, it's a *war*. The guy wasn't Heidi — he had a weapon, right? It's a tough thing, for sure, but you got to cut out that staring."

Then he said, "Maybe you better lie down a minute."

Then after a long empty time he said, "Take it slow. Just go wherever the spirit takes you."

The butterfly was making its way along the young man's forehead, which was spotted with small dark freckles. The nose was undamaged. The skin on the right cheek was smooth and fine-grained and hairless. Frail-looking, delicately boned, the young man had never wanted to be a soldier and in his heart had feared that he would perform badly in battle. Even as a boy growing up in the village of My Khe, he had often worried about this.

He imagined covering his head and lying in a deep hole and closing his eyes and not moving until the war was over. He had no stomach for violence. He loved mathematics. His eyebrows were thin and arched like a woman's, and at school the boys sometimes teased him about how pretty he was, the arched eyebrows and long shapely fingers, and on the playground they would mimic a woman's walk and make fun of his smooth skin and his love for mathematics. He could not make himself fight them. He often wanted to, but he was afraid, and this increased his shame. If he could not fight little boys, he thought, how could he ever become a soldier and fight the Americans with their airplanes and helicopters and bombs? It did not seem possible. In the presence of his father and uncles, he pretended to look forward to doing his patriotic duty, which was also a privilege, but at night he prayed with his mother that the war might end soon. Beyond anything else, he was afraid of disgracing himself, and therefore his family and village. But all he could do, he thought, was wait and pray and try not to grow up too fast.

20 "Listen to me," Kiowa said. "You feel terrible, I know that."

21 Then he said, "Okay, maybe I *don't* know."

22 Along the trail there were small blue flowers shaped like bells. The young man's head was wrenched sideways, not quite facing the flowers, and even in the shade a single blade of sunlight sparkled against the buckle of his ammunition belt. The left cheek was peeled back in three ragged strips. The wounds at his neck had not yet clotted, which made him seem animate even in death, the blood still spreading out across his shirt.

23 Kiowa shook his head.

24 There was some silence before he said, "Stop *staring*."

25 The young man's fingernails were clean. There was a slight tear at the lobe of one ear, a sprinkling of blood on the forearm. He wore a gold ring on the third finger of his right hand. His chest was sunken and poorly muscled — a scholar, maybe. For years, despite his family's poverty, the man I killed had been determined to continue his education in mathematics. The means for this were arranged, perhaps, through the village liberation cadres, and in 1964 the young man began attending classes at the university in Saigon, where he avoided politics and paid attention to the problems of calculus. He devoted himself to his studies. He spent his nights alone, wrote romantic poems in his journal, took pleasure in the grace and beauty of differential equations. The war, he knew, would finally take him, but for the time being he would not let himself think about it. He had stopped praying; instead, now, he waited. And as he waited, in his final year at the university, he fell in love with a classmate, a girl of seventeen, who one day

told him that his wrists were like the wrists of a child, so small and delicate, and who admired his narrow waist and the cowlick that rose up like a bird's tail at the back of his head. She liked his quiet manner; she laughed at his freckles and bony legs. One evening, perhaps, they exchanged gold rings.

Now one eye was a star.

"You okay?" Kiowa said.

The body lay almost entirely in the shade. There were gnats at the mouth, little flecks of pollen drifting above the nose. The butterfly was gone. The bleeding had stopped except for the neck wounds.

Kiowa picked up the rubber sandals, clapping off the dirt, then bent down to search the body. He found a pouch of rice, a comb, a fingernail clipper, a few soiled piastres, a snapshot of a young woman standing in front of a parked motorcycle. Kiowa placed these items in his rucksack along with the grey ammunition belt and rubber sandals.

Then he squatted down.

"I'll tell you the straight truth," he said. "The guy was dead the second he stepped on the trail. Understand me? We all had him zeroed. A good kill — weapon, ammunition, everything." Tiny beads of sweat glistened at Kiowa's forehead. His eyes moved from the sky to the dead man's body to the knuckles of his own hands. "So listen, you have to pull your shit together. Can't just sit there all day."

Later he said, "Understand?"

Then he said, "Five minutes, Tim. Five more minutes and we're moving out."

The one eye did a funny twinkling trick, red to yellow. His head was wrenched sideways, as if loose at the neck, and the dead young man seemed to be staring at some distant object beyond the bell-shaped flowers along the trail. The blood at the neck had gone to a deep purplish black. Clean fingernails, clean hair — he had been a soldier for only a single day. After his years at the university, the man I killed returned with his new wife to the village of My Khe, where he enlisted as a common rifleman with the 48th Vietcong Battalion. He knew he would die quickly. He knew he would see a flash of light. He knew he would fall dead and wake up in the stories of his village and people.

Kiowa covered the body with a poncho.

"Hey, Tim, you're looking better," he said. "No doubt about it. All you needed was time — some mental R&R."

Then he said, "Man, I'm sorry."

Then later he said, "Why not talk about it?"

39   Then he said, "Come on, man, talk."
40   He was a slim, dead, almost dainty young man of about twenty. He lay with one leg bent beneath him, his jaw in his throat, his face neither expressive nor inexpressive. One eye was shut. The other was a star-shaped hole.
41   "Talk to me," Kiowa said.

1991

NOTES

Although the title is "The Man *I* Killed" (my italics), you will find the "I" used only twice, both times in the repetition of the title phrase. There is a certain detachment or objectivity in the telling when the narrator hides the self ("I"). The focus is on the dead soldier.

R & R Rest and recreation.

Heidi A female character in the classic children's story *Heidi* (1881) by Johanna Spyri (1829–1901). She is sweet, friendly, and helpful.

Tim O'Brien uses some of his own war experiences as the foundation for this story and for others in the collection *The Things They Carried*. He even uses his own name for the character of the storyteller. He adds a wrinkle here. The dead Vietcong's life as imagined by the soldier Tim is really what happened to Tim O'Brien the writer. If you remove local references, the core is autobiographical.

Tim the soldier is projecting his own story onto the dead Vietcong. Projection is a psychological term that describes how a person having certain experiences or feelings attributes them to someone or something else.

Quang Ngai A province in Vietnam.

Trung sisters Two widows, Trung Trac and Trung Nhi, who led an uprising against foreign rule in 39 A.D.

Tran Hung Dao The Vietnamese general (1213–1300) who defeated Kublai Khan's army of Mongols.

Le Loi A Vietnamese emperor (1428–1433) and hero for his fight against the Chinese.

COMPREHENSION AND DISCUSSION

1. What is the theme of this story?
2. Who are the two friends of the protagonist? How are they different from one another?
3. How are the three characters' attitudes revealed? What are their attitudes toward the dead man?
4. What story does the protagonist create about the dead man? Why does he make up such a story? Who is the narrator really talking about?
5. Observe Kiowa's speech. How does he change? How does the writer make this obvious?
6. Why does the writer have the character repeat certain details in his description of the dead soldier?
7. Why does the writer choose to open the story with the aftermath of an ambush? Should the writer have described the attack in detail?
8. What is the tone of this story?

LITERARY TECHNIQUES

Autobiographical fiction is a literary category in which the writer recounts aspects of his life in fictional form. However, these events probably did not occur exactly as the writer presents them in the story. It is important to realize that the story is fictional even though it may contain biographical events.

This story is static in that Tim the soldier does not move; even Kiowa and Azar have limited movement and action. The extended paragraphs reveal Tim's thoughts; the dialogue is reserved for his two buddies. The story then is, therefore, a psychological study.

Sentence structure The opening sentence beginning with "His jaw..." and concluding with "...this wound that had killed him" (p. 170) is not only long but also detailed in its description of the dead soldier. Long sentences tend to be descriptive and informative; short sentences, emphatic, attention-getting, and succinct. Notice the shorter sentences near the end of the paragraph. Because of their brevity, the sentences sound choppy, thus changing the rhythm or flow.

Paragraphing O'Brien has three very long paragraphs in which he talks about the dead enemy. This technique merits mentioning. First, like the long sentence, the lengthy paragraph reveals the workings of Tim the soldier's mind. Second, Tim the soldier imagines a life that the dead Vietcong never had. The first half of a long paragraph is description and the last half is the invented life Tim gives to the fallen soldier. In the first paragraph the word "maybe" begins the imagined biography. Each successive long paragraph adds different details to the Vietcong's "life."

Repetition Repeating words and ideas shows Tim the soldier's preoccupation with his first kill. The recurring images of the butterfly, the star-shaped wound, and fingers gain symbolic value: the delicacy of the man and the fragility of life.

Language There is sharp contrast in the thoughts of Tim the soldier and in the speeches by his two buddies, especially Azar's. In Tim's mind, the diction and vocabulary are almost formalized, whereas in the dialogues, the expletive words and phrases reveal a coarse reality.

ASSIGNMENTS

1. What does this story say about war and combat, or about soldiers?
2. This story has no action in the traditional sense. Analyze the story to show how the writer captures the reader's attention and interest.
3. Explain the ending in which Kiowa says: "Talk to me" (p. 174). How has he changed even though Tim never spoke to him at all?
4. David Arnason's "A Girl's Story" (p. 22) is metafiction, writing that refers to the process of writing. Does O'Brien's story have elements of this technique? If so, how?
5. Read George Orwell's "Shooting an Elephant" (p. 314). How do both stories focus on states of mind? Explain the similarities.

The Cask of Amontillado
Edgar Allan Poe

The thousand injuries of Fortunato I had borne as I best could, but when he ventured upon insult I vowed revenge. You, who so well know the nature of my soul, will not suppose, however, that I gave utterance to a threat. *At length* I would be avenged; this was a point definitely settled—but the very definitiveness with which it was resolved precluded the idea of risk. I must not only punish but punish with impunity. A wrong is unredressed when retribution overtakes its redresser. It is equally unredressed when the avenger fails to make himself felt as such to him who has done the wrong.

It must be understood that neither by word nor deed had I given Fortunato cause to doubt my goodwill. I continued, as was my wont, to smile in his face, and he did not perceive that my smile *now* was at the thought of his immolation.

He had a weak point—this Fortunato—although in other regards he was a man to be respected and even feared. He prided himself on his connoisseurship in wine. Few Italians have the true virtuoso spirit. For the most part their enthusiasm is adopted to suit the time and opportunity, to practise imposture upon the British and Austrian *millionaires*. In painting and gemmary, Fortunato, like his countrymen, was a quack, but in the matter of old wines he was sincere. In this respect I did not differ from him materially;—I was skillful in the Italian vintages myself, and bought largely whenever I could.

It was about dusk, one evening during the supreme madness of the carnival season, that I encountered my friend. He accosted me with excessive warmth, for he had been drinking much. The man wore motley. He had on a tight-fitting parti-striped dress, and his head was surmounted by the conical cap and bells. I was so pleased to see him that I thought I should never have done wringing his hand.

I said to him—"My dear Fortunato, you are luckily met. How remarkably well you are looking today! But I have received a pipe of what passes for Amontillado, and I have my doubts."

"How?" said he. "Amontillado? A pipe? Impossible! And in the middle of the carnival!"

"I have my doubts," I replied; "and I was silly enough to pay the full Amontillado price without consulting you in the matter. You were not to be found, and I was fearful of losing a bargain."

8 "Amontillado!"
9 "I have my doubts."
10 "Amontillado!"
11 "And I must satisfy them."
12 "Amontillado!"
13 "As you are engaged, I am on my way to Luchresi. If anyone has a critical turn it is he. He will tell me—"
14 "Luchresi cannot tell Amontillado from Sherry."
15 "And yet some fools will have it that his taste is a match for your own."
16 "Come, let us go."
17 "Whither?"
18 "To your vaults."
19 "My friend, no; I will not impose upon your good nature. I perceive you have an engagement. Luchresi—"
20 "I have no engagement;—come."
21 "My friend, no. It is not the engagement, but the severe cold with which I perceive you are afflicted. The vaults are insufferably damp. They are encrusted with nitre."
22 "Let us go, nevertheless. The cold is merely nothing. Amontillado! You have been imposed upon. And as for Luchresi, he cannot distinguish Sherry from Amontillado."
23 Thus speaking, Fortunato possessed himself of my arm; and putting on a mask of black silk and drawing a *roquelaure* closely about my person, I suffered him to hurry me to my palazzo.
24 There were no attendants at home; they had absconded to make merry in honour of the time. I had told them that I should not return until the morning, and had given them explicit orders not to stir from the house. These orders were sufficient, I well knew, to insure their immediate disappearance, one and all, as soon as my back was turned.
25 I took from their sconces two flambeaux, and giving one to Fortunato, bowed him through several suites of rooms to the archway that led into the vaults. I passed down a long and winding staircase, requesting him to be cautious as he followed. We came at length to the foot of the descent, and stood together on the damp ground of the catacombs of the Montresors.
26 The gait of my friend was unsteady, and the bells upon his cap jingled as he strode.
27 "The pipe," said he.
28 "It is farther on," said I; "but observe the white webwork which gleams from these cavern walls."
29 He turned towards me, and looked into my eyes with two filmy orbs that distilled the rheum of intoxication.

"Nitre?" he asked at length.

"Nitre," I replied. "How long have you had that cough?"

"Ugh! ugh! ugh!—ugh! ugh! ugh!—ugh! ugh! ugh!—ugh! ugh! ugh!—ugh! ugh! ugh!"

My poor friend found it impossible to reply for many minutes.

"It is nothing," he said at last.

"Come," I said, with decision, "we will go back; your health is precious. You are rich, respected, admired, beloved; you are happy, as once I was. You are a man to be missed. For me it is no matter. We will go back; you will be ill, and I cannot be responsible. Besides, there is Luchresi—"

"Enough," he said; "the cough is a mere nothing; it will not kill me. I shall not die of a cough."

"True—true," I replied; "and, indeed, I had no intention of alarming you unnecessarily—but you should use all proper caution. A draught of this Médoc will defend us from the damps."

Here I knocked off the neck of a bottle which I drew from a long row of its fellows that lay upon the mould.

"Drink," I said, presenting him the wine.

He raised it to his lips with a leer. He paused and nodded to me familiarly, while his bells jingled.

"I drink," he said, "to the buried that repose around us."

"And I to your long life."

He again took my arm, and we proceeded.

"These vaults," he said, "are extensive."

"The Montresors," I replied, "were a great and numerous family."

"I forget your arms."

"A huge human foot d'or, in a field azure; the foot crushes a serpent rampant whose fangs are imbedded in the heel."

"And the motto?"

"Nemo me impune lacessit."

"Good!" he said.

The wine sparkled in his eyes and the bells jingled. My own fancy grew warm with the Médoc. We had passed through long walls of piled skeletons, with casks and puncheons intermingling, into the inmost recesses of the catacombs. I paused again, and this time I made bold to seize Fortunato by an arm above the elbow.

"The nitre!" I said; "see, it increases. It hangs like moss upon the vaults. We are below the river's bed. The drops of moisture trickle among the bones. Come, we will go back ere it is too late. Your cough—"

"It is nothing," he said; "let us go on. But first, another draught of the Médoc."

54 I broke and reached him a flagon of De Grâve. He emptied it at a breath. His eyes flashed with a fierce light. He laughed and threw the bottle upward with a gesticulation I did not understand.

55 I looked at him in surprise. He repeated the movement—a grotesque one.

56 "You do not comprehend?" he said.

57 "Not I," I replied.

58 "Then you are not of the brotherhood."

59 "How?"

60 "You are not of the masons."

61 "Yes, yes," I said; "yes, yes."

62 "You? Impossible! A mason?"

63 "A mason," I replied.

64 "A sign," he said, "a sign."

65 "It is this," I answered, producing from beneath the folds of my *roquelaure* a trowel.

66 "You jest," he exclaimed, recoiling a few paces. "But let us proceed to the Amontillado."

67 "Be it so," I said, replacing the tool beneath the cloak and again offering him my arm. He leaned upon it heavily. We continued our route in search of the Amontillado. We passed through a range of low arches, descended, passed on, and descending again, arrived at a deep crypt, in which the foulness of the air caused our flambeaux rather to glow than flame.

68 At the most remote end of the crypt there appeared another less spacious. Its walls had been lined with human remains, piled to the vault overhead, in the fashion of the great catacombs of Paris. Three sides of this interior crypt were still ornamented in this manner. From the fourth the bones had been thrown down, and lay promiscuously upon the earth, forming at one point a mound of some size. Within the wall thus exposed by the displacing of the bones, we perceived a still interior crypt or recess, in depth about four feet, in width three, in height six or seven. It seemed to have been constructed for no especial use within itself, but formed merely the interval between two of the colossal supports of the roof of the catacombs, and was backed by one of their circumscribing walls of solid granite.

69 It was in vain that Fortunato, uplifting his dull torch, endeavoured to pry into the depth of the recess. Its termination the feeble light did not enable us to see.

70 "Proceed," I said; "herein is the Amontillado. As for Luchresi—"

"He is an ignoramus," interrupted my friend, as he stepped unsteadily forward, while I followed immediately at his heels. In an instant he had reached the extremity of the niche, and finding his progress arrested by the rock, stood stupidly bewildered. A moment more and I had fettered him to the granite. In its surface were two iron staples, distant from each other about two feet, horizontally. From one of these depended a short chain, from the other a padlock. Throwing the links about his waist, it was but the work of a few seconds to secure it. He was too much astounded to resist. Withdrawing the key I stepped back from the recess.

"Pass your hand," I said, "over the wall; you cannot help feeling the nitre. Indeed it is *very* damp. Once more let me *implore* you to return. No? Then I must positively leave you. But I must first render you all the little attentions in my power."

"The Amontillado!" ejaculated my friend, not yet recovered from his astonishment.

"True," I replied; "the Amontillado."

As I said these words I busied myself among the pile of bones of which I have before spoken. Throwing them aside, I soon uncovered a quantity of building stone and mortar. With these materials and with the aid of my trowel, I began vigorously to wall up the entrance of the niche.

I had scarcely laid the first tier of the masonry when I discovered that the intoxication of Fortunato had in a great measure worn off. The earliest indication I had of this was a low moaning cry from the depth of the recess. It was *not* the cry of a drunken man. There was a long and obstinate silence. I laid the second tier, and the third, and the fourth; and then I heard the furious vibrations of the chain. The noise lasted for several minutes, during which, that I might hearken to it with the more satisfaction, I ceased my labours and sat down upon the bones. When at last the clanking subsided, I resumed the trowel, and finished without interruption the fifth, the sixth, and the seventh tier. The wall was now nearly upon a level with my breast. I again paused, and holding the flambeaux over the masonwork, threw a few feeble rays upon the figure within.

A succession of loud and shrill screams, bursting suddenly from the throat of the chained form, seemed to thrust me violently back. For a brief moment I hesitated, I trembled. Unsheathing my rapier, I began to grope with it about the recess; but the thought of an instant reassured me. I placed my hand upon the solid fabric of the catacombs, and felt satisfied. I reapproached the wall; I replied to the yells of him who clamoured. I re-echoed, I aided, I surpassed them in volume and in strength. I did this, and the clamourer grew still.

78   It was now midnight, and my task was drawing to a close. I had completed the eighth, the ninth, and the tenth tier. I had finished a portion of the last and the eleventh; there remained but a single stone to be fitted and plastered in. I struggled with its weight; I placed it partially in its destined position. But now there came from out the niche a low laugh that erected the hairs upon my head. It was succeeded by a sad voice, which I had difficulty in recognizing as that of the noble Fortunato. The voice said—

79   "Ha! ha! ha!—he! he! he!—a very good joke, indeed—an excellent jest. We will have many a rich laugh about it at the palazzo—he! he! he!—over our wine—he! he! he!"

80   "The Amontillado!" I said.

81   "He! he! he!—he! he! he!—yes, the Amontillado. But is it not getting late? Will not they be awaiting us at the palazzo, the Lady Fortunato and the rest? Let us be gone."

82   "Yes," I said, "let us be gone."

83   *"For the love of God, Montresor!"*

84   "Yes," I said, "for the love of God!"

85   But to these words I hearkened in vain for a reply. I grew impatient. I called aloud—

86   "Fortunato!"

87   No answer. I called again—

88   "Fortunato!"

89   No answer still. I thrust a torch through the remaining aperture and let it fall within. There came forth in return only a jingling of the bells. My heart grew sick; it was the dampness of the catacombs that made it so. I hastened to make an end of my labour. I forced the last stone into its position; I plastered it up. Against the new masonry I re-erected the old rampart of bones. For the half of a century no mortal has disturbed them. *In pace requiescat!*

1846

NOTES

Edgar Alan Poe (1809–1849) was an American writer; he is known for scary stories and poems.

Roquelaure   A knee-length cloak of the 18th century. It was a popular garment, often adorned with silk and fur.

Palazzo Italian for "a stately home, a palace."

D'or French for "of gold."

Nemo me impune lacessit Latin for "no one hurts me without penalty." Poe has taken this motto from the royal arms of Scotland and the Order of the Thistle.

Fortunato's reference to the masons' brotherhood is to the Free and Accepted Masons, popularly known as Freemasons, an international organization with secret signs and rituals. This secret society has a long and colourful history. Because Montresor is not a member, he has reason to fear reprisals should the masons discover his crime.

Montresor shows the trowel to Fortunato and declares himself a mason. The avenger's meaning is different from the victim's. This trowel foreshadows events to follow.

Catacomb An underground cemetery with long tunnels and recesses for graves. During the persecution of early Christians by the Romans, catacombs were popular places of sanctuary and made convenient burial grounds.

In pace requiescat! Latin for "May he rest in peace!" Note the irony as Montresor says this prayer.

COMPREHENSION AND DISCUSSION

1. What kind of insult would make Montresor plot his revenge?
2. Show the various steps that Montresor has taken to secure vengeance.
3. Does Montresor know human behaviour? How? Cite at least three examples.
4. Explain the importance of Fortunato's costume to the story.
5. Does Fortunato deserve his fate?
6. How do you know that this story is told in flashback? Why is this technique effective?
7. To whom is Montresor confessing this dastardly crime? Why? What punishment does he wish to evade, now at his deathbed?
8. Is there a surprise ending here? Or, why are you not surprised? Is there suspense?

LITERARY TECHNIQUES

The names of characters are important to the telling of the story. *Montresor* means "my treasure" in French, and everything about him shows that his treasure is himself. He and his whole family are vain and egotistical. Note the declaration in the Montresors' coat of arms. On the other hand, *Fortunato*, which means "the lucky one," is used ironically; he is a most unlucky man.

The Latin mottoes and expressions lend authenticity to setting, show the social status of the characters, and imply a classical education.

To create an atmosphere of dread, Poe has both Montresor and Fortunato descend deeper into the catacombs. This downward movement can be a metaphor for the depths of hell or of the human soul. In addition, the dampness and Fortunato's persistent cough suggest it is an unhealthy place to be.

Poe uses first-person narration. The speaker and main character is Montresor, the villain. Usually, in first-person point of view, the protagonist is good or virtuous so that the reader can identify with the hero. However, Poe gives a twist to this convention: by having Montresor as the narrator, the author reveals the twisted mind of his character.

The "you" addressed in the opening does not refer to the reader, although that is the usual interpretation upon first reading. "You" is made clear at the end when Montresor confesses his 50-year-old crime to a priest. This sleight of hand is deliberate so that the story sounds more intimate than it is.

ASSIGNMENTS

1. Discuss the common elements of horror stories present in this story.
2. Explain the concept of revenge. When is it justified? There is a saying that revenge is a dish best enjoyed cold. Discuss the validity of this saying.
3. A short film has been made of this story. Watch it and write a critique.
4. Read another of Poe's stories and compare it with this one.
5. Research the Freemasons and write a short explanatory essay.
6. Read Pico Iyer's "Of Weirdos and Eccentrics" (p. 289). Is Montresor an eccentric or a weirdo? Why?

7. Horror stories are usually a study of abnormal people or ordinary people put in an abnormal situation. Is this statement valid? Write a persuasive paper using any of these classic stories of terror: "The Lottery" (p. 105), "The Monkey's Paw" (p. 116), or "The Cask of Amontillado."

The Open Window

Saki (H.H. Munro)

1. "My aunt will be down presently, Mr. Nuttel," said a very self-possessed young lady of fifteen; "in the meantime you must try and put up with me."

2. Framton Nuttel endeavoured to say the correct something which should duly flatter the niece of the moment without unduly discounting the aunt that was to come. Privately he doubted more than ever whether these formal visits on a succession of total strangers would do much towards helping the nerve cure which he was supposed to be undergoing.

3. "I know how it will be," his sister had said when he was preparing to migrate to this rural retreat; "you will bury yourself down there and not speak to a living soul, and your nerves will be worse than ever from moping. I shall just give you letters of introduction to all the people I know there. Some of them, as far as I can remember, were quite nice."

4. Framton wondered whether Mrs. Sappleton, the lady to whom he was presenting one of the letters of introduction, came into the nice division.

5. "Do you know many of the people round here?" asked the niece, when she judged that they had had sufficient silent communion.

6. "Hardly a soul," said Framton. "My sister was staying here, at the rectory, you know, some four years ago, and she gave me letters of introduction to some of the people here."

7. He made the last statement in a tone of distinct regret.

8. "Then you know practically nothing about my aunt?" pursued the self-possessed young lady.

9. "Only her name and address," admitted the caller. He was wondering whether Mrs. Sappleton was in the married or widowed state. An undefinable something about the room seemed to suggest masculine habitation.

10. "Her great tragedy happened just three years ago," said the child; "that would be since your sister's time."

11. "Her tragedy?" asked Framton; somehow in this restful country spot tragedies seemed out of place.

12. "You may wonder why we keep that window wide open on an October afternoon," said the niece, indicating a large French window that opened on to a lawn.

"It is quite warm for the time of the year," said Framton, "but has that window got anything to do with the tragedy?"

"Out through that window, three years ago to a day, her husband and her two young brothers went off for their day's shooting. They never came back. In crossing the moor to their favourite snipe-shooting ground they were all three engulfed in a treacherous piece of bog. It had been that dreadful wet summer, you know, and places that were safe in other years gave way suddenly without warning. Their bodies were never recovered. That was the dreadful part of it." Here the child's voice lost its self-possessed note and became falteringly human. "Poor aunt always thinks that they will come back some day, they and the little brown spaniel that was lost with them, and walk in at that window just as they used to do. That is why the window is kept open every evening till it is quite dusk. Poor dear aunt, she has often told me how they went out, her husband with his white waterproof coat over his arm, and Ronnie, her youngest brother, singing 'Bertie, why do you bound?' as he always did to tease her, because she said it got on her nerves. Do you know, sometimes on still, quiet evenings like this, I almost get a creepy feeling that they will all walk in through that window—"

She broke off with a little shudder. It was a relief to Framton when the aunt bustled into the room with a whirl of apologies for being late in making her appearance.

"I hope Vera has been amusing you?" she said.

"She has been very interesting," said Framton.

"I hope you don't mind the open window," said Mrs. Sappleton briskly; "my husband and brothers will be home directly from shooting, and they always come in this way. They've been out for snipe in the marshes today, so they'll make a fine mess over my poor carpets. So like you menfolk, isn't it?"

She rattled on cheerfully about the shooting and the scarcity of birds, and the prospects for duck in the winter. To Framton it was all purely horrible. He made a desperate but only partially successful effort to turn the talk on to a less ghastly topic, he was conscious that his hostess was giving him only a fragment of her attention, and her eyes were constantly straying past him to the open window and the lawn beyond. It was certainly an unfortunate coincidence that he should have paid his visit on this tragic anniversary.

"The doctors agree in ordering me complete rest, an absence of mental excitement, and avoidance of anything in the nature of violent physical exercise," announced Framton, who laboured under the tolerably widespread delusion that total strangers and chance acquaintances are hungry for the least detail of one's ailments and infirmities, their cause and cure. "On the matter of diet they are not so much in agreement," he continued.

21 "No?" said Mrs. Sappleton, in a voice which only replaced a yawn at the last moment. Then she suddenly brightened into alert attention — but not to what Framton was saying.

22 "Here they are at last!" she cried. "Just in time for tea, and don't they look as if they were muddy up to the eyes!"

23 Framton shivered slightly and turned towards the niece with a look intended to convey sympathetic comprehension. The child was staring out through the open window with dazed horror in her eyes. In a chill shock of nameless fear Framton swung round in his seat and looked in the same direction.

24 In the deepening twilight three figures were walking across the lawn towards the window; they all carried guns under their arms, and one of them was additionally burdened with a white coat hung over his shoulders. A tired brown spaniel kept close at their heels. Noiselessly they neared the house, and then a hoarse young voice chanted out of the dusk: "I said, Bertie, why do you bound?"

25 Framton grabbed wildly at his stick and hat; the hall door, the gravel drive, and the front gate were dimly noted stages in his headlong retreat. A cyclist coming along the road had to run into the hedge to avoid imminent collision.

26 "Here we are, my dear," said the bearer of the white mackintosh, coming in through the window, "fairly muddy, but most of it's dry. Who was that who bolted out as we came up?"

27 "A most extraordinary man, a Mr. Nuttel," said Mrs. Sappleton; "could only talk about his illnesses, and dashed off without a word of good-bye or apology when you arrived. One would think he had seen a ghost."

28 "I expect it was the spaniel," said the niece calmly; "he told me he had a horror of dogs. He was once hunted into a cemetery somewhere on the banks of the Ganges by a pack of pariah dogs, and had to spend the night in a newly dug grave with the creatures snarling and grinning and foaming just above him. Enough to make anyone lose their nerve."

29 Romance at short notice was her speciality.

1914

NOTES

Saki is the pen name of H.H. Munro (1870–1916), an English writer.

What is described as a "French window" in the story we would more likely call "French doors."

Letters of introduction were used to gain access into upper-middle-class and aristocratic society. They were not only a formality but a necessity in doing business and in social gatherings.

Notice the use of the word "romance" in the last sentence. We think of the word to mean "a love story," but other meanings of the word refer to fiction and storytelling.

COMPREHENSION AND DISCUSSION

1. What caused the girl, Vera, to spin such a tale? Would she have done so if Framton was not a stranger in these parts?
2. Why does Framton believe the girl's story?
3. Discuss Framton's character. If this story were to be filmed, which actors would be suitable to play the part of Framton, and which would be unlikely? Explain your reasoning.
4. What kind of person is Mrs. Sappleton?
5. Explain the humour in the story.
6. Why is this story effectively told?

LITERARY TECHNIQUES

Names that reflect character or personality traits are a staple method writers use as shortcuts to character development. The technique is like stereotyping. For example, the name "Framton Nuttel" immediately cues the reader to his character. His name suggests a weak person. His surname is a play on the words "nut all."

The name "Vera" comes from the Latin word for truth, *veritas*. Thus, the young lady who tells tall tales is ironically named "truth."

Although written in the third-person singular, much of this story is told through dialogue. Since Framton Nuttel has come to visit the Sappletons and therefore is expected to socialize by talking, the medium is conversation, an oral delivery of information. It is logical then to have Framton reveal his weakness and Vera to spin her tale in dialogue.

ASSIGNMENTS

1. Read Stephen Leacock's "My Financial Career" (p. 145). Compare the narrator in Leacock's story with Framton Nuttel.
2. Describe a practical joke, or hoax, you have played on someone or have experienced yourself. What is required to make a hoax a success?
3. Find another short story by Saki and compare it with "The Open Window."
4. Compare the short film of "The Open Window" with the original story.
5. Vera has taken advantage of Nuttel. Write a paragraph defending the visitor, or admonishing the girl.
6. Comedy or humour has a cruel streak. Someone or something is ridiculed, mocked, and made fun of all for a laugh. Debate the issue of what makes people laugh. Perhaps you can compare this story with a current situation comedy on TV.
7. Research 19th-century etiquette for visiting. Choose one aspect, such as calling cards or letters of introduction, and write an explanation.

Red Plaid Shirt
Diane Schoemperlen

RED PLAID SHIRT that your mother bought you one summer in Banff. It is 100% Pure Virgin Wool, itchy but flattering against your pale skin, your black hair. You got it in a store called Western Outfitters, of the sort indigenous to the region, which stocked only *real* (as opposed to designer) blue jeans, Stetson hats, and $300 hand-tooled cowboy boots with very pointy toes. There was a saddle and a stuffed deer-head in the window.

Outside, the majestic mountains are sitting all around, magnanimously letting their pictures be taken by ten thousand tourists wielding Japanese cameras and eating ice-cream cones. You had tricked your mother into leaving her camera in the car so she wouldn't embarrass you, who lived there and were supposed to be taking the scenery for granted by now.

You liked the red plaid shirt so much that she bought you two more just like it, one plain green, the other chocolate brown. But these two stayed shirts, never acquiring any particular significance, eventually getting left unceremoniously behind in a Salvation Army drop-box in a grocery-store parking lot somewhere along the way.

The red plaid shirt reminded you of your mother's gardening shirt, which was also plaid and which you rescued one winter when she was going to throw it away because the elbows were out. You picture her kneeling in the side garden where she grew only flowers — bleeding hearts, roses, peonies, poppies — and a small patch of strawberries. You picture her hair in a bright babushka, her hands in the black earth with her shirtsleeves rolled up past the elbow. The honeysuckle hedge bloomed fragrantly behind her and the sweet peas curled interminably up the white trellis. You are sorry now for the way you always sulked and whined when she asked you to help, for the way you hated the dirt under your nails and the sweat running into your eyes, the sweat dripping down her shirtfront between her small breasts. You kept her old shirt in a bag in your closet for years, with a leather patch half-sewn onto the left sleeve, but now you can't find it.

5   You were wearing the red plaid shirt the night you met Daniel in the tavern where he was drinking beer with his buddies from the highway construction crew. You ended up living with him for the next five years. He was always calling it your "magic shirt," teasing you, saying how it was the shirt that made him fall in love with you in the first place. You would tease him back, saying how you'd better hang on to it then, in case you had to use it on somebody else. You've even worn it in that spirit a few times since, but the magic seems to have seeped out of it and you are hardly surprised.

6   You've gained a little weight since then or the shirt has shrunk, so you can't wear it any more, but you can't throw or give it away either.

7   RED: crimson carmine cochineal cinnabar sanguine scarlet red ruby rouge my birthstone red and blood-red brick-red beet-red bleeding hearts Queen of fire god of war Mars the colour of magic my magic the colour of iron flowers and fruit the colour of meat dripping lobster cracking claws lips nipples blisters blood my blood and all power.

8   **BLUE COTTON SWEATSHIRT**
that says "Why Be Normal?" in a circle on the front. This is your comfort shirt, fleecy on the inside, soft from many washings, and three sizes too big so you can tuck your hands up inside the sleeves when they're shaking or cold. You like to sit on the couch with the curtains closed, wearing your comfort shirt, eating comfort food: vanilla ice cream, macaroni and cheese, white rice with butter and salt, white toast with CheezWhiz and peanut butter. Sometimes you even sleep in it.

9   This is the shirt you wore when you had the abortion three days before Christmas. They told you to be there at nine in the morning and then you didn't get into the operating room until nearly twelve-thirty. So you wore it in the waiting room with the other women also waiting, and the weight you had already gained was hidden beneath it while you pretended to read *Better Homes and Gardens* and they wouldn't let you smoke. After you came to, you put the shirt back on and waited in another waiting room for your friend Alice to come and pick you up because they said you weren't capable yet of going home alone. One of the other women was waiting there too, for her boyfriend, who was always late, and when he finally got there, first she yelled at him briefly and then they decided to go to

McDonald's for a hamburger. At home, Alice pours you tea from the porcelain pot into white china cups like precious opaque stones.

None of this has diminished, as you feared it might, the comfort this shirt can give you when you need it. Alice always puts her arms around you whenever she sees you wearing it now. She has one just like it, only pink.

> BLUE: azure aqua turquoise delft and navy-blue royal-blue cerulean peacock-blue indigo ultramarine cobalt-blue Prussian-blue cyan the sky and electric a space the colour of the firmament and sapphire sleeping silence the sea and blues my lover plays the saxophone cool blue he plays the blues.

PALE GREY TURTLENECK
that you bought when you were seeing Dwight, who said one night for no apparent reason that grey is a mystical colour. You took this judgement to heart because Dwight was more likely to talk about hockey or carburetors and you were pleasantly surprised to discover that he might also think about other things. You spotted the turtleneck the very next day on sale at Maggie's for $9.99.

You took to wearing it on Sundays because that was the day Dwight was most likely to wander in, unannounced, on his way to or from somewhere else. You wore it while you just happened to put a bottle of good white wine into the fridge to chill and a chicken, a roast, or a pan of spinach lasagna into the oven to cook slowly just in case he showed up hungry. You suppose now that this was pathetic, but at the time you were thinking of yourself as patient and him as worth waiting for.

Three Sundays in a row you ended up passed out on the couch, the wine bottle empty on the coffee table, the supper dried out, and a black-and-white movie with violin music flickering on the TV. In the coloured morning, the pattern of the upholstery was imprinted on your cheek and your whole head was hurting. When Dwight finally did show up, it was a Wednesday and you were wearing your orange flannelette nightie with all the buttons gone and a rip down the front, because it was three in the morning, he was drunk, and you had been in bed for hours. He just laughed and took you in his arms when you told him to get lost. Until you said you were seeing someone else, which was a lie, but one that you both wanted to believe because it was an easy answer that let both of you gingerly off the hook.

15. You keep meaning to wear that turtleneck again sometime because you know it's juvenile to think it's a jinx, but then you keep forgetting to iron it.

16. Finally you get tough and wear it, wrinkled, grocery-shopping on Saturday afternoon. You careen through the aisles like a crazed hamster, dodging toddlers, old ladies, and other carts, scooping up vegetables with both hands, eating an apple you haven't paid for, leaving the core in the dairy section. But nothing happens and no one notices your turtleneck: the colour or the wrinkles.

17. Sure enough, Dwight calls the next day, Sunday, at five o'clock. You say you can't talk now, you're just cooking supper: prime rib, wild rice, broccoli with Hollandaise. You have no trouble at all hanging quietly up on him while pouring the wine into the crystal goblet before setting the table for one with the Royal Albert china your mother left you in her will.

18. GREY: oyster pewter slate dull lead dove-grey pearl-grey brain my brains silver or simple gone into the mystic a cool grey day overcast with clouds ashes concrete the aftermath of airplanes gunmetal-grey granite and gossamer whales elephants cats in the country the colour of questions the best camouflage the opaque elegance an oyster.

19. WHITE EMBROIDERED BLOUSE
that you bought for $80 to wear with your red-flowered skirt to a Christmas party with Peter, who was working as a pizza cook until he could afford to play his sax full-time. You also bought a silken red belt with gold beads and tassels, a pair of red earrings with dragons on them, and ribbed red stockings which are too small but you wanted them anyway. This striking outfit involves you and Alice in a whole day of trudging around downtown in a snowstorm, holding accessories up in front of mirrors like talismans.

20. You spend an hour in the bathroom getting ready, drinking white wine, plucking your eyebrows, dancing like a dervish, and smiling seductively at yourself. Peter calls to say he has to work late but he'll meet you there at midnight.

By the time he arrives, you are having a complex anatomical conversation with an intern named Fernando who has spilled a glass of red wine down the front of your blouse. He is going to be a plastic surgeon. Your blouse is soaking in the bathtub and you are wearing only your white lace camisole. Fernando is feeding you green grapes and little squares of cheese, complimenting your cheekbones, and falling in love with your smooth forehead. You are having the time of your life and it's funny how you notice for the first time that Peter has an inferior bone structure.

> WHITE: ivory alabaster magnolia milk the moon is full and chalk-white pure-white snow-white moonstone limestone rime and clay marble many seashells and my bones are china bones precious porcelain lace white magic white feather the immaculate conception of white lies wax white wine as a virtue.

YELLOW EVENING GOWN
that you bought for your New Year's Eve date with Fernando. It has a plunging neckline and a dropped sash which flatteringly accentuates your hips. You wear it with black hoop earrings, black lace stockings with seams, and black high-heels that Alice forced you to buy even though they hurt your toes and you are so uncoordinated that you expect you will have to spend the entire evening sitting down with your legs crossed, calves nicely flexed.

You spend an hour in the bathroom getting ready, drinking pink champagne, applying blusher with a fat brush according to a diagram in a women's magazine that shows you how to make the most of your face. You practise holding your chin up so it doesn't sag and look double. Alice French-braids your hair and teaches you how to waltz like a lady. Fernando calls to say he has to work late but he'll meet you there before midnight.

You go to the club with Alice instead. They seat you at a tiny table for two so that when you sit down, your knees touch hers. You are in the middle of a room full of candles, fresh flowers, lounge music, and well-groomed couples staring feverishly into each others' eyes. The meal is sumptuous: green salad, a whole lobster, home-made pasta, fresh asparagus, and warm buns wrapped in white linen in a wicker basket. You eat everything and then you get the hell out of there, leaving a message for Fernando.

26 You go down the street to a bar you know where they will let you in without a ticket even though it's New Year's Eve. In the lobby you meet Fernando in a tuxedo with his arm around a short homely woman in black who, when you ask, "Who the hell are you?", says, "His wife." In your black high-heels you are taller than both of them and you know your gown is gorgeous. When the wife says, "And who the hell are *you*?", you point a long finger at Fernando's nose and say, "Ask him." You stomp away with your chin up and your dropped sash swinging.

27 Out of sight, you take off your high-heels and walk home through the park and the snow with them in your hands, dangling. Alice follows in a cab. By the time you get there, your black lace stockings are in shreds and your feet are cut and you are laughing and crying, mostly laughing.

28 YELLOW: jonquil jasmine daffodil lemon and honey-coloured corn-coloured cornsilk canary crocus the egg yolk in the morning the colour of mustard bananas brass cadmium yellow is the colour of craving craven chicken cats' eyes I am faint-hearted weak-kneed lily-livered or the sun lucid luminous means caution or yield.

29 BLACK LEATHER JACKET
that you bought when you were seeing Ivan, who rode a red Harley-Davidson low-rider with a suicide shift, his black beard blowing in the wind. The jacket has rows of diagonal pleats at the yoke and a red leather collar and cuffs.

30 Ivan used to take you on weekend runs with his buddies and their old ladies to little bars in other towns where they were afraid of you: especially of Ivan's best friend, Spy, who had been hurt in a bike accident two years before and now his hands hung off his wrists at odd angles and he could not speak, could only make guttural growls, write obscene notes to the waitress on a serviette, and laugh at her like a madman, his eyes rolling back in his head, and you could see what was left of his tongue.

31 You would come riding up in a noisy pack with bugs in your teeth, dropping your black helmets like bowling balls on the floor, eating greasy burgers and pickled eggs, drinking draft beer by the jug, the foam running down your chin. Your legs, after the long ride, felt like a wishbone waiting to be sprung. If no one would rent you a room, you slept on picnic tables in the

campground, the bikes pulled in around you like wagons, a case of beer and one sleeping bag between ten of you. In the early morning, there was dew on your jacket and your legs were numb with the weight of Ivan's head on them.

You never did get around to telling your mother you were dating a biker (she thought you said "baker"), which was just as well, since Ivan eventually got tired, sold his bike, and moved back to Manitoba to live with his mother, who was dying. He got a job in a hardware store and soon married his high school sweetheart, Betty, who was a dental hygienist. Spy was killed on the highway: drove his bike into the back of a tanker truck in broad daylight; there was nothing left of him.

You wear your leather jacket now when you need to feel tough. You wear it with your tight blue jeans and your cowboy boots. You strut slowly with your hands in your pockets. Your boots click on the concrete and you are a different person. You can handle anything and no one had better get in your way. You will take on the world if you have to. You will die young and in flames if you have to.

> BLACK: ebon sable charcoal jet lamp-black blue-black bruises in a night sky ink-black soot-black the colour of my hair and burning rubber dirt the colour of infinite space speeding blackball blacklist black sheep blackberries ravens eat crow black as the ace of spades and black is black I want my baby back before midnight yes of course midnight that old black dog behind me.

BROWN CASHMERE SWEATER

that you were wearing the night you told Daniel you were leaving him. It was the week between Christmas and New Year's which is always a wasteland. Everyone was digging up recipes called Turkey-Grape Salad, Turkey Soufflé, and Turkey-Almond-Noodle Bake. You kept vacuuming up tinsel and pine needles, putting away presents one at a time from under the tree. You and Daniel sat at the kitchen table all afternoon, drinking hot rum toddies, munching on crackers and garlic sausage, playing Trivial Pursuit, asking each other questions like:

What's the most mountainous country in Europe?
Which is more tender, the left or right leg of a chicken?
What race of warriors burned off their right breasts in Greek legend?

Daniel was a poor loser and he thought that Europe was a country, maybe somewhere near Spain.

36   This night you have just come from a party at his friend Harold's house. You are sitting on the new couch, a loveseat, blue with white flowers, which was Daniel's Christmas present to you, and you can't help thinking of the year your father got your mother a coffee percolator when all she wanted was something personal: earrings, a necklace, a scarf for God's sake. She spent most of the day locked in their bedroom, crying noisily, coming out every hour or so to baste the turkey, white-lipped, tucking more Kleenex up her sleeve. You were on her side this time and wondered how your father, whom you had always secretly loved the most, could be so insensitive. It was the changing of the guard, your allegiance shifting like sand from one to the other.

37   You are sitting on the new couch eating cold pizza and trying to figure out why you didn't have a good time at the party. Daniel is accusing you alternately of looking down on his friends and sleeping with them. He is wearing the black leather vest you bought him for Christmas and he says you are a cheapskate.

38   When you tell him you are leaving (which is a decision you made months ago but it took you this long to figure out how you were going to manage it and it has nothing to do with the party, the couch, or the season), Daniel grips you by the shoulders and bangs your head against the wall until the picture hung there falls off. It is a photograph of the mountains on a pink spring morning, the ridges like ribs, the run-off like incisions or veins. There is glass flying everywhere in slices into your face, into your hands pressed over your eyes, and the front of your sweater is spotted and matted with blood.

39   On the way to the hospital, he says he will kill you if you tell them what he did to you. You promise him anything, you promise him that you will love him forever and that you will never leave.

40   The nurse takes you in to the examining room. Daniel waits in the waiting room, reads magazines, buys a chocolate bar from the vending machine, then a Coke and a bag of ripple chips. You tell the nurse what happened and the police take him away in handcuffs with their guns drawn. In the car on the way to the station, he tells them he only did it because he loves you.

The officer who takes down your report tells you this and he just keeps shaking his head and patting your arm. The police photographer takes pictures of your face, your broken fingers, your left breast which has purple bruises all over it where he grabbed it and twisted and twisted.

By the time you get to the women's shelter, it is morning and the blood on your sweater has dried, doesn't show. There is no way of knowing. There, the other women hold you, brush your hair, bring you coffee and cream-of-mushroom soup. The woman with the broken cheekbone has two canaries in a gold cage that she carries with her everywhere like a lamp. She shows you how the doors are steel, six inches thick, and the windows are bulletproof. She shows you where you will sleep, in a room on the third floor with six other women, some of them lying now fully dressed on their little iron cots with their hands behind their heads, staring at the ceiling as if it were full of stars or clouds that drift slowly westward in the shape of camels, horses, or bears. She shows you how the canaries will sit on your finger if you hold very still and pretend you are a tree or a roof or another bird.

BROWN: ochre cinnamon coffee copper caramel the colour of my Christmas cake chocolate mocha walnut chestnuts raw sienna my suntan burnt umber burning toast fried fricasseed sautéed grilled I baste the turkey the colour of stupid cows smart horses brown bears brown shirt brown sugar apple brown betty brunette the colour of thought and sepia the colour of old photographs the old earth and wood.

GREEN SATIN QUILTED JACKET
in the Oriental style with mandarin collar and four red frogs down the front. This jacket is older than you are. It belonged to your mother, who bought it when she was the same age as you are now. In the black-and-white photos from that time, the jacket is grey but shiny and your mother is pale but smooth-skinned, smiling with her hand on her hip or your father's thigh.

You were always pestering her to let you wear it to play dress-up, with her red high-heels and that white hat with the feathers and the little veil that covered your whole face. You wanted to wear it to a Halloween party at school where all the other girls would be witches, ghosts, or princesses and you would be the only mandarin, with your eyes, you imagined, painted up slanty and two sticks through a bun in your hair. But she would never let you. She would just keep on cooking supper, bringing carrots, potatoes, cabbages up from the root cellar, taking peas, beans, broccoli out of the freezer in labelled dated parcels, humming, looking out through the slats of the Venetian blind at the black garden and the leafless rose bushes. Each year, at least one of them would be winter-killed no matter how hard she had tried to protect them. And she would dig it up in the spring by the dead roots and the thorns would get tangled in her hair, leave long bloody scratches all down her arms. And the green jacket stayed where it was, in the cedar chest with the hand-made lace doilies, her grey linen wedding suit, and the picture of your father as a small boy with blond ringlets.

45   After the funeral, you go through her clothes while your father is outside shovelling snow. You lay them out in piles on the bed: one for the Salvation Army, one for the second-hand store, one for yourself because your father wants you to take something home with you. You will take the green satin jacket, also a white mohair cardigan with multicoloured squares on the front, a black-and-white striped shirt you sent her for her birthday last year that she never wore, an imitation-pearl necklace for Alice, and a dozen unopened packages of pantyhose. There is a fourth pile for your father's friend Jack's new wife, Frances, whom your mother never liked, but your father says Jack and Frances have fallen on hard times on the farm since Jack got emphysema, and Frances will be glad of some new clothes.

46   Jack and Frances drop by the next day with your Aunt Jeanne. You serve tea and the shortbread cookies Aunt Jeanne has brought. She makes them just the way your mother did, whipped, with a sliver of maraschino cherry on top. Jack, looking weather-beaten or embarrassed, sits on the edge of the couch with his baseball cap in his lap and marvels at how grown-up you've got to be. Frances is genuinely grateful for the two green garbage bags of clothes, which you carry out to the truck for her.

47   After they leave, you reminisce fondly with your father and Aunt Jeanne about taking the toboggan out to Jack's farm when you were small, tying it to the back of the car, your father driving slowly down the country lane, towing you on your stomach, clutching the front of the toboggan which curled like a wooden wave. You tell him for the first time how frightened you were of the black tires spinning the snow into your face, and he says he had no idea, he thought you were having fun. This was when Jack's first wife, Winnifred, was still alive. Your Aunt Jeanne, who knows everything,

tells you that when Winnifred was killed in that car accident, it was Jack, driving drunk, who caused it. And now when he gets drunk, he beats Frances up, locks her out of the house in her bare feet, and she has to sleep in the barn, in the hay with the horses.

You are leaving in the morning. Aunt Jeanne helps you pack. You are anxious to get home but worried about leaving your father alone. Aunt Jeanne says she'll watch out for him.

The green satin jacket hangs in your front hall closet now, between your black leather jacket and your raincoat. You can still smell the cedar from the chest and the satin is always cool on your cheek like clean sheets or glass.

One day you think you will wear it downtown, where you are meeting a new man for lunch. You study yourself in the full-length mirror on the back of the bathroom door and you decide it makes you look like a different person: someone unconventional, unusual, and unconcerned. This new man, whom you met recently at an outdoor jazz festival, is a free spirit who eats health food, plays the dulcimer, paints well, writes well, sings well, and has just completed an independent study of eastern religions. He doesn't smoke, drink, or do drugs. He is pure and peaceful, perfect. He is even teaching you how to garden, how to turn the black soil, how to plant the seeds, how to water them, weed them, watch them turn into lettuce, carrots, peas, beans, radishes, and pumpkins, how to get the kinks out of your back by stretching your brown arms right up to the sun. You haven't even told Alice about him yet because he is too good to be true. He is bound to love this green jacket, and you in it too.

You get in your car, drive around the block, go back inside because you forgot your cigarettes, and you leave the green jacket on the back of a kitchen chair because who are you trying to kid? More than anything, you want to be transparent. More than anything, you want to hold his hands across the table and then you will tell him you love him and it will all come true.

> GREEN: viridian verdigris chlorophyll grass leafy jade mossy verdant apple-green pea-green lime-green sage-green sea-green bottle-green emeralds avocadoes olives all leaves the colour of Venus hope and jealousy the colour of mould

mildew envy poison and pain and snakes the colour of everything that grows in my garden fertile nourishing sturdy sane and strong.

1990

NOTES

Banff A small town and popular tourist resort, located in the mountains of Alberta.

The lists of colours are significant. They relate to the narrator's moods and states of mind. At other times, they function as foreshadowing and as momentary flashbacks.

COMPREHENSION AND DISCUSSION

1. Why are these articles of clothing important to the story and to the narrator?
2. How do the colours of the clothing relate to the episodes in this woman's life?
3. Why is food so important to the narrator?
4. The narrator leaves a lot of clues about her degenerating relationship with Daniel. Can you list them?
5. What is Schoemperlen's purpose in bringing in the story of Jack and his two wives?
6. How do you know the ending is not the real ending? (Hint: Look for the china dishes.)
7. Can you unscramble the episodes and make a logical, linear progression of this story?
8. Can you identify which of all the young men with names is the perfect man the woman talks about in the conclusion?
9. Describe the narrator's personality. Is she like her mother?

LITERARY TECHNIQUES

The usual points of view in telling a story are first-person and third-person. Schoemperlen has chosen the second-person, "you." By doing so, she has created a narrator who disassociates herself from her own experience. In short, the anonymous speaker sees herself almost as another person so she can talk about herself. Otherwise, she may not because the experience and emotions are so raw. In psychological terms, this is a defence mechanism. Second, "you" suggests that the speaker is talking to someone. It is possible she is in counselling. The second person is also used in English to refer to people in general.

The narrator's name is hidden from the reader. This method has on occasion caused readers to believe that the writer is the narrator. It shouldn't. The anonymous speaker becomes a metaphor for all young women in society with similar experiences. In short, the "you" narrator is everywoman.

Schoemperlen has borrowed the dramatic monologue from poetry. A dramatic monologue has one speaker and a silent listener. In the course of the monologue, the speaker reveals her innermost thoughts and feelings, even her soul. Note that Schoemperlen's story has no dialogue, only indirect speeches as related by the speaker.

This is not a linear story; in short, the chronology is scrambled on purpose. The beginning is not entirely the beginning and the ending is definitely not the ending of the story. Neither are some of the episodes in this young woman's life in any logical order. From the associations of clothing and colours, she speaks from memory, and memory does not always follow chronology. Schoemperlen imitates the movement of the mind, or stream of consciousness.

This story is rich in symbolism. A symbol is a concrete representation of an abstraction or quality. To illustrate, in this story, the main recurrent symbols are food, clothing, and colours. Sumptuous food stands for sustenance, for the narrator's nurturing trait, for her expression of love. Each piece of clothing represents different aspects of her personality at different times: adventurous, vulnerable, glamorous, foolish, and hopeful. Similarly, the colours symbolize her feelings.

ASSIGNMENTS

1. Compare this story with the article "Exiled in Paradise" (p. 337) by Ellen Singer. How do both writers deal with the issue of abusive men? How do these writers portray women who have abusive partners?

2. If this story were told from a man's point of view, how would it be written? What would be emphasized? What would be left out?
3. Write a paragraph describing an article of clothing you owned and its significance in your life.
4. David Arnason's "A Girl's Story" (p. 22) also emphasizes colours and clothing in Linda, the heroine. How is that story similar to or different from Schoemperlen's?
5. How important is love, or finding someone to love? What illusions do you hold about love, even in the face of reality?

Ralphie at the Races
Sam Selvon

Ralphie lost his image standing in front of the narrow mirror on the bathroom door of his apartment. No matter how much he twisted his head and hunched his shoulders to try and get a glimpse of the skin at the back of his neck, as he leaned sideways the upper part of his body just vanished off the mirror as if it had never existed. Eventually, persevering in the contortions, he was rewarded with his head at an awkward angle, but he froze in the position and gingerly brushed his fingertips on the area.

There was no doubt about it. He, a landed immigrant from tropical Trinidad only eleven degrees off the Equator, was sunburnt. The thin outer pigment of black was peeled away to reveal pink and even white patches.

What made matters worse as he stood there examining the rest of his body was the discovery of bumps on his arms from mosquito bites. In spite of himself Ralphie had to laugh. Sunburnt, *and* mosquito-bitten. Here he was in Calgary, in the "frozen north," just beginning to get accustomed to the weather, and if he wrote a letter home to tell them it was so hot he was sunburnt for the first time in his life, and itching with mosquito bites, they would never believe him.

It was Friday morning, and in a way the hot summer was responsible for an unusual chain of circumstances which had started for Ralphie at the beginning of the week. On Monday, listening to the weather forecast predict an indefinite run of fine weather, he got to thinking that he was falling into a rut. He felt he should make some effort to get up and about, as there was so much he hadn't done or seen since he settled down in Calgary. He didn't want to be like so many other immigrants who get into a routine the day they find a job and a place to live and lose their original interest in the new environment and exploring the things about them. A good example was his best friend Angus, a fellow Trinidadian, who had been living in Calgary for seven years and was now a Canadian citizen, and hadn't even been up to the top of the Calgary Tower.

When Ralphie explained his feelings, Angus merely shrugged.

"I see the tower every day, man," he said, "what I want to go up there for, to catch birds?"

"You don't feel funny that you living here so long and up to now you haven't been?" Ralphie asked him.

8   "Why I should feel funny? I bet a lot of other people who born here haven't been either. Besides boy, the weather too hot these days to do anything."

9   "Too hot?" Ralphie scoffed. "A Trinidadian like you complaining that it's too hot?"

10   "Weather like this, the best place to be is the racetrack," Angus said. "Let the horses and the jockeys provide the action while you sit back, and at the same time you could come away with a few bucks in your pocket."

11   "You could also lose the shirt off your back," Ralphie reminded him, knowing that Angus spent all his spare time at the races.

12   "Not a bad idea in this kind of weather," Angus laughed.

13   "That's the trouble with you guys," Ralphie said, "you make a joke of everything. But I bet by the time the summer is over, I will know more about Calgary than you do."

14   "Good luck," Angus said, still laughing, "maybe you will be able to take me on a conducted tour of the city to see the sights and places of historic interest!"

15   "Laugh all you want," Ralphie retorted, "but I intend to take advantage of this good weather we're having."

16   But he almost had to give up the idea when he was driving to work on the Wednesday and his car broke down. Ironically enough, the damage was caused by his engine getting overheated with the temperature soaring into the upper twenties. And it was more trouble than he thought when he found it couldn't start. He had to be towed away, and the people at the garage told him it would take a couple of days and cost a hundred and fifty bucks.

17   It had not taken Ralphie long to realize that in this country without transport one might as well be stranded on a desert island. The only walking anyone did was to and from a parking lot, or shopping in the malls. But where would he find that sort of money with payday not until the following week? And what about his plans to get about and see the local sights? He had been thinking of driving to the mountains over the weekend — he'd heard about the cool mountain lakes, and felt sure that he would have no trouble tempting Angus to go along with him to get away from the hot and humid city for a while.

18   As he thought of Angus it occurred to him that friends were there to help a guy get out of a jam, and he phoned him and explained the situation. Angus said he didn't have the money right away, but he was sure he would have it by Friday and would lend it to him, no sweat.

19   Ralphie was so relieved that he did not mind having to leave the car. One of his workmates gave him a drop home that evening, but when he got

up on Thursday he had to get to work by bus. It was only when he was using his own two feet to get to the bus stop that he realized how hot it really was. He was perspiring and out of breath. I must be out of shape, he thought, I ought to be doing some exercise.

That was why, during the lunch hour, instead of sitting in the cafeteria around the corner as he usually did, he bought a sandwich and took a stroll in the neighbourhood. It turned out to be more of an exploration, for he saw shops and business places that he never knew existed, and suddenly, at the end of the street, he came across a greenbelt area. It excited him — this was exactly the sort of thing he was telling Angus about, calling yourself a Calgarian, but ignorant of what the city was like just a couple of blocks or so from the place where you worked!

In spite of the heat Ralphie lingered in the area. There were other people about, some of them stretched out on the grass in the open baking in the sun... why should *he* grumble?

When he got home that evening he headed straight for the fridge, dying for an ice-cold beer, only to discover he had run short. If he had the car he could easily drive down to the liquor store. The thought was irritating — and so was his body, sore and itchy from his unaccustomed walk in the sun. Anyway, tomorrow was Friday, he'd get the money from Angus to pay for the car, thank God for that.

He reminded himself of this in the morning when he discovered the results of his lunchtime walk, and gave thanks again that the car was equipped with air conditioning. He was almost consoled when the phone rang and he answered.

It was Angus.

"You're early," Ralphie said.

"Yeah, I wanted to catch you before you went to work."

Something in Angus' tone alarmed Ralphie and he asked abruptly: "You got the money?"

"That's what I called about. I went to the races last night..." *and here it comes, Ralphie thought...* "and I lost. A streak of bad luck, boy..."

"Go on," Ralphie said, as Angus' voice trailed away.

"What d'you mean, 'go on?' That's it, all I got left is about fifty bucks."

"You call yourself a friend?" Ralphie said bitterly, scratching his arm. "I got sunburn and mosquito bite walking about in the heat, and now you let me down. I was planning to go to the Rockies tomorrow, too."

"Look Ralphie, I'm sure I'll have it for you tonight. I can't be so bad-luck-ed twice in a row."

33 "You mean you're going back?"

34 "Sure. I can't miss the Wild Rose Stakes meeting, the stands will be packed. Why don't you give it a whirl?"

35 "I never been to a racetrack in my life, and I don't intend to start now."

36 "You could dump that old Chevvy and buy a new car."

37 "Yeah, I could lose the little money I got, too."

38 "At least think about it. With an expert like me you can't go wrong. If you change your mind give me a call and I'll pick you up after work."

39 All morning, as he went about his job in a downtown repository, Ralphie thought of Angus with mixed feelings. He was disappointed in his friend, but he could not help a grudging admiration for his carefree style and having the nerve to gamble on horses. Perhaps he himself was being too cautious, and should take a chance for once — how else could he pay for the car short of a miracle? If he tightened his belt, he could afford to risk about twenty-five dollars. Would that be enough? He had the faintest clue. Maybe he'd have to dress for it — Canadians seemed to have special clothing for every damn thing, curling, golfing, baseball, fishing, ice-skating...why not horse-racing? As his resistance weakened, he began to think of it as just another way to get out of the routine and do something different, which was just what he was planning all along.

40 Late in the afternoon he phoned Angus. "Look, about this evening..."

41 Angus didn't wait for him to finish. "That's great, boy, maybe you'll have beginner's luck."

42 "I haven't even been near a horse all my life, Angus. I don't even know where the racetrack is."

43 "Stampede Park — I said I'd pick you up."

44 "Have I got to wear a jockey cap or something?"

45 Angus laughed so loudly Ralphie had to shift the phone off his ear. "Come on Ralphie, you're not as dumb as all that. Look, just get a paper and study the form, if you like. I'll pick you up after work, okay?"

46 Before Ralphie could raise any more objections or questions Angus hung up on him.

47 When they got to Stampede Park that evening, Ralphie had made up his mind about two things. The first was he wasn't going to make himself appear a complete fool to Angus even if he had to bluff and bluster. The second was that he was going to be careful and hold on tight to his money. No bets in the first race, or the second, or even the third and fourth. He would case the joint, as it were, and feel his way into this new experience before he invested any part of his twenty-five bucks — well, twenty-three, he corrected himself, deducting the two-dollar entrance fee which he felt

Angus should have paid, and thinking uneasily that he was down two bucks already and he hadn't even seen a horse or heard one neigh.

Angus was anxious to get doing. He wore a cap which he assured Ralphie had nothing to do with the attire of racegoers ("it always bring me good luck if I wear it") and a pair of binoculars dangled on his chest from a leather strap around his neck ("I will lend it to you now and then if you want to get a close-up of the race; I bought it with my first winnings").

As they went through the turnstiles and walked towards the pavilion, Angus said, "We mustn't miss the daily double."

"Yeah," Ralphie muttered, feeling ill-at-ease and gazing around at the crowds of people moving about in complete familiarity with their surroundings. He also suspected that Angus was trying to impress him, putting on airs as if he was the Chief Steward of the meeting or something: as they were passing some stairs he gestured and said, "When I'm in the money I go up there to the clubhouse, but seeing as this is your first visit I'll stick around with you — or rather, you stick around with me."

"I'll be okay, don't worry about me," Ralphie said.

They went out to the open stands and Angus led Ralphie to his usual place in the back row of the yellow section. Once seated he immediately became engrossed in studying the form, checking the list of horses and jockeys, what time they made at previous meetings, and what tips he could get from the newspapers: he even looked up at the sky as if seeking a sign from the few puffy clouds that drifted above the park. All of which had Ralphie baffled, he could not make head or tail of it as Angus frowned and concentrated like he was trying to work out Einstein's theory of relativity. Ralphie looked across the central stage or platform at the tote board flashing figures and letters on and off giving information which was totally useless to him, how could anyone make sense of it?

Suddenly a woman came out on the platform, dressed up like English people when they are going to chase the foxes with the hounds. She had a bugle under her arm and she marched up like a soldier to a microphone and she played a little tune, army reveille or something it sounded like to Ralphie.

"Where's the rest of the band?" Ralphie asked, hopeful for some music to divert his thoughts.

"Ten minutes to go," Angus muttered, "you putting anything on the daily double?"

"I will hold my horses for a while," Ralphie said, unconsciously making a pun.

The riders began to come out on the track to warm up and get in position for the start.

58 "Number five look good," Ralphie volunteered, for no other reason than feeling that he had to say something.

59 "You think so?" Angus frowned like a man tortured by indecisions and consulted the program. "Two point eleven...two point ten...that's the worse time in the lot."

60 "All the same, if I was you I would put my money on number five," Ralphie persisted.

61 "I am taking number three, and number six for the second race," Angus said. "Take it from me, that's the best bet."

62 "Six is an unlucky number," Ralphie was beginning to enjoy his deception. "I would choose seven if I was you."

63 Angus chuckled. "Boy, I could understand why you keep away from the racetrack, and leave it to the experts like me!" And he went off to place his bet.

64 Needless to say, number five came in first, and in the second race, number seven finished a whole length in front of the others.

65 "And they're paying three hundred bucks for the double," Angus said mournfully.

66 "What!" Ralphie sat up. He couldn't believe it, although Angus pointed it out on the toteboard, and said that if he had only had a little guts to bet a mere two dollars, he would have had three hundred in his pocket now.

67 "Three hundred and twenty-three, including my capital," Ralphie choked.

68 Angus was too much the regular gambler to let it upset him, but Ralphie did a hop and a dance in dismay.

69 "I lost my chance, I lost my chance!" He wailed.

70 "It got other races," Angus said. "And besides, look at all the other losers."

71 "I don't see any! Everybody win excepting me!"

72 "Cool it. Can't you see all those bits of paper scattered around," Angus waved a hand about the stands, already the ground was strewn with discarded tickets. "Forget what's gone, man, that's spilt milk, water under the bridge. See what you could do in the next race."

73 "That's easy for a hardened gambler like you to say," Ralphie could not recover from the blow. He got up and wandered about the stands with his hands in his pockets, kicking disgustedly at any tickets he saw on the ground. Lady Luck had smiled at him and he had spurned her advances. He went out on the grounds and leaned against the rails, and as the horses came around the last bend he imagined they were running the first two races again and this time he had bet every cent he had.

He was so bitter and disappointed he was tempted to get out of Stampede Park and go home, but he came across the Rodeo Bar as he strayed about. Perhaps a double scotch chased with a beer might console him.

As he sipped the drink he did feel better, and he thought, what the hell, I might as well have another, at least I'm enjoying this instead of trusting my money on jockeys and horses that I know nothing about—and I'm not the only one, if you ask me the bar is doing more business than the races!

"I had the daily double," he said conversationally to a stranger standing next to him.

"Yeah?" the man replied, "you caught them, eh?"

"Yeah." Ralphie drained his glass. "But I didn't bet."

"Tough luck." He gave Ralphie a curious glance and turned back to his own friends.

Ralphie wasn't sure how long he'd been away, but when he got back Angus asked him if he'd won anything.

"I wasn't betting," he replied. "Just moseying around."

"Well, a quinella is coming up now."

"Quin-ella? Where?"

"Pick two horses, it doesn't matter which comes in first or second."

"Oh yeah, quinella...how've you been doing, you make a big kill yet?"

"Not too good, Ralphie. You better start betting if you want that car for the weekend. You didn't pick up any tips on your wanderings?"

Ralphie took a random peep at the program. "Sure, I heard two Chinese guys arguing about *Ruby Morning* and *Victor Brave Boy* for that quinella thing."

"Yeah?" Angus was too experienced a punter to take any tip lightly, no matter from what source. Many times he'd stood behind some Chinese guy in the payout line and seen him strain to pick up the load of notes he'd won. But when he looked up the card selections he read "continues to disappoint" for one, and "needs mini-miracle" for the other. He shook his head and went back to his own convictions and calculations.

The girl in the fox-hunting garb came out and blew her bugle and the horse came out for a preliminary canter. Ralphie was too miserable to care. He had ten dollars left and was just impatient to get home and forget the whole thing.

"Jesus!" Angus exclaimed as the race ended, tossing away his tickets like so many other. "Victor Brave Boy and Ruby Morning! Man, this is *twice* you make a correct forecast and you didn't bet!"

91   "Because I am a moron, the most stupid man in Calgary!" This time Ralphie was on the verge of tears.

92   "The most stupid here today, that's for sure. I don't know how you do it, boy, but whatever it is, it works. And you better stop depending on me to take the car out, I just lost again."

93   "Let's go home." Ralphie was dejected. "I never coming back to this racetrack again. This must be a sign that I should never gamble."

94   "The last race is coming up," Angus said. "Cowards die many times before their deaths is one saying, but they have another, which is 'third time lucky.' In fact, I will go against my better judgement and back your tip. Look at this list of eight horses and pick the winner."

95   But Ralphie had nothing to say. He hung his head in utter despair, and his eyes couldn't even focus properly on the clusters of unlucky tickets lying at his feet and around him. If he had had the courage to buy one, *just one*, his worries would have been over.

96   Suddenly he stood up and without a word to Angus he strode off determinedly to the nearest betting window. For a moment he paused, wondering what to say. Then he pulled the ten dollars out and put the money down and shut his eyes and said, "All that on the last race."

97   The girl looked at him. "What bet?"

98   "Oh. Ah. To win."

99   "What horse... what number?"

100 "Er... number ten."

101 She smiled a little. "There's no number ten running in this race."

102 "Oh. What's the next number, nine?" he asked.

103 "You want ten dollars on number nine to win?"

104 "Yeah, yeah. That's it."

105 He rejoined Angus silently and sat down.

106 Angus left him alone, except for a quick glance of sympathy. Like a true punter, he appreciated what agonies a man suffered when he did not take advantage of an inspired forecast and watched the horse come in a winner. Ralphie had a lot to learn, though, he should not give up, he should take his blows like a man and come out fighting in the next rounds.

107 Through the race Ralphie kept his head down and forced himself to think of anything but horses. Already he was regretting his rashness, he would be leaving the racetrack without a cent in his pocket, couldn't even afford to buy some lotion from the drugstore for his sunburn, though it didn't bother him much unless he touched the tender skin... as for driving to the mountain over the weekend, well, it was just too bad, he would have to wait until next payday...

He tried not to listen to the commentator's excited voice as the race progressed, but Angus's yelling was too close to shut out.

"Number eight! Come on eight! That's it baby, come on! It's eight! Eight in the lead!"

And that's the end of that, he told himself, let it be a lesson to you, better to spend your money on women and drink...

Then he heard Angus swearing. "Oh hell... it's a photo-finish, there's an inquiry..."

Photo-finish? Inquiry? Was that the name of a horse or something? Perhaps they would have to run the race again, and this time... this time...

After what seemed ages he heard Angus swearing again. "Blast it! Eight come in second... nine is the winner!"

Ralphie looked up and gaped at Angus. "Nine? Win?"

"Yeah. You bet on nine?"

He couldn't speak. He was trembling with excitement and could barely lift his hand to show Angus the ticket.

"Jesus, nine was a rank outsider. Ralphie! You must have hit it rich, boy!"

As they moved to go inside Angus was so elated for his bewildered friend that he clapped him heartily on the shoulders and was about to voice congratulations again when Ralphie let out a mighty yell of pain.

"Oh Christ, Angus, my sunburn!" He hunched and staggered a little and the ticket slipped from his nervous fingers, but he grabbed wildly on the ground for it, elbowing in the jostling crowd.

"Sorry, Ralphie... I forgot all about that in the excitement... I'll just check the full results on the telly, you better join the payline before it get too big."

Ralphie was among the first winners, so excited that he was breathing in short gasps and trying to control his body from shaking.

When he put his ticket down the cashier looked at it closely then frowned at him.

"You've made a mistake."

"Yeah." He was grinning all over his face and the words did not register until she spoke again.

"This is for the ninth race, and it isn't a winning number. Move aside and check it, please."

Looking for Ralphie, Angus found him down on all fours near the spot where he had dropped the ticket, scrambling about hopelessly in the litter of betting tickets and muttering to himself like a madman.

1983

NOTES

Landed immigrant A person who can legally live in Canada but has not yet become a citizen.

Sunburn An inflammation of the skin caused by too much exposure to the sun. There is a common but incorrect belief that dark-skinned people cannot get a sunburn.

Calgary Tower A free-standing tower, with a rotating observation area for tourists, similar to the CN Tower in Toronto, Ontario.

Greenbelt area A track of land, usually in an urban setting, that has trees and grass for public use.

Wild Roses Stakes Name of a horse-racing event where people can place bets.

Punter A person who lays bets or gambles.

"Just moseying around" Slang for just looking about without any particular purpose.

"Cowards die many times before their deaths" is from Shakespeare's *Julius Caesar*, 2.2.32–33. The complete lines are as follows:
   Cowards die many times before their deaths;
   The valiant never taste of death but once.

COMPREHENSION AND DISCUSSION

1. Where is this story set?
2. How are Ralphie and Angus similar? How do they differ?
3. Name some things immigrants to Canada do not expect or are not prepared for.
4. Why is Raphie's expression—"You could also lose the shirt off your back" (p. 206)—prophetic?
5. Why is a car important in Canada?
6. What does Ralphie discover when he has to walk rather than drive?
7. Why does Ralphie let Angus talk him into going to the races?

8. Is there a lesson in this story about gambling?
9. Do you believe in Lady Luck? Like Angus with his cap, do you carry lucky objects? Discuss the reasons for superstition.
10. Is there any relationship between Ralphie's sunburn and his gambling? What do you consider to be gambling?
11. Would this story be the same if Ralphie were not an immigrant? Explain.
12. How does Selvon create humour? What different techniques does the writer use?

LITERARY TECHNIQUES

The writer uses a time-honoured method in plotting: cause and effect. He does so consistently. For example, Ralphie's car breaking down leads him to get a sunburn and to go with Angus to the horse races, and so on.

Second, Selvon limits his characters to two. Not only is this economical storytelling, but it also gives a sharper contrast between Ralphie and Angus. Their attitudes toward life are different.

ASSIGNMENTS

1. Why are some people superstitious? Why do people often carry lucky charms? Recount some superstitions you have observed or practised.
2. Why is gambling so popular? Can you compare playing the ponies with getting married as a form of gambling? If so, why? If not, why not?
3. Is gambling addictive? Is it a disease? If so, why are so many provincial governments running lotteries and opening up casinos? Research some of the latest findings on this topic.
4. Compare the immigrant experience that Selvon writes about with Rosie DiManno's in "Growing Up on Grace" (p. 250) or with Garry Engkent's "Chickens for Christmas" (p. 63).
5. Compare the use of "three" in this story with Jacobs's "The Monkey's Paw" (p. 116). Why is "three" so often used in literature and in life?
6. Compare Selvon's use of humour with Stephen Leacock's in "How We Kept Mother's Day" (p. 140) or "My Financial Career" (p. 145).

The Use of Force

William Carlos Williams

1. They were new patients to me, all I had was the name, Olson. Please come down as soon as you can, my daughter is very sick.

2. When I arrived I was met by the mother, a big startled looking woman, very clean and apologetic who merely said, Is this the doctor? and let me in. In the back, she added. You must excuse us, doctor, we have her in the kitchen where it is warm. It is very damp here sometimes.

3. The child was fully dressed and sitting on her father's lap near the kitchen table. He tried to get up, but I motioned for him not to bother, took off my overcoat and started to look things over. I could see that they were all very nervous, eyeing me up and down distrustfully. As often, in such cases, they weren't telling me more than they had to, it was up to me to tell them; that's why they were spending three dollars on me.

4. The child was fairly eating me up with her cold, steady eyes, and no expression to her face whatever. She did not move and seemed, inwardly, quiet; an unusually attractive little thing, and as strong as a heifer in appearance. But her face was flushed, she was breathing rapidly, and I realized that she had a high fever. She had magnificent blonde hair, in profusion. One of those picture children often reproduced in advertising leaflets and the photogravure sections of the Sunday papers.

5. She's had a fever for three days, began the father and we don't know what it comes from. My wife has given her things, you know, like people do, but it don't do no good. And there's been a lot of sickness around. So we tho't you'd better look her over and tell us what is the matter.

6. As doctors often do I took a trial shot at it as a point of departure. Has she had a sore throat?

7. Both parents answered me together, No... No, she says her throat don't hurt her.

8. Does your throat hurt you? added the mother to the child. But the little girl's expression didn't change nor did she move her eyes from my face.

9. Have you looked?

10. I tried to, said the mother, but I couldn't see.

11. As it happens we had been having a number of cases of diphtheria in the school to which this child went during that month and we were all, quite apparently, thinking of that, though no one had as yet spoken of the thing.

Well, I said, suppose we take a look at the throat first. I smiled in my best professional manner and asking for the child's first name I said, come on, Mathilda, open your mouth and let's take a look at your throat.

Nothing doing.

Aw, come on, I coaxed, just open your mouth wide and let me take a look. Look, I said opening both hands wide, I haven't anything in my hands. Just open up and let me see.

Such a nice man, put in the mother. Look how kind he is to you. Come on, do what he tells you to. He won't hurt you.

At that I ground my teeth in disgust. If only they wouldn't use the word "hurt" I might be able to get somewhere. But I did not allow myself to be hurried or disturbed but speaking quietly and slowly I approached the child again.

As I moved my chair a little nearer suddenly with one catlike movement both her hands clawed instinctively for my eyes and she almost reached them too. In fact she knocked my glasses flying and they fell, though unbroken, several feet away from me on the kitchen floor.

Both the mother and father almost turned themselves inside out in embarrassment and apology. You bad girl, said the mother, taking her and shaking her by one arm. Look what you've done. The nice man...

For heaven's sake, I broke in. Don't call me a nice man to her. I'm here to look at her throat on the chance that she might have diphtheria and possibly die of it. But that's nothing to her. Look here, I said to the child, we're going to look at your throat. You're old enough to understand what I'm saying. Will you open it now by yourself or shall we have to open it for you?

Not a move. Even her expression hadn't changed. Her breaths however were coming faster and faster. Then the battle began. I had to do it. I had to have a throat culture for her own protection. But first I told the parents that it was entirely up to them. I explained the danger but said that I would not insist on a throat examination so long as they would take the responsibility.

If you don't do what the doctor says you'll have to go to the hospital, the mother admonished her severely.

Oh yeah? I had to smile to myself. After all, I had already fallen in love with the savage brat, the parents were contemptible to me. In the ensuing struggle they grew more and more abject, crushed, exhausted while she surely rose to magnificent heights of insane fury of effort bred of her terror of me.

The father tried his best, and he was a big man but the fact that she was his daughter, his shame at her behaviour and his dread of hurting her made him release her just at the critical times when I had almost achieved success, till I wanted to kill him. But his dread also that she might have diphtheria made him tell me to go on, go on though he himself was almost fainting, while the mother moved back and forth behind us raising and lowering her hands in an agony of apprehension.

24 Put her in front of you on your lap, I ordered, and hold both her wrists.

25 But as soon as he did the child let out a scream. Don't, you're hurting me. Let go of my hands. Let them go I tell you. Then she shrieked terrifyingly, hysterically. Stop it! Stop it! You're killing me!

26 Do you think she can stand it, doctor! said the mother.

27 You get out, said the husband to his wife. Do you want her to die of diphtheria?

28 Come on now, hold her, I said.

29 Then I grasped the child's head with my left hand and tried to get the wooden tongue depressor between her teeth. She fought, with clenched teeth, desperately! But now I also had grown furious — at a child. I tried to hold myself down but I couldn't. I know how to expose a throat for inspection. And I did my best. When finally I got the wooden spatula behind the last teeth and just the point of it into the mouth cavity, she opened up for an instant but before I could see anything she came down again and gripping the wooden blade between her molars she reduced it to splinters before I could get it out again.

30 Aren't you ashamed, the mother yelled at her. Aren't you ashamed to act like that in front of the doctor?

31 Get me a smooth-handled spoon of some sort, I told the mother. We're going through with this. The child's mouth was already bleeding. Her tongue was cut and she was screaming in wild hysterical shrieks. Perhaps I should have desisted and come back in an hour or more. No doubt it would have been better. But I have seen at least two children lying dead in bed of neglect in such cases, and feeling that I must get a diagnosis now or never I went at it again. But the worst of it was that I too had got beyond reason. I could have torn the child apart in my own fury and enjoyed it. It was a pleasure to attack her. My face was burning with it.

32 The damned little brat must be protected against her own idiocy, one says to one's self at such times. Others must be protected against her. It is a social necessity. And all these things are true. But a blind fury, a feeling of adult shame, bred of a longing for muscular release are the operatives. One goes on to the end.

33 In a final unreasoning assault I overpowered the child's neck and jaws. I forced the heavy silver spoon back of her teeth and down her throat till

she gagged. And there it was — both tonsils covered with membrane. She had fought valiantly to keep me from knowing her secret. She had been hiding that sore throat for three days at least and lying to her parents in order to escape just such an outcome as this.

Now truly she was furious. She had been on the defensive before but now she attacked. Tried to get off her father's lap and fly at me while tears of defeat blinded her eyes.

34

1938

NOTES

William Carlos Williams (1883 – 1963) was an American physician and writer. He is well known for his poetry. Drawing from his medical practice and experience, Williams wrote a number of short stories, often composing them between medical appointments.

Unlike today when patients go to the doctor's office or clinic, in the past, doctors made house calls or visits to the patients' homes.

Diphtheria is a highly contagious, air-borne bacterial disease that can infect the throat and skin. A common childhood illness of the 1930s, diphtheria causes difficulty in breathing, creates fast heart beating, and enlarges the lymph glands. It can cause asphyxiation and death.

The name "Mathilda" comes from Teutonic and means "brave" or "mighty in battle." Note how the meaning suits the little girl.

COMPREHENSION AND DISCUSSION

1. How do you know that the Olson family is poor? Give at least three examples.
2. Why does the doctor dislike the parents, but admire the little girl?
3. When does this struggle between doctor and patient become personal?
4. Is the doctor justified in using force on the little girl?
5. Why does Mathilda leap at the doctor?
6. Are Mathilda's parents ineffectual in their parenting skills?
7. How would you have handled the situation?

8. Does Mathilda have diphtheria? How would the story change if the opposite were true?

LITERARY TECHNIQUES

The story is told in first person. The main character is the doctor, and we see everything from his point of view. We know his thoughts but not the Olson family members'. Moreover, the story moves in a linear fashion; that is, there are minimal flashbacks and they are done quickly just to give background information.

Note that Williams does not use quotation marks to show dialogue. Quotation marks to frame direct speech is a convention used in English literature to distinguish narrative from dialogue. Most writers adhere to it; others prefer the European method of a dash (—) to signal direct speech. Some, like Williams, ignore it all together.

The physical action of the story is simple and deceptive. The parents are not aware of the contest of wills between the doctor and their daughter. This psychological conflict parallels the physical. Williams draws on a faint echo of the David and Goliath story here, with the giant winning the battle.

The conclusion is open-ended. There are several interpretations for it; depending on your explanation and supporting evidence from the story, each has validity. For example, Mathilda is ungrateful to the doctor for saving her life and attacks him; the doctor's bullying tactics force the girl to retaliate the only way she can to preserve her dignity.

ASSIGNMENTS

1. Look up the case of Tyrell Dueck, a Saskatchewan boy who refused conventional medical help. Write an essay on personal choice in medicine.
2. Discuss alternative medicine such as homeopathic, naturopathic, herbal, and home remedies (passed down the generations).
3. How should Canadians pay for medical treatment? Pay by cash on a per-service fee? Government medicare system? Private medical insurance plan? What proposals do you have to change or fix the current health care system?

4. In what situations would the use of force be acceptable?
5. Nobody likes to have things forced upon him. Read George Orwell's essay "Shooting an Elephant" (p. 314). Can you see the similarity between that article and this short story?

PART TWO
READING NON-FICTION

READING NON-FICTION

INTRODUCTION

The world of books is divided into fiction and non-fiction. The library and the bookstore both use this essential classification. In television, fiction is in the form of dramas and situation comedies, while non-fiction is in the form of documentaries and news programs. The term "fiction" comes from the Latin *fictio,* "the act of shaping, a feigning, that which is feigned." In English, fiction then is something made up, imaginary; so non-fiction is, essentially, reality. The writer may be expressing a strange view of the subject matter, but the events he or she is discussing are true ones.

Most writing is non-fiction. Every day, we give information, express our thoughts, or share our experiences with others. You may want to tell your friend about the wonderful movie you saw, so you e-mail him or write a letter. What you have written is non-fiction. The message you have sent is grounded in reality and is true.

You read different kinds of non-fiction. A newspaper story reports an accident, the results of a study, or a political situation. An essay or an editorial gives the writer's opinions on the news story. A textbook gives you information on the subject you are studying and directs your learning. A manual tells you how to operate your car, appliances, or electronic gadget. A biography tells the story of a person's life.

DISTINGUISHING FICTION AND NON-FICTION

While the world of literature is divided into fiction and non-fiction, sometimes it is not easy to tell the difference. For example, Garry Engkent's short stories, like "Chickens for Christmas" (p. 63), have often been incorrectly classified as non-fiction essays because they are based on true events and because the narrator is a person similar to the author. However, if you compare this story with Rosie DiManno's "Growing Up on Grace" (p. 250), you can see the difference. Engkent uses dialogue to tell his story, whereas reminiscences are rarely presented with so much dialogue. How many of us could remember the exact words our mother said to us when we were children?

The line between fiction and non-fiction can be blurred. Docudramas on television re-create real events, but they are still "re-creations." Journalists sometimes make up a character that represents several real people to give sharper focus to the article or column, even though that person does not exist. Sometimes a fictional character like Scrooge seems real because so many people have heard of him so often.

Writers of non-fiction essays can use narrative to tell a story, as Rosie DiManno and George Orwell do. Truman Capote's book *In Cold Blood* is called a non-fiction novel. A celebrity biography may stretch the truth so much that the book seems to belong on the fiction shelves. Two history books can have very different versions of reality. Old science and medical books can be based on so much inaccurate information that they resemble works of fiction. It is even said that truth is stranger than fiction.

However, even though the fiction/non-fiction distinction may not always hold fast, it is still a useful one. The majority of works you read will clearly belong to one camp or the other, and the more experience you have as a reader, the easier it will be to see the difference.

TYPES OF NON-FICTION

Writing can be categorized according to different rhetorical modes or types. Essay writers generally use more than one rhetorical mode in a piece. For instance, to describe a process, the writer uses definition and description to make the process clear. These types of essays are discussed again, from a writing point of view, in Chapter 4 of Part Three.

Exposition Explaining something that the writer knows. "Exposition" means to expose or show ideas and information. Often it is an umbrella term that includes all other modes of writing. Examples from this text include:
"Canadian Tire Money" (p. 280)
"Don't You Think It's Time to Start Thinking?" (p. 268)
"The End of Manual Labour" (p. 355)
"Grey Owl's Magnificent Masquerade" (p. 232)
"I'll Decide What's Broken" (p. 326)
"The Joys of Keeping in Touch, Virtually" (p. 272)
"What Is an Idea?" (p. 283)

Example/illustration Giving specific models or details to support ideas or to give readers a clearer picture. Readings that use illustration include:
"The End of Manual Labour" (p. 355)
"I'll Decide What's Broken" (p. 326)
"Junk Food Heaven" (p. 245)
"The Joys of Keeping in Touch, Virtually" (p. 272)

Definition Giving clear meanings of concepts, words, or practices. Readings that use definition include:
   "Of Weirdos and Eccentrics" (p. 289)
   "Possessed by Stuff" (p. 345)
   "Toothpaste" (p. 241)
   "What Is an Idea?" (p. 283)

Classification/division Separating items or concepts into categories for easier identification. It is a kind of definition. For example, writing may be separated into fiction and non-fiction: the work of imagination and the work of reality. Moreover, it may be further broken down into kinds of fiction or kinds of non-fiction, such as detective stories and romances in fiction, and cookbooks and literary critiques in non-fiction. Examples of classification can be found in:
   "Of Weirdos and Eccentrics" (p. 289)
   "Possessed by Stuff" (p. 345)
   "Toothpaste" (p. 241)

Compare/contrast Drawing similarities or differences between two or more items. Examples appear in:
   "Am I Blue?" (p. 349)
   "The End of Manual Labour" (p. 355)
   "Of Weirdos and Eccentrics" (p. 289)

Cause/effect Demonstrating relationships and consequences so that readers can see connections. Examples can be found in:
   "The Golden Years of Electronic Helps" (p. 258)
   "Growing Up on Grace" (p. 250)
   "Exiled in Paradise" (p. 337)
   "Have Wheels, Will Go A-Wooing" (p. 322)
   "The Patterns of Eating" (p. 262)
   "Shooting an Elephant" (p. 314)

Description Detailing information, usually visual information, so that readers can make a mental picture of the item or get a good idea of what it is like. You can find examples of description in:
   "Am I Blue?" (p. 349)
   "Junk Food Heaven" (p. 245)
   "The Story of Service" (p. 301)
   "Toothpaste" (p. 241)

Narration Telling a story, describing an incident or action. Examples of narration in the reading selections include all the short stories and the following essays:
"Am I Blue?" (p. 349)
"Exiled in Paradise" (p. 337)
"Growing Up on Grace" (p. 250)
"Have Wheels, Will Go A-Wooing" (p. 322)
"I'll Decide What's Broken" (p. 326)
"Junk Food Heaven" (p. 245)
"The Patterns of Eating" (p. 262)
"Shooting an Elephant" (p. 314)
"The Story of Grey Owl" (p. 330)
"Truth and Consequences" (p. 236)

Argumentation/persuasion Trying to make readers accept a certain point of view. The readings that use argument include:
"Don't Say Cheese!" (p. 276)
"The Golden Years of Electronic Helps" (p. 258)
"Grey Owl's Magnificent Masquerade" (p. 232)
"Have Wheels, Will Go A-Wooing" (p. 322)
"Our Father Who Art in Classrooms: No" (p. 294)
"Our Father Who Art in Classrooms: Yes" (p. 296)
"Rediscovering Christmas" (p. 359)
"Don't You Think It's Time to Start Thinking?" (p. 268)

Process/instruction Showing how something works, and telling readers how to perform certain tasks. The readings that use process/instruction include:
"Canadian Tire Money" (p. 280)
"The Patterns of Eating" (p. 262)
"The Story of Service" (p. 301)
"Toothpaste" (p. 241)

DETERMINING MAIN IDEAS

When you read an essay, you will be asked to determine the author's main point. Ask yourself why the writer wrote the article, what message he or she is trying to communicate to the audience. You should be able to express the main idea in one complete sentence, which could also be called a summary statement. Do not confuse the main idea with the topic. If you say something like "this article is about...," you are probably going to give the topic, not the main point.

> In "The Golden Years of Electronic Helps," Fred Donnelly talks about technological advancements. (topic)

> In "The Golden Years of Electronic Helps," Fred Donnelly shows that computers and other electronic inventions can help older people live fuller lives. (main idea)

As you read the non-fiction articles, determine the main idea of each. Write it down in your reading notes.

ANALYZING ESSAYS

Just as you examine the techniques used by short-story writers, you can analyze essays. You can start by determining the rhetorical modes used, the author's purpose (the main idea), and the intended audience of the piece. You look carefully at the content — what is said and how it is organized. How does the writer support her statements? What kind of background information does she give? Is the essay clear?

In addition to looking at content, you must examine tone and style. Is the article conversational or academic? Do the words carry strong connotations? For instance, an anti-abortionist might use the term "baby-killer" to refer to doctors that perform abortions. Does the author have a distinctive style — favouring puns or word play, for example?

Some patterns of organization are typical for certain kinds of writing. Magazine articles, for example, often start with an anecdote, a story, before they move on to more general information. Newspaper stories are arranged in a spiral: the headline tells the story briefly, the first paragraph or two tells the story again, but in full sentences, and the rest of the article repeats the story with more information. News stories rarely have proper conclusions because sometimes they must be chopped off at the end in order to fit the space.

ANSWERING READING COMPREHENSION QUESTIONS

Reading requires more than just the ability to pass your eyes over a piece of text and recognize all the words. You must be able to absorb ideas and information from the printed page. You must understand what you read. You must be able to follow the logic of the information. To find out whether you have understood something, your instructor will test you. This testing can be as simple as answering a few questions orally in class, or it can be a written exam or assignment.

Paraphrasing is an important test of reading comprehension. You can't put something in your own words if you do not understand it. In an assignment or exercise, you may be asked to paraphrase a particular passage. Other times, in a test, you may just have to put the author's ideas in your own words. It is not sufficient to simply copy the words directly from the text; this tells the instructor little about your understanding of the text.

For example, here are two possible answers to the question, "How does Bill Bryson find the taste of the junk food he so rashly buys?" ("Junk Food Heaven," p. 245):

1. Bryson finds the taste of the food awful. It seemed discouragingly pallid or disgustingly sickly.

2. Bryson dislikes the food because it has little taste or is too cloying.

Answer 1 uses words and phrases from the original text: "awful" and "seemed discouragingly pallid or disgustingly sickly" use little of the student's wording. This answer would receive few, or no, marks. Answer 2 is the better one.

In addition to such short-answer questions, you might be asked multiple choice or true-or-false questions. While some questions may focus on content, others might require you to analyze and interpret the text. You may have to identify the writer's thesis or comment on the techniques used in the essay. Writing a summary is also a test of reading comprehension.

SKIMMING AND SCANNING

Skimming and scanning are useful reading techniques when you need to get the general idea of a piece or are looking for a specific piece of information. When you skim a text, you let your eyes pass quickly over the words. You don't worry about understanding everything; you are just trying to get the gist of what is said. In scanning, you look for specific words. For instance, you might look for the name of a place or a specific date.

Skimming and scanning also include selective reading. You can read subtitles, the first sentences of paragraphs, and chapter introductions and summaries to get an idea of what material is covered. The table of contents and index can help you find specific points.

Effective skimming and scanning are skills you develop through practice. As a student, you need these skills in order to deal with the volumes of reading material for your courses.

Grey Owl's Magnificent Masquerade

John Barber

1   The colourful lies and personal failures that marked the career of the pseudo-Native Grey Owl did nothing to diminish his reputation when they flashed into view after his premature death in 1938. "Grey Owl had cockney accent and four wives," one headline read. As many of his eulogists accurately predicted, the fabrications served mainly to enhance his legacy.

2   "His attainments as a writer and naturalist will survive," *The Ottawa Citizen* editorialized at the time, "and when in later years our children's children are told of the strange masquerade — if it was a masquerade — their wonder and their appreciation will grow."

3   The time of those children's children has now come. Beginning tomorrow, they will be munching popcorn in front of a frankly hagiographic blockbuster devoted to the life and times of Grey Owl — a film that never would have been made had Archie Belaney not "written" his life according to the improbable conventions of Hollywood melodrama.

4   Grey Owl's many champions say that he misrepresented himself in order to attract attention to the causes of animal rights and wilderness conservation. No one would have paid attention to a plain old Englishman gone native in the Canadian North, they say; but a mystical "Red Indian" could really put it across. So, despite his lies, he did good.

5   In fact, there is no "despite" about it. The lies and the message are inextricable. The truth is, Grey Owl did good because he lied. Or, to make that statement more palatable, incorporate the euphemism favoured for lies we approve of: Grey Owl helped create the mythology that made the modern environmental movement possible.

6   The most powerful myth he created was that Native North Americans are the exemplars of environmental consciousness. Of all the variants of the "noble savage" cultural stereotype, invented by 18th-century Europeans for their own political and cultural purposes, it is by far the most durable. Despite what we know — and there is basically no anthropological evidence to support the notion — we can't let it go.

7   The best example is that of Chief Seattle, famous for an inspiring speech that brilliantly and poetically captures all the core beliefs of modern environmentalism. ("The Earth does not belong to man; man belongs to the Earth,"

et cetera.) Supposedly delivered in 1854, it was actually written around 1970 by U.S. screenwriter Ted Perry—and based on a poetic rendition that itself was based on an "improved" version of a highly dubious transcription made by a romantic Englishman 30 years after the actual words were uttered.

"Why are we so willing to accept a text like that if it's attributed to a Native American?" Mr. Perry has wondered. More to the point, why do so many people still vehemently insist on its authenticity?

Reading Grey Owl today, it is blazingly obvious (as many of this Native friends knew at the time) that he was no half-Apache wanderer who lacked formal education and, as late as his teenage years, had nothing better than pidgin English. His contemporary readers engaged in a suspension of disbelief that was more than willing—it was fierce.

It is less obvious, but equally true, that Grey Owl was no Canadian. The movement that he joined included many Canadians, most prominently the artists of the Group of Seven; and he learned his entire shtick from the writings of Ernest Thompson Seton (especially *Two Little Savages,* a manual on living like an Indian that Archie Belaney read as a boy and put into practice brilliantly). But to modern readers, his preoccupations seem wholly English.

Until Grey Owl, for instance, issues of animal rights were basically unknown on this side of the pond. (Even the famous John James Audubon shot every bird he ever painted.) In extolling the virtues of the "little folk" of the forest, especially the beavers he made into pets, Grey Owl was clearly following the example of his English grandfather and namesake, a crusading anti-vivisectionist—and not, as he claimed, traditional Native ways.

Grey Owl was surely the only Ojibwa of the 1930s to hold passionate views on the morality of English fox hunting.

None of that matters now. Grey Owl endures as a true Canadian hero, a foreigner who helped reveal the beauty of a magnificent landscape to scandalously blinkered nationals. He endures as a Native hero, not in his blood but in attitudes and beliefs that we still believe to be authentic. More than anything, he is an environmental hero, one who helped change the "real world" fundamentally through a magnificent act of the imagination.

1999

NOTES

Hagiographic blockbuster A huge Hollywood movie that portrays its hero as a saint. Barber is referring to the 1999 film starring Pierce Brosnan, which was just due to come out when this article was written.

Archie Belaney (1888–1938) An Englishman who lived in Canada, adopted the name Grey Owl, and wrote about environmental issues.

Red Indian A term to distinguish Native North Americans from East Indians, people from India. European settlers kept the generic misnomer of "Indian" for the North American Native peoples but distinguished them by the colour of their skin, which they saw as "red." This term is now considered a racial slur.

Noble savage A term coined by European writers and philosophers who idealized the North American Indian as being in touch with nature and unspoiled by civilization.

Chief Seattle (1786–1866) A famous Suquamish Native American who befriended settlers in the Pacific Northwest. He is revered as an environmentalist because of the speech he supposedly made.

Group of Seven (1920–1933) Famous Canadian artists who painted the wilderness of Canada.

Ernest Thompson Seton (1860–1946) A Canadian writer who wrote about animals and nature. His best-known works are *Wild Animals I Have Known* (1898) and *Two Little Savages: Being the Adventures of Two Boys Who Lived as Indians and What They Learned* (1906).

John James Audubon (1785–1851) An American naturalist and artist, famous for his study of birds.

COMPREHENSION AND DISCUSSION

1. What is Barber's attitude toward Grey Owl?
2. Does the writer try to balance his article with pros and cons about his subject? How?
3. Explain the paradox: "The truth is, Grey Owl did good because he lied" (p. 232). When is a lie acceptable? Do you believe that the end justifies the means?
4. Why did Grey Owl's words mean more than Archie Belaney's words would have? In other words, why was the masquerade necessary?
5. Why would modern readers be less likely to believe the masquerade?

6. Put this statement in your own words: "His contemporary readers engaged in a suspension of disbelief that was more than willing — it was fierce" (p. 233).

LITERARY TECHNIQUES

Barber makes his opinion clear by the positive words he uses, right from the title phrase "magnificent masquerade." Although he does not omit Belaney's character faults, he deals with them lightly and emphasizes the man's good deeds.

Oxymoron A literary device, a deliberate joining of two contradictory words or ideas, such as true lies or a healthy illness, to draw attention. Sometimes an oxymoron is used to create humour; at other times, to heighten the truth in the contradiction. For example, Barber states: "The truth is, Grey Owl did good because he lied" (p. 232). Since Grey Owl's life is full of such contraries, the oxymoron is appropriate.

ASSIGNMENTS

1. Make a vocabulary list for this article. Write down the words you are not familiar with and find definitions and synonyms.
2. One of the greatest impostors in recent history is Ferdinand Demara. Research his story. Find out his Canadian connections. Write a brief account of his exploits and life.
3. Read "Truth and Consequences" (p. 236) and "The Story of Grey Owl" (p. 330). How do the three writers differ in their tone and approach to the topic?
4. Read "The Loons" (p. 128). In this short story, Vanessa thinks that Piquette knows the secrets of nature because of the stereotype of Native people. Discuss the stereotype and explain what impact it has in our society.

Truth and Consequences
Brian Bethune

1   Almost as soon as the man known as Grey Owl died in a Prince Albert, Saskatchewan, hospital on April 13, 1938, his many secrets began to emerge into the open air. That same day, *The North Bay Nugget* ran a story it had sat on for three years, revealing that the famous Indian naturalist was actually an Englishman named Archie Belaney. And not just any Englishman, it eventually turned out, but a binge-drinking bigamist who had had five "wives." His closest supporters, especially Lovat Dickson, the Canadian-born London publisher who had made Grey Owl a household name in Britain, were devastated. They were desperately worried that all the good Grey Owl had done the cause of conservation would now be interred with his bones. But the twists and turns of Archie Belaney's strange saga by no means ended with his death.

2   Belaney was born in the English Channel port of Hastings in 1888, the son of a teenage bride and a reprobate father who soon left his family. Raised by two strict maiden aunts, Archie early on began to develop elaborate fantasies about his absent father, entwining the elder Belaney with his own love of animals and fascination with North American Natives. Those fantasies became the basis of Grey Owl's imaginary ancestry as the Mexican-born son of a Scots frontiersman and an Apache woman—Belaney's standard account of himself within two years of his arrival alone at age 17 in Northern Ontario in 1906. In 1910, Belaney married an Ojibwa woman, Angele Egwuna, his first and only legal wife. The next year, already drinking heavily, he abandoned her and their daughter, Alice.

3   During the next four poorly documented years of his life, Belaney strove to eradicate his English accent. He also had a son with a Métis woman, who died of tuberculosis soon after giving birth. Belaney next emerged in Digby, Nova Scotia, in May 1915, when he enlisted in the Canadian army. There he told the army recruiters that he was unmarried, thereby depriving Angele and Alice of government financial support. Belaney was out of the trenches in a year, after losing a toe to a possibly self-inflicted rifle wound. While convalescing near his aunts' home in Hastings, he re-met a childhood friend, Ivy Holmes, and married her in February 1917. When he returned to Canada that September, he told Ivy he would send for her. They never saw each other again.

After the war, Belaney continued to fine-tune his identity as an Indian. He dyed his hair black and coloured his skin with henna. His disgust with civilization, made almost complete by his combat experience, only deepened his concern for the shrinking forests of the North and the disappearing beaver. Under the influence of his fourth wife, an Iroquois variously called Pony or Anahareo, Belaney abandoned trapping. In 1929, he wrote a successful article for the British magazine *Country Life* about the passing wilderness way of life. The magazine's editors suggested he write a book. During the two years he worked on *The Men of the Last Frontier,* Belaney told his editors first that he lived among Indians, next that he had been adopted by Indians, and finally, in 1931, that he *was* an Indian. After a stab at the name White Owl, he settled on Grey Owl. From the book's publication until his death from pneumonia seven years later, he was an international superstar, one of the most famous Canadians of his day.

During his glory years, Grey Owl wrote more best-sellers, two of which—*Pilgrims of the Wild* and *The Adventures of Sajo and Her Beaver People*—are still regarded as classics. He made movies. Yousuf Karsh photographed him, even though Grey Owl missed a dinner engagement with Karsh and a clutch of Ottawa VIPs because of his involvement in a drunken brawl in a hotel bar. Grey Owl did manage to dine with Prime Minister William Lyon Mackenzie King, and he conducted two triumphant lecture tours of the British Isles, culminating in a three-hour audience with the Royal Family, including the future Queen Elizabeth II.

All the ironies of Archie Belaney's deceptive life came into play in that time. Certainly his key message of preservation of wilderness and wildlife struck a responsive chord, especially in animal-loving Britain. And in the time-honoured Canadian fashion, success in Britain brought acclaim back home. But what gained him a hearing in the first place was his assumed identity as an exotic noble savage, buttressed by his compelling storytelling power, itself polished through years of lying. His real upbringing provided him with his graceful prose. Grey Owl may have looked and sounded Indian, at least to urban audiences, but he wrote like the Hastings Grammar School graduate he was. (Only one contemporary critic noticed Grey Owl's rarefied English, however, and enraged Belaney—who could not admit the truth—by suggesting the untutored Native had had the aid of a ghostwriter.)

Throughout the 1930s, dozens of people, including almost every Indian who encountered him, knew the truth about Archie Belaney. Yet none ever exposed him publicly. Angele willingly admitted the facts to anyone who asked, including a *North Bay Nugget* reporter in 1935, but she did not initiate an open scandal. Those who knew Belaney either liked him—even the abandoned wives—or like the *Nugget*'s city editor and Indian leaders who appreciated Grey Owl's support for Natives, thought his message too important to risk harming. And when his death freed the *Nugget* to publish, setting off an international media frenzy, the Canadian response was surprisingly positive. "Of course, the value of his work is not jeopardized. His attainments as a writer and naturalist will survive," concluded *The Ottawa Citizen,* in an opinion widely shared in the national press.

8   That didn't stop a generation of neglect, however, as another world war and unprecedented economic growth pushed wilderness Canada out of the public consciousness. But the dawning environmental movement of the late 1960s found inspiration in Grey Owl's work. "Grey Owl was a superb propagandist for the natural world," says University of Calgary historian Donald Smith, author of *From the Land of Shadows: The Making of Grey Owl.* "He was the first to get it right—our uniqueness, our wonderful forests and rivers, what we were doing wrong—the first to tell mainstream Canada, 'Remember you belong to Nature, not it to you.' "

9   In the early 1970s, Grey Owl's books came out in new editions and in 1972 CBC-TV aired a documentary on him. His books remain in print, and new works about their author continue to appear, including Smith's 1990 biography and Jane Billinghurst's lavishly illustrated *Grey Owl* (1999). Even Parks Canada, which had allowed Grey Owl's last home, Beaver Lodge in Prince Albert National Park, to fall into disrepair, was roused to action. It made the area around Beaver Lodge a protected wilderness sanctuary and restored the cabin itself. That was a gesture that might have moved the enigmatic Archie Belaney. In a lifetime of deceit, love of the wilderness may have been his only genuine emotion.

1999

NOTES

Bigamist A person who is married to more than one spouse at the same time. Bigamy is illegal.

The North Bay Nugget A newspaper published in North Bay, Ontario.

Yousuf Karsh (1908–) A famous Canadian photographer, renowned for his photographs of famous people.

Noble savage A term invented and used by Europeans at the beginning of the 17th century to denote an Aboriginal person with high principles, who lives in the wilds but is civilized.

The Ottawa Citizen A daily newspaper published in Ottawa.

COMPREHENSION AND DISCUSSION

1. Who is Archie Belaney? (Summarize his biography as given in this article.)
2. How did he hone his Native persona? (A persona is a voice or character developed by a writer, or a role that one assumes in public.)
3. What did he do for Canada?
4. Why did people who knew him not expose him as a fraud?
5. Why is he still controversial?
6. How do you view Grey Owl—as a hero or a fraud? What is the most important aspect of his life?

LITERARY TECHNIQUES

Biography The story of a person's life. This article is biographical, more so than the articles by John Barber and Colin Ross. Note how the biography begins with Grey Owl's death. This technique is a common one. From here the writer can review Grey Owl's life and evaluate his contributions or achievements.

Chronology The sequence of events in a time line. Bethune goes from birth to death and elaborates the significant events in Grey Owl's life. Note that the writer does not jump back and forth at this time because doing so may confuse the reader. In addition, the references to dates help the reader get a bearing as Bethune gathers events together.

Quotations Actual words spoken or written about someone or something. Quotations inserted in an article tend to authenticate and advance the writer's views on the subject. They lend credence to opinions and explanations; they also offer another point of view. Sometimes writers pepper their articles with quotations to show that they have done extensive research on this subject and that the reader can depend on its veracity.

Slant This term refers to a bias or point of view in the writing. It can be favourable or unfavourable, depending on the approach the writer takes to the topic. Although most expository writing tends to be neutral or objective, a writer cannot help but put a bias or slant in it. Sometimes this bias occurs with the choice of material or point of view; sometimes, the leaning is unintentional. When the slant is decidedly one way, the writer intends it to be so (as in Colin Ross's article on Grey Owl, p. 330).

ASSIGNMENTS

1. Read the other two articles on Grey Owl: John Barber's "Grey Owl's Magnificent Masquerade" (p. 232) and Colin Ross's "The Story of Grey Owl" (p. 330). Explain the viewpoints each writer holds about Grey Owl.
2. Read "Of Weirdos and Eccentrics" (p. 289). Does Grey Owl qualify as eccentric? Support your view in a brief essay.
3. Research and write a short biography about another controversial Canadian, such as William Lyon Mackenzie King, Sir John A. Macdonald, Louis Riel, Margaret Trudeau, Amor De Cosmos, Nellie McClung, or Gerta Munsinger. Evaluate the person's place in history.
4. Find and read a sample of Grey Owl's writing or Chief Seattle's speech and analyze why it makes an effective environmental message.
5. Watch the motion picture *Grey Owl* (1999) starring Pierce Brosnan. Write a critique of the movie. What do you think Archie Belaney would think of the movie?

Toothpaste
David Bodanis

Into the bathroom goes our male resident, and after the most pressing need is satisfied it's time to brush the teeth. The tube of toothpaste is squeezed, its pinched metal seams are splayed, pressure waves are generated inside, and the paste begins to flow. But what's in this toothpaste, so carefully being extruded out?

Water mostly, 30 to 45 percent in most brands: ordinary, everyday simple tap water. It's there because people like to have a big gob of toothpaste to spread on the brush, and water is the cheapest stuff there is when it comes to making big gobs. Dripping a bit from the tap onto your brush would cost virtually nothing; whipped in with the rest of the toothpaste the manufacturers can sell it at a neat and accountant-pleasing $2 per pound equivalent. Toothpaste manufacture is a very lucrative occupation.

Second to water in quantity is chalk: exactly the same material that schoolteachers use to write on blackboards. It is collected from the crushed remains of long-dead ocean creatures. In the Cretaceous seas chalk particles served as part of the wickedly sharp outer skeleton that these creatures had to wrap around themselves to keep from getting chomped by all the slightly larger other ocean creatures they met. Their massed graves are our present chalk deposits.

The individual chalk particles — the size of the smallest mud particles in your garden — have kept their toughness over the eons, and now on the toothbrush they'll need it. The enamel outer coating of the tooth they'll have to face is the hardest substance in the body — tougher than skull, or bone, or nail. Only the chalk particles in toothpaste can successfully grind into the teeth during brushing, ripping off the surface layers like an abrading wheel grinding down a boulder in a quarry.

The craters, slashes, and channels that the chalk tears into the teeth will also remove a certain amount of built-up yellow in the carnage, and it is for that polishing function that it's there. A certain amount of unduly enlarged extra-abrasive chalk fragments tear such cavernous pits into the teeth that future decay bacteria will be able to bunker down there and thrive; the quality control people find it almost impossible to screen out these errant super-chalk pieces, and government regulations allow them to stay in.

6   In case even the gouging doesn't get all the yellow off, another substance is worked into the toothpaste cream. This is titanium dioxide. It comes in tiny spheres, and it's the stuff bobbing around in white wall paint to make it come out white. Splashed onto your teeth during the brushing, it coats much of the yellow that remains. Being water soluble it leaks off in the next few hours and is swallowed, but at least for the quick glance up in the mirror after finishing it will make the user think his teeth are truly white. Some manufacturers add optical whitening dyes — the stuff more commonly found in washing machine bleach — to make extra sure that that glance in the mirror shows reassuring white.

7   These ingredients alone would not make a very attractive concoction. They would stick in the tube like a sloppy white plastic lump, hard to squeeze out as well as revolting to the touch. Few consumers would savour rubbing in a mixture of water, ground-up blackboard chalk, and the whitener from latex paint first thing in the morning. To get around that finicky distaste the manufacturers have mixed in a host of other goodies.

8   To keep the glop from drying out, a mixture including glycerine glycol — related to the most common car anti-freeze ingredient — is whipped in with the chalk and water, and to give *that* concoction a bit of substance (all we really have so far is wet coloured chalk) a large helping is added of gummy molecules from the seaweed *Chondrus crispus*. This seaweed ooze spreads in among the chalk, paint, and anti-freeze, then stretches itself in all directions to hold the whole mass together. A bit of paraffin oil (the fuel that flickers in camping lamps) is pumped in with it to help the moss ooze keep the whole substance smooth.

9   With the glycol, ooze, and paraffin we're almost there. Only two minor chemicals are left to make the refreshing, cleansing substance we know as toothpaste. The ingredients so far are fine for cleaning, but they wouldn't make much of the satisfying foam we have come to expect in the morning brushing.

10   To remedy that, every toothpaste on the market has a big dollop of detergent added too. You've seen the suds detergent will make in a washing machine. The same substance added here will duplicate that inside the mouth. It's not particularly necessary, but it sells.

11   The only problem is that by itself this ingredient tastes, well, too like detergent. It's horribly bitter and harsh. The chalk put in toothpaste is pretty foul-tasting too for that matter. It's to get around that gustatory discomfort that the manufacturers put in the ingredient they tout perhaps the most of all. This is the flavouring, and it has to be strong. Double rectified peppermint oil is used — a flavourer so powerful that chemists know better than to sniff

it in the raw state in the laboratory. Menthol crystals and saccharin or other sugar simulators are added to complete the camouflage operation.

Is that it? Chalk, water, paint, seaweed, anti-freeze, paraffin oil, detergent, and peppermint? Not quite. A mix like that would be irresistible to the hundreds of thousands of individual bacteria lying on the surface of even an immaculately cleaned bathroom sink. They would get in, float in the water bubbles, ingest the ooze and paraffin, maybe even spray out enzymes to break down the chalk. The result would be an uninviting mess. The way manufacturers avoid that final obstacle is by putting something in to kill the bacteria. Something good and strong is needed, something that will zap any accidentally intrudant bacteria into oblivion. And that something is formaldehyde — the disinfectant used in anatomy labs.

So it's chalk, water, paint, seaweed, anti-freeze, paraffin oil, detergent, peppermint, formaldehyde, and fluoride (which can go some way towards preserving children's teeth) — that's the usual mixture raised to the mouth on the toothbrush for a fresh morning's clean. If it sounds too unfortunate, take heart. Studies show that thorough brushing with just plain water will often do as good a job.

1986

NOTES

Cretaceous The last period of the Mesozoic era, about 70 million years ago.

COMPREHENSION AND DISCUSSION

1. Why does Bodanis want to give you all this information about toothpaste? Can you see the broader ramifications?
2. How does Bodanis arrange the information for you? Why does he choose this method?
3. Explain how the ingredients work together to clean your teeth.
4. What can you do with this information? How does it affect you?
5. What qualities in toothpaste are important to you, and which could you do without?
6. How does this information make you look at other products you use? Which products would you like to know more about?

LITERARY TECHNIQUES

Bodanis begins his thesis with a rhetorical question: "But what's in this toothpaste, so carefully being extruded out?" (p. 241). He answers this question in the rest of the article. A rhetorical question grabs the attention and curiosity of the reader.

Process analysis or description is a rhetorical mode that explains in detail how something works or how something is made or done. Its purpose is to give you an understanding of the workings of the subject. It is methodical in that it is a step-by-step explanation. Unlike a set of instructions, the process description does not tell you what to do.

Classification and division are two other methods used in this article. Division is the categorizing of ideas or things into smaller units. For example, a large company may divide itself up into the electronics division, the parts division, and so on. Classification is the breakdown of one unit into smaller components. For example, Bodanis uses one unit—toothpaste—and separates it into its components: water, chalk, detergent, and so on.

Diction is the choice of words used in an article. In this case, Bodanis prefers informal, plain English rather than technical language because his audience does not require it. Moreover, scientific jargon might frustrate or confuse his readers. Appropriate vocabulary is important in writing.

ASSIGNMENTS

1. Read Jessica Mitford's "The Story of Service" (p. 301). Note how she reveals a process that we would prefer not to know more about—embalming. Compare the two articles.
2. Research another cosmetic product and write an essay about its ingredients.
3. Read "Junk Food Heaven" (p. 245). Find out more about the ingredients in junk food and write an essay describing preservatives and other additives.
4. Write a process analysis paragraph or essay on how a food product goes from original ingredients to your table. For example, track coffee from the plantation to your cup.
5. Food manufacturers must list their ingredients on the package. No such stipulation exists for cosmetic manufacturers, however. Write an argument essay on whether cosmetic manufacturers should list ingredients.

Junk Food Heaven
Bill Bryson

I decided to clean out the fridge the other day. We don't usually clean out our fridge — we just box it up every four or five years and send it off to the Centers for Disease Control in Atlanta with a note to help themselves to anything that looks scientifically promising — but we hadn't seen one of the cats for a few days and I had a vague recollection of having glimpsed something furry on the bottom shelf towards the back. (Turned out to be a large piece of Gorgonzola.)

So there I was, down on my knees unwrapping pieces of foil and peering cautiously into Tupperware containers, when I came across an interesting product called a breakfast pizza and I examined it with a kind of rueful fondness, as you might regard an old photograph of yourself dressed in clothes that you cannot believe you ever thought were stylish. The breakfast pizza, you see, represented the last surviving relic of a bout of very serious retail foolishness on my part.

Some weeks ago I announced to my wife that I was going to the supermarket with her next time she went because the stuff she kept bringing home was — how can I put this? — not fully in the spirit of American eating. Here we were living in a paradise of junk food — the country that gave the world cheese in a spray can — and she kept bringing home healthy stuff like fresh broccoli and packets of Ryvita.

It was because she was English, of course. She didn't really understand the rich, unrivalled possibilities for greasiness and goo that the American diet offers. I longed for artificial bacon bits, melted cheese in a shade of yellow unknown to nature, and creamy chocolate fillings, sometimes all in the same product. I wanted food that squirts when you bite into it or plops onto your shirt front in such gross quantities that you have to rise carefully from the table and limbo over to the sink to clean yourself up. So I accompanied her to the supermarket and while she was off squeezing melons and pricing shiitake mushrooms I made for the junk food section — which was essentially all the rest of the store. Well, it was heaven.

The breakfast cereals alone could have occupied me for most of the afternoon. There must have been 200 types, and I am not exaggerating. Every possible substance that could be dried, puffed, and coated with sugar was there. The most immediately arresting was a cereal called Cookie Crisp, which tried to pretend it was a nutritious breakfast but was really just chocolate chip cookies that you put in a bowl and ate with milk. Brilliant.

6   Also of note were cereals called Peanut Butter Crunch, Cinnamon Mini Buns, Count Chocula ("with Monster Marshmallows"), and a particularly hardcore offering called Cookie Blast Oat Meal, which contained *four* kinds of cookies. I grabbed one of each of the cereals and two of the oatmeal — how often I've said that you shouldn't start a day without a big steaming bowl of cookies — and sprinted with them back to the trolley.

7   "What's that?" my wife asked in the special tone of voice with which she often addresses me in retail establishments.

8   I didn't have time to explain. "Breakfast for the next six months," I panted as I dashed past, "and don't even *think* about putting any of it back and getting muesli."

9   I had no idea how the market for junk food had proliferated. Everywhere I turned I was confronted with foods guaranteed to make you waddle, most of which were entirely new to me — jelly creme pies, moon pies, pecan spinwheels, peach mellos, root beer buttons, chocolate fudge devil dogs, and a whipped marshmallow sandwich spread called Fluff, which came in a tub large enough to bath a baby in.

10 You really cannot believe the bounteous variety of non-nutritious foods available to the American supermarket shopper these days or the quantities in which they are consumed. I recently read that the average American eats 17.8 *pounds* of pretzels every year.

11 Aisle seven ("Food for the Seriously Obese") was especially productive. It had a whole section devoted exclusively to a product called Toaster Pastries, which included, among much else, eight different types of toaster strudel. And what exactly is toaster strudel? Who cares? It was coated in sugar and looked drippy. I grabbed an armload.

12 I admit I got a little carried away — but there was so much and I had been away so long.

13 It was the breakfast pizza that finally made my wife snap. She looked at the box and said, "No."

14 "I beg your pardon, my sweet?"

15 "You are not bringing home something called breakfast pizza. I will let you have" — she reached into the trolley for some specimen samples — "root beer buttons and toaster strudel and..." She lifted out a packet she hadn't noticed before. "What's this?"

16 I looked over her shoulder. "Microwave pancakes," I said.

17 "Microwave pancakes," she repeated, but with less enthusiasm.

18 "Isn't science wonderful?"

"You're going to eat it all," she said. "Every bit of everything that you don't put back on the shelves now. You do understand that?"

"Of course," I said in my sincerest voice.

And do you know she actually made me eat it. I spent weeks working my way through a symphony of American junk food, and it was all awful. Every bit of it. I don't know whether American junk food has got worse or whether my taste buds have matured, but even the treats I'd grown up with now seem discouragingly pallid or disgustingly sickly.

The most awful of all was the breakfast pizza. I tried it three or four times, baked it in the oven, zapped it with microwaves, and once in desperation served it with a side of marshmallow Fluff, but it never rose beyond a kind of limp, chewy listlessness. Eventually I gave up altogether and hid the box in the Tupperware graveyard on the bottom shelf of the fridge.

Which is why, when I came across it again the other day, I regarded it with mixed feelings. I started to chuck it out, then hesitated and opened the lid. It didn't smell bad — I expect it was pumped so full of chemicals that there wasn't any room for bacteria — and I thought about keeping it a while longer as a reminder of my folly, but in the end I discarded it. And then, feeling peckish, I went off to the larder to see if I couldn't find a nice plain piece of Ryvita and maybe a stick of celery.

1997

NOTES

Bill Bryson is an American who lived in England for almost twenty years. In 1996, he moved back to the United States with his family. Then he wrote a column for a British magazine about his rediscovery of his homeland.

Vocabulary can vary greatly from one dialect to another. American and British English are distinct varieties of English. Canadian English is similar to American English in vocabulary and expression, but it is not identical. And of course, there are different varieties of American, British, and Canadian English, so you cannot generalize too much. However, as an example, here is a list of British terms that are different in American and Canadian English:

British	American and Canadian
bonnet	hood (of a car)
boot	trunk (of a car)

flat	apartment
lift	elevator
trousers	pants, slacks
knickers	underpants

You can easily find more examples in dictionaries and books on language. On the Internet, you can use the search terms "Britishisms" or "Americanisms."

COMPREHENSION AND DISCUSSION

1. How do you know that Bryson is exaggerating in the first paragraph? Explain the exaggeration.
2. Make a list of other exaggerations — things that could not possibly be true — in his article.
3. What words would a Canadian or an American use for "peckish," "larder," and "trolley"?
4. What kind of foods does his wife choose at the supermarket? What kind does he long for? Are his descriptions of the food appetizing?
5. Why does Bryson write a dialogue between his wife and himself?
6. How have the author's tastes changed?
7. What do you consider junk food? What is the difference between junk food and fast food?

LITERARY TECHNIQUES

Humour often depends on exaggeration, or stretching the truth in order to make a point. For example, Bryson did not really expect to find the cat in the refrigerator. Humour is also cultural. Something may be hilarious in one culture, but meaningless or not funny at all in another. Much of the humour comes from Bryson's description of the foods and his relationship to such junk food.

Use of "I" (first person) Usually in non-fiction writing (such as articles, essays, scholarly monographs), the "I" may be identified as the author of the piece. In this case, the "I" is Bill Bryson. Such may not be the case in fiction.

ASSIGNMENTS

1. Write a humorous account of some facet of everyday life in Canada.
2. Write a process essay describing a grocery shopping trip or the preparation of a meal.
3. Are you an adventurous eater? What foods do you find disgusting? Explain why. Consider such foods as yogurt, horse, dog, eel, insects, pizza, tofu, sugared cereal, liver, tripe, brain, and tongue.
4. Read Farb and Armelagos's "The Patterns of Eating" (p. 262). How is this treatment of food different from Bryson's?
5. Given what Farb and Armelagos (p. 262) say about the evolution of table manners and utensils, speculate on such tools and etiquette at the dinner table in twenty years' time, using Bryson's article as a guideline.
6. Describe a strange food that you have encountered and tell of your experience eating (or not eating) it.

Growing Up on Grace

Rosie DiManno

1. I was about 6 years old when I discovered that I was a Canadian.

2. This came as a rude shock.

3. Insofar as I had a vague image of a huge world with a bunch of different countries in it, I thought I was an American.

4. My parents are Italian immigrants and I was born in Toronto, grew up on Grace St. downtown, but didn't learn English until I started school. In my household, whenever the adults spoke of leaving their old country for this new one, it was always put in these terms: We came to *America*. They made no distinction between the United States and Canada, or maybe I just didn't grasp it.

5. *America*. Sometimes it was said with regret and sadness, other times in terms of a bold adventure, but never with a sense of belonging. It was always this alien place in which they found themselves, and to which they were grateful for whatever comforts they had acquired. But their suspicions and their sense of isolation lingered. It's why they — and every other ethnic group that ventures to this city — clustered in self-contained, unilingual neighbourhoods, both to shun and to defend themselves from shunning. They weren't cultural ghettos; they were outposts of the familiar, like pioneer forts in a hostile land. The land of the *Inglese*.

6. It was the early '60s. I watched American TV beamed from Buffalo: *Captain Kangaroo* and *Commander Tom*. Sitcoms like *Petticoat Junction* and *The Honeymooners* — which had no similarities to our own existence on Grace St., but which I misunderstood as that larger American reality, from which I was excluded only because of my parentage, not by geographic boundaries. And certainly not because these were phony, idealized domestic situations that only existed within a television tube.

7. This, I thought — flipping between *Leave It to Beaver* and *I Love Lucy* — is how people *really* live, except on my street: The privileged people, not the interlopers (like us), the imposters (like us); the ones who have proprietary first dibs on the country, the ones who drink milk at the dinner table, who have cereal for breakfast, who make sandwiches from pre-sliced white bread, who wear high heels in the house.

8. There was no Canadian flag, remember, as the most visible national icon. At Clinton Public School, they flew the Union Jack, but I thought that was just a weird variation on the Stars and Stripes. There was a pho-

tograph of the Queen at the head of the class, and this got me to thinking about the relationship between the Queen and the president, who was also familiar to me from American TV news. We sang "God Save the Queen" in school, but at night, when the TV stations signed off, it was the American national anthem that accompanied the fade to black. There was no "O Canada."

Perhaps my main problem is that I never watched the CBC.

It dawned on me, somewhere around Grade 1, that I was not American at all, although this growing suspicion was something I kept to myself for awhile. It's not the kind of thing you ask an adult about, lest you appear colossally stupid, and I was not in the habit of asking my parents anything. They were probably more alien to me than the Ricardos.

When I was forced to accept this reality, it was with a sense of loss. Here I had been trying to visualize myself growing up and fitting into this bustling American lifestyle, this energetic and self-confident and purposeful country. But I was stuck with dreary old/young Canada. Second-rate by ancestry, third-rate by an accident of birth.

This dismay wore off, of course. Certainly, it was shed abruptly when I met my bosom friend Barbara Zloty, in Grade 5. She really was an American but had moved to Toronto with her mother to stay with relatives because her father was fighting in Vietnam. I could not imagine having a father fighting a war in a distant country, maybe getting killed, maimed. Eventually, Barbara's father was wounded, and they returned to El Paso.

Barbara made me my first grilled-cheese sandwich, which seemed terribly decadent and decidedly *Inglese*. My mother, who did not believe that we should ever enter the homes of anyone outside the extended family — and rarely were any of us invited — had forbidden me to have lunch at Barbara's. I went anyway. When I got home from school that afternoon, my mother met me halfway up the street and hit me with her shoe.

This is supposed to be a narrative about My Canada, yet I'm not sure what that means. I can tell you only small stories about growing up in a small piece of the country, as insular as any tumbleweed-tossed Prairie town or desolate Maritime hamlet.

I grew up not in a country but on a street. My territory stretched from Bloor to Harbord, with traffic lights at either end, Christie Pits to the north, Bickford Park directly across from the house, Montrose Park to the south. Bickford Park, where I climbed every tree, had no amenities: no playground, no pool, no soccer pitch. Just a weary little softball diamond, one drinking fountain, and a huge sewer grate that was cool against your face when you lay across it on hot summer days.

16 And yet the park fascinated us, we over-protected young children who were never allowed to roam beyond the busy thoroughfares at either end of Grace. Once I saw a man running through the park with his mangled left arm hanging by just a few strands of sinew. Once I found a gold signature pin that said: Rosalba. That is my real name, abbreviated and Anglicized once I started school, in a desperate attempt to be less Italian, more English. It fills me with wonder, still, that I should have found such a pin, with that odd name, in the grass at Bickford Park.

17 There were many Italians on that street, some relatives, some merely *paisans,* some with no ancestral connection but part of the cultural fraternity that kept Us separate from Them. There were several Jewish families, too, and I remember feeling a kinship with them, because they were also aliens. (Later on, in my teens, we would move to a predominantly Jewish neighbourhood in Downsview. This resulted in one curious anomaly: My mother now speaks English with a Yiddish accent and is as likely to make a brisket for dinner as lasagna.)

18 I was mortified, in those days, by our Italian-ness. I begged my mother to shave her legs, to which she finally acquiesced, although she never did understand the fuss. I hated the tomatoes and tangle of vegetables in our backyard and longed for the banality of a grass carpet. I hated the pepper and onions that my mother would string like braids on the front porch.

19 In late spring, my father—a farmer and shepherd before emigrating—would dump a load of manure on the front lawn because this is the world's best fertilizer. On those occasions, returning from school, I would walk right past my house lest any classmates realize that I lived in such a Munsters-like place.

20 My father—and I respect him for this only in retrospect—never attempted to ingratiate himself with the *Inglese* by being less Italian or by altering the rhythms of his life, although he was impeccably hospitable and generous.

21 He hunted, not for sport, but for food, and I can see him now, skinning jackrabbits over the cellar sink. In the fall, he would slaughter a pig; at Easter, a lamb.

22 My parents made sausages and strung them to dry inside a makeshift smokehouse. Prosciutto would be salted and hung for a year in the wine cellar. My mother would spend weeks slicing fresh tomatoes and bottling them for sauce, sterilizing the bottles in a steel drum of boiling water in the backyard, stoking the fire underneath. She'd pickle cucumbers and artichokes, cauliflower and olives.

23 I loved all these foods, so common now in Italian restaurants and grocery stores, but I was ashamed of them then. I would throw away my lunch

at school and starve rather than expose these peculiar items to my *Inglese* friends. I pined for peanut-butter sandwiches.

Sometimes, I would go grocery shopping with my mother just so I could persuade her to buy all this ostensibly tasty English stuff that I saw advertised on TV: jelly rolls, Cap'n Crunch cereal, Pop Tarts, Wonderbread, SpaghettiOs, Campbell's soup, Kraft macaroni and cheese, marshmallows. It all tasted foul, it made me gag. But if this is what it took to be *Inglese,* I would suffer for my pride.

In autumn, after weeks of consultation and innumerable taste-testing expeditions, the crates of grapes would be delivered to the house: hundreds of them, stacked on the lawn. California grapes for homemade wine. Families would help each other out in the complicated wine-making process, churning and pressing and sifting and decanting. It was, I suppose, a different version of the barn-building efforts in other cultures, a community event.

Invariably, I would step on a nail.

Menstruating women were not allowed near the mulch, lest they spoil the wine. I, still a child, was humiliated on behalf of these women, who would be sent upstairs to make themselves otherwise useful. I only realized later that they considered it a blessing to be so ostracized from such backbreaking work, and the constant curses of the men.

I rebelled against all of it. The religious processions that were the highlight of the calendar year; refusing to parade along the street in my bridelike Communion gown; refusing to attend the Catholic school in which I had been enrolled (hiding out in the sewer pipes at Christie Pits) until my mother threw up her hands in defeat; refusing to kiss the aunts and the uncles (all of whom had chin whiskers); refusing to eat anything that had a hint of tomato in it; refusing to speak Italian.

Education was not valued highly in our family, which possibly made us, our sub-group of Italian immigrants, different from other ethnic groups washing ashore in Canada. Education was feared by these Italians — a fear nurtured and encouraged by the Catholic church. Education would take children away from their parents, the priests said, would make them question authority, would draw them into the outside world, which was a forbidden place.

Yet every week, from the time I was very small, my mother would take me, in a clandestine venture, to the St. George main library, a good 20-block hike from our house. She could barely read Italian but she wanted me to learn something from the ridiculed pleasure of books.

An education, particularly a post-secondary education, was considered a waste on a girl. If I were to have any profession at all, it was decided on my behalf, I would become a teacher: a feminine profession, respectable, akin to mothering. I played along and planned my escape.

32   So there came a time when the street, and the neighbourhood, became too small and too cramped an existence for me. Symbolically, it was enough for my parents. They finally felt safe and entrenched. They knew nothing about the rest of the country and did not care. They didn't know the difference between a city and a province.

33   They were clueless about the vastness of Canada, although they had come to Toronto from Halifax by train. They never ventured outside the city, rarely strayed from the neighbourhood. The most ambitious foray I can recall is one winter when we took the streetcar to the College St. Eaton's store — the most WASPish of establishments — to buy me a typewriter. I'd never seen an escalator before.

34   My parents never took a vacation — in 45 years, my father has yet to return to Italy for a visit — never mingled with another ethnic group (save for an Indian friend who was my dad's hunting companion, and the Jewish family in whose coin laundry my mother had once worked), never had any curiosity about politics or social issues or even the most innocent of *Inglese* pleasures. My father has never been to a movie, never gone to a hockey game, never attended a parent night at school.

35   When I'm being generous, I convince myself that he was merely shy, that he felt ignorant in this English culture. But I'm more included to believe that he lived completely within himself, and even his family was an intrusion.

36   Perhaps I have inherited his discomfort, his diffidence, because I don't feel particularly connected to this country, either, although I have a genuine fondness for it.

37   Too long an outsider, faking it, beseeching entry. Relentlessly *Inglese* in attitude and tastes, irredeemably Italian in my genes. But not hyphenated, never hyphenated. A clumsy hybrid, maybe.

38   I used to fret so much, in my younger days, about how I could ever reconcile these two cultures, how I could be Rosalba and Rosie and still stay intact. The struggle doesn't seem very important any more.

39   But I am constantly astonished by third-generation Italian Canadians who seem more proud of their ancestral homeland than the country of their birth, who chatter in Italian on St. Clair Ave., who seem more Italian to me now than my parents did 30 years ago. Cultural pride is one thing, but so much of this overt Italian sensibility seems to me to be a betrayal — of Canada, and to those of us who broke all the rules so that we didn't have to stay insularly Italian, imprisoned by culture, in this country.

I don't wave flags and I find the notion of Canada Day contrived, if sweet. But I have felt moments of intense patriotism. Little moments, like spotting a Maple Leaf on a teenager's backpack in Europe. Grand moments, like when a Canadian wins a gold medal at the Olympics. Aching moments, like when I visit the Canadian war cemetery in Cassino, just down the mountain from my parents' village. (As children, they survived the battle of Monte Cassino.) And historical moments, like covering the referendum in Montreal in 1995, and feeling a sudden swell of anxiety, as if we were letting something very precious slip away, through carelessness and self-absorption.

As an adult, when I visit my ancestral village in Italy — which lost half its population to Toronto after the war — they always ask about life in *America*. I have given up trying to make the distinction. It just doesn't seem significant, from the perspective of a mountain top south of Naples.

It's funny, though. From the first time I set foot on Italian soil, I felt as if I belonged. I looked like everyone else, my name didn't sound foreign. I felt a thousand years of history rushing through my blood. But I couldn't live there.

And every time I come through Canada Customs, travel back across the border, I breathe a sigh of relief. Home.

My parents are Canadian citizens now. Grace St. is long ago and far away. They are living the good, Canadian life: a suburban home, a cottage, two cars, a truck, money in the bank. They take occasional trips, mostly church-organized, and are finally seeing a little more of the country. They vote. And they try very hard to pretend that we are not a fractured, dysfunctional family.

They do not read English. They will not read this story. They have never read a word I have written.

1997

NOTES

Rosie DiManno is a columnist and sports writer for *The Toronto Star*. She is known for her outspokenness and brashness.

America Many immigrant groups refer to both Canada and the United States as America. The Chinese, for example, use the term *gum san,* which translates as "golden mountain," to refer to Canada and the United States.

Union Jack The British flag. The three crosses of England, Scotland, and Ireland combine to make this symbol of the United Kingdom. These crosses respectively belong to St. George, St. Andrew, and St. Patrick.

Stars and Stripes The flag of the United States of America. Originally, it had only thirteen stars and stripes (one for each of the thirteen colonies at the time of the American Revolution). Now the flag has 50 stars, one for each state in the union.

Ricardo The family name in the popular American TV series *I Love Lucy*. It was one of the first ethnically mixed marriages on TV.

The Munsters A popular TV comedy series of the mid-1960s, featuring a family of monsters (a Frankenstein monster, vampire, witch, and were-wolf) trying to fit into the typical American society.

Prosciutto An Italian variation of ham.

Christie Pits An area in Metro Toronto.

WASP An acronym for "White Anglo-Saxon Protestant."

COMPREHENSION AND DISCUSSION

1. Why did the young Rosie DiManno believe she was American instead of Canadian?
2. What are some general criticisms DiManno has about Canada and Canadians?
3. How do the DiMannos preserve their old country ways?
4. Why did the author want to become part of the establishment and reject her Italian heritage?
5. Describe or explain DiManno's mixed feelings when she returned to Monte Cassino, Italy.
6. How does DiManno define her identity now?
7. Explain what DiManno means in her conclusion. Can you see this in a larger context about the immigrant experience?

LITERARY TECHNIQUES

Memoirs Thoughts, reflections, and feelings recounted in written form. Often they are synonymous with autobiography or biography, diaries, and letters.

Autobiography The story of a person's life written by that person.

"Write what you know" is the standard advice for writers. Many authors write about their childhood. The topic is familiar and easily researched. All the writer needs to do is draw from memory — most of the time.

ASSIGNMENTS

1. Write a narrative about a childhood experience. What particular incident do you remember vividly and wish to put into words for your readers?
2. What did you want to be when you were a child growing up, and what changed for you?
3. If you are an immigrant or if your parents are immigrants, what are some of the hardest things to change and to accept?
4. Read the short stories "Chickens for Christmas" (p. 63) and "Ralphie at the Races" (p. 205). Compare the non-fiction and the fiction portrayals of immigrant life. What are the distinguishing characteristics?
5. What makes you Canadian?
6. Some people argue that there is no distinctive Canadian culture. Do you agree? What is Canadian culture?
7. What aspects of your ethnic heritage do you want to keep for yourself and your children? Why? Or, what parts of your ethnic background would you want to drop? Why?

The Golden Years of Electronic Helps

Fred Donnelly

1. The baby-boom generation is about to cross one of the great thresholds of family life: In the next two decades many of them will see the death of their parents. Even before that happens, the aging of those parents will bring with it a number of difficult problems, including greater needs for medical services, nursing care, and alternative means of transportation, to name a few.

2. As a pre-boomer, born just a year after the end of the Second World War, I recently went through this difficult period. My parents lived until their early 80s, and both died of natural causes last year.

3. In the years just before their deaths they had a particular problem I called the technology gap. My father retired at age 60, expecting to live to 70 or so. Instead he lived almost a quarter of a century after his withdrawal from the work force. Confronted with new gadgets, high-tech appliances and especially computers, he tended to ignore them.

4. Why bother? He was sure he would be long gone before he had time to master the use of these newfangled gizmos.

5. The result was an ever-increasing technology gap between my parents' household operation and that of much of the developed world. They knew next to nothing about home computers, e-mail, and telephone-answering machines. They didn't know how to use the bank's automatic teller machine.

6. Things such as VCRs and microwave ovens (gifts from their sons) sat unused on counters. They simply occupied space until a visitor turned them on. My father, I recall, used the terms "CD" and "cassette" interchangeably, so it took me some time to realize he didn't know what a CD player was.

7. For years the technology gap was of no great significance to them. But it just kept getting wider. Then came the day when my aging parents were having trouble maintaining their cherished, independent life in their own home. They lost the ability to walk any significant distance, and at the same time could no longer drive their car. Soon they were trapped in their house, unable to venture out alone.

8. The irony of all this was that the new electronic technology held the solution to many of the mobility problems of their later days. They could have done their banking electronically from a home computer. Instead they

were dependent on others to drive them to the bank, where my mother, especially, would draw out large amounts of cash. The next trip to the bank might be far off, so they reasoned it was better to have a little more money on hand. The security problem presented by the situation was a further worry for our family.

Some shopping and most bill-paying could have been done electronically. Likewise, they could have used e-mail both to keep in touch with distant friends and carry on general household correspondence. As they couldn't walk to a mailbox, this was important.

As my father's physical condition deteriorated, he gradually lost manual dexterity. Writing became difficult and finally impossible. And yet I think he could have stayed active longer by working the keyboard of a personal computer. As they gradually slipped into the life of shut-ins, I am certain the computer could have provided a great source of entertainment.

The solution to many of my parents' problems was readily available in the new technology of electronic devices. Yet their generation, understandably enough, is the last to be largely computer-illiterate; the practical application of that technology was beyond their grasp.

For our aging seniors to hold on to an independent, mentally active life as long as possible, we need to devise ways to close the technology gap.

I wish I had been able to do that for my parents.

1998

NOTES

Baby boom Three decades (1946–1963) of an unprecedented increase in birthrates around the world, particularly in Canada and the United States.

Gizmo A generic slang term to mean anything mechanical or technological.

COMPREHENSION AND DISCUSSION

1. What is the attitude of seniors when they confront the latest technological product on the market? Why is this so?
2. What problems can occur when seniors do not adapt to new technology?
3. How would technology have helped the author's parents live more comfortably?

4. What technological products should older people need to have and know how to use? Why?
5. Have you encountered attitudes similar to those held by Donnelly's parents? Explain.

LITERARY TECHNIQUES

Donnelly uses the example of his parents to make general points about technology and older people. Notice how the first paragraph and the second-last paragraph contain generalizations, sandwiching the story of his parents.

Problem and solution In the section about his aging parents, Donnelly uses the problem/solution method to advance his point. He identifies the difficulty his parents were having and then in another paragraph offers the solution. For example, he states that his father and mother could no longer travel to the bank; then he draws attention to electronic banking, which could have allowed them to stay at home and still have access to their money.

One-sentence paragraphs They are used to emphasize or to show a transition from one unit of information to another. In this case, the concluding paragraph, in one sentence, serves to underscore the advantages of technology for the elderly and shut-ins. Such short paragraphs are common in newspaper and magazine articles because they break up the prose to make it easier to read in narrow columns. In academic writing, however, these short paragraphs would likely be part of longer, developed paragraphs.

ASSIGNMENTS

1. Write an essay stating the advantages or disadvantages of technological change.
2. Read Margaret Wente's "The End of Manual Labour" (p. 355). How does her approach to the topic of technology differ from Donnelly's?
3. Compare Donnelly's view of technology with that of Spider Robinson (p. 326).
4. If all electronic devices suddenly stopped functioning (as was feared for the Y2K problem), how would you survive? What changes in your life would you have to make?

5. Write an essay explaining why one of the following products is essential to modern life: computer, automobile, cellular phone, pager, answering machine, Walkman, fax machine, photocopier, home security alarm, microwave oven.

The Patterns of Eating
Peter Farb and George Armelagos

1. Among the important societal rules that represent one component of cuisine are table manners. As a socially instilled form of conduct, they reveal the attitudes typical of a society. Changes in table manners through time, as they have been documented for western Europe, likewise reflect fundamental changes in human relationships. Medieval courtiers saw their table manners as distinguishing them from crude peasants; but by modern standards, the manners were not exactly refined. Feudal lords used their unwashed hands to scoop food from a common bowl and they passed around a single goblet from which all drank. A finger or two would be extended while eating, so as to be kept free of grease and thus available for the next course, or for dipping into spices and condiments—possibly accounting for today's "polite" custom of extending the finger while holding a spoon or small fork. Soups and sauces were commonly drunk by lifting the bowl to the mouth; several diners frequently ate from the same bread trencher. Even lords and nobles would toss knawed bones back into the common dish, wolf down their food, spit onto the table (preferred conduct called for spitting under it), and blew their noses into the tablecloth.

2. By about the beginning of the sixteenth century, table manners began to move in the direction of today's standards. The importance attached to them is indicated by the phenomenal success of a treatise, *On Civility in Children*, by the philosopher Erasmus, which appeared in 1530; reprinted more than thirty times in the next six years, it also appeared in numerous translations. Erasmus' idea of good table manners was far from modern, but it did represent an advance. He believed, for example, that an upper-class diner was distinguished by putting only three fingers of one hand into the bowl, instead of the entire hand in the manner of the lower class. Wait a few moments after being seated before you dip into it, he advises. Do not poke around in your dish, but take the first piece you touch. Do not put chewed food from your mouth back on your place; instead, throw it under the table or behind your chair.

3. By the time of Erasmus, the changing table manners reveal a fundamental shift in society. People no longer ate from the same dish or drank from the same goblet, but were divided from one another by a new wall of constraint. Once the spontaneous, direct, and informal manners of the Middle Ages had been repressed, people began to feel shame. Defecation

and urination were now regarded as private activities; handkerchiefs came into use for blowing the nose; nightclothes were now worn, and bedrooms were set apart as private areas. Before the sixteenth century, even nobles ate in their vast kitchens; only then did a special room designated for eating come into use away from the bloody sides of meat, the animals about to be slaughtered, and the bustling servants. These new inhibitions became the essence of "civilized" behaviour, distinguishing adults from children, the upper classes from the lower, and Europeans from the "savages" then being discovered around the world. Restraint in eating habits became more marked in the centuries that followed. By about 1800, napkins were in common use, and before long they were placed on the thighs rather than wrapped around the neck; coffee and tea were no longer slurped out of the saucer; bread was genteelly broken into small pieces with the fingers rather than cut into large chunks with a knife.

Numerous paintings that depict meals — with subjects such as the Last Supper, the wedding at Cana, or Herod's feast — show what dining tables looked like before the seventeenth century. Forks were not depicted until about 1600 (when Jacopo Bassano painted one in a Last Supper), and very few spoons were shown. At least one knife is always depicted — an especially large one when it is the only one available for all the guests — but small individual knives were often at each place. Tin disks or oval pieces of wood had already replaced the bread trenchers. This change in eating utensils typified the new table manners in Europe. (In many other parts of the world, no utensils at all were used. In the Near East, for example, it was traditional to bring food to the mouth with the fingers of the right hand, the left being unacceptable because it was reserved for wiping the buttocks.) Utensils were employed in part because of a change in the attitude toward meat. During the Middle Ages, whole sides of meat, or even an entire dead animal, had been brought to the table and then carved in view of the diners. Beginning in the seventeenth century, at first in France but later elsewhere, the practice began to go out of fashion. One reason was that the family was ceasing to be a production unit that did its own slaughtering; as that function was transferred to specialists outside the home, the family became essentially a consumption unit. In addition, the size of the family was decreasing, and consequently whole animals, or even large parts of them, were uneconomical. The cuisines of Europe reflected these social and economic changes. The animal origin of meat dishes was concealed by the arts of preparation. Meat itself became distasteful to look upon, and carving was moved out of sight to the kitchen. Comparable changes had already taken place in Chinese cuisine, with meat being cut up beforehand, unobserved by the diners. England was an exception to the change in Europe, and in its former colonies — the United States, Canada, Australia, and South Africa — the custom has persisted of bringing a joint of meat to the table to be carved.

5   Once carving was no longer considered a necessary skill among the well-bred, changes inevitably took place in the use of the knife, unquestionably the earliest utensil used for manipulating food. (In fact, the earliest English cookbooks were not so much guides to recipes as guides to carving meat.) The attitude of diners toward the knife, going back to the Middle Ages and the Renaissance, had always been ambivalent. The knife served as a utensil, but it offered a potential threat because it was also a weapon. Thus taboos were increasingly placed upon its use: It was to be held by the point with the blunt handle presented; it was not to be placed anywhere near the face; and most important, the uses to which it was put were sharply restricted. It was not to be used for cutting soft foods such as boiled eggs or fish, or round ones such as potatoes, or to be lifted from the table for courses that did not need it. In short, good table manners in Europe gradually removed the threatening aspect of the knife from social occasions. A similar change had taken place much earlier in China when the warrior was supplanted by the scholar as a cultural model. The knife was banished completely from the table in favour of chopsticks, which is why the Chinese came to regard Europeans as barbarians at their table who "eat with swords."

6   The fork in particular enabled Europeans to separate themselves from the eating process, even avoiding manual contact with their food. When the fork first appeared in Europe, toward the end of the Middle Ages, it was used solely as an instrument for lifting chunks from the common bowl. Beginning in the sixteenth century, the fork was increasingly used by members of the upper classes — first in Italy, then in France, and finally in Germany and England. By then, social relations in western Europe had so changed that a utensil was needed to spare diners from the "uncivilized" and distasteful necessity of picking up food and putting it into the mouth with fingers. The addition of the fork to the table was once said to be for reasons of hygiene, but this cannot be true. By the sixteenth century people were no longer eating from a common bowl but from their own plates, and since they also washed their hands before meals, their fingers were now every bit as hygienic as a fork would have been. Nor can the reason for the adoption of the fork be connected with the wish not to soil the long ruff that was worn on the sleeve at the time, since the fork was also adopted in various countries where ruffs were not then in fashion.

7   Along with the appearance of the fork, all table utensils began to change and proliferate from the sixteenth century onward. Soup was no

longer eaten directly from the dish, but each diner used an individual spoon for that purpose. When a diner wanted a second helping from the serving dish, a ladle or a fresh spoon was used. More and more special utensils were developed for each kind of food: soup spoons, oyster forks, salad forks, two-tined fondue forks, blunt butter knives, special utensils for various desserts and kinds of fruit, each one differently shaped, or a different size, with differently numbered prongs and with blunt or serrated edges. The present European pattern eventually emerged, in which each person is provided with a table setting of as many as a dozen utensils at a full-course meal. With that, the separation of the human body from the taking of food became virtually complete. Good table manners dictated that even the cobs of maize were to be held by prongs inserted in each end, and the bones of lamb chops covered by ruffled paper pantalettes. Only under special conditions — as when Western people consciously imitate an earlier stage in culture at a picnic, fish fry, cookout, or campfire — do they still tear food apart with their fingers and their teeth, in a nostalgic reenactment of eating behaviours long vanished.

Today's neighbourhood barbecue recreates a world of sharing and hospitality that becomes rarer each year. We regard as a curiosity the behaviour of hunters in exotic regions. But every year millions of North Americans take to the woods and lakes to kill a wide variety of animals — with a difference, of course: What hunters do for survival we do for sport (and also for proof of masculinity, for male bonding, and for various psychological rewards). Like hunters, too, we stuff ourselves almost whenever food is available. Nibbling on a roasted ear of maize gives us, in addition to nutrients, the satisfaction of participating in culturally simpler ways. A festive meal, however, is still thought of in Victorian terms, with the dominant male officiating over the roast, the dominant female apportioning vegetables, the extended family gathered around the table, with everything in its proper place — a revered picture, as indeed it was so painted by Norman Rockwell, yet one that becomes less accurate with each year that passes.

1980

NOTES

This reading is an excerpt from the book *Consuming Passions: The Anthropology of Eating*.

Erasmus (1469–1536) A Dutch humanist philosopher of the Renaissance and Reformation. His famous work is *The Praise of Folly*.

Last Supper, the wedding at Cana, and Herod's feast Three paintings depicting episodes found in the New Testament in the Bible.

Norman Rockwell (1894–1978) An American painter who depicted a nostalgic past. He was famous for his illustrations on the cover of *The Saturday Evening Post* magazine.

COMPREHENSION AND DISCUSSION

1. What is the thesis of this article?
2. Why do we need table manners?
3. How is moving from the kitchen to a dining room a major step in social change?
4. Explain: "Once the spontaneous, direct, and informal manners of the Middle Ages had been repressed, people began to feel shame" (paragraph 3, p. 262).
5. Explain the evolving nature of the fork and the knife at the dinner table.
6. How is the barbecue a throwback to the Middle Ages in terms of cuisine?

LITERARY TECHNIQUES

Extended paragraph The length of a paragraph varies, depending on the function and style of the article. However, in academic writing, a developed paragraph runs about 150 to 200 words. The extended paragraph is longer and has more details. It is not a common style in modern writing and requires rhetorical skill to sustain its length properly. Individual sentences also tend to be longer in this style.

Cause/effect This technique explains progression. Cause is usually what starts something to happen; effect is the consequence of the action. Or, cause is the reason for an action; effect is the result of it.

Process analysis This method shows how things happen. Like cause-effect, it explains the logical sequence of events with as much detail as needed.

Diction Word choice. To set the tone of a piece, a writer must select the appropriate words. Note the formal use of language in this article. However, the words are not so technical as to force the reader to a dictionary.

ASSIGNMENTS

1. In "Junk Food Heaven" (p. 245), Bill Bryson talks about "food that squirts when you bite into it or plops onto your shirt front in such gross quantities that you have to rise carefully from the table and limbo over to the sink to clean yourself up." Describe the etiquette of eating messy food.
2. Besides good table manners, what other things can you think of that would define a society as civilized or refined?
3. How is this article similar to David Bodanis's "Toothpaste" (p. 241) or Bill Bryson's "Junk Food Heaven" (p. 245)?
4. Farb and Armelagos show how our attitudes toward meat have changed. Some people have gone even further and embraced vegetarianism. Write an essay for or against the principles behind vegetarianism.
5. While some cultures use the knife and fork at mealtimes, the use of chopsticks or fingers is the preferred method of eating in some cultures. Compare these methods, explaining the advantages and disadvantages.

Don't You Think It's Time to Start Thinking?

Northrop Frye

1. A student often leaves high school today without any sense of language as a structure.

2. He may also have the idea that reading and writing are elementary skills that he mastered in childhood, never having grasped the fact that there are differences in levels of reading and writing as there are in mathematics between short division and integral calculus.

3. Yet, in spite of his limited verbal skills, he firmly believes that he can think, that he has ideas, and that if he is just given the opportunity to express them he will be all right. Of course, when you look at what he's written you find it doesn't make any sense. When you tell him this he is devastated.

4. Part of his confusion here stems from the fact that we use the word "think" in so many bad, punning ways. Remember James Thurber's Walter Mitty who was always dreaming great dreams of glory. When his wife asked him what he was doing he would say, "Has it ever occurred to you that I might be thinking?"

5. But, of course, he wasn't thinking at all. Because we use it for everything our minds do, worrying, remembering, daydreaming, we imagine that thinking is something that can be achieved without any training. But again it's a matter of practice. How well we can think depends on how much of it we have already done. Most students need to be taught, very carefully and patiently, that there is no such thing as an inarticulate idea waiting to have the right words wrapped around it.

6. They have to learn that ideas do not exist until they have been incorporated into words. Until that point you don't know whether you are pregnant or just have gas on the stomach.

7. The operation of thinking is the practice of articulating ideas until they are in the right words. And we can't think at random either. We can only add one more idea to the body of something we have already thought about. Most of us spend very little time doing this, and that is why there are so few people whom we regard as having any power to articulate at all. When such a person appears in public life, like Mr. Trudeau, we tend to regard him as possessing a gigantic intellect.

8. A society like ours doesn't have very much interest in literacy. It is compulsory to read and write because society must have docile and obedient cit-

izens. We are taught to read so that we can obey the traffic signs and to cipher so that we can make out our income tax, but development of verbal competency is very much left to the individual.

And when we look at our day-to-day existence we can see that there are strong currents at work against the development of powers of articulateness. Young adolescents today often betray a curious sense of shame about speaking articulately, of framing a sentence with a period at the end of it.

Part of the reason for this is the powerful anti-intellectual drive which is constantly present in our society. Articulate speech marks you out as an individual, and in some settings this can be rather dangerous because people are often suspicious and frightened of articulateness. So if you say as little as possible and use only stereotyped, ready-made phrases you can hide yourself in the mass.

Then there are various epidemics sweeping over society which use unintelligibility as a weapon to preserve the present power structure. By making things as unintelligible as possible, to as many people as possible, you can hold the present power structure together. Understanding and articulateness lead to its destruction. This is the kind of thing that George Orwell was talking about, not just in *Nineteen Eighty-Four,* but in all his work on language. The kernel of everything reactionary and tyrannical in society is the impoverishment of the means of verbal communication.

The vast majority of things that we hear today are prejudices and clichés, simply verbal formulas that have no thought behind them but are put up as pretence of thinking. It is not until we realize these things conceal meaning, rather than reveal it, that we can begin to develop our own powers of articulateness.

The teaching of humanities is, therefore, a militant job. Teachers are faced not simply with a mass of misconceptions and unexamined assumptions. They must engage in a fight to help the student confront and reject the verbal formulas and stock responses, to convert passive acceptance into active, constructive power. It is a fight against illiteracy and for the maturation of the mental process, for the development of skills which once acquired will never become obsolete.

1986

NOTES

Northrop Frye (1912–1991) is considered one of the foremost academics of the 20th century. His writings reflect astute scholarship and original thinking, and his lectures at the University of Toronto were erudite and dynamic. This article appeared in *The Toronto Star*, so it was written for the general reader but with students in mind.

James Thurber (1894–1961) An American satirist and humorist in the earlier half of the 20th century. His most famous short story is "The Secret Life of Walter Mitty."

Walter Mitty The main character in Thurber's story. He is a middle-aged, hen-pecked daydreamer. We still allude to Walter Mitty to describe people with similar traits.

Pierre Elliott Trudeau (1919–2000) A prime minister of Canada from 1967 to 1983.

George Orwell (1903–1950) The pseudonym of Eric Blair, a British writer and satirist. His often reprinted writings are *1984, Animal Farm,* "Shooting an Elephant" (p. 314), and "Politics and the English Language."

Humanities A group of subjects in education including culture, language, literature, religion, philosophy, the arts, and history.

COMPREHENSION AND DISCUSSION

1. According to Frye, what does the average student "see" as "thinking"?
2. What is daydreaming? Define.
3. Explain Frye's phrase: "powers of articulateness."
4. Paraphrase this statement: "Most students need to be taught, very carefully and patiently, that there is no such thing as an inarticulate idea waiting to have the right words wrapped around it" (p. 268).
5. Why is thinking important to the individual and to society?
6. Frye criticizes our society by saying it is anti-intellectual and not really interested in literacy. Do you agree or disagree? Give examples to support your point of view.
7. Do you think Frye's criticism of students is justified?

LITERARY TECHNIQUES

This is an argument paper for a general audience. The tone is casual as evidenced by the vocabulary and by colloquial speech patterns such as shifts in pronoun with "you" and "we." His choice of examples are everyday, and he uses familiar allusions, such as Walter Mitty and George Orwell's *1984*.

Frye begins with the specific and moves to the general. He captures the reader's interest by focusing on a typical student and then widening his point to include society. By doing so, he reinforces his point about the necessity of teaching the humanities to help the process of thinking.

Because this article is written for a newspaper (in fact, *The Toronto Star*), Frye uses shorter paragraphs than those used in a periodical. He does so primarily because short paragraphs are easier to read and they fit better in narrow columns. Note that the first two paragraphs have only one sentence each. In addition, if you gather the first five paragraphs together into one, you will find a well-written developed introduction to his topic on thinking.

In short, the medium is as important as the message. In other words, how things are written is as significant as the content or ideas. In our textbook, we advocate the essay, a formal and structured way of writing for college and university students. However, the essay is not the only form of writing. As you can see here, an academic like Frye can shift into another style effortlessly.

ASSIGNMENTS

1. Read "What Is an Idea?" (p. 283). Compare it with Frye's article on subject matter and treatment.
2. Some people think that computer technology improves students' ability to think. In an essay, agree or disagree with this point of view.
3. Explain how reading is a mental exercise.
4. Frye says intellectuals are not valued in our society. What does our society value?
5. In Alice Munro's "An Ounce of Cure" (p. 153), the protagonist does not think logically. Would she have benefited from reading Frye's article?
6. Read James Thurber's short story "The Secret Life of Walter Mitty" (or see the 1947 film by the same name, starring Danny Kaye). Does daydreaming fulfill a useful purpose?

The Joys of Keeping in Touch, Virtually

Charles Gordon

1. Already the backlash has begun. Call it a virtual backlash. A *New Yorker* writer tells a chilling true story of a romance carried on by e-mail, a relationship that cannot survive face-to-face contact. The writer of an opinion piece in *The Toronto Star* talks disparagingly of the old friends who have contacted him by e-mail. "Virtual friends," he calls them, and "annoying social relics." He doesn't want to have anything to do with them, and how he wishes the technology that brought them together would go away.

2. There are other negative reports from the field. A newspaper executive has an e-mail address and makes a point of never looking in his e-mailbox. He figures anybody who has anything important to say to him will speak to him personally, telephone, or write a real letter. A university administrator refuses to have anything to do with e-mail, thinks it debases correspondence and increases the already excessive capacity of people to deal impersonally with each other.

3. Meanwhile, people all over the globe are happily e-mailing each other—exchanging gossip, passing along the latest joke that someone has passed along to them, telling everybody in the office that the big scissors are missing from the reception desk or that someone is selling candy bars again to send his daughter's recorder trio to the national finals. Most of these people think of e-mail as one of technology's better gifts of late. True, the odd dark cloud is appearing on the horizon—they are tired of having their labours interrupted by the latest word about the scissors, and they are beginning to see commercial intruders and political obsessives in their mailboxes, attempting to sell this and that. But a lot of e-mailers are willing to forgive all that for the feeling of being instantly in touch.

4. True, being instantly in touch means that people are instantly in touch with you, but they are in touch in a way that is far less invasive than the telephone solicitation at supper time. The e-mail intruder can usually be ignored and is at least quiet.

5. Plus, there is something to be said for having the ability, even if you don't use it, to reconnect with your past. Those who moved often in their childhood or who now live far from their home towns are happy to find and be found by friends and even acquaintances they had thought were long lost. As a result of

e-mail and the Internet, we will be seeing an increase in things like high-school reunions and, more important, an increase in post-reunion contact among friends. Some may find this frivolous, some may find it even intrusive, but there is nothing intrinsically wrong and a lot intrinsically right in being able to reconnect with your past, and your childhood. To do so takes you out of yourself, takes you away from the job and the TV out into the world where people you used to know are thinking about different things in different places.

It's true that one can be overpowered by this new toy. You can spend all your time in the past, huddled in front of the screen. Worse still, you can live your whole emotional life by e-mail, mistaking the pixels on the screen for the living molecules of genuine relationship. When the people on the screen become more important than the people around you, you, and those close to you, have lost your battle with technology.

Still, it is only technology. And e-mail is only a form of communication. What is communicated is up to you, not it. There is debate, even this early in the game, about the quality of communication. Everyone concedes that e-mail facilitates correspondence. Some go so far as to say that e-mail has resurrected the art of letter writing. Others note the casual haste with which today's e-mail correspondence is carried on and contrast it negatively with the elegant and thoughtful letters that are assumed to have been the norm in the days of pen-and-ink.

And so on and so on. Still, it is only a means of communication. You could even argue that the breezy, instantaneous mood of e-mail correspondence is, in at least some cases, an improvement over the slow, ponderous, and pretentious voice of yesterday's formal correspondence.

One point over which there can be no dispute at all is that tomorrow's historians will face a mountainous and largely unrewarding task sifting through the e-mails of their subjects. Given the electronic pack rat-ism that afflicts today's generation, only the failure of computer hard drives holds out any hope of relief from massive information overload.

There are other, less negative, reports from the field. A parent of children who attend overseas schools reports on their newfound ability to stay in touch by e-mail with friends who have moved to other continents. It is likely that the widening of the wired world and the ease of correspondence by e-mail will mean that friendships have a better chance of being forever. The once-in-a-lifetime bittersweetness of the high-school reunion will give way to the small daily pleasures of the electronic update. This may not be all for the better—how many friends is too many and how many virtual commercials will we have to wade through to contact them when the world of commerce learns to seize the technological opportunity? But who can know yet in these caveman days?

11   Concerning this stuff and the larger world of the Internet, the questions are so many and the answers so few that it is impossible even to discuss the growing gap between the technological haves and have-nots in the world. The gap is there, both within and between nations; that much is obvious. The people with computers and good phone lines can do things that the people without can't. What we don't know yet is which side of the gap is the worse off.

1997

NOTES

Charles Gordon is a writer for *The Ottawa Citizen*. He writes a column, "Another View," in *Maclean's* magazine, where this essay appeared.

COMPREHENSION AND DISCUSSION

1. Explain what Gordon means by a "backlash." To what is he referring? Why does he use this term?
2. What are some of the negative reactions to e-mail? What are some of the positive effects of e-mail?
3. How does e-mail connect with the past?
4. Paraphrase this statement: "Given the electronic pack rat-ism that afflicts today's generation, only the failure of computer hard drives holds out any hope of relief from massive information overload" (p. 273).
5. What is Gordon's conclusion? Is he in favour of e-mail?
6. Explain "the growing gap between the technological haves and have-nots" (above).
7. This article was written in 1997. Given that technology changes so rapidly, are Gordon's comments about e-mail still valid today?
8. Have you ever had an e-mail message misconstrued because the reader did not have the benefit of a tone of voice or facial expressions? Discuss your experiences.

LITERARY TECHNIQUES

Figure of speech Way of expressing something without being literal. Often these figures of speech liven up a statement or idea. For example, Gordon's clause "the odd dark cloud is appearing on the horizon" (p. 272) is more colourful and visual than saying "it is possible that a problem will show up."

Gordon presents two opposing points of view in this article. He presents the views in a conversational way, going back and forth between the positive and negative aspects about e-mail. He uses simple transition words between the different sections, switching sides with simple words like "but," "still" (in the sense of "however"), and "true." Go through the article and find the places where he switches between positive and negative points. Note how he marks each transition.

While this essay is a column from a magazine, it uses developed paragraphs, unlike many magazine articles. Gordon is addressing a general audience and is using an informal style. For instance, he starts sentences with "still," "and," and "but," giving the piece a conversational tone.

ASSIGNMENTS

1. Write a paragraph or short essay giving the advantages or disadvantages of e-mail. Do not just repeat the ideas from the article. Or, compare e-mail with other forms of communication. For example, how is e-mail more like conversation than other forms of writing?
2. Besides e-mail, how else has the Internet affected human behaviour?
3. In the 1960s, Marshall McLuhan said that telecommunication has made the world a global village. Is this still true, or have we gone beyond the global village?
4. Read "The Golden Years of Electronic Helps" by Fred Donnelly (p. 258). Compare it with Gordon's article. How do their views on the new technology differ?
5. Has e-mail made you a more careful or sloppier writer? Why? How?
6. Research the privacy issue in relation to e-mail. For example, do your employers have the right to open your e-mail? Does your service provider have the right to censor your e-mail? Is e-mail really secure and private?
7. Speculate on the future of e-mail and electronic communication. How will technological advancements affect other methods of communication?

Don't Say Cheese!
Shinan Govani

1. I am not a big shot, and here's why.
2. I don't own a camera. I say this with the same dill-pickled smugness that some people use when they announce that they don't own a television set.
3. My disenchantment with the camera began rather early, when it occurred to me that birthday parties and school events were more about getting "the shot" than anything else.
4. The disenchantment heightened during my high-school graduation when I looked around and saw that people were not savouring this seminal moment, but were rather too busy posing for pictures that would somehow help to invoke memories of a moment when, funnily enough, they were posing for pictures.
5. My position hardened finally, irretrievably, during my stock coming-of-age trip to Europe, when I witnessed countless souls who never seemed to come up from behind their lens to actually experience anything, types who never really *saw* the San Marco Plaza in Venice or the Cote d'Azur in France.
6. While any kind of photography runs the danger of turning into a kind of false grist for remembrance (a soon-to-be-married friend mused recently that she felt like she was having a wedding primarily to take pictures), I find photographs to be particularly vexing during vacations and trips.
7. People often ask: "Don't you want pictures of your trips so that you can share your memories with others?"
8. No, I can tell others about them. You remember narrative, don't you? They say storytelling is a lost art.
9. "Well," I'm asked, "aren't you afraid that you'll forget what you've seen?"
10. Well, to be honest, I'd rather forget what I haven't actually seen in the first place than hang on to some pictures, which are, at best, a microwaved version of the real thing.
11. "But a picture is worth a thousand words," they object.
12. Well, that may be true in one sense of the word "worth." In another sense, I'm a writer and I can sell words, but unless you're a professional photographer, you can't hawk your snaps to pay for the trip. So why not just purchase a really good memorabilia book of photographs (or even a bunch of postcards) of the places you've visited by people who are actually deft at taking pictures?

And while it's true that members of the species Homo sapiens have been smitten with documenting themselves ever since they daubed the walls of caves with drawings, photographs are different. For many people, photographs are no longer a means of invoking the journey but instead the aim of the journey, and the camera the chariot that takes them there. Documentation has become the destination. The photo has become the pilgrimage.

I even heard a frightening story recently about one family that pulled up to the Grand Canyon in a minivan. A man jumped out of the vehicle, took a picture and just as he stopped to pause a bit to take in the grandeur, his wife pulled him back in. "You don't have to stop. We can look at the pictures when we get home," she bellowed.

It's all a bit like being at a sumptuous feast and being too worried about having some stuff for leftovers than actually taking the time to relish the spread itself.

For a culture obsessed with gadgetry, cameras are nifty toys to help people who are experience-challenged to have an experience. In particular, it allows them to bring home replicas of the same shots that they've seen a hundred times in movies or in their friends' albums, giving them the sensation that they've entered into a common experience with everyone who has come before them.

It validates the trip.

The taking of the picture, in this sense, is a ceremonial ritual, a verbal spell, an ecstatic chant. And in the same way that some people are famous for being famous, some places, it seems to me, are photographed now because they're famous for being photographed.

1999

NOTES

It is traditional for photographers to tell their subjects to "Say cheese!" so that they will smile for the picture. In order to say "cheese" the mouth must pull the cheek muscles and expose teeth. Thus, the person makes his face into a "smile."

Big shot A slang term for someone important. Since we also refer to "shots" in photography, Govani is playing on the term.

Snaps Short for snapshots or photographs.

COMPREHENSION AND DISCUSSION

1. What is the Govani's main point in this article?
2. Why doesn't Govani take pictures when he is on trips?
3. What do you think he means by "dill-pickled smugness" (p. 276)? Explain the imagery in the term.
4. Are his arguments reasonable? Explain.
5. Put into your own words: "Documentation has become the destination. The photo has become the pilgrimage" (p. 277). What does Govani mean?
6. Find synonyms for these words: seminal, memorabilia, Homo sapiens, smitten, nifty.
7. Why do you take photographs?
8. Does Govani's argument discourage you from taking pictures? Why? Or why not?

LITERARY TECHNIQUES

Chronological sequence One method of organizing ideas in writing. Note how Govani begins at childhood birthday parties and moves to a wedding. These steps not only are logical but also require the passage of time.

Rhetorical questions Questions posed and answered by the writer. This method engages the reader. Govani gives a variation on the question-and-answer method in the middle of the essay when he has an imaginary argument with those who hold an opposing view.

Analogy A comparison, a method whereby the writer draws on something familiar to explain the unfamiliar to the reader. It can be brief or extended, depending on the complexity of the original idea.

Govani draws attention to his article with a single statement: "I am not a big shot, and here's why" (p. 276).

ASSIGNMENTS

1. Read Katherine Govier's "The Immaculate Conception Photography Gallery" (p. 76). How does the view of photography in that story differ from Govani's?

2. Write a description of a photograph that is meaningful for you.
3. Govani mentions the trip to Europe as a typical "coming-of-age" experience (p. 276). What is the importance of such an experience? Describe other ways people mark becoming an adult.
4. Speculate on the implications of digital cameras and digitized photographs. How will this technology change our society?

Canadian Tire Money
Wayne Grady

1. You know how, when you pay cash for something at a Canadian Tire store, you get Canadian Tire money back, even if you pay for the thing with Canadian Tire money in the first place? Say you're buying a hammer for $10. You count out twenty 50¢ coupons, give them to the cashier, she puts them in one drawer, then opens another drawer, takes out a fresh 50¢ coupon, and hands it back to you.

2. Here's an experiment. The next time you're in Canadian Tire, try giving the cashier $9.50 worth of Canadian Tire money and say, "Just keep the one you were going to give me." And the cashier will say: "I'm sorry, but we can't do that."

3. That's just the way Murial Billes wanted it. The wife of Alfred Jackson Billes — who, with his brother John William, founded the Canadian Tire Corporation in 1922 — Murial invented Canadian Tire money when the store opened its first gas bar in Toronto in 1958. Rather than give customers a dinner plate or a toaster, as rival service stations were doing, Murial thought (I'm paraphrasing here): "Why not give them a coupon worth 5 percent of their purchase, *redeemable only at Canadian Tire?*"

4. That's why Murial would have rejected my experiment — because it reduces the coupon to a simple discount. Canadian Tire money is more than that, more even than a customer-loyalty program. Canadian Tire money is a metaphysical construct. It keeps you going back to Canadian Tire, since, theoretically at least, that's the only place you can spend it. Yet the more Canadian Tire money you spend, the more you get back. You can't leave without it. It sticks to you like fly paper.

5. Canadian Tire likes the program because it compels us to spend like Santa but makes us think we're saving like Scrooge. Canadians like Canadian Tire money, however, because we can thwart the cycle; we can turn the money to our own use. It's become our unofficial second currency, because we've figured out ways to spend it that Murial Billes never intended. We've all heard the one about the guy who paid an unsuspecting cab driver in Mexico with Canadian Tire money. A bar in Cornwall, Ontario, used to accept Canadian Tire money for beer, before it burned down last year. And I know of a school that got parents to donate their Canadian Tire money; when the teachers had collected $500 worth, they took it to Canadian Tire and bought a bicycle, then raffled off the bicycle, raising

$1200 in real money. Then they bought sports equipment for the school—from Canadian Tire, which earned them $60 in Canadian Tire money.

I don't know what the teachers did with the $60. Maybe they went back and spent it at Canadian Tire. But I hope they took it to that bar in Cornwall, before it burned down.

1999

NOTES

Scrooge The main character in Charles Dickens's classic tale *A Christmas Carol* (1843), in which a miser learns the true spirit of Christmas in 19th-century England. The term "Scrooge" is synonymous with being a miser. Canadian Tire has run a long, successful ad campaign with the slogan "Give like Santa, save like Scrooge."

COMPREHENSION AND DISCUSSION

1. Who are the Billes?
2. When was the first Canadian Tire money given out? Who thought up this marketing scheme and why? How was it different from what other companies were doing?
3. In what inventive ways have customers used this money?
4. Do you consider Canadian Tire money legitimate currency?
5. Explain what Grady means when he compares Canadian Tire money to fly paper.

LITERARY TECHNIQUES

This piece is written in a very conversational style. Notice the use of expressions such as "you know how" and "say." The use of "you" and the present tense in the first paragraph is colloquial. It also serves to draw you into the article.

Expository essay A piece of writing that gives information on a certain topic or subject matter. Note how the writer begins with the familiar—Canadian Tire money—and then gives information you may not know, such as the origins and history of this marketing strategy.

Example and illustration Both offer information and details to support general statements in a paragraph or essay. An example is specific and often more concise (note the sentence about the Canadian tourist in Mexico). An illustration is equally exact but can be expanded or more elaborate. For instance, Grady draws on the schoolteachers' inventive use of Canadian Tire money to raise funds for sports equipment.

Conclusion Grady follows the time-honoured method of wrapping up the topic by referring to something said in the body of the article. In this case, he combines two examples—the teachers and the bar owner—of people who have used Canadian Tire money inventively.

ASSIGNMENTS

1. Write a descriptive paragraph on what Canadian Tire money looks like.
2. What recent marketing campaigns have caught your attention or imagination? Evaluate their effectiveness.
3. Write a brief expository piece on one of the following items of Canadian culture: timbits, poutine, the Stanley Cup, pablum, toques, Hockey Night in Canada.
4. As often happens in family businesses, the second generation of Billes have had some problems and disagreements. Research the family and write an expository essay about their history.
5. Read "Toothpaste" (p. 241). Both articles discuss a single product. How are the treatments different?

What Is an Idea?
Marshall W. Gregory and Wayne C. Booth

"I've got an idea; let's go get a hamburger." "All right, now, as sales representatives we must brainstorm for ideas to increase profits." "The way Ray flatters the boss gives you the idea he's bucking for a promotion, doesn't it?" "Hey, listen to this: I've just had an idea for attaching the boat to the top of the car without having to buy a carrier." "The idea of good defence is to keep pressure on the other team without committing errors ourselves." "What did you say that set of books was called? *The Great Ideas?* What does that mean?"

The word *idea,* as you can see, is used in a great many ways. In most of the examples just mentioned it means something like "intention," "opinion," or "mental image." The "idea" of going for a hamburger is really a mental picture of a possible action, just as the "idea" of a boat carrier is a mental image of a mechanical device. The "ideas" of good defence and Ray the flatterer are really opinions held by the speakers, while the appeal for "ideas" about how to increase profits is really an appeal for opinions (which may also involve mental images) from fellow workers. None of these examples, however, encompasses the meaning of *idea* as it has always been used by those who engage in serious discussions of politics, history, intellectual movements, and social affairs. Even the last example, an allusion to the famous set of books edited by Robert Maynard Hutchins and Mortimer Adler at the University of Chicago, does not yet express an idea; it only directs us toward a source where ideas may be encountered.

These uses of *idea* are entirely appropriate in their contexts. Words play different roles at different times. One can "fish" for either trout or compliments; and a scalp, an executive, and a toilet (in the Navy) are all "heads." Usually these different uses have overlapping, not opposed, meanings. For example, we wouldn't know what fishing for compliments meant unless we already knew what fishing for trout meant, and the "heads" we just referred to are all indications of position or place. In the same way, the different uses of the word *idea* overlap. Even the most enduring ideas may appear to some as "mere opinion." What, then, does *idea* mean in the context of serious talk, and what keeps some opinions and mental images from being ideas in our sense?

Three central features distinguish an idea from other kinds of mental constructs:

1. An idea is always connected to other ideas that lead to it, follow from it, or somehow support it. *Like a family member, an idea always exists amid a network of ancestors, parents, brothers, sisters, and cousins.* An idea could no more spring into existence by itself than a plant could grow without a seed, soil, and a suitable environment. For example, the idea that acts of racial discrimination are immoral grows out of and is surrounded by a complex of other, related ideas about the nature of human beings and the nature of moral conduct: Racial differences are irrelevant to human nature, the sort of respect that is due to any human being *as* a human being is due equally to *all* human beings, it is immoral to deny to any human being the rights and privileges due to every human being, and so on. You can see that a great many other ideas surround, support, and follow from the leading idea.
2. An idea always has the capacity to generate other ideas. Ideas not only have ancestors and parents, but progeny. The idea that *racial* discrimination is immoral, for example, is the offspring of the idea that *any* sort of bigotry is wrong.
3. An idea is always capable of yielding more than one argument or position. An idea never has a fixed, once-and-for-all meaning, and it always requires interpretation and discussion. Whenever interpretation is required and discussion permitted, disagreements will exist. Ideas are always to some degree controversial, but the kind of controversy produced by the clash of ideas — unlike the kind of controversy produced by the clash of prejudices — is one in which reasons are offered and tested by both sides in the debate. As reasons are considered, positions that seemed fixed turn into ideas that move with argument.

5   In recent years, for example, the idea that racial discrimination is immoral, combined with the idea that past discriminations should be compensated for, has led to the follow-up idea that minority groups should, in some cases, receive preferred treatment, such as being granted admission to medical school with lower scores than those of competing applicants from majority groups. Some people have charged that this is "reverse discrimination," while others advance arguments for such actions with great intellectual and moral vigour. Regardless of where you stand on this issue, you can see that interpretations of ideas yield a multiplicity of positions.

6   There are obviously many kinds of mental products that do not qualify as ideas according to these criteria. "Two plus two equals four," for example, is not an idea. Without reference to the ideas that lie behind it, it

can neither be interpreted nor used. In and of itself, "two plus two equals four" is simply a brute fact, not an idea. However, as a statement it is clearly the product of ideas: the idea of quantity, the idea that the world can be understood and manipulated in terms of systems of numbers, and so on.

Many of our everyday notions, opinions, and pictures of things also fail to qualify as ideas. "I hate John" may be an intelligible utterance—it conveys the feelings of the speaker—but it is not an idea. The "parents" of this utterance lie in the psychology or biography of the speaker, not in other ideas, and it can neither yield its own offspring nor support an argument. "Catholics are sheep," "All communists are traitors," "Christianity is the only true religion," "Republicans stink," "Most people on welfare are cheaters," and "Premarital sex is OK if you know what you're doing" are all such non-ideas. With appropriate development or modification, some of these opinions could be turned into ideas, but what keeps them from qualifying as ideas in their present form is that they are only minimally related (and in some instances totally unrelated) to other ideas. One sign that you are being offered mindless, bigoted, or fanatical opinions, not ideas, is the presence of emotion-charged generalizations, unsupported by evidence or argument. Catchwords, clichés, and code phrases ("welfare cheaters," "dumb jocks," "typical woman," "mad scientist") are a sure sign that emotions have shoved ideas out of the picture.

A liberal education is an education in ideas—not merely memorizing them, but learning to move among them, balancing one against the other, negotiating relationships, accommodating new arguments, and returning for a closer look. Writing is one of the primary ways of learning how to perform this intricate dance *on one's own.* In American education, where the learning of facts and data is often confused with an education in ideas, thoughtful writing remains one of our best methods for learning how to turn opinions into ideas.

The attempt to write well forces us to clarify our thoughts. Because every word in an essay (unlike those in a conversation) can be retrieved in the same form every time and then discussed, interpreted, challenged, and argued about, the act of putting words down on paper is more deliberate than speaking. It places more responsibility on us, and it threatens us with greater consequences for error. Our written words and ideas can be thrown back in our faces, either by our readers or simply by the page itself as we re-read. We are thus more aware when writing than when speaking that every word is a *choice,* one that commits us to a meaning in a way that another word would not.

10   One result is that writing forces us to develop ideas more systematically and fully than speaking does. In conversation we can often get away with canyon-sized gaps in our arguments, and we can rely on facial expression, tone, gesture, and other "body language" to fill out our meanings when our words fail. But most of these devices are denied to us when we write. To make a piece of writing effective, every essential step must be filled in carefully, clearly, and emphatically. We cannot grab our listeners by the lapel or charm them with our ingratiating smile. The "grabbing" and the "charm" must somehow be put into words, and that always requires greater care than is needed in ordinary conversation.

11   Inexperienced writers often make the mistake of thinking that they have a firmer grasp on their ideas than on their words. They frequently utter the complaint, "I know what I want to say; I just can't find the words for it." This claim is almost always untrue. It is easy to confuse an intuitive sense that you have something to say with the false sense that you already know precisely what that something is. When a writer is stuck for words, the problem is rarely a problem only of words. Inexperienced writers may think they need larger vocabularies when what they really need are clearer ideas and intentions. Being stuck for words indicates that the thought you want to convey is still vague, unformed, cloudy, and confused. Once you finally discover your concrete meaning, you will discover the proper words for expressing it at the same time. You may revise words later as meanings become *more* clear to you, but no writer ever stands in full possession of an idea without having enough words to express it.

12   Ideas are to writing as strength and agility are to athletic prowess: They do not in themselves guarantee quality, but they are the muscle in all good writing prowess. Not all strong and agile athletes are champions, but all champion athletes are strong and agile. Not everyone who has powerful ideas is a great writer, but it is impossible for any writer even to be effective, much less achieve greatness, without them.

1992

NOTES

This essay comes from the introduction to *The Harper & Row Reader,* a college textbook by Gregory and Booth. It tells students what they need in their writing. Ideas, as defined in this essay, are the basis of topic sentences and thesis statements.

COMPREHENSION AND DISCUSSION

1. Why do Gregory and Booth feel the need to define "idea"?
2. What are the three features of an idea?
3. Explain "reverse discrimination."
4. Why is writing important to ideas? How is writing different from speech?
5. Why do the authors dismiss the claim that people have ideas but not the words to explain them?
6. What message do the authors have for students?
7. Does this article convince you of the value of essay writing as an academic exercise? Why or why not?

LITERARY TECHNIQUES

Gregory and Booth begin with a selection of quotations, all common phrases and statements made in relation to their topic: the concept of idea. Having done that, the authors use another strategy: the rhetorical question to pique the interest of the reader.

Definition Explaining a term or idea so that the reader can understand it. The method can be formal or informal in structure, brief or extended, technical or common. Note that defining requires the inclusion of other writing techniques, such as classification, example and illustration, comparison, and exposition.

Negation is often helpful in showing difference or revealing what something is not. As the authors define "idea," they elaborate by showing what it is not, for example, in paragraph 7: "Many of our everyday notions, opinions, and pictures of things also fail to qualify as ideas" (p. 285). The authors then proceed to itemize what cannot be included as an idea.

Analogy A comparison in which the writer uses something common or familiar to explain the unknown or unfamiliar. This reading ends with an analogy, using the idea of athletic prowess to explain writing. The assumption is that the readers know more about athletics than about writing.

Paragraphing The developed paragraph has two features: a clear topic sentence and expanded support for that main idea. Unlike Frye's newspaper article (p. 268), Gregory and Booth's academic essay prefers paragraphs of more than 150 words each. The length of a paragraph then determines what can be included to make the point clear.

ASSIGNMENTS

1. Read Northrop Frye's "Don't You Think It's Time to Start Thinking?" (p. 268) and compare the points the two essays make.
2. Analyze Gregory and Booth's last paragraph (p. 286). What are these writers saying? What techniques of writing do they use?
3. Using the points in this reading, write an essay explaining the value of writing an essay, or of the value of a liberal arts education.
4. Compare speaking and writing.

Of Weirdos and Eccentrics
Pico Iyer

Charles Waterton was just another typical eccentric. In his 80s the eminent country squire was to be seen clambering around the upper branches of an oak tree with what was aptly described as the agility of an "adolescent gorilla." The beloved 27th lord of Walton Hall also devoted his distinguished old age to scratching the back part of his head with his right big toe. Such displays of animal high spirits were not, however, confined to the gentleman's later years. When young, Waterton made four separate trips to South America, where he sought the wourali poison (a cure, he was convinced, for hydrophobia), and once spent months on end with one foot dangling from his hammock in the quixotic hope of having his toe sucked by a vampire bat.

James Warren Jones, by contrast, was something of a weirdo. As a boy in the casket-making town of Lynn, Indiana, he used to conduct elaborate funeral services for dead pets. Later, as a struggling preacher, he went from door to door, in bow tie and tweed jacket, selling imported monkeys. After briefly fleeing to South America (a shelter, he believed, from an imminent nuclear holocaust), the man who regarded himself as a reincarnation of Lenin settled in Northern California and opened some convalescent homes. Then, one humid day in the jungles of Guyana, he ordered his followers to drink a Kool-Aid-like punch soured with cyanide. By the time the world arrived at Jonestown, 911 people were dead.

The difference between the eccentric and the weirdo is, in its way, the difference between a man with a teddy bear in his hand and a man with a gun. We are also, of course, besieged by other kinds of deviants—crackpots, oddballs, fanatics, quacks, and cranks. But the weirdo and the eccentric define between them that invisible line at which strangeness acquires an edge and oddness becomes menace.

The difference between the two starts with the words themselves: eccentric, after all, carries a distinguished Latin pedigree that refers, quite reasonably, to anything that departs from the centre; weird, by comparison, has its mongrel origins in the Old English *wyrd,* meaning fate or destiny; and the larger, darker forces conjured up by the term—*Macbeth*'s weird sisters and the like—are given an extra twist with the slangy, bastard suffix -o. Beneath the linguistic roots, however, we feel the differences in our pulses. The eccentric we generally regard as something of a donny, dotty, harmless type, like the British peer who threw over his Cambridge fellowship in order to live in a bath. The weirdo is an altogether more shadowy figure—Charles Manson acting out his messianic visions. The eccentric is a distinctive presence; the weirdo something of an absence, who casts no reflection in society's mirror. The eccentric raises a smile; the weirdo leaves a chill.

5   All too often, though, the two terms are not so easily distinguished. Many a criminal trial, after all, revolves around precisely that grey area where the two begin to blur. Was Bernhard Goetz just a volatile Everyman, ourselves pushed to the limit, and then beyond? Or was he in fact an aberration? Often, besides, eccentrics may simply be weirdos in possession of a VIP pass, people rich enough or powerful enough to live above convention, amoral as Greek gods. Elvis Presley could afford to pump bullets into silhouettes of humans and never count the cost. Lesser mortals, however, must find another kind of victim.

6   To some extent too, we tend to think of eccentricity as the prerogative, even the hallmark, of genius. And genius is its own vindication. Who cared that Glenn Gould sang along with the piano while playing Bach, so long as he played so beautifully? Even the Herculean debauches of Babe Ruth did not undermine so much as confirm his status as a legend.

7   Indeed, the unorthodox inflections of the exceptional can lead to all kinds of dangerous assumptions. If geniuses are out of the ordinary and psychopaths are out of the ordinary, then geniuses are psychopaths and vice versa, or so at least runs the reasoning of many dramatists who set their plays in loony bins. If the successful are often strange, then being strange is a way of becoming successful, or so believe all those would-be artists who work on eccentric poses. And if celebrity is its own defence, then many a demagogue or criminal assures himself that he will ultimately be redeemed by the celebrity he covets.

8   All these distortions, however, ignore the most fundamental distinction of all: the eccentric is strange because he cares too little about society, the weirdo because he cares too much. The eccentric generally wants nothing more than his own attic-like space in which he can live by his own peculiar lights. The weirdo, however, resents his outcast status and constantly seeks to get back into society, or at least get back at it. His is the rage not of the bachelor but the divorcé.

9   Thus the eccentric hardly cares if he is seen to be strange; that in a sense is what makes him strange. The weirdo, however, wants desperately to be taken as normal and struggles to keep his strangeness to himself. "He was always such a nice man," the neighbours ritually tell reporters after a sniper's rampage. "He always seemed so normal."

And because the two mark such different tangents to the norm, their incidence can, in its way, be an index of a society's health. The height of British eccentricity, for example, coincided with the height of British power, if only, perhaps, because Britain in its imperial heyday presented so strong a centre from which to depart. Nowadays, with the empire gone and the centre vanishing, Britain is more often associated with the maladjusted weirdo — the orange-haired misfit or the soccer hooligan.

At the other extreme, the relentless and ritualized normalcy of a society like Japan's — there are only four psychiatrists in all of Tokyo — can, to Western eyes, itself seem almost abnormal. Too few eccentrics can be as dangerous as too many weirdos. For in the end, eccentricity is a mark of confidence, accommodated best by a confident society, whereas weirdness inspires fear because it is a symptom of fear and uncertainty and rage. A society needs the eccentric as much as it needs a decorated frame for the portrait it fashions of itself; it needs the weirdo as much as it needs a hole punched through the middle of the canvas.

1988

NOTES

Theophrastus (370–285 B.C.), a Greek philosopher, began a form of writing called character sketches. He took stereotypical traits of people from every walk of life and described them. He used physiognomy, the art of revealing personality from bodily features, usually the face. This concept caught the fancy of later writers and became quite popular in the 18th century. It is still used in literature.

James Warren Jones (1931–1978) More commonly known as Jim Jones. His cult was called the People's Temple. The deaths in Jonestown, Guyana, occurred in 1978.

Charles Manson The charismatic leader of a group called "the family" that, in 1969, killed several people including actress Sharon Tate, wife of famed director Roman Polanski.

Bernhard Goetz The New York "subway vigilante." In 1984 he shot five black teenagers, who, he believed, were going to rob him on a subway train. He was found not guilty of attempted murder.

Glenn Gould (1932–1982) A great Canadian pianist, known for odd behaviour such as wearing many layers of clothing, even in the summertime.

Babe Ruth (1895–1948) Nickname for George Herman Ruth Jr., an American baseball pitcher and hitter, one of the best players ever.

COMPREHENSION AND DISCUSSION

1. Explain Iyer's distinction between weirdo and eccentric.
2. Explain: "[E]ccentrics may simply be weirdos in possession of a VIP pass, people rich enough or powerful enough to live above convention."
3. Is perceiving someone as a weirdo or eccentric just a personal opinion or a societal one?
4. Why would Britain have more eccentrics than Japan?
5. Describe an example of eccentric or weird behaviour you have witnessed.

LITERARY TECHNIQUES

Compare/contrast To compare is to look for similarities in two or more items; to contrast is to look for differences. This technique is helpful in drawing together or in separating one thing from another. In this case, Iyer shows the differences between weirdos and eccentrics.

Definition Making the meaning of a term or idea clear and distinct so the reader can understand it. The method can be formal or informal in structure, brief or extended, technical or common. Defining requires the inclusion of other writing techniques such as classification, example and illustration, comparison, and exposition.

Examples Note how the writer opens with an extended example to catch the reader's attention. An example is defined as a specific piece of information used to support a general statement.

Etymology How a word comes into use. Often in definition the writer explains the history of the word and its origins. Note Iyer's etymological explanation of "weird" in paragraph 4 (p. 289). The root or source of a word can enlighten the reader to its current usage.

ASSIGNMENTS

1. Would Iyer classify the narrator of "We So Seldom Look on Love" (p. 86) as a weirdo or an eccentric? Support your opinion in a short essay or paragraph.
2. See the readings about Grey Owl (pp. 232, 236, and 330). Was Grey Owl a weirdo or an eccentric?
3. Write an essay defining two different kinds of people: tourist/traveller, cook/chef, amateur/professional athlete, gourmet/gourmand, doctor/nurse, secretary/assistant, children/adults.
4. Is it fair to categorize people by physical appearance, behaviour, or personality types? Why or why not?
5. How much eccentricity can our society accept? What boundaries are necessary?
6. Research a famous person who exhibits or exhibited eccentric behaviour. Explain the eccentricity. Should that person be vilified or accepted? How does the person's celebrity status affect the eccentricity? Some examples: Michael Jackson, Elvis Presley, Doug Henning, Howard Hughes, Glenn Gould, William Lyon Mackenzie King, Amor de Cosmos, Ludwig van Beethoven, Dennis Rodman.

Our Father Who Art in Classrooms: No
Keith Knight

1. Prayer is one's conversation with a higher being. For Christians, it involves a conversation with God.

2. Early Christ followers, not sure just exactly how they should pray, asked Jesus Christ for instructions. He taught them a profoundly simple, yet all-encompassing prayer which we know today as the Lord's Prayer. It is a prayer to be offered by those who believe in Jesus Christ as the Son of God and as their personal saviour.

3. Religion and faith once played a significant role in the public education system. Egerton Ryerson, considered the father of Ontario's public school system, focused on academics and structure when he set out in the 1840s to organize education. But he also believed in teaching Christian morality as one of the underlying values of education. Those values were a reflection of a white, Protestant Ontario in the mid-1800s. Subsequently, a Roman Catholic education system was also put in place to reflect those values.

4. As the province became more multicultural and less Christian, there was a growing notion that religious teaching belonged in the home, church, synagogue, or mosque rather than in the classroom.

5. The question of religious instruction in the public school system has always been a strong bone of contention, but legislation in 1971 again made this a possibility. The act provided for about an hour of religious instruction per week, but this was usually used up with five-minute sessions loosely termed as "opening exercises." They generally involved Bible reading and prayer, depending on the school principal and the board of education.

6. School boards tended to shy away from a course in religious instruction because many schools consisted of a kaleidoscope of beliefs and it would be impossible to do justice to all of them. Consequently, some schools, especially those in rural areas where populations tended to remain essentially white and Protestant, offered opening exercises which included the Lord's Prayer and perhaps even Bible reading. Today, that practice is left to the discretion of the principal.

7. Just as today we no longer speak one language, we also don't serve one God. The church no longer serves as a focal point for mainstream Ontario society. Religion and faith are becoming increasingly irrelevant.

Consequently, the public school system has adopted a humanist perspective, encouraging students to make their own religious and faith decisions apart from the classroom. The classroom has become a place where cultures and faith perspectives meet, and where children are encouraged to respect each other as individuals, without determining which belief is "right" or "wrong."

Does the Lord's Prayer belong in the classroom? Only if all those students and the teacher truly believed what they pray. That is why Christian schools exist. And Jewish schools. And Muslim schools. These are schools where faith and religion permeate the curriculum. The teaching perspective is not humanist, it is Christian, or Jewish, or Muslim, or whatever.

Those who advocate a return of the Lord's Prayer to the classroom live with the mistaken notion that our society in general and the public school system specifically are indeed Christian. Check out Reginald Bibby's books on church attendance and the role of the Christian faith in Canadian society. They confirm that Canada is no longer considered a Christian nation.

Those nine Saskatoon parents have right to complain. Neither they nor their children believe in God. To have them recite the Lord's Prayer could be considered an act of blasphemy. Saskatoon rabbi Roger Pavey is right: "Prayer as an act of worship has to be engaged, in order to be meaningful, as a voluntary act of faith. Here it is a coercive act of worship, which is meaningless."

The Lord's Prayer belongs in a school setting where faith and religion play a significant role. And just as our society celebrates our multiculturalism, so we should also celebrate our religious diversity and our desire to educate our children with those perspectives in mind. If we honour diversity, we should acknowledge that an educational system with just two ideological streams — humanist and Roman Catholic — does not reflect the Ontario of the 21st century.

1999

Our Father Who Art in Classrooms: Yes

Raheel Raza

1. I learned the Lord's Prayer at a very young age in school—not here in Canada, but in Pakistan at the convent school where I was educated. This was at a time and place where the words diversity or multiculturalism had no meaning; I'm talking predominant Muslim ideology in a small town.

2. When the recent furor in Saskatoon schools came to a head, I realized that with the passage of time, I'd forgotten all but my favourite part of the prayer "forgive us our trespasses as we forgive those that trespass against us...." I asked a colleague to refresh my memory and recite the Lord's Prayer for me. Glancing at me suspiciously, she recited the prayer. I wanted to convince myself there is nothing amiss in a non-Christian like me reciting the Lord's Prayer which I did happily for many years, not because I was forced to—we had a choice of abstaining—but because I liked to.

3. The Christian students at school used to stand in line, fold their hands, bow their heads, and softly recite the prayer with the nuns. We Muslim students were not required to, but I always joined in and revered the experience. One day I announced to my mother that I knew the Lord's Prayer and proudly recited it from beginning to end. My mother smiled and said, "It's always nice to know that all of us, despite different faiths, believe in the same Lord."

4. I don't believe my psyche, my freedom, or my faith have suffered from the impact of the Lord's Prayer. The handful of parents agitating against the practice of reciting the Lord's Prayer in Saskatoon schools must be a very sorry lot. As Jews, Unitarians, and Muslims, surely they don't believe in a Lord *other* than the one referred to in the Torah, Bible, and Quran. If their children in school were being *forced* to recite prayers, it's a different matter. But they have the choice to abstain. Most kids from diverse backgrounds face some form of ridicule for their differences—whether it be caste, colour, creed, or costume. This is what teaches them to be strong in their own beliefs—provided they show the same respect to others.

5. Minorities in Canada have the liberty to build their own place of prayer, ask for special exemption for their kids in school, and have total freedom to preach and practise their faith openly. Some of them come

from countries where they were persecuted for practising a particular faith. Yet they are questioning the faith practice of a community that has been doing the same for a long time, and are forcing the majority to change the law.

The Saskatoon Human Rights Commission declared the prayers discriminatory because "they interfere with the freedom of religion for all students." I understand freedom of religion in a different way, that is, the freedom to practise any religion, anywhere and anytime. This is what I thought Canada was all about, not just multicultural but multifaith as well. On the one hand, there is a major push to promote tolerance and understanding between all the people who have made Canada their home. At the same time, the practices of the people for whom Canada was home long before we came here are being questioned.

This is similar to the furor about calling Christmas by its name, saying "Happy Holidays" (which we only do to people going on vacation!), and having Christmas trees in public places. What is the matter with Canadians? In trying to accommodate the rights and freedoms of all the diverse groups coming to Canada, are they going to let their own rights and freedoms be compromised? Recently there was even talk about taking God out of the Constitution.

Perhaps the best solution is to do what a teacher friend has implemented in her multicultural school in London. Everyday at assembly, a different faith group recites a short prayer (including the Lord's Prayer), so kids are exposed to a variety of faiths, learn to respect each other's beliefs, and understand that all religions teach good values and basically stem from the same root. This has created a better relationship and understanding not only among students, but between teachers and parents, and has been lauded as a great approach for the new millennium.

My suggestion to people with a chip on their shoulder about other faiths is to leave the Lord alone. Instead of taking faith out of lives, let us adjust to fit our lives around the Lord. After all, the Lord doesn't need us — we need Him. Amen.

1999

NOTES

Keith Knight works for the Presbyterian Church in Canada. Raheel Raza belongs to the Islamic faith.

Humanist A person whose philosophy focuses on human values rather than on religious grounds.

Saskatoon controversy Began in 1993 when some Saskatoon parents objected to the recitation of "The Lord's Prayer" in the classroom. The issue was somewhat resolved by a ruling by a Board of Inquiry on July 27, 1999.

COMPREHENSION AND DISCUSSION

1. How does Knight begin his article? When does he come to his thesis?
2. How does Raza begin her article? When does she come to her thesis?
3. Why did *The Toronto Star* newspaper choose Keith Knight and Raheel Raza to oppose each other on this topic?
4. Knight states: "The church no longer serves as a focal point for mainstream Ontario society. Religion and faith are becoming increasingly irrelevant" (p. 294). How valid is this statement?
5. Raza states: "In trying to accommodate the rights and freedoms of all the diverse groups coming to Canada, are they [Canadians] going to let their own rights and freedoms be compromised?" (p. 297). How valid is this statement?
6. Who presents the stronger argument? With whom do you agree?
7. Does religion have a place in public education? Argue for or against it.
8. Should there be religious schools in Canada? Why or why not?

LITERARY TECHNIQUES

Pro and con (for and against) Two opposing sides on a controversial topic. It is a form of debate on an issue. Each writer argues for his or her side, and the reader is left to decide which presents the stronger case. Note that in this kind of debate the writers do not respond to each other's points.

Note how Knight presents his side. After introducing his topic in a single statement, he gives a brief history of Christianity and its role in public education in two subsequent paragraphs. Then he turns to a general discussion of religious instruction in the schools. In it he explains the recent changes in a diverse population and the need to reflect the new reality. All this is background for the reader, who may not be aware of the controversy. His main point begins after the rhetorical question "Does the Lord's Prayer belong in the classroom?" (p. 295). The last paragraph makes his position clear.

Note how Raza presents her side. She introduces her topic with a personal experience before she informs the reader of the recent controversy. Moreover, she makes it clear she is Muslim, not Christian. She continues with a personal anecdote about her mother. From her own classroom experience as a child, she now questions the suggestion of harm done in reciting the Christian prayer. She makes the point that minorities have choices and can exercise their rights. She questions the right of the minority to force the established majority to make changes. Finally, she offers a solution for the classroom teacher, and reiterates her argument.

Argumentation All writing has the implicit element of persuasion; however, in an argument paper, the writer unabashedly wants to win the reader over, so the writing is designed to make persuasive points.

There are common elements in an argument paper:

- stating a position on the issue
- giving background information for the reader
- gathering persuasive support in some logical order
- confronting the main opposing arguments
- reiterating the position

ASSIGNMENTS

1. Summarize the two sides of the argument in a paragraph for each. Your paragraphs should be less than 100 words each.
2. In an essay, suggest guidelines for the role of religion in a multicultural society.
3. Why is religion such a controversial topic? Explain.
4. As an intellectual exercise, it is good training to argue both sides of an issue. Write two short essays, one on each side of a controversial issue. For instance, you can write about gun control, school uniforms, government spending, or any local issue. Alternatively, hold a formal debate in the class on the issue.
5. In 2000, the Ontario government wanted to make singing the national anthem and reciting the oath of citizenship a mandatory part of the

school day. Because of the controversy surrounding the oath, especially the pledge to the Queen, the government removed that requirement. What do you think of requiring school children to recite an oath, sing an anthem, or say a prayer before school? Research the topic and write an argument essay.

6. Read "Rediscovering Christmas" (p. 359). Do you think Almas Zakiuddin would agree with Raza? Explain.

The Story of Service
Jessica Mitford

There was a time when the undertaker's tasks were clear-cut and rather obvious, and when he billed his patrons accordingly. Typical late-nineteenth-century charges, in addition to the price of merchandise, are shown on bills of the period as: "Services at the house (placing corpse in the coffin), $1.25," "Preserving remains on ice, $10," "Getting permit, $1.50." It was customary for the undertaker to add a few dollars to his bill for being "in attendance," which seems only fair and right. The cost of embalming was around $10 in 1880. An undertaker, writing in 1900, recommends these minimums for service charges: washing and dressing, $5; embalming, $10; hearse, $8 to $10. As Robert W. Habenstein and William M. Lamers, the historians of the trade, have pointed out, "The undertaker had yet to conceive of the value of personal service offered professionally for a fee, legitimately claimed." Well, he has now so conceived with a vengeance.

When weaving in the story of service as it is rendered today, spokesmen for the funeral industry tend to become so carried away by their own enthusiasm, so positively lyrical and copious in their declarations, that the outsider may have a little trouble understanding it all. There are indeed contradictions. Preferred Funeral Directors International has prepared a talk designed to inform people about service: "The American public receive the services of employees and proprietor alike, nine and one half days of labour for every funeral handled, they receive the use of automobiles and hearses, a building including a chapel and other rooms which require building maintenance, insurance, taxes and licences, and depreciation, as well as heat in the winter, cooling in the summer, light and water." The writer goes on to say that while the process of embalming takes only about three hours, "it would be necessary for one man to work two forty-hour weeks to complete a funeral service. This is coupled with an additional forty hours of service required by members of other local allied professions, including the work of the cemeteries, newspapers, and, of course, the most important of all, the service of your clergyman. These some 120 hours of labour are the basic value on which the cost of funerals rests."

Our informant has lumped a lot of things together here. To start with "the most important of all, the service of your clergyman": the average religious funeral service lasts no more than twenty-five minutes. Furthermore, it is not, of course, paid for by the funeral director. The "work of cemeteries" presumably means the opening and closing of a grave. This now mechanized operation, which takes fifteen to twenty minutes, is likewise not billed as part of the funeral director's costs. The work of "newspapers"? This is a puzzler. Presumably, reference is made here to the publication of an obituary notice on the vital statistics page. It is, incidentally, surprising to learn that newspaper work is considered an "allied profession."

4   Just how insurance, taxes, licences, and depreciation are figured in as part of the 120 man-hours of service is hard to tell. The writer does mention that his operation features "65 items of service." In general, the funeral salesman is inclined to chuck in everything he does under the heading of "service." For example, in a typical list of "services" he will include items like "securing statistical data" (in other words, completing the death certificate and finding out how much insurance was left by the deceased), the "arrangements conference" (in which the sale of the funeral to the survivors is made), and the "keeping of records," by which he means his own bookkeeping work. Evidently, there is some confusion here between items that properly belong in a cost-accounting system and items of actual service rendered in any given funeral. In all likelihood, the idle time of employees is figured in and prorated as part of the "man-hours." The up-to-date funeral home operates on a twenty-four-hour basis, and the prepared speech contains this heartening news:

> The funeral service profession of the United States is proud of the fact that there is not a person within the continental limits of the United States who is more than two hours away from a licensed funeral director and embalmer. That's one that even the fire-fighting apparatus of our country cannot match.

5   While the hit-or-miss rhetoric of the foregoing is fairly typical of the prose style of the funeral trade as a whole, and while the statement that 120 man-hours are devoted to a single funeral may be open to question, there really is a fantastic amount of service accorded the dead body and its survivors.

6   Having decreed what sort of funeral is right, proper, and nice, and having gradually appropriated to himself all the functions connected with it, the funeral director has become responsible for a multitude of tasks—beyond the obvious one of "placing corpse in the coffin" recorded in our nineteenth-century funeral bill. His self-imposed duties fall into two main categories: attention to the corpse itself, and the stage-managing of the funeral.

The drama begins to unfold with the arrival of the corpse at the mortuary.

Alas, poor Yorick! How surprised he would be to see how his counterpart of today is whisked off to a funeral parlour and is in short order sprayed, sliced, pierced, pickled, trussed, trimmed, creamed, waxed, painted, rouged, and neatly dressed — transformed from a common corpse into a Beautiful Memory Picture. This process is known in the trade as embalming and restorative art, and is so universally employed in the United States and Canada that for years the funeral director did it routinely, without consulting corpse or kin. He regards as eccentric those few who are hardy enough to suggest that it might be dispensed with. Yet no law requires embalming, no religious doctrine commends it, nor is it dictated by considerations of health, sanitation, or even of personal daintiness. In no part of the world but in North America is it widely used. The purpose of embalming is to make the corpse presentable for viewing in a suitably costly container; and here too the funeral director routinely, without first consulting the family, prepares the body for public display.

Is all this legal? The processes to which a dead body may be subjected are, after all, to some extent circumscribed by law. In most states, for instance, the signature of next of kin must be obtained before an autopsy may be performed, before the deceased may be cremated, before the body may be turned over to a medical school for research purposes; or such provision must be made in the decedent's will. In the case of embalming, permission is required (under Federal Trade Commission rules) only if a charge is to be made for the procedure. Embalming is not, as funeral providers habitually claim, a legal requirement even when the body of the deceased is to be on display in an open casket. A textbook, *The Principles and Practices of Embalming,* comments on this: "There is some question regarding the legality of much that is done within the preparation room." The author points out that it would be most unusual for a responsible member of a bereaved family to instruct the mortician, in so many words, to "embalm" the body of a deceased relative. The very term "embalming" is so seldom used that the mortician must rely on custom in the matter. The author concludes that unless the family specifies otherwise, the act of entrusting the body to the care of a funeral establishment carries with it an implied permission to go ahead and embalm.

Embalming is indeed a most extraordinary procedure, and one must wonder at the docility of Americans who each year pay hundreds of millions of dollars for its perpetuation, blissfully ignorant of what it is all about, what is done, and how it is done. Not one in ten thousand has any idea of what actually takes place. Books on the subject are extremely hard to come by. You will not find them in your neighbourhood bookshop or library.

11   In an era when huge television audiences watch surgical operations in the comfort of their living rooms, when, thanks to the animated cartoon, the geography of the digestive system has become familiar territory even to the nursery-school set, in a land where the satisfaction of curiosity about almost all matters is a national pastime, surely the secrecy surrounding embalming cannot be attributed to the inherent gruesomeness of the subject. Custom in this regard has within this century suffered a complete reversal. In the early days of American embalming, when it was performed in the home of the deceased, it was almost mandatory for some relative to stay by the embalmer's side and witness the procedure. Today, family members who might wish to be in attendance would certainly be dissuaded by the funeral director. All others, except apprentices, are usually barred by law from the preparation room.

12   A close look at what actually does take place may explain in large measure the undertaker's intractable reticence concerning a procedure that has become his major raison d'être. Is it possible he fears that public information about embalming might lead patrons to wonder if they really want this service? If the funeral men are loath to discuss the subject outside the trade, the reader may, understandably, be equally loath to go on reading at this point. For those who have the stomach for it, let us part the formaldehyde curtain.

13   The body is first laid out in the undertaker's morgue — or, rather, Mr. Jones is reposing in the preparation room to be readied to bid the world farewell.

14   The preparation room in any of the better funeral establishments has the tiled and sterile look of a surgery, and indeed the embalmer/restorative artist who does his chores there is beginning to adopt the term "dermasurgeon" (appropriately corrupted by some mortician-writers as "demi-surgeon") to describe his calling. His equipment — consisting of scalpels, scissors, augers, forceps, clamps, needles, pumps, tubes, bowls, and basins — is crudely imitative of the surgeon's, as is his technique, acquired in a nine- or twelve-month post–high school course at an embalming school. He is supplied by an advanced chemical industry with a bewildering array of fluids, sprays, pastes, oils, powders, creams, to fix or soften tissue, shrink or distend it as needed, dry it here, restore the moisture there. There are cosmetics, waxes, and paints to fill and cover features, even plaster of Paris to replace entire limbs. There are ingenious aids to prop and stabilize the cadaver: a VariPose Head Rest, the Edwards Arm and Hand Positioner, the

Repose Block (to support the shoulders during the embalming), and the Throop Foot Positioner, which resembles an old-fashioned stocks.

Mr. John H. Eckels, president of the Eckels College of Mortuary Science, thus describes the first part of the embalming procedure: "In the hands of a skilled practitioner, this work may be done in a comparative short time and without mutilating the body other than by slight incision so slight that it scarcely would cause serious inconvenience if made upon a living person. It is necessary to remove the blood, and doing this not only helps in the disinfecting, but removes the principal cause of disfigurements due to discoloration."

Another textbook discusses the all-important time element: "The earlier this is done, the better, for every hour that elapses between death and embalming will add to the problems and complications encountered. ..." Just how soon should one get going on the embalming? The author tells us, "On the basis of such scanty information made available to this profession through its rudimentary and haphazard system of technical research, we must conclude that the best results are to be obtained if the subject is embalmed before life is completely extinct — that is, before cellular death has occurred. In the average case, this would mean within an hour after somatic death." For those who feel that there is something a little rudimentary, not to say haphazard, about this advice, a comforting thought is offered by another writer. "Speaking of fears entertained in the early days of premature burial," he points out, "one of the effects of embalming by chemical injection, however, has been to dispel fears of live burial." How true; once the blood is removed, chances of live burial are indeed remote.

To return to Mr. Jones, the blood is drained out through the veins and replaced by embalming fluid pumped in through the arteries. As noted in *The Principles and Practices of Embalming*, "Every operator has a favourite injection and drainage point — a fact which becomes a handicap only if he fails or refuses to forsake his favourites when conditions demand it." Typical favourites are the carotid artery, femoral artery, jugular vein, and subclavian vein. There are various choices of embalming fluid. If Flextone is used, it will produce a "mild, flexible rigidity. The skin retains a velvety softness, the tissues are rubbery and pliable. Ideal for women and children." It may be blended with B. and G. Products Company's Lyf-Lyk tint, which is guaranteed to reproduce "nature's own skin texture...the velvety appearance of living tissue." Suntone comes in three separate tints: Suntan; Special Cosmetic Tint; moderately pink.

About three to six gallons of a dyed and perfumed solution of formaldehyde, glycerin, borax, phenol, alcohol, and water is soon circulating through Mr. Jones, whose mouth has been sewn together with a "needle directed upward between the upper lip and gum and brought out through the left nostril," with the corners raised slightly "for a more pleasant expression." If he should be buck-toothed, his teeth are cleaned with Bon Ami and coated with colourless nail polish. His eyes, meanwhile, are closed with flesh-tinted eye caps and eye cement.

19   The next step is to have at Mr. Jones with a thing called a trocar. This is a long, hollow needle attached to a tube. It is jabbed into the abdomen and poked around the entrails and chest cavity, the contents of which are pumped out and replaced with "cavity fluid." This done, and the hole in the abdomen having been sewn up, Mr. Jones's face is heavily creamed (to protect the skin from burns which may be caused by leakage of chemicals), and he is covered with a sheet and left unmolested for a while. But not for long—there is more, much more, in store for him. He has been embalmed, but not yet restored, and the best time to start the restorative work is eight to ten hours after embalming, when the tissues have become firm and dry.

20   The object of all this attention to the corpse, it must be remembered, is to make it presentable for viewing in an attitude of healthy repose. "Our customs require the presentation of our dead in the semblance of normality... unmarred by the ravages of illness, disease, or mutilation," says Mr. J. Sheridan Mayer in his *Restorative Art*. This is rather a large order since few people die in the full bloom of health, unravaged by illness and unmarked by some disfigurement. The funeral industry is equal to the challenge: "In some cases the gruesome appearance of a mutilated or disease-ridden subject may be quite discouraging. The task of restoration may seem impossible and shake the confidence of the embalmer. This is the time for intestinal fortitude and determination. Once the formative work is begun and affected tissues are cleaned or removed, all doubts of success vanish. It is surprising and gratifying to discover the results which may be obtained."

21   The embalmer, having allowed an appropriate interval to elapse, returns to the attack, but now brings into play the skill and equipment of sculptor and cosmetician. Is a hand missing? Casting one in plaster of Paris is a simple matter. "For replacement purposes, only a cast of the back of the hand is necessary; this is within the ability of the average operator and is quite adequate." If a lip or two, a nose, or an ear should be missing, the embalmer has at hand a variety of restorative waxes with which to model replacements. Pores and skin texture are simulated by stippling with a little brush, and over this cosmetics are laid on. Head off? Decapitation cases are rather routinely handled. Ragged edges are trimmed, and head joined to torso with

a series of splints, wires, and sutures. It is a good idea to have a little something at the neck — a scarf or high collar — when time for viewing comes. Swollen mouth? Cut out tissue as needed from inside the lips. If too much is removed, the surface contour can easily be restored by padding with cotton. Swollen neck and cheeks are reduced by removing tissue through vertical incisions made down each side of the neck. "When the deceased is casketed, the pillow will hide the suture incisions.... [A]s an extra precaution against leakage, the suture may be painted with liquid sealer."

The opposite condition is more likely to present itself — that of emaciation. His hypodermic syringe now loaded with massage cream, the embalmer seeks out and fills the hollowed and sunken areas by injection. In this procedure, the backs of the hands and fingers and the under-chin area should not be neglected.

Positioning the lips is a problem that recurrently challenges the ingenuity of the embalmer. Closed too tightly, they tend to give a stern, even disapproving expression. Ideally, embalmers feel, the lips should give the impression of being ever so slightly parted, the upper lip protruding slightly for a more youthful appearance. This takes some engineering, however, as the lips tend to drift apart. Lip drift can sometimes be remedied by pushing one or two straight pins through the inner margin of the lower lip and then inserting them between the two front upper teeth. If Mr. Jones happens to have no teeth, the pins can just as readily be anchored in his Armstrong Face Former and Denture Replacer. Another method to maintain lip closure is to dislocate the lower jaw, which is then held in its new position by wire run through holes which have been drilled through the upper and lower jaws at the midline. As the French are fond of saying, *il faut souffrir pour être belle.*

If Mr. Jones has died of jaundice, the embalming fluid will very likely turn green. Does this deter the embalmer? Not if he has intestinal fortitude. Masking pastes and cosmetics are heavily laid on, burial garment and casket interiors are colour-correlated with particular care, and Jones is displayed beneath rose-coloured lights. Friends will say, "How *well* he looks." Death by carbon monoxide, on the other hand, can be rather a good thing from the embalmer's viewpoint: "One advantage is the fact that this type of discoloration is an exaggerated form of a natural pink coloration." This is nice because the healthy glow is already present and needs but little attention.

The patching and filling completed, Mr. Jones is now shaved, washed, and dressed. A cream-based cosmetic, available in pink, flesh, suntan, brunette, and blond, is applied to his hands and face, his hair is shampooed and combed (and, in the case of Mrs. Jones, set), his hands manicured. For the horny-handed son of toil, special care must be taken; cream should be applied to remove ingrained grime, and the nails cleaned. "If he were not in the habit of having them manicured in life, trimming and shaping is advised for better appearance — never questioned by kin."

26 Jones is now ready for casketing (this is the present participle of the verb "to casket"). In this operation his right shoulder should be depressed slightly "to turn the body a bit to the right and soften the appearance of lying flat on the back." Positioning the hands is a matter of importance, and special rubber positioning blocks may be used. The hands should be cupped slightly for a more lifelike, relaxed appearance. Proper placement of the body requires a delicate sense of balance. It should lie as high as possible in the casket, yet not so high that the lid, when lowered, will hit the nose. On the other hand, we are cautioned, placing the body too low "creates the impression that the body is in a box."

27 Jones is next wheeled into the appointed slumber room, where a few last touches may be added — his favourite pipe placed in his hand, or, if he was a great reader, a book propped into position. (In the case of little Master Jones, a teddy bear may be clutched.) Here he will hold open house for a few days, visiting hours 10 A.M. to 5 P.M.

28 All now being in readiness, the funeral director calls a staff conference to make sure that each assistant knows his precise duties. Mr. Wilber Krieger writes: "This makes your staff feel that they are a part of the team, with a definite assignment that must be properly carried out if the whole plan is to succeed. You never heard of a football coach who failed to talk to his entire team before they go on the field. They have been drilled on the plays they are to execute for hours and days, and yet the successful coach knows the importance of making even the bench-warming third-string substitute feel that he is important if the game is to be won." The winning of *this* game is predicated upon a glass-smooth handling of the logistics. The funeral director has notified the pallbearers, whose names were furnished by the family, has arranged for the presence of a clergyman, organist, and soloist, has provided transportation for everybody, has organized and listed the flowers sent by friends. In *Psychology of Funeral Service,* Mr. Edward A. Martin points out: "He may not always do as much as the family thinks he is doing, but it is his helpful guidance that they appreciate in knowing they are proceeding as they should.... The important thing is how well his services can be used to make the family believe they are giving unlimited expression to their own sentiment."

29 The religious service may be held in a church or in the chapel of the funeral home; the funeral director vastly prefers the latter arrangement, for not only is it more convenient for him, but it affords him the opportunity to show off his beautiful facilities to the gathered mourners. After the cler-

gyman has had his say, the mourners queue up to file past the casket for a last look at the deceased. The family is not asked whether they want an open-casket ceremony; in the absence of instruction to the contrary, this is taken for granted. Consequently, well over 68 percent of all American funerals in the mid-1990s featured an open casket — a custom unknown in other parts of the world. Foreigners are astonished by it. An Englishwoman living in San Francisco described her reaction in a letter to the writer:

> I myself have attended only one funeral here — that of an elderly fellow worker of mine. After the service I could not understand why everyone was walking towards the coffin (sorry, I mean casket), but thought I had better follow the crowd. It shook me rigid to get there and find the casket open and poor old Oscar lying there in his brown tweed suit, wearing a suntan makeup and just the wrong shade of lipstick. If I had not been extremely fond of the old boy, I have a horrible feeling that I might have giggled. Then and there I decided that I could never face another American funeral — even dead.

The casket (which has been resting throughout the service on a Classic Beauty Ultra Metal Casket Bier) is now transferred by a hydraulically operated device called Porto-Lift to a balloon-tired, Glide Easy casket carriage which will wheel it to yet another conveyance, the Cadillac Funeral Coach. This may be lavender, cream, light green. Black, once de rigeur, is coming back into fashion. Interiors, of course, are colour-correlated, "for the man who cannot stop short of perfection."

At graveside, the casket is lowered into the earth. This office, once the prerogative of friends of the deceased, is now performed by a patented mechanical lowering device. A "Lifetime Green" artificial grass mat is at the ready to conceal the sere earth, and overhead, to conceal the sky, is a portable Steril Chapel Tent ("resists the intense heat and humidity of summer and the terrific storms of winter... available in Silver Grey, Rose, or Evergreen"). Now is the time for the ritual scattering of the earth over the coffin, as the solemn words "earth to earth, ashes to ashes, dust to dust" are pronounced by the officiating cleric. This can today be accomplished "with a mere flick of the wrist with the Gordon Leak-Proof Earth Dispenser. No grasping of a handful of dirt, no soiled fingers. Simple, dignified, beautiful, reverent! The modern way!" The Gordon Earth Dispenser is of nickel-plated brass construction. It is not only "attractive to the eye and long wearing"; it is also "one of the 'tools' for building better public relations" if presented as "an appropriate non-commercial gift" to the clergy. It is shaped something like a saltshaker.

32   Untouched by human hand, the coffin and the earth are now united.

33   It is in the function of directing the participants through this maze of gadgetry that the funeral director has assigned to himself his relatively new role of "grief therapist." He has relieved the family of every detail, he has revamped the corpse to look like a living doll, he has arranged for it to nap for a few days in a slumber room, he has put on a well-oiled performance in which the concept of *death* has played no part whatsoever — unless it was inconsiderately mentioned by the clergyman who conducted the religious service. He has done everything in his power to make the funeral a real pleasure for everybody concerned. He and his team have given their all to score an upset victory over death.

34   Dale Carnegie has written that in the lexicon of the successful man there is no such word as "failure." So have the undertakers managed to delete the word "death" and all its associations from their vocabulary. They have from time to time published lists of In and Out words and phrases to be memorized and used in connection with the final return of dust to dust; then, still dissatisfied with the result, they have elaborated and revised the list. Thus, a 1916 glossary substitutes "prepare body" for "handle corpse." Today, though, "body" is Out and "remains" or "Mr. Jones" is In.

35   "The use of improper terminology by anyone affiliated with a mortuary should be strictly forbidden," declares Edward A. Martin. He suggests a rather thorough overhauling of the language; his deathless words include: "service, not funeral; Mr., Mrs., Miss blank, not corpse or body; preparation room, not morgue; casket, not coffin; funeral director or mortician, not undertaker; reposing room, not showroom; baby or infant, not stillborn; deceased, not dead; autopsy or post-mortem, not 'post'; coach, not hearse; shipping case, not shipping box; flower car, not flower truck; cremains or cremated remains, not ashes; clothing, dress, suit, etc., not shroud; drawing room, not parlour."

36   This rather basic list was refined in 1956 by Victor Landig in his *Basic Principles of Funeral Service.* He enjoins the reader to avoid using the word "death" as much as possible, even when such avoidance may seem impossible; for example, a death certificate should be referred to as a "vital statistics form." One should speak not of the "job" but rather of the "call." We do not "haul" a dead person, we "transfer" or "remove" him — and we do this in a "service car," not a "body car." We "open and close" his grave rather than dig and fill it, and in it we "inter" rather than bury him. This is not done in a graveyard or cemetery, but rather in a "memorial park." The deceased is beautified, not with makeup, but with "cosmetics." Anyway, he didn't die, he "expired." An important error to guard against, cautions

Mr. Landig, is referring to "cost of the casket." The phrase "amount of investment in the service" is a wiser usage here.

Miss Anne Hamilton Franz, writing in *Funeral Direction and Management,* adds an interesting footnote on the use of the word "ashes" to describe (in a word) ashes. She fears this usage will encourage scattering (for what is more natural than to scatter ashes?), and prefers to speak of "cremated remains" or "human remains." She does not like the word "retort" to describe the container in which cremation takes place, but prefers "cremation chamber" or "cremation vault," because this "sounds better and softens any harshness to sensitive feelings."

As for the Loved One, poor fellow, he wanders like a sad ghost through the funeral men's pronouncements. No provision seems to have been made for the burial of a Heartily Disliked One, although the necessity for such must arise in the course of human events.*

---

* The funeral people, ever alert to fill a need, have come up with a casket that can be written on. The York "Expressions" casket, introduced at the 1996 convention of the National Funeral Directors Association, features "a smooth surface with a special coating on which those who gather may write one last farewell to the departed." The caskets come with a set of permanent markers and a Memorial Guide that rashly invites "those who gather" to "make known their hidden thoughts." As happens when chums are invited to autograph a schoolmate's surgical cast, there will predictably be the occasional nonconformist who is unable to resist the temptation to use the permanent marker to express his hidden thoughts, however derogatory.

1998

NOTES

This reading is Chapter 5 of the book *The American Way of Death Revisited* by Jessica Mitford (1917–1996). The book was a second edition of the 1963 book, an exposé of funeral practices. This selection appears in some anthologies as "Behind the Formaldehyde Curtain."

Alas, poor Yorick A quote from Shakespeare's play *Hamlet.* Hamlet is regarding the skull of Yorick in this famous gravedigger scene.

Raison d'être Reason for being or purpose (French).

Il faut souffrir pour être belle It is necessary to suffer in order to be beautiful (French).

COMPREHENSION AND DISCUSSION

1. Why does Mitford call this chapter of her book a "drama" (p. 303)?
2. Why does Mitford comment on the legality of embalming?
3. Why is preserving the "natural" appearance of the deceased important?
4. What is the difference in meaning between "dermasurgeon" and "demi-surgeon" (paragraph 14, p. 304)?
5. Is there a real Mr. Jones? Why does Mitford refer to the deceased as Mr. Jones?
6. Explain: "He [the funeral director] and his team have given their all to score an upset victory over death" (p. 310).
7. Is Mitford's tone objective and neutral or sarcastic and disapproving?
8. What message does Mitford want to give her readers?
9. What is your opinion on the importance of various funeral practices — embalming, restoration, visitation, open casket, wake, funeral service, interment?

LITERARY TECHNIQUES

Process analysis Mitford is describing the process of embalming. Process is the methodical description of some task, action, or event. The reader does not necessarily need to do anything, but upon reading the piece he or she can understand the process. Here, Mitford's intention is to give the lay reader information he or she may not have.

Quotations and references In a serious, investigative piece of writing, quoting specific experts in the field serves to authenticate the information presented. Moreover, detailed references to texts and manuals lend greater credibility to what is said.

Present tense Note that this process description is written in the present tense. First, it gives immediacy to the topic; second, it suggests a sense of continuity — that is, this process will be used in the future; and third, it is the proper tense to use in analysis and exposition.

Testimonial Like quotations and references, the testimonial supports the writer's thesis. For example, the Englishwoman's comment underscores the point that open-casket ceremonies are unique to North America.

ASSIGNMENTS

1. Research funeral costs and evaluate them. What expenses are reasonable? Are funeral directors taking advantage of the bereaved?
2. Consider environmental issues surrounding funerals — for traditional burials, cremations, and the latest trend, woodland burial in cardboard caskets.
3. How does this article differ from Barbara Gowdy's "We So Seldom Look on Love" (p. 86) in its explanation of the embalming process?
4. Compare Mitford's article with Bodanis's "Toothpaste" (p. 241). Explain the similarities or differences in writing techniques.
5. Write a process description of a task that you have performed in one of your jobs.

Shooting an Elephant

George Orwell

1   In Moulmein, in Lower Burma, I was hated by large numbers of people — the only time in my life that I have been important enough for this to happen to me. I was sub-divisional police officer of the town, and in an aimless, petty kind of way anti-European feeling was very bitter. No one had the guts to raise a riot, but if a European woman went through the bazaars alone somebody would probably spit betel juice over her dress. As a police officer I was an obvious target and was baited whenever it seemed safe to do so. When a nimble Burman tripped me up on the football field and the referee (another Burman) looked the other way, the crowd yelled with hideous laughter. This happened more than once. In the end the sneering yellow faces of young men that met me everywhere, the insults hooted after me when I was at a safe distance, got badly on my nerves. The young Buddhist priests were the worst of all. There were several thousands of them in the town and none of them seemed to have anything to do except stand on street corners and jeer at Europeans.

2   All this was perplexing and upsetting. For at that time I had already made up my mind that imperialism was an evil thing and the sooner I chucked up my job and got out of it the better. Theoretically — and secretly, of course — I was all for the Burmese and all against their oppressors, the British. As for the job I was doing, I hated it more bitterly than I can perhaps make clear. In a job like that you see the dirty work of Empire at close quarters. The wretched prisoners huddling in the stinking cages of the lock-ups, the grey, cowed faces of the long-term convicts, the scarred buttocks of the men who had been flogged with bamboos — all these oppressed me with an intolerable sense of guilt. But I could get nothing into perspective. I was young and ill-educated and I had had to think out my problems in the utter silence that is imposed on every Englishman in the East. I did not even know that the British Empire is dying, still less did I know that it is a great deal better than the younger empires that are going to supplant it. All I know was that I was stuck between my hatred of the empire I served and my rage against the evil-spirited little beasts who tried to make my job impossible. With one part of my mind I thought of the British Raj as an unbreakable tyranny, as something clamped down, *in saecula saeculorum,* upon the will of prostrate peoples; with another part I thought that the greatest joy in the world would be to drive a bayonet into

a Buddhist priest's guts. Feelings like these are the normal by-products of imperialism; ask any Anglo-Indian official, if you can catch him off duty.

One day something happened which in a roundabout way was enlightening. It was a tiny incident in itself, but it gave me a better glimpse than I had had before of the real nature of imperialism — the real motives for which despotic governments act. Early one morning the sub-inspector at a police station the other end of the town rang me up on the phone and said that an elephant was ravaging the bazaar. Would I please come and do something about it? I did not know what I could do, but I wanted to see what was happening and I got on to a pony and started out. I took my rifle, an old .44 Winchester and much too small to kill an elephant, but I thought the noise might be useful *in terrorem*. Various Burmans stopped me on the way and told me about the elephant's doings. It was not, of course, a wild elephant, but a tame one which had gone "must." It had been chained up as tame elephants always are when their attack of "must" is due, but on the previous night it had broken its chain and escaped. Its mahout, the only person who could manage it when it was in that state, had set out in pursuit, but he had taken the wrong direction and was now twelve hours' journey away, and in the morning the elephant had suddenly reappeared in the town. The Burmese population had no weapons and were quite helpless against it. It had already destroyed somebody's bamboo hut, killed a cow, and raided some fruit-stalls and devoured the stock; also it had met the municipal rubbish van, and when the driver jumped out and took to his heels, had turned the van over and inflicted violence upon it.

The Burmese sub-inspector and some Indian constables were waiting for me in the quarter where the elephant had been seen. It was a very poor quarter, a labyrinth of squalid bamboo huts, thatched with palm-leaf, winding all over a steep hillside. I remember that it was a cloudy stuffy morning at the beginning of the rains. We began questioning the people as to where the elephant had gone, and, as usual, failed to get any definite information. That is invariably the case in the East; a story always sounds clear enough at a distance, but the nearer you get the scene of events the vaguer it becomes. Some of the people said that the elephant had gone in one direction, some said that he had gone in another, some professed not even to have heard of any elephant. I had almost made up my mind that the whole story was a pack of lies, when we heard yells a little distance away. There was a loud, scandalized cry of "Go away, child! Go away this instant!" and an old woman with a switch in her hand came round the corner of a hut, violently shooing away a crowd of naked children. Some more women followed, clicking their tongues and exclaiming; evidently there was something there that the children ought not to have seen. I rounded the hut and saw a man's dead body sprawling in the mud. He was an Indian, a black Dravidian coolie, almost naked, and he could not have been dead many minutes. The people said that the elephant had come suddenly upon him round the corner of the hut, caught him with its trunk, put its foot on his back, and ground him into the earth. This was the rainy season and the ground was soft, and his face had scored a trench a foot deep and a couple of yards long. He was lying on his belly with arms crucified and head sharply twisted to one side. His face was coated with mud, the eyes wide open, the teeth bared, and grinning with an expression of unendurable agony. (Never tell me, by the way, that the dead look peaceful. Most of the corpses I have seen looked devilish.) The friction of the great beast's foot had stripped the skin from his back as neatly as one skins a rabbit. As soon as I saw the dead man I sent an orderly to a friend's house nearby to borrow an elephant rifle. I had already sent back the pony, not wanting it to go mad with fright and throw me if it smelled the elephant.

5   The orderly came back in a few minutes with a rifle and five cartridges, and meanwhile some Burmans had arrived and told us that the elephant was in the paddy fields below, only a few hundred yards away. As I started forward practically the whole population of the quarter flocked out of their houses and followed me. They had seen the rifle and were all shouting excitedly that I was going to shoot the elephant. They had not shown much interest in the elephant when he was merely ravaging their homes, but it was different now that he was going to be shot. It was a bit of fun to them, as it would be to an English crowd; besides, they wanted the meat. It made me vaguely uneasy. I had no intention of shooting the elephant — I had merely sent for the rifle to defend myself if necessary — and it is always unnerving to have a crowd following you. I marched down the hill, looking and feeling a fool, with the rifle over my shoulder and an ever-growing army of people jostling at my heels. At the bottom when you got away from the huts there was a metalled road and beyond that a miry waste of paddy fields a thousand yards across, not yet ploughed but soggy from the first rains and dotted with coarse grass. The elephant was standing eighty yards from the road, his left side towards us. He took not the slightest notice of the crowd's approach. He was tearing up bunches of grass, beating them against his knees to clean them, and stuffing them into his mouth.

6   I had halted on the road. As soon as I saw the elephant I knew with perfect certainty that I ought not to shoot him. It is a serious matter to shoot a working elephant — it is comparable to destroying a huge and costly piece of machinery — and obviously one ought not to do it if it can possibly be

avoided. And at that distance, peacefully eating, the elephant looked no more dangerous than a cow. I thought then and I think now that his attack of "must" was already passing off; in which case he would merely wander harmlessly about until the mahout came back and caught him. Moreover, I did not in the least want to shoot him. I decided that I would watch him for a little while to make sure that he did not turn savage again, and then go home.

But at that moment I glanced round at the crowd that had followed me. It was an immense crowd, two thousand at the least and growing every minute. It blocked the road for a long distance on either side. I looked at the sea of yellow faces above the garish clothes—faces all happy and excited over this bit of fun, all certain that the elephant was going to be shot. They were watching me as they would watch a conjurer about to perform a trick. They did not like me, but with the magical rifle in my hands I was momentarily worth watching. And suddenly I realized that I should have to shoot the elephant after all. The people expected it of me and I had got to do it; I could feel their two thousand wills pressing me forward, irresistibly. And it was at this moment, as I stood there with the rifle in my hands, that I first grasped the hollowness, the futility of the white man's dominion in the East. Here was I, the white man with his gun, standing in front of the unarmed native crowd—seemingly the leading actor of the piece; but in reality I was only an absurd puppet pushed to and fro by the will of those yellow faces behind. I perceived in this moment that when the white man turns tyrant it is his own freedom that he destroys. He becomes a sort of hollow, posing dummy, the conventionalized figure of a sahib. For it is the condition of his rule that he shall spend his life in trying to impress the "natives" and so in every crisis he has got to do what the "natives" expect of him. He wears a mask, and his face grows to fit it. I had got to shoot the elephant. I had committed myself to doing it when I sent for the rifle. A sahib has got to act like a sahib; he has got to appear resolute, to know his own mind and do definite things. To come all that way, rifle in hand, with two thousand people marching at my heels, and then to trail feebly away, having done nothing—no, that was impossible. The crowd would laugh at me. And my whole life, every white man's life in the East, was one long struggle not to be laughed at.

But I did not want to shoot the elephant. I watched him beating his bunch of grass against his knees, with the preoccupied grandmotherly air that elephants have. It seemed to me that it would be murder to shoot him. At that age I was not squeamish about killing animals, but I had never shot an elephant and never wanted to. (Somehow it always seems worse to kill a *large* animal.) Besides, there was the beast's owner to be considered. Alive, the elephant was worth at least a hundred pounds; dead, he would only be worth the value of his tusks — five pounds, possibly. But I had got to act quickly. I turned to some experienced-looking Burmans who had been there when we arrived, and asked them how the elephant had been behaving. They all said the same thing: he took no notice of you if you left him alone, but he might charge if you went too close to him.

9   It was perfectly clear to me what I ought to do. I ought to walk up to within, say, twenty-five yards of the elephant and test his behaviour. If he charged I could shoot, if he took no notice of me it would be safe to leave him until the mahout came back. But also I knew that I was going to do no such thing. I was a poor shot with a rifle and the ground was soft mud into which one would sink at every step. If the elephant charged and I missed him, I should have about as much chance as a toad under a steam-roller. But even then I was not thinking particularly of my own skin, only the watchful yellow faces behind. For at that moment, with the crowd watching me, I was not afraid in the ordinary sense, as I would have been if I had been alone. A white man mustn't be frightened in front of "natives"; and so, in general, he isn't frightened. The sole thought in my mind was that if anything went wrong those two thousand Burmans would see me pursued, caught, trampled on, and reduced to a grinning corpse like that Indian up the hill. And if that happened it was quite probable that some of them would laugh. That would never do. There was only one alternative. I shoved the cartridges into the magazine and lay down on the road to get a better aim.

10   The crowd grew very still, and a deep, low, happy sigh, as of people who see the theatre curtain go up at last, breathed from innumerable throats. They were going to have their bit of fun after all. The rifle was a beautiful German thing with cross-hair sights. I did not know that in shooting an elephant one should shoot to cut an imaginary bar running from ear-hole to ear-hole. I ought, therefore, as the elephant was sideways on, to have aimed straight at his ear-hole; actually I aimed several inches in front of this, thinking the brain would be further forward.

11   When I pulled the trigger I did not hear the bang or feel the kick — one never does when a shot goes home — but I heard the devilish roar of glee that went up from the crowd. In that instant, in too short a time, one would have thought, even for the bullet to get there, a mysterious, terrible change had come over the elephant. He neither stirred nor fell, but every line of his body altered. He looked suddenly stricken, shrunken, immensely old, as though the frightful impact of the bullet had paralyzed him without knocking him down. At last, after what seemed a long time — it might have been

five seconds, I dare say — he sagged flabbily to his knees. His mouth slobbered. An enormous senility seemed to have settled upon him. One could have imagined him thousands of years old. I fired again into the same spot. At the second shot he did not collapse but climbed with desperate slowness to his feet and stood weakly upright, with legs sagging and head drooping. I fired a third time. That was the shot that did for him. You could see the agony of it jolt his whole body and knock the last remnant of strength from his legs. But in falling he seemed for a moment to rise, for as his hind legs collapsed beneath him he seemed to tower upwards like a huge rock toppling, his trunk reaching skyward like a tree. He trumpeted, for the first and only time. And then down he came, his belly towards me, with a crash that seemed to shake the ground even where I lay.

I got up. The Burmans were already racing past me across the mud. It was obvious the elephant would never rise again, but he was not dead. He was breathing very rhythmically with long rattling gasps, his great mound of a side painfully rising and falling. His mouth was open wide — I could see far down into caverns of pale pink throat. I waited a long time for him to die, but his breathing did not weaken. Finally I fired my two remaining shots into the spot where I thought his heart must be. The thick blood welled out of him like red velvet, but still he did not die. His body did not even jerk when the shots hit him, the tortured breathing continued without a pause. He was dying, very slowly and in great agony, but in some world remote from me where not even a bullet could damage him further. I felt that I had got to put an end to that dreadful noise. It seemed dreadful to see the great beast lying there, powerless to move and yet powerless to die, and not even to be able to finish him. I sent back for my small fire and poured shot after shot into his head and down his throat. They seemed to make no impression. The tortured gasps continued as steadily as the ticking of a clock.

In the end I could not stand it any longer and went away. I heard later that it took him half an hour to die. The Burmans were arriving with dahs and baskets even before I left, and I was told they had stripped his body almost to the bones by the afternoon.

Afterwards, of course, there were endless discussions about the shooting of the elephant. The owner was furious, but he was only an Indian and could do nothing. Besides, legally I had done the right thing, for a mad elephant has be to killed, like a mad dog, if its owner fails to control it. Among the Europeans opinion was divided. The older men said I was right, the younger men said it was a damn shame to shoot an elephant for killing a coolie, because an elephant was worth more than any damn Coringhee coolie. And afterwards I was very glad that the coolie had been killed; it put me legally in the right and it gave me sufficient pretext for shooting the elephant. I often wondered whether any of the others grasped that I had done it solely to avoid looking a fool.

1936

NOTES

George Orwell (1903–1950) is a British author known for the books *Animal Farm* and *1984* and for the essays "Politics and the English Language" and "A Hanging." This essay came out of his experiences in Burma, where he served in the 1920s.

Betel juice A very staining red juice.

In saecula saeculorum Generation of generations, or since time immemorial (Latin).

In terrorem To scare away, to frighten off (Latin).

Must In animals, a frenzied condition caused by sexual arousal.

Mahout Elephant keeper and driver (Hindi).

Sahib Hindi term for white, European master.

Dahs Knives about the size of machetes.

COMPREHENSION AND DISCUSSION

1. Why was Orwell in Burma? Why was he so hated by the local people?
2. Summarize the events that led up to Orwell's confronting the elephant.
3. Was the elephant a menace to human life when Orwell decided to shoot it? Why did he not want to kill this beast?
4. What justifications does he give for shooting the elephant? What was his real reason?
5. Why did the Burmese want him to slaughter the animal?
6. What if Orwell had decided not to shoot? Speculate on the aftermath.
7. When is it justified to hunt animals such as black bears, deer, moose, and wolves?
8. Should sports hunting of all types be banned entirely?

LITERARY TECHNIQUES

Narration Telling a story. Storytelling requires not only the chronological ordering of events but also the explanatory information that the reader may not know. For example, Orwell informs the reader why he is hated by the Burmese, and this piece of information later plays an important role in his shooting the elephant. Moreover, the writer tells the reader about elephants, about their behaviour in calm and in "must," and about this rogue elephant's rampage.

Orwell is not simply telling a story. He has two points to make: First, although he is in charge of the situation with the elephant, he is also being manipulated. Second, he tells of the underlying unease between Europeans and the Burmese, caused by British imperialism.

Latin phrases The scattering of Latin phrases was a common practice in learned and formal writing. The phrases speak to a time when Latin was widely taught in the British educational system and readers were likely to understand them.

ASSIGNMENTS

1. Write a narrative of an experience you have had.
2. Compare the treatment and fate of the elephant with the horse in "Am I Blue?" (p. 349).
3. Have you ever been coerced by others into doing something you didn't want to do? Describe the situation.
4. Read Tim O'Brien's "The Man I Killed" (p. 170). Compare the reactions of the shooter in that story with Orwell's.

Have Wheels, Will Go A-Wooing

Kurt Preinsperg

1. On a Saturday morning the woman from my dance class called to suggest meeting for coffee. I had given her my business card a few days earlier and was delighted she called.

2. "We have to meet in my area," she said. "I don't have a car to get to your part of town."

3. "Great," I replied. "I don't have a car either, but I'm happy to take the bus to your part of town."

4. "What?" she said. "You don't have a car?"

5. "Actually, I don't like driving," I said, sensing another potential romance fizzle as I offered reasons for being ideologically opposed to cars. I sounded defensive, eccentric, and pathetic even to my own ears.

6. Being a non-driver is readily equated, in our society, with being too poor to afford a car. And evidence that a man is poor is not too charitably received during the early stages of courtship.

7. The woman's diminished enthusiasm was palpable when we met at the Art Gallery café. Her attitude was one of suspicion. (What's wrong with him? A man in his forties, and he doesn't own a car?)

8. Later, a colleague said: "Yep, a man gotta have his own wheels. Otherwise women think you're either cheap or kooky."

9. So here I was, middle-aged, single, employed, trying to explain to my date why I hadn't owned a car in years. Pretty soon I found myself slipping into a lecture about the adverse effects of cars.

10. First, the stress. I had several small accidents and near-accidents as a roving college instructor when, for seven years, I drove hundreds of kilometres each week as far from Vancouver as Chilliwack. Navigating through heavy traffic is so absorbing that one often isn't even aware of one's wasted nervous energy. My stress level went way down without a car.

11. Second, the cost. These days, a college instructor's salary is high enough to support a car, but low enough to make this a sizable expense. No wonder the middle class is emotionally invested in car ownership: We always value most what we make sacrifices for.

12. Third, the worries. A car accident can be crippling or even deadly to oneself or others, especially pedestrians. Cars usually involve repeat visits

to such uninspiring places as repair shops, gas stations, Air Care centres, insurance offices, parking garages, and the impound lots of towing companies. Not having to worry about breakdowns, parking, car security, speeding tickets, and so forth can take real clutter off one's mind.

Fourth, the environmental damage. Billions of people around the world live in a poison cloud of exhaust fumes in areas of urban sprawl, which is both caused by cars and makes cars ever more necessary.

Fifth, the missed romance of bus travel. To be sure, there are indignities associated with bus travel: waiting in the rain while smoke-belching cars roar past, or spending an hour on a trip that would take ten minutes by car. But public transport not only frees time for reading, it often leads to meeting people. The bus, like the dance floor, is one of the few places where people can invade each other's space without affront. And bus travel frequently offers the delight of glimpsing a stranger whose looks resonate with some deep esthetic reflex inside one's psyche.

Impressed by the down side of car ownership, I vowed to live without a car—and to choose a partner partly on the basis of whether she could accept that.

Well, the evidence is in. The pickings have been slim. The lesson I learned is that a car is almost a necessity for a single man, both as a symbol of respectable masculinity and as a practical courtship tool.

A woman doesn't want to shiver at a bus stop on the way to and from a movie. A car is a cozy enclosure against the elements where two people can talk and negotiate the next step. Asking a woman " Do you want a ride home?" is a powerful code for saying "I'm interested in you." Without a car, a man deprives himself of one of our culture's most effective courtship manoeuvres.

In what follows, I want to generalize about men and women as statistical aggregates only, stressing that many exceptional men and women do not fit. Over the years I've come to believe in a kind of "sexual Marxism," heavily tinged with the influence of Freud, Foucault, and evolutionary psychology. Marx was partly wrong. It is not one's place in the system of economic production that fundamentally controls the shaping of a person's identity, but one's rank in the hierarchy of desirability to the opposite sex.

Members of both sexes compete for what are perceived to be desirable partners. It is no accident that most men's sexual interest is easily ignited by almost any healthy fertile-looking woman, whereas most women's more selective sexuality responds in part to a man's promise as a protector and provider.

20 Both men and women are strongly motivated to satisfy each other's mating preferences, but male sexual demand invariably faces a scarcity of female supply. This gender dynamic is the single most important driving force underlying all social life.

21 I'm sometimes tempted to think the human world is a veiled gynocracy and only superficially a patriarchy. Women's sexual power is the basic power; other kinds of power are largely derivative. A great deal of women's behaviour can be understood from the perspective of the possession or diminution of sexual power, and a great deal of men's behaviour can be understood from the perspective of the quest for a woman's sexual favours.

22 The economic and political spheres are just part of the superstructure of the sexual sphere; and the political and economic dominance of men is best explained, in large part, as a reaction to the sexual power of women. A very small proportion of men have any significant economic or political power; a much larger proportion of women have significant sexual power.

23 That is why most young men, propelled by a deep yearning to make themselves more acceptable to young women, are desperate to have a car. The humiliations of being outside the car-owning mainstream send all but the most stubborn idealists off to a car dealership as soon as they have enough funds or credit.

24 A few weeks ago, on a Sunday, it so happened that I felt shamed, belittled, rejected by three different women for not owning a car. That triggered an internal dialogue. Subconsciously, did I perhaps resist buying a car to punish myself? By not buying a car, was I really caught up in a perverse self-sabotage? In any case, I was clearly forgoing the satisfaction of basic emotional needs for the sake of utterly futile idealism.

25 The following Monday, I went to a place called Healthy Wheels and bought a used Toyota.

26 And judging from a recent turn of events, lonely times will soon be past. The carbon monoxide and other pollutants I add to Vancouver's air suddenly seem like a small price for my enhanced masculinity.

1997

NOTES

A-wooing An old form, in which the *a-* prefix shows that someone is engaged in an activity. You won't see it very often, so don't worry about it too much. It shows up in old folksongs like "Frog went a-courtin'."

COMPREHENSION AND DISCUSSION

1. What are the five reasons why the author does not want a car? Are his reasons valid?
2. Why is a car essential to dating?
3. Put this statement in your own words: "It is not one's place in the system of economic production that fundamentally controls the shaping of a person's identity, but one's rank in the hierarchy of desirability to the opposite sex" (p. 323). What does Preinsperg mean?
4. As well as being a writer, Preinsperg teaches philosophy. What clues are there in the essay as to his profession?
5. Do you think the author made the right decision when he bought a car?
6. What else is important to make someone attractive to the opposite sex? What do you value in a prospective date?

LITERARY TECHNIQUES

Anecdotal opening To catch your attention, Preinsperg gives a personal experience relevant to the topic of his article.

ASSIGNMENTS

1. Read Boyle's "Greasy Lake" (p. 35) and compare it with this article on the topic of cars and their uses.
2. What price in terms of health and sanity are you willing to pay to own a car? What does a car really mean to you?
3. North American society is too dependent on cars. Suggest ways to change this.
4. Can you function without one or several of these technological items: VCR, TV, radio, cellular phone, pager, computer and Internet access, Walkman, credit or debit card? Why? How?

I'll Decide What's Broken

Spider Robinson

1. Like many writers, I'm a *serious* coffee drinker. The only secret of good coffee (besides avoiding Starbucks beans) is fanatic cleanliness: I clean my trusty Black & Decker drip coffeemaker with a damp paper towel at least twice a day.

2. Still, brown mung inevitably builds up on the underside of the drizzler (pardon these technical terms) and also in those ribbed channels on the floor of the filter basket. I usually buy a new machine every year or so.

3. I've been trying to for days, and it's the damndest thing, but apparently you can't buy a good one anymore. All the ones I've seen, even this year's Black & Decker, now seem to have that damn "drip-stop" feature.

4. It is, always, a catastrophic malfunction waiting to happen: a flimsy 5-cent bit of plastic and spring whose inevitable failure will necessitate replacing the whole furshlugginer machine.

5. Meanwhile, it collects brown mung, concentrates it at the worst possible place, and cannot be cleaned effectively. Above all, it's unnecessary: if you absolutely MUST have coffee before the cycle finishes, why not just replace the carafe with your cup, then swap back again when it's full?

6. They solved a problem I didn't have — poorly — and now it appears they've forced the flawed solution on me.

7. To my horror, I discover they're now claiming to have improved audio CDs. Two competing, and naturally incompatible, new systems are lurching your way right now. (Eerily echoing the old VHS/Betamax debacle, it's Sony versus everybody else, and again Sony's system is technically superior, but too expensive.)

8. Once that's sorted out, we can all settle down to replacing our entire music collection, again — like we did when CDs first came out, and before that when cassettes got good, and before that when consumer reel-to-reel decks appeared. Don't even mention eight-track.

9. We'll probably do it, too. Listen, one of these new systems samples music a bajillion times a second at eight bits, and the other umpty-two bajillion at one bit! (Don't ask what these things mean...or they will tell you.) With smokin' gear like that around, you're not gonna stick with that cheap piece of crap you got now, are you, dude?

10. Yes, I am...for as long as I can hold out. Whichever system wins the war, I predict there will be perhaps 20 people in Canada capable of telling

it from my present piece of crap in a blindfold test. (And they'll all have sour faces: Ears that acute must be a dreadful curse.) Present audio CDs already deliver sound as accurate as my ears can register — "improvement" is pointless.

There *is,* mind you, a hypothetical improvement to CDs for which I would willingly upgrade to new gear. Tommy, can you hear me? I want a player that'll let me alter the track-order of an album... *and save my changes,* so the disc will follow that new lineup every time I insert it, *without* my having to reprogram it manually each time. I've wanted that feature for years. But nobody's ever asked me.

Then there's TV. You know about that one, right? Within a maximum of five years, you're going to have to throw out — not sell, not give to the less fortunate, but scrap — all your TVs and their attendant VCRs and other peripherals, and replace everything with much more expensive digital models. You have no choice: It's a done deal, and cannot be reversed now.

To be sure, digital TV, unlike the new audio CDs, offers value in return. For one thing, the picture actually is perceptibly sharper. This will prove to be a terrible disaster for the entire TV industry, network and cable alike... and may prove to be the deathblow for the CBC, if somehow it should last that long.

Have you ever spent time on a TV set? Yes, and I kept falling off. Okay, I'll rephrase that: Have you ever visited premises where a TV show was being broadcast or videotaped? If so, you probably noticed something. News studio, talk-show set, or location lot — network, cable, or specialty channel — all sets have one thing in common. Everything looks a *lot* crummier than it will appear on TV.

Now, that is. Soon, every single television studio or set in the world is going to have to be substantially, expensively rebuilt — lest viewers see just how cheesy, tacky, and unconvincing it really is. You tell me: Can the CBC survive one more major hemorrhage?

And television itself — desperately in need of improvement — will *not be improved one iota* by all this effort and expense. It will merely be a bit clearer. For a fraction of what that will cost us all, we might have gotten better writing, acting, directing, and production instead. That's what I'd have voted for... if I'd been consulted.

Isn't there some way for us to communicate with the people who're inventing our future: Designers, and the industries who pay them? Wouldn't they welcome a little help in identifying our real desires, the better to pander to them? Wouldn't it be more efficient to sell us things we actually want to buy, and thus be able to fire half the advertising and marketing weasels? Present market research techniques simply aren't working — again and again techno-wizards solve problems we didn't have, and fail to guess our actual needs or desires.

18 I fantasize about a huge Web site, with a page for every consumer industry, and links galore — a sort of perpetual town meeting. Someplace where innovators can run proposed new technologies past interested consumers... and we can object before it's too late. Where we can tell companies what we hate about their present products and suggest improvements we'd actually like — or even propose new products altogether.

19 I wish someone would offer to sell me a continuously self-tuning acoustic guitar, for instance. Or a word-processing program that does not force me to pay for (and waste hard-disk space on) elaborate and powerful page layout, graphics, table, sound, video, outlining, voice annotation, and mail-merge functions I'll never use.

20 Or a self-cleaning coffeepot. Without those mung-collecting little ribs on the floor of the filter basket...

1999

NOTES

Spider Robinson is a well-known science fiction writer, as well as a newspaper columnist.

Furshlugginer A word made up by Robinson to mean useless.

Eight-track A cassette tape player, now obsolete.

Bajillion A word made up by Robinson to mean uncountable numbers.

Tommy, can you hear me? Famous line in The Who's rock opera *Tommy* (1969) about a deaf, blind, and mute pinball player.

COMPREHENSION AND DISCUSSION

1. Robinson is complaining about which specific items?
2. In general, what is his point? Where does he make it?
3. Why does he begin with his coffeemaker? What is the organization of this article?

4. Will Robinson get his wish? Explain.
5. What expressions in the article tell you that Robinson is not technologically inclined?
6. Do you sympathize with Robinson? Why or why not?

LITERARY TECHNIQUES

Rant Speaking wildly or vehemently at length on a particular subject. Usually rants are complaints that move from the personal to the general.

Slang Colloquial speech patterns in oral communication adapted to the written word. Nonstandard spelling and vocabulary, made-up words, and ungrammatical constructions characterize slang.

Personal pronouns Note how Robinson shifts from "I" to "we" as he progresses in his rant. When he distinguishes himself from the crowd, he uses "I"; when he wants to include everyone, he switches to "we." When he directly addresses the reader and the public at large, he uses "you."

As in Wayne Grady's article, "Canadian Tire Money" (p. 280), Robinson's conclusion comes full circle to his coffeemaker. Robinson wraps up the topic by referring to something said in the body of the article. By doing so, he reminds the reader of the topic and ends the article on a light note.

ASSIGNMENTS

1. Choose a gadget, machine, or software program that you use frequently. Write a paragraph describing the good and bad points of its design.
2. Read Kurt Preinsperg's "Have Wheels, Will Go A-Wooing" (p. 322), Fred Donnelly's "The Golden Years of Electronic Helps" (p. 258), and Isaac Asimov's "The Fun They Had" (p. 30). How do these three readings contrast with or complement Robinson's article? Focus on technology and gadgetry.
3. Write a cause-effect essay on the theme of "new and improved" products foisted on the consumer.

The Story of Grey Owl

Colin Ross

1   Once upon a time there was a pervert called Grey Owl, who lived in the Canadian woods. He is famous because he came to Canada and learned how to imitate the Indians—he wore a disguise and grew his hair long. The white people in Canada know so little about Indians, and about their own woods, that Grey Owl fooled them all for a long time. But even after they found out that the famous Indian was really only Archie Belaney from England, even then they still respected him. Canadians have so few heroes that they decided to have Archie Belaney for a hero—they said to themselves, "Old Archie sure fooled us, didn't he? What a great man he was, to be able to fool us all, and live like an Indian."

2   Archie was only like an Indian on the outside though. That's why the Canadians liked him, and made him a hero. They wanted to have a hero who played little boy's games in the woods, and made friends with animals just like in a story book. Canadians don't like Indians, on the outside or on the inside. That's why they like Archie so well, and still do—they know that he's just a pleasant Englishman on the inside, just like them. When they know that, then they can love his Indian clothes and his Indian canoe, and even think that maybe his Indian life is very beautiful. When it's only harmless old Archie Belaney inside that Indian costume, then the Canadian ladies have nothing to be afraid of. Why *there's* an Indian who would just *love* to talk to them, and tell them about his friendly animal pets in the woods.

3   The Canadian ladies may live in Canada, but they don't like Canada—they don't like the cold, they don't like the bears, they don't like the lonely prairies, they don't like the forest. They're afraid of all those things and places. They don't have to be afraid of Archie Belaney—he writes nice books for them, that sound just like Henry Williamson, and other nice Englishmen who love nature. Archie Belaney had a very big heart, not like Indians—if the Canadian ladies ever tried to talk to an Indian, that Indian's heart wouldn't like them. They wouldn't like the Indian either.

4   All the Canadians are very grateful to Archie Belaney. His books are such a relief for them. When they read his books then they're not afraid of nature anymore—Archie makes them feel that nature is tame and friendly and safe. The only difference between Archie's life in the woods and Mrs. Smith's life in the city is that Archie has beavers for pets. Mrs. Smith, and her neighbour Mrs. MacKenzie, both keep budgies. The Canadian ladies

are *very* grateful to Archie for keeping beavers for pets. Beavers seem like the best symbol Canada could have, when you think of Archie Belaney's friendly pets. All those Indians care about is killing the poor beavers, and selling their skins.

"Yes sir, those Indians are awful," says Mrs. MacKenzie. "Why if they came to our city they'd probably eat my budgies. Those poor friendly beavers and rabbits that live in our beautiful forests, the Indians hunt and kill them. And Indians never write lovely books like Grey Owl does. Isn't it a shame that they never learned how to write!"

"Quite a shame," says one of the ladies.

"Yes," says Mrs. Smith. "You know, we should form a club to help those poor Indians. They have no books and no shoes, and all they ever eat is rabbits and wild things. We should help them. It's a shame. They're people too you know, just like us. Let's gather up some money and give it to the Indians to buy food and clothes. It would be *such* a good thing to do."

"Very good," says another one of the ladies.

The bridge party was at Mrs. MacKenzie's house that day. Mr. MacKenzie wasn't feeling well so he was at home. Mr. MacKenzie is a fireman. Mr. MacKenzie was serving the ladies tea and cakes — he had gotten up too early to bake them.

Mr. MacKenzie is very proud of being a Canadian man. He's very tough. He fights fires in the city, and in the fall he takes his holidays and goes hunting just like an Indian. Just like Grey Owl. Mr. MacKenzie spoke up and said, "The Indians were good people. They only killed the friendly animals in the woods because they needed them for food and clothes. They couldn't let their children go hungry. The Indians were good people, and very good hunters. They just weren't very smart, that's all — they weren't quite as high up as we are in the family tree of man." Mr. MacKenzie was talking to his wife, explaining about Indians to her. All the other ladies were listening.

"As a matter of fact," continued Mr. MacKenzie, "we're at the top. Yes, ladies, it's true. Now if the Indians had been able to build cars and houses like us, then I'm sure they wouldn't have killed so many of the poor animals in nature. They would have loved them just like you love your budgies."

The ladies knew Mr. MacKenzie was a very good fireman, and they listened to what he said with a great deal of respect. Mrs. MacKenzie knew her husband went hunting in the fall though. She didn't like the poor dead wild animals he brought back, and she wondered how he could ever bring himself to pull the trigger. But Mr. Mackenzie is so tough and strong that he still has hunting instincts just like a real Indian. Just like Grey Owl. You can't expect him to stop hunting just because of the Canadian ladies. After all Mr. MacKenzie loves nature in his own way, and who is Mrs. MacKenzie to say his way is wrong?

13   The Canadian ladies are *very* grateful to Archie Belaney. They had some bad feelings about nature, and about Indians, but after they read his books they felt all right. The bad feelings went away. After the Canadian ladies read Archie's books they felt that the woods and the Indians were safe and friendly after all. And Archie Belaney was so concerned about his animal friends he went *all* the way to England, just to talk about them. Wasn't that a great thing for Canada!

14   Mr. MacKenzie doesn't have much time for books. But his wife and the other ladies have said such nice things about Grey Owl that *he* admires Grey Owl too. Mr. MacKenzie would never call Grey Owl just old Archie Belaney. If he did that then his wife's bad feelings about Indians might come back. That wouldn't be nice.

15   Mr. MacKenzie and his friends were so grateful to Archie for making the bad feelings go away that they got together. They made Archie into a hero, and promised never to call him anything but Grey Owl. If they called him just old Archie Belaney, then he might seem like just another Englishman.

16   Yes, it was a good day for Canada when Archie Belaney came over here and started pretending to be an Indian. There was quite a mystery to his life you know, not like the Indians, who just sneak around in the woods in a bad mood killing things. Let me show you what a nice guy Archie was—here's some of his writing. This is from his wonderful book which he called *Tales from an Empty Cabin:*

> There was a wood-chuck, a special chum of mine, who year after year made her home under the upper cabin, where she had every Spring a brood of wood-chucklets, or whatever they are called. She was an amiable old lady, who used often to watch me at my work and allowed me a number of privileges, including the rare one of handling her young ones. But if a stranger came, she would spread herself out so as to quite fill the entrance to her domicile, to keep the youngsters in, and when the stranger left she would emit a shrill whistling sound at his retreating back, very sure that she had frightened him away. She too has gone, her time fulfilled, and another has taken over her old home; a well-built, very trim young matron who stands up straight and very soldierly before her doorway and tries to look in windows.

Old Archie sure was a tame Indian wasn't he. *Isn't* Mrs. Smith grateful for that? When Archie Belaney left his three aunts in England and came over to Canada Mrs. Smith really felt good. She loved nature then. "Good!" she thought to herself. Mr. Smith and Mr. MacKenzie were so grateful they gave Archie a place to live in a special park, and paid him for the rest of his life to keep on playing games with animals. They never paid any real Indians.

When Archie writes a book, he writes just like an Englishman. That's the nicest way. He makes the woodchucks sound just like the ladies who read his books. Archie Belaney dressed up like an Indian and pretended to be one himself. The Canadian ladies loved him for that. But inside Archie was all the time an Englishman who called the woodchucks his chums. Archie had lots of friends. Some had feathers. Some had fur. Some wore hats to church. They were all one big happy family, Archie and Mr. Smith, and Mrs. Smith, and Mr. MacKenzie, and his wife, and Mrs. Woodchuck, and her woodchucklets. Archie sure had a nice time in nature. Wouldn't it be beautiful to live like an Indian too?

Indians are really very lovable people. If Mr. MacKenzie was an Indian he would be able to say wonderful things about nature too. Just like Archie and Geronimo. Archie Belaney was brought up by his three aunts in England. This was bad for little Archie — there were too many ladies around all the time. So when Archie got the chance he decided he'd *really* show his aunts he didn't need them. He'd go over to Canada and be a wild Indian, and no aunties would tell *him* what to do. Archie Belaney was one guy who sure was tough. He didn't need a bunch of aunties to take care of *him*. He was a wild Indian who lived by himself in nature and showed everybody. After he showed them real good, he came back to England.

Yes, Archie came back to England as an Indian, and gave speeches and went to dinners. He even went to dinner with that white man the King, and he sure didn't show him any respect. How could you expect a wild Indian to stand up when the King walked in the room? Boy, Archie really showed his aunts that time, when he went back to England.

Even when Archie was a little boy in England he used to play at being an Indian. But he couldn't play Indians in England and still live with his aunts when he was thirty or forty. Everyone would laugh at him. Archie was smart. He went over to Canada and played at being an Indian over there. No one laughed at him in Canada; in fact he fooled them all and played the game for the rest of his life. Trouble was, he wasn't really an Indian on the inside. Inside Archie Belaney was an Englishman who got lonely for his aunts. What do you think he did? Well, he made friends with all the animals, then he never got lonely again, not for the rest of his life. When he wrote about his animal friends, in his books, he used words like "domicile," "chum," "youngsters," "matron," and maybe even "auntie."

22   The Canadian ladies are *very* grateful. They were worried about living in this country. But Archie helped them. He wrote books, and in his books he showed the Canadian ladies that all the wild animals are really just as warm and friendly as an aunt or a grandma. Wasn't that wonderful! Mr. MacKenzie and Mrs. Smith were grateful too. All the Canadian people loved Archie Belaney for doing this great thing, and promised *never* to call him anything but Grey Owl. And that's just what they did.

1979

NOTES

Indians A term referring to the Native peoples of North America. It is not considered politically or historically correct, even though there is no term that can neatly replace it.

Geronimo (1829 – 1909) A legendary Apache who fought against the U.S. cavalry.

COMPREHENSION AND DISCUSSION

1. How does the word "pervert" in the opening sentence set the tone of the article?
2. Why does Ross address Archie Belaney as "Archie" rather than the formal family name "Belaney" throughout?
3. How does Ross denigrate Grey Owl's achievements?
4. Show how, according to Ross, Archie Belaney won over the white middle-class Canadians of the 1930s.
5. How much of the mockery is directed at Canadians rather than at Archie Belaney/Grey Owl?
6. How does Ross, in the dialogues, reflect the underlying prejudice that white Canadians have for the Native peoples?
7. How does Ross show the tone of condescension (patronizing, superior attitude) of Mr. and Mrs. MacKenzie, Mrs. Smith, and the author himself?
8. Why doesn't Ross admire Archie Belaney/Grey Owl?
9. What do you think Ross's ethnic background is? Why do you think so?

LITERARY TECHNIQUES

Satire A biting commentary or analysis that ridicules or mocks a person, institution, idea, or thing. Satirists use exaggeration, innuendo, sarcasm, invective, and inversion to draw attention to the subject's flaws. Often satire attempts to bring about change or conformity through wit and humour.

"Just like" Note the mocking tone in this comparison: "[Mr. MacKenzie] fights fires in the city, and in the fall he takes his holidays and goes hunting just like an Indian. Just like Grey Owl" (p. 331).

Fairy-tale opening, "once upon a time" Ross wants to accomplish a number of things here. The fairy-tale opening creates a sense of unreality (which is undercut and contradicted by the real-life Archie Belaney). It permits Ross to use simplistic language and a sarcastic tone at the same time. It also lets Ross blend fact and fiction.

Composite characters Ross creates fictitious persons such as the MacKenzies and Smiths in order to give a concrete basis to a general statement; that is, these people represent a major portion of white Canadians of the time. This technique is legitimate for this article because the writer focuses on exposing attitudes more than real people (other than Archie Belaney).

ASSIGNMENTS

1. Read the other two articles about Grey Owl: "Grey Owl's Magnificent Masquerade" (p. 232) and "Truth and Consequences" (p. 236). Which essay is the most effective of the three? Which did you enjoy the most? Explain.
2. All three articles mention the writing style of Grey Owl's books. Ross gives you a sample. Explain how the writing style betrays the writer, showing that he could not possibly be who he says he is. Search out more samples of his writing.
3. Explain the techniques Ross uses to ridicule Grey Owl and the people who believed in him.
4. Read Jessica Mitford's "The Story of Service" (p. 301). How does Ross's exposé of Grey Owl differ from Mitford's revelations about the funeral establishment?
5. Using Pico Iyer's definitions of weirdos and eccentrics (p. 289), to which category would Archie Belaney belong according to Ross?

6. Read Stephen Leacock's "How We Kept Mother's Day" (p. 140). How is the mockery similar to or different from Ross's?
7. Appropriation of voice is a controversial issue in literature. For example, some people say that a white author should not write about the experience of non-whites. A famous recent example is the novel "Memoirs of a Geisha," which is told in the first person by the author Arthur Golden, who is neither female nor Japanese. Discuss the issue in an essay.

Exiled in Paradise
Ellen Singer (pseudonym)

Some mornings, I dance among the kelp and flirt with the salted waves that peek beneath my skirt and dare dawn's sun to colour my shoulders tourist-red. Only then can I pretend that I am enjoying a moment's solitude between snorkelling and mambo lessons included in a Caribbean holiday package. Only then can I forget that there is no return plane ticket tucked inside my hotel-room safe, that my itinerary does not include maid service nor, on many days, a meal plan.

But reality returns at tide's ebb. I am grounded here in paradise, and the reason is hellish: I am in exile from a country that could not, would not protect me from the psychopathic stalker who was once my husband. I am at the beach looking for shells or driftwood that might be fashioned into quick-sale souvenirs so I can buy today's groceries. My once-freckled skin is solid umber and my feet, once treated to weekly pedicures, are now leathered by the sand. This is not life as I had planned it.

Once upon a time I was an award-winning journalist and associate professor of English. Those were my day jobs. I moonlighted as the wife of a sadist and master manipulator whose idea of a joke was to lock me in a room and leave a howling baby on the other side of the door. Thomas also claimed he was just teaching me survival skills by arranging to have the telephone, gas, and hydro service disconnected an hour after he left for a mid-winter trip to Florida. He did leave a car, but it was drained of gas, a discovery I made after shovelling my way through four-foot snowdrifts in order to open the driver's door. My two daughters, then 4 and 1, spent the week in my bed. We were plenty warm — we all had fevers from the flu.

The Florida-trip incident was neither the least nor worst of Thomas's torments. By the time it occurred, I had known Thomas for 13 years and had been married to him for eight. I was not only accustomed to accepting and excusing Thomas's cruelties, I was worn down by them. I fantasized daily about Thomas's death by car crash or cancer, but I lacked the strength to leave him. He promised to make my life hell if I divorced him, and I was certain that he would keep that vow. I was also embarrassed. A perfectionist still chagrined because of the two Bs I received in university courses, how could I admit to a mistake as colossal as marrying a man who earned a six-figure income but emptied my purse of cash every morning? And who would believe me? My charismatic spouse convinced friends and neighbours that he was the best catch since the one Willy Mays made for New

York against Cleveland in the 1954 World Series, and I never corrected the impression.

5   Four years later, in early 1992, some maternal or survival instinct kicked in, and I found the courage to leave. I was sick—again, this time with a fever of 103, and Karen and Courtney were sneaking lukewarm soup and cold toast up to my bedroom after their pleas that Thomas feed me were rebuffed. ("If she wants to eat, she can get her ass down here or she can stay up there and starve to death. I'm not going to wait on her.") Something about this act of bravery and the stoicism with which my babies carried it out pierced my numb façade; three weeks later, I fled with my daughters to Hiatus House, a shelter for battered women and their children in Windsor, Ontario.

6   We stayed six weeks, and somewhere amid the literature, the lectures, the counselling sessions, and casual conversations about domestic violence, I was visited by two long-forgotten allies: determination and strength. As physically and emotionally fragile as I was (my voice, for example, even when shouting in anger, could not rise above a whisper), I was fortified by my vow to protect Karen and Courtney from my mistake and grew stronger with each action I took toward that goal and away from Thomas. I pushed myself and prodded persons at every level in Canadian and United States officialdom; faxed and phoned lawyers, psychologists, children's advocates, celebrity survivors of abuse, newspaper columnists, even a couple of convicted wife-killers. I filed complaints, secured orders of protection, recorded phone conversations, kept a diary.

7   I literally became a poster woman for survivors of domestic violence (an image of my face, photographed the day after Thomas broke my nose, cheekbone, jaw, and eardrum, and below the caption, "Don't Apply Makeup. Apply the Law," hangs in the foyer at Hiatus House and a dozen other institutions and has appeared in newspapers and on television shows.) I did everything The System told me to do in order to restore my safety and self-respect, and believed the poster's tag line: Take the Fight Out of an Abuser by Taking Him to Court. I did. It worked. Today, though, I'd attach this addendum: Sometimes. Sort of. Not for Me.

8   The System is seriously flawed, especially for battered women who have children. Imagine a judge ordering a mugging victim to (a) reveal his address and phone number to his convicted attacker, (b) to forever remain in the same location unless a proposed move is approved by the court or agreed to by the attacker, and further, that (c) the mugging victim must meet his attacker at Tim Hortons every Saturday. And jail time is the penalty for the victim who fails to comply with these attacker-friendly orders. Sound

ludicrous? Well, because judges generally deem a man's right to visit his kids more important than a woman's right to survival, such orders are routinely meted out to women who were beaten, bloodied, and broken by men who fathered their children. Sure, some cities have established visitation centres for supposed neutral exchanges of children, but it is up to the custodial parent to request such an arrangement and the court to approve it.

In my case, I applied for participation in Windsor's pick-up and drop-off centre before it opened, but 18 months passed before a judge approved the request. By this time, Thomas had been banned from Canada for assaulting and threatening to kill me, so I had to agree to let Thomas's girlfriend pick up Karen and Courtney and drive them across the border into Detroit, even though, since she was not a party to the divorce case, the Ontario court could not bind her to any of its rulings, and despite the fact that three psychologists and four social workers had concluded that the girls should never spend time alone with their father. And when Thomas was ordered to spend four Saturdays working on a Michigan chain gang for violating terms of his probation in a separate conviction for throwing me onto a roadway, pummelling my face into the pavement, and abandoning me in front of 40-miles-per-hour traffic, I faced contempt charges for refusing to alter Thomas's visiting schedule so that it would not interfere with what he called "weekend landscaping duties."

Windsor judges also decreed that Thomas be given my address and telephone number and that I reside in Windsor permanently, ignoring my arguments that: Thomas didn't need my address since he wasn't permitted in the country; and a person deemed too dangerous to be in Canada should not have the addresses of its citizens, particularly those he has previously tried to kill.

Thomas used the phone to harass and stalk me, once calling 87 times in a single evening and often leaving messages praising an outfit or criticizing an activity I had performed that day.

Karen and Courtney were old enough to call their father; his telephone privileges were not dependent on knowledge of my name.

It made no sense that I be forced to live in Windsor when Thomas did not, and I could find no full-time work within commuting distance of my home. I ended up on public dole after a year of waiting for Ontario to enforce child-support payments. Since Thomas lived outside the country, the province's Family Support Plan could not collect the debt. For nearly two years, I pursued payment through Michigan's Friend of the Court; four months after a reciprocal support agreement was signed and enforced, Thomas claimed his income had dropped by 80 percent and petitioned to have support payments ended entirely.

14   Between early 1992 and mid-1994, my efforts to protect my daughters and myself from Thomas within legal parameters consumed $100 000, four drawers of my lawyer's filing cabinets, and 6000 hours of my time. I fought longer, harder, and smarter than most battered women and was treated slightly better than average by the courts. My claims were bolstered by the province's top family-assessment team, argued by its best lawyers, and backed by the highest ranks in the House of Commons. Neither Thomas nor his attorney were even permitted to appear at the divorce trial, which made it shorter but by no means a rousing victory for me. I got what most battered women do: custody of the children, no money, no protection. Thomas received what most batterers do: the right to visit his children and the tools (phone numbers and addresses) to harass, stalk, and harm me.

15   Six months later, a flawed court decision that allowed a London, Ontario, woman to move in order to take a job created one of those clichéd windows of opportunity for me to move. My lawyer advised me to get a job — a good job, in my field — and get it quickly because he was certain the London decision would be overturned. I made a lot of phone calls, begged and called in favours from anyone who answered the phone, and landed a job in New York. The move was approved, with the condition that I forfeit child support and fly Karen and Courtney back to Detroit once a month.

16   We moved on the first available 21-day-advance-purchase flight, and I felt safe for the first time in memory. Thomas would not know our address, our phone number, or where I worked and I would resume a freelance writing career in North America's writing capital. I was successful enough to afford a doorman apartment in the city's highest rent district, tropical vacations, theatre tickets, and daily restaurant dining. During their first semester of school, one of my daughters was asked to audition for a Broadway musical; the other won a city-wide art contest. We planned to live there forever, free from Thomas, free of fear.

17   But Thomas's obsession with me — unabated by his remarriage and the birth of another daughter — was further fed by a new weapon: modern technology. Every time I withdrew money from an ATM machine, shopped with a credit card, made plane reservations, placed a long-distance phone call, or rented a video, I left Hansel-and-Gretel crumbs for Thomas to follow.

18   So Thomas used cyberspace to shrink the 500 actual miles that separated us and became my constant companion of terror. He sent champagne to our hotel room in the Bahamas and pizza to a log cabin in the Poconos. He sent flowers to Karen and Courtney at school and called me at each of three unlisted home phone numbers. He greeted me at airports when I had told no one of my destination. He was my personal, unending bomb scare; I did not answer

a telephone, open a door, or unseal an envelope without dread. I did everything possible to spare Karen and Courtney my anxiety. I said the champagne was a hotel courtesy, the pizza delivery a fluke; I had trained school personnel and apartment doormen to reroute all packages and mail to me.

For more than a year, I deluded my daughters about their safety. I kept vigil every night, sleeping only during my daughters' school hours. I walked both to their school playgrounds and pretended to leave with the other parents, but stayed until a security guard signalled that both had reached their classrooms. At 3 each afternoon, my pulse rate soared until a flash of scarf or a glimpse of their hair assured me that Karen and Courtney had survived another day. But I maintained the casual air of a busy New York mama and never limited their outings or activities. Stress was mine, and innocence belonged to them until the morning Thomas accosted me outside their school as I kissed them goodbye. They never spent another unguarded moment in New York. They looked over their shoulders and scanned the face of every dark-haired man. They checked and rechecked our apartment locks each night and kept the blinds down on our 12th-floor apartment windows. For weeks, Courtney would go to school only if I remained inside her classroom throughout the day. One of them awoke screaming each night. (More than a year previously, Courtney, and six months previously, Karen, had refused to continue visits with their father and the girls were not expecting ever to see him again.)

I reported all this to New York police, armed with my orders of protection from Canada and Michigan. But the city had no stalking laws, and my paperwork was meaningless there. Then I started noticing that my daughters and I were photographed at nearly every public event. This was the Big Apple, not Mayberry, so I thought we were receiving undue attention. I also thought I was being paranoid and possibly delusional. This continued for more than a year. Then, for several weeks, we were photographed daily and by the same person. I confessed these occurrences as well as my fears of going crazy to my therapist, who replied with a few calculated hmmmms. A month later, she asked me to describe the photographer. I provided details, including a vehicle description; she told me the same person had taken her photograph that morning. I wasn't paranoid, she said, but I might be in peril.

I traced the car, a rental, and its driver, a German citizen with a hitman reputation. My life had officially become a B-movie, and I had to do something to change the ending. Professionals who reviewed my history with Thomas said my options for staying alive were limited to these: Kill him or disappear. Not one suggested a way I could safely remain in New York. Not one predicted that Thomas's obsession would end until one of us was dead.

22   I opted to hide and, after months and months of planning, I walked out of my apartment one afternoon, picked up my daughters from school, hailed a cab, and disappeared. No suitcases, no moving boxes, no notice of resignation, no goodbyes to friends or family. Hello to a life without a name, credit cards, chequing accounts, or home-delivered pizza. I can't get a regular job because a social-security number would reveal my address (and no matter what my level of poverty, I can't collect welfare for the same reason). I don't send away for rebates or request refunds in stores that require drivers' licences. I am more than a little out of sync with the modern world.

23   The life I have chosen is hard, more severe than I imagined it would be. My Thomas-inflicted injuries have left me incapable of performing relatively high-paying housecleaning or waitressing jobs. My six years of higher education are wasted on furniture refinishing, but perhaps help me to supplement my income with bartering. I handle my landlord's bookkeeping and tax preparation in exchange for rent, and I traded free tutoring for Courtney's piano lessons. So, we get by. And, though I could justly curse the unfairness of my situation, I choose to be thankful for children who laugh easily and often, who are strong and outspoken, and who sleep without nightmares. Some day, they will return to their stage and easel. Some time, I will resume my writing career. Some year, perhaps, laws will make it easier for battered women to get out, stay out, and stay alive. Until then, I'll be searching for seashells and holding onto serenity. And, some mornings, I will dance among the kelp.

All the names, including that of the writer, have been changed to protect the author and her children.

2000

NOTES

The author is writing under a pseudonym to protect her identity. In other words, Ellen Singer is not her real name. Writers wishing to hide their real identities adopt a fictitious name to use as authors. The reasons are varied: some want to separate their private lives from the public eye; some want to distinguish one kind of book from another in order not to confuse readership; some want to hide from vengeful people who may retaliate for exposing them to public scrutiny.

"Once upon a time" is a traditional opening for a fairy tale, usually with a happy ending. Singer uses this phrase ironically. Her past life is no fairy tale and has no happy ending.

Willy Mays Famous baseball player who played for the New York Giants.

Hansel and Gretel A fairy tale about two resourceful children, abandoned in the woods, who find their way home by leaving a trail of bread crumbs as markers.

Big Apple A popular term for New York City.

Mayberry The name of a fictitious small town in the situation comedy series *The Andy Griffith Show* (1960–1968). The name evokes innocence and idyllic living.

B-movie A second-rate motion picture, often filled with predictable clichés and plots.

COMPREHENSION AND DISCUSSION

1. How long had Ellen Singer been with Thomas, her husband? Why did she stay with him after so many incidents of vicious abuse?
2. What made her finally break from her husband?
3. Explain in your own words why the law is inadequate in protecting her. In short, why did the courts and judges fail to help her?
4. Speculate why her ex-husband would spend so much time, money, and energy in making her life and the children's lives miserable.
5. How is Singer different from many battered wives?
6. If the situation were reversed, do you think a woman could do this to a man? Why or why not?
7. After reading Singer's story, what do you think of the social, legal, and political safety nets for battered women? Should policies be changed?

LITERARY TECHNIQUES

Narrative essay Singer tells the story of her history with her husband. It is told simply, but effectively, with little dramatization.

Juxtapositioning Arrangement — putting two ideas, two words, or two of something side by side to create an effect. These can be similar, but more often they are opposites. Sometimes, the writer throws in the unexpected; for example, "We were plenty warm — we all had fevers from the flu" (p. 337). The effect is to make the reader feel off-kilter, just as her life is off-kilter.

Tone In most cases, the reader can sense whether the tone of the piece is serious, flippant, informal, ironic, or solemn by word choice, expression, and content. On the surface, Singer speaks calmly of her ordeals with her husband and the court system, but the underlying tone has tinges of anger and desperation.

Openings and closings Openings must catch the readers' interest or curiosity within the first sentence or paragraph. Closings should quickly make the readers reflect on the topic discussed in the body of the article. Given the subject matter, Singer tries to end on a hopeful note. More than that, she comes full circle by repeating the ideas expressed in the opening: "And, some mornings, I will dance among the kelp" (p. 342).

ASSIGNMENTS

1. If Singer's children were to write this story about their mother, how would they see it?
2. Research stalking laws in your area. Are they sufficient for the victims' protection? How would you improve them?
3. Research the problem of wife battering. Discuss the causes and effects in an essay.
4. Read Diane Schoemperlen's "Red Plaid Shirt" (p. 191). How are the women in the story and in the essay similar?
5. Play the devil's advocate. Write a justification for the husband's actions from his point of view.

Possessed by Stuff
Lynn Van der Water

I have a friend who believes the human race will meet its doom not at the hands of any of the usual suspects (war, pestilence, famine) but because of stuff: An inexorably swelling tide of potpourri sachets, Welsh souvenir coaster sets, Beanie Babies, and floppy velvet berets trimmed with peacock feathers.

A garage sale provides the ideal opportunity to study our relationship with stuff at its most primal. Garage sale merchandise is cheap and sells without ad campaigns or brand names to lend it glamour, succeeding solely on the seemingly universal belief that everyone else's stuff is better than your own.

At our garage sale, I observed three major categories of stuff-seekers. If you're having a sale of your own this summer, you might want to keep an eye out for these: dealers, utilitarians, and dreamers.

Dealers take a detached, even superior, attitude toward stuff. They don't need or want your stuff, but they know what other people might be willing to pay for it. They rifle through old books and snap up what you thought was unremarkable old china with intimidating decisiveness. Then they pay the asking price with an expression so close to pity that you will spend the rest of the day wondering how much they're going to mark up those items when they put them on display in their "antique" shops. But it's important to remember that the dealers are not really superior. They're just earning money to buy themselves stuff somewhere else.

Then there are the utilitarians, who really believe they need your stuff. On the surface, they may seem quite sensible, but these are the people who get hung up on something for sale cheap at a garage sale that they'd never look twice at in a store. The utilitarians' need to find a bargain, at any cost, leads to the reverse psychology of stuff: Whatever you thought was truly useless garbage will be sold right away, while stuff you secretly thought was kind of neat (like, say, a wooden platter with a handle carved in the shape of a leaping fish) will be ignored.

During our sale, I witnessed, and encouraged, a bidding war over a wicker chair, the Morticia Addams-type found in every student household but never actually sat in. And as the sale progressed, rusted metal toolboxes, failed pottery experiments, old linguistics textbooks all leapt improbably off the shelves, thanks in part to the utilitarians.

7. The dreamers take the attitude that "this stuff needs *me*." Dreamers scan objects carefully to discover their hidden potential. Everything must have a purpose and so must be rescued from the scrap heap. They will stand frozen, staring up with unseeing eyes at the suburban summer sky, trying, no doubt, to channel the wise-woman spirit of bric-a-brac, who will reveal the exact use of the one-handled straw tote bag.

8. Dreamers dwell on another plane of awareness. At our sale, a pleasant woman in her mid-40s picked up a book on Vancouver and remarked, "I used to live in Vancouver. In White Rock, actually. I found it very dull." I was just about to agree with her when she pulled something out of her wallet. It was an underexposed photo of an old tree trunk. She pointed to a shadow. "See? This is one here. You can just see her head. And over here is a troll. And in the back is another fairy." It turned out what she had said about White Rock was, "I found a fairy dell."

9. The dreamer and I had quite a chat, during which she found even more useless stuff that needed a home. It looked like we'd be unloading even the hard-to-sell items and I was brimming with the deceptive satisfactions of holding a garage sale. For one thing, I was feeling just a tad superior to my clientele, in spite of the fact that, technically, I was a dreamer, utilitarian, and dealer rolled into one. After all, I had actually bought some of this stuff once, and now I was trying to make money on it. Furthermore, with cash trickling in and junk moving out, I was beginning to believe that it's actually possible to get rid of stuff.

10. This is an illusion. At every moment, the universal tide of stuff is building toward the inevitable apocalyptic deluge my friend warned about. Once you've sold that butter dish shaped like an oyster shell, or the complete set of *Partridge Family* trading cards, they don't really go away — they simply move from your basement to someone else's, and the cycle continues. That's how I know that somewhere out there, on some hot summer evening, some poor soul will be standing knee-deep in stuff, wondering what price to put on that wooden platter with a handle carved in the shape of a leaping fish.

1999

NOTES

Beanie babies Small, stuffed toys that were a popular collector's item in the 1990s.

Morticia Addams The Addams family was the creation of a *New Yorker* cartoonist Charles Addams (1912–1988) and was later made into a 1960s TV series and two 1990s movies. Morticia's chair was wicker with a very high back.

The Partridge Family This TV series, about a family that formed a rock 'n' roll band, was popular in the early 1970s.

COMPREHENSION AND DISCUSSION

1. How does Van der Water introduce her topic? Does it catch your attention or curiosity?
2. Summarize the three categories of "stuff seekers."
3. Can you add to the writer's categories?
4. Why does she categorize herself as "a dreamer, utilitarian, and dealer rolled into one" (p. 346)?
5. Explain the image the writer creates with "the inevitable apocalyptic deluge" (p. 346).
6. Oscar Wilde once defined a cynic as "a man who knows the price of everything and the value of nothing." Can this definition be applied to the sellers or buyers at garage sales?
7. What aspects of human nature does the writer capture in this article?
8. If you have held a garage sale, talk about your experiences. Do they match Van der Water's?

LITERARY TECHNIQUES

Classification and definition Van der Water classifies her garage sale customers into three categories, defining each one.

Classification A method of categorizing. Classification is the breakdown of one unit into smaller components. Here the writer distinguishes the kinds of buyers: dealers, utilitarians, and dreamers.

Definition Explaining a term or idea so that the reader can understand it. The method can be formal or informal in structure, brief or extended, technical or common. Note that defining requires the inclusion of other writing techniques such as classification, example and illustration, comparison, and exposition. Here, Van der Water characterizes the three classifications of buyers.

ASSIGNMENTS

1. Do you have too much junk in your home? Write a descriptive paragraph about some "stuff" that you own or owned.
2. Write a brief narrative about an experience you had at a garage sale or flea market.
3. Compare this classification essay with Pico Iyer's "Of Wierdos and Eccentrics" (p. 289).
4. Write a research essay about one type of collectible (Beanie babies, *Star Wars* toys, Depression-era glassware, baseball cards, Barbie dolls, etc.). Explain its popularity and its investment potential.
5. Write a process analysis about how someone can hold a garage sale, shop at garage sales, or participate in an auction.

Am I Blue?
Alice Walker

For about three years my companion and I rented a small house in the country that stood on the edge of a large meadow that appeared to run from the end of our deck straight into the mountains. The mountains, however, were quite far away, and between us and them there was, in fact, a town. It was one of the many pleasant aspects of the house that you never really were aware of this.

It was a house of many windows, low, wide, nearly floor to ceiling in the living room, which faced the meadow, and it was from one of these that I first saw our closest neighbour, a large white horse, cropping grass, flipping its mane, and ambling about—not over the entire meadow, which stretched well out of sight of the house, but over the five or so fenced-in acres that were next to the twenty-odd that we had rented. I soon learned that the horse, whose name was Blue, belonged to a man who lived in another town, but was boarded by our neighbours next door. Occasionally, one of the children, usually a stocky teenager, but sometimes a much younger girl or boy, could be seen riding Blue. They would appear in the meadow, climb up on his back, ride furiously for ten or fifteen minutes, then get off, slap Blue on the flanks, and not be seen again for a month or more.

There were many apple trees in our yard, and one by the fence that Blue could almost reach. We were soon in the habit of feeding him apples, which he relished, especially because by the middle of summer the meadow grasses—so green and succulent since January—had dried out from lack of rain, and Blue stumbled about munching the dried stalks half-heartedly. Sometimes he would stand very still just by the apple tree, and when one of us came out he would whinny, snort loudly, or stamp the ground. This meant, of course: I want an apple.

It was quite wonderful to pick a few apples, or collect those that had fallen to the ground overnight, and patiently hold them, one by one, up to his large, toothy mouth. I remained as thrilled as a child by his flexible dark lips, huge, cubelike teeth that crunched the apples, core and all, with such finality, and his high, broad-breasted *enormity;* beside which, I felt small indeed. When I was a child, I used to ride horses, and was especially friendly with one named Nan until the day I was riding and my brother deliberately spooked her and I was thrown, head first, against the trunk of a tree. When I came to, I was in bed and my mother was bending worriedly over me; we silently agreed that perhaps horseback riding was not the safest sport for me. Since then I have walked, and prefer walking to horseback riding — but I had forgotten the depth of feeling one could see in horses' eyes.

5 I was therefore unprepared for the expression in Blue's. Blue was lonely. Blue was horribly lonely and bored. I was not shocked that this should be the case; five acres to tramp by yourself, endlessly, even in the most beautiful of meadows — and his was — cannot provide many interesting events, and once rainy season turned to dry that was about it. No, I was shocked that I had forgotten that human animals and nonhuman animals can communicate quite well; if we are brought up around animals as children we take this for granted. By the time we are adults we no longer remember. However, the animals have not changed. They are in fact *completed* creations (at least they seem to be, so much more than we) who are not likely to change; it is their nature to express themselves. What else are they going to express? And they do. And, generally speaking, they are ignored.

6 After giving Blue the apples, I would wander back to the house, aware that he was observing me. Were more apples not forthcoming then? Was that to be his sole entertainment for the day? My partner's small son had decided he wanted to learn how to piece a quilt; we worked in silence on our respective squares as I thought...

7 Well, about slavery: about white children, who were raised by black people, who knew their first all-accepting love from black women, and then, when they were twelve or so, were told they must "forget" the deep levels of communication between themselves and "mammy" that they knew. Later they would be able to relate quite calmly, "My old mammy was sold to another good family." "My old mammy was ——— ———." Fill in the blank. Many more years later a white woman would say: "I can't understand these Negroes, these blacks. What do they want? They're so different from us."

8 And about the Indians, considered to be "like animals" by the "settlers" (a very benign euphemism for what they actually were), who did not understand their description as a compliment.

9 And about the thousands of American men who marry Japanese, Korean, Filipina, and other non-English-speaking women and of how happy they report they are, "*blissfully,*" until their brides learn to speak English, at which point the marriages tend to fall apart. What then did the men see, when they looked into the eyes of the women they married, before they could speak English? Apparently only their own reflections.

10 I thought of society's impatience with the young. "Why are they playing the music so loud?" Perhaps the children have listened to much of the

music of oppressed people their parents danced to before they were born, with its passionate but soft cries for acceptance and love, and they have wondered why their parents failed to hear.

I do not know how long Blue had inhabited his five beautiful, boring acres before we moved into our house; a year after we had arrived — and had also travelled to other valleys, other cities, other worlds — he was still there.

But then, in our second year at the house, something happened in Blue's life. One morning, looking out the window at the fog that lay like a ribbon over the meadow, I saw another horse, a brown one, at the other end of Blue's field. Blue appeared to be afraid of it, and for several days made no attempt to go near. We went away for a week. When we returned, Blue had decided to make friends and the two horses ambled or galloped along together, and Blue did not come nearly as often to the fence underneath the apple tree.

When he did, bringing his new friend with him, there was a different look in his eyes. A look of independence, of self-possession, of inalienable *horse*ness. His friend eventually became pregnant. For months and months there was, it seemed to me, a mutual feeling between me and the horses of justice, of peace. I fed apples to them both. The look in Blue's eyes was one of unabashed "this is *it*ness."

It did not, however, last forever. One day, after a visit to the city, I went out to give Blue some apples. He stood waiting, or so I thought, though not beneath the tree. When I shook the tree and jumped back from the shower of apples, he made no move. I carried some over to him. He managed to half-crunch one. The rest he let fall to the ground. I dreaded looking into his eyes — because I had of course noticed that Brown, his partner, had gone — but I did look. If I had been born into slavery, and my partner had been sold or killed, my eyes would have looked like that. The children next door explained that Blue's partner had been "put with him" (the same expression that old people used, I had noticed, when speaking of an ancestor during slavery who had been impregnated by her owner) so that they could mate and she conceive. Since that was accomplished, she had been taken back by her owner, who lived somewhere else.

Will she be back? I asked.

They didn't know.

Blue was like a crazed person. Blue *was,* to me, a crazed person. He galloped furiously, as if he were being ridden, around and around his five beautiful acres. He whinnied until he couldn't. He tore at the ground with his hooves. He butted himself against his single shade tree. He looked always and always toward the road down which his partner had gone. And then, occasionally, when he came up for apples, or I took apples to him, he looked at me. It was a look so piercing, so full of grief, a look so *human*, I almost laughed (I felt too sad to cry) to think there are people who do not know that animals suffer. People like me who have forgotten, and daily forget, all that animals try to tell us. "Everything you do to us will happen to you; we are your teachers, as you are ours. We are one lesson" is essentially it, I think. There are those who never once have even considered animals' rights: those who have been taught that animals actually want to be used and abused by us, as small children "love" to be frightened, or women "love" to be mutilated and raped.... They are the great-grandchildren of those who honestly thought, because someone taught them this: "Women can't think," and "niggers can't faint." But most disturbing of all, in Blue's large brown eyes was a new look more painful than the look of despair: the look of disgust with human beings, with life; the look of hatred. And it was odd what the look of hatred did. It gave him, for the first time, the look of a beast. And what that meant was that he had put up a barrier within to protect himself from further violence; all the apples in the world wouldn't change that fact.

18   And so Blue remained, a beautiful part of our landscape, very peaceful to look at from the window, white against the grass. Once a friend came to visit and said, looking out on the soothing view: "And it *would* have to be a *white* horse; the very image of freedom." And I thought, yes, the animals are forced to become for us merely "images" of what they once so beautifully expressed. And we are used to drinking milk from containers showing "contented" cows, whose real lives we want to hear nothing about, eating eggs and drumsticks from "happy" hens, and munching hamburgers advertised by bulls of integrity who seem to command their fate.

19   As we talked of freedom and justice one day for all, we sat down to steaks. I am eating misery, I thought, as I took the first bite. And spit it out.

1986

NOTES

Alice Walker is an American writer, famous for her novel *The Color Purple*, which was made into a 1985 movie by Steven Spielberg, starring Whoopi Goldberg.

Blue is more than just a colour. It has associations with feelings and moods, especially sad, unhappy, or downcast states. Note how Walker impresses several ideas into the one colour: the name of the horse, her state of mind and her mood, her similarity to the horse's situation, and the literary technique of imagery.

COMPREHENSION AND DISCUSSION

1. In paragraph 2 (p. 349), Walker begins to focus on the horse. Why does she give so much information about the absent owner who boards the animal, and the occasional riders? Why is this opening relevant to her later discussion about slavery and freedom?
2. When does Walker became aware of the emotional state of the horse? What does the writer begin to associate with the horse? Show the steps in her thinking.
3. How does Walker make Blue seem like a person, a human being?
4. Explain this statement: "And we are used to drinking milk from containers showing 'contented' cows, whose real lives we want to hear nothing about, eating eggs and drumsticks from 'happy' hens, and munching hamburgers advertised by bulls of integrity who seem to command their fate" (p. 352).
5. What have you learned from reading this article? Will you see animals in a more compassionate way? Will you see the relationship between humanity and beast? Will you stop eating meat?
6. Will Walker become a vegetarian because of this experience?

LITERARY TECHNIQUES

Narration Telling a story or anecdote that may be either factual or fictional. In this case, Walker's article is the former. Note that even in a "real" piece, the selection of ideas and organization of information are important.

Concatenation A linking of different events, things, or ideas that at first do not seem to be related but have a core of commonality. As a literary technique, it creates suspense and momentary confusion for the reader that is readily cleared up by the writer. Note how Walker links horses to slavery, to racial attitude, to freedom, to marriage, to sex, to loneliness, to advertisements, and to our eating habits. These all come back to the title "Am I Blue?"

Analogy A comparison and illustration. Usually in an analogy, a common or easily understood concept is given first, then followed by a more difficult idea. One is used to clarify the other. Walker is making an analogy when she compares animals to slaves.

ASSIGNMENTS

1. Walker shows similarities between humans and animals. What makes people different from animals then?
2. How do you think animals should be treated? Write an essay explaining guidelines for such treatment.
3. Read Morley Callaghan's "All the Years of Her Life" (p. 47). This story and Walker's article speak of awareness and understanding. Recount an experience you have had in which you suddenly felt enlightened.
4. Read Diane Schoemperlen's "Red Plaid Shirt" (p. 191). She too uses colours in her story. Which writer makes use of colour imagery more effectively? Why?
5. Garry Engkent's "Chickens for Christmas" (p. 63) also deals with live, domestic animals — in this case, chickens. How does that story differ from Walker's?
6. Visit a zoo, a farm, or an abattoir and see how animals are kept or slaughtered. Then, keeping in mind Walker's article, write about your observations and feelings.

The End of Manual Labour
Margaret Wente

The only times I truly laboured for my living were the summers I waitressed during college. At the end of my shift I would count up all my tips (dimes and quarters; a dollar was a bonanza), tithe the counterman, and stagger home, where I would collapse in a stupor of honest physical exhaustion.

I was an outstanding waitress. I had stamina and could carry three plates at once in my left hand, a trick that still impresses my friends. It's the only useful manual skill I have.

Like most affluent boomers, I am physically soft and manually incompetent. I'm a sturdy person. Full of peasant genes. Built to pull a plow. But I don't even push a pencil any more. I tap away on an ergonomically friendly keyboard and have a headset for my phone, so that I don't actually have to lift the receiver.

When Y2K leaves the world freezing in the dark, I will be the first to die. That's because I am totally deskilled. I have none of the craft, knowledge, experience, or physical proficiency necessary for even the most primitive means of subsistence. Without supermarkets or electricity, I would be helpless as an infant.

The decline of manual skills in the modern world has been swift and relentless. My great-great-grandmothers were German farmers. Not only could they work both ends of a plow, they could also produce and make everything necessary to support the family. They threshed wheat and baked bread, slaughtered pigs, sewed the family's clothes, made their own soap from ashes and lye, churned butter, drove horses, made the furniture and the mattresses for their beds, shot varmints, built their own houses, and pulled their own teeth. They lived to be 85 and I doubt they ever suffered a moment of depression in their lives. No time.

My grandmother had all the competencies of a typical Depression-era housewife. She cooked and canned and preserved, raised chickens and beans, and was an able seamstress. She tried to show me the ropes once, when I had to make a skirt for Grade 7 Home Ec. It had to have darts. I hated the whole experience. I flunked, and, for the first and only time I remember, she lost her temper. She simply could not understand how such an intelligent girl could be such a hopeless dolt with a needle.

But now, manual labour is making a comeback of sorts. For boomers, it has turned into the ultimate status symbol — something that only those with time and money are able to cultivate. My most affluent friends are streaming back to the countryside, where they spend all their spare time hacking, hewing, and improving. They buy tractors and play at farming, or buy cows and play at breeding and herding. They speak knowledgeably about husbandry and fertilizers. They sink large fortunes into places where they can go feel like men and women of the soil from Friday to Sunday.

8   If you can't afford it, at least you can read about it. There's a reason why Frances Mayes's book *Under the Tuscan Sun* has become a runaway bestseller. It's not simply the romance of the Italian countryside, or the middle-aged romance that Frances strikes up with the mysterious and omnicompetent Ed. It's also the romance of hard manual labour, described with lyrical sensuality. Here is Ed, lovingly waxing and refinishing the 98 original chestnut beams of their ruined ancient country house. Here is Frances, clipping rosemary and preparing hearty Tuscan feasts for 18 from the bounty of the countryside and making wedding cake from scratch. There are Ed and Frances, hauling stone and harvesting their very own olives. Where the heck did they learn how to do all those things? They're only English professors.

9   For the vast middle classes, though, the joys of manual labour will remain a luxury beyond reach. Worse, most of us are doomed to watch whatever pitiful remnants of skills we still possess wither and die. I can scarcely remember how to cook without a microwave (my nieces and nephews never learned). My new microwave doesn't even require me to guess the cooking time. I just push Defrost, or Soup, or Potato. "Enjoy your meal," it says a few minutes later, in English or Spanish.

10 In Silicon Valley, they're working on the next generation of smart chips, which they promise will simplify (i.e., deskill) life even more. These chips will start your morning coffee for you, but not if you're out of town. They will be built into your refrigerator, and order more food when supplies get low. If the dishwasher breaks, the chip in it will call up the repairman. In another decade the only time you'll have to touch food is when you eat it.

11 I can't say that I'm nostalgic for waitressing. But there is something to be said for work that, done properly, makes you tired. No doubt my great-great-grandmothers would say it was the only honest work I ever did.

1999

NOTES

Margaret Wente is a columnist and editor of *The Globe and Mail*.

Y2K Note that this article was written before the year 2000 (Y2K). It was feared that the flaw in computer dating would cause electronic devices to stop operating, leaving people without power on January 1, 2000.

To show someone the ropes A nautical term in which sailors learn to tie different kinds of knots for different purposes on a sailing ship. As an idiomatic expression, it means to teach someone the way to do things.

Home Ec. Short for Home Economics, a high-school class, usually for teenage girls. In this course, students learn to cook, sew, make a budget, shop wisely, and so on, all to prepare them for domestic life.

Heck A euphemism for the stronger swear word "hell."

COMPREHENSION AND DISCUSSION

1. Why is waitressing such a physically demanding job? Is it also mentally demanding? Why or why not?
2. Why does the author no longer have to exert herself physically?
3. What could her grandparents do that she no longer can?
4. Why is there a renewed interest in manual labour?
5. Do you believe weekend farmers are as capable as real farmers in cultivating the land?
6. What skills do you regret that you did not learn or that you do not possess now? Why?
7. Explain this statement: "For the vast middle classes, though, the joys of manual labour will remain a luxury beyond reach. Worse, most of us are doomed to watch whatever pitiful remnants of skills we still possess wither and die" (p. 356).

LITERARY TECHNIQUES

Illustration The act of explaining or showing. Like the example, the illustration offers longer explanations in order to clarify the main idea or topic. Generally, an illustrative essay gives a range of scenarios and related narratives.

"here is," "there are" (paragraph 8, p. 356) Used in this context, these openings are demonstrative; that is, they point out. They are also emphatic.

ASSIGNMENTS

1. How do Wente and Fred Donnelly (in "The Golden Years of Electronic Helps," p. 258) agree?
2. Describe a skill that you wish you had (such as sewing, driving, speaking another language) and explain why it would be important in your life.
3. What do you consider to be "honest work"?
4. Explain why physical work is not valued in our society.
5. The deskilling of jobs is an important issue in the workplace. Write a report on a job that has been deskilled because of the use of computers.
6. In an essay, explain the popularity of handicrafts and the work of Martha Stewart.

Rediscovering Christmas
Almas Zakiuddin

It was my first winter in Toronto and so cold it froze the frown on my face. I frowned a lot in those days, before I rediscovered Christmas. Of course, I always knew about Christmas. I had read about it, even seen people celebrate Christmas. I was a typical convent-school-English-educated South Asian, brought up in a family that combined Muslim postcolonial nationalism with heady tales of the good old British Raj. Which meant that we used knives and forks at the table, but said our *isha* prayers before sitting down to dinner. I was (and still am) a Muslim.

Before I came to Canada, I was under the impression that I was not supposed to celebrate Christmas; it was not the done thing. I told no one, certainly not my parents, but once in a while I used to wonder: What if I had been born in a family that celebrated Christmas? Like the family of (let's call her) Jennifer McDonald.

I was 15 years old, a plump, pimply day student at a convent school for girls in Karachi, Pakistan. Jennifer McDonald was that kind of person known as an "anglo," of mixed South Asian–British ancestry. She had golden-tan skin, light brown curly hair and hazel eyes. She wore lipstick (my mother said only "fast" girls wore lipstick), a skin-tight beige skirt, and an even tighter white blouse to school. I was made to wear a loose beige tunic, with baggy trousers called a *shalwar* and a white scarf.

Jennifer McDonald appeared at our end-of-term charity bazaar in the school gym in this incredible, short, fluffy, pink dress with frills that swished when she moved. She flounced to the centre of the room, tossed her curls, crossed her legs. "So what're yoa'll doin' fer Christmas, men?" she asked. ("Men" was a favourite term of endearment among anglos.) "I'm gonna have a bloody good time!" she laughed. ("Bloody" was another favourite anglo term.)

It was almost four decades later that I thought again about Jennifer McDonald. I was in a different country, almost a different civilization.

"And what are you doing for Christmas then?" asked the young woman at the corner store near my subway stop in Toronto. If I looked up in surprise it was because the young woman had not said a word to me in the six weeks I had been patronizing her store. "Oh, Christmas...? I don't know really. I'm...uh..." I mumbled, unsure of my plans. Someone wanted a jar of honey from the top shelf and the young woman disappeared. I wasn't sure why she had asked about my Christmas plans: It might have been because she wanted to be friendly.

7   It occurred to me, then, that people in Canada change during Christmas, becoming almost friendly. I mean, they talk to strangers, even smile at them, occasionally. All this in spite of the cold, the wind-chill factor (minus 24 that evening), and the reality that I was yet another addition to the swelling ranks of hyphenated, multicultural Canada.

8   In the next week or so, I found myself experiencing a different kind of Canada. There were new sounds, new sights, new smells, and new flavours, and they all connected, somehow, with Christmas. There were lights everywhere, there was mistletoe, decorations, tiny marzipan angels, tinsel. There were stockings waiting to be filled and red bows for doorways, and a bright costume for the old man, Father Christmas, Santa Claus. There was an air of fun that had not existed before. Neighbours appeared where none had been noticeable before, inviting me into their homes, showing me their lights, their decorations, their preparations. I went and got my own lights and spent a weekend doing up my front window — my tiny apartment looked quite festive when they were on.

9   As the holiday season progressed, I watched the people around me, of all ages and backgrounds, people at the parties to which I was invited, people shopping, going to the cinema, ice skating, people at work. Everyone walked and talked with a little spring in their step. I turned on the radio, and the carols were beautiful, full of hope and joy. I quietly gave a few extra coins to an old man on the street, more conscious of the need to share the good things of life. Not a gloomy sign did I see, anywhere in these otherwise dark and bitterly cold days in Canada. I stopped frowning all the time. There was something happening here, something that I had not seen before. People were participating in a festival that was universal — or could be, if we allowed ourselves to make it so.

10   And this is when I rediscovered Christmas. During my first winter in Canada, I realized that you don't have to be a Christian to celebrate Christmas. After all, Christmas hardly belongs exclusively to Christianity. By all accounts, the feast is originally pagan Roman, the tree of German innovation, the sleigh and reindeer Scandinavian. Santa himself is a mythical Nordic invention, the trimmings are now probably shipped from Bangladesh, and the carols recorded in Taiwan on digital equipment made in Hong Kong!

11   Christmas might trace some of its roots to an Anglo-Saxon heritage, but so do the days of the week, the English language, the pizza, and the ballpoint pen — all of which are pretty essential to my personal survival. It is as ludicrous to expect me to forgo any benefit from these things sim-

ply because their inventors were not of my race or religion as it is to expect the western world to stop counting because the modern world's numerals originally "belonged" to the Arabs.

Indeed, Christmas does not "belong" to anyone. At an office party later that week, I heard the many different languages, dialects, and accents. We were as multicultural a bunch of human beings as could exist on God's earth. There were Christians of various denominations — Greek Orthodox to Catholic — and the Jewish, Muslim, Hindu, and Parsi faiths, as well as people from virtually every continent.

This is when she came to mind, my classmate from a previous life, Jennifer McDonald, she of the pink, frilly, swishing dress who first made me want to celebrate Christmas — who first made me want to be different. I realized we were all, in one way or another, like Jennifer. Each of us has taken something — a ritual or a tradition or a tool, an item of food — from someone other than our "pure laine" ancestors.

I realized that it was okay to be a little "anglo." Here in Canada, you can be a Muslim, as I am. You can be a Canadian, as I am. This is the only country in the world where you can be everything you are and want to be.

And I realized that here, in Canada, you can celebrate Christmas, if you want to. Or not, if you don't want to.

1999

NOTES

Raj Short for "raja," an East Indian term for ruler or prince. During British rule in the far East, European men of position or rank were called a "raj" or "raja."

Fast A colloquial or slang term for someone with loose morals.

Anglos A colloquial term for white people or for people who speak only English.

Bloody A British expression, considered swearing. It is not commonly used in North America. In the past, "bloody" had a stronger emphasis than today.

Pure laine Literally, meaning "100 percent wool" (French). It has become a term used in Quebec to mean those Québécois who are descended from the early French settlers. It excludes recent immigrants of different nationalities and races and anglophone Quebeckers.

COMPREHENSION AND DISCUSSION

1. How old (approximately) is the writer at the time of this article?
2. Who is Jennifer McDonald? Why do you think the writer picked this name?
3. According to the author, what makes the sales clerk suddenly become friendly?
4. How does she discount the notion that Christmas only belongs to the Christians? Note the origins of the various Christmas traditions.
5. Is Christmas truly universal? Do you celebrate Christmas as a secular or a religious holiday? Or not at all? Explain.
6. Why is the Muslim point of view in this article important? Would the article be the same if it had been written by a Christian?

LITERARY TECHNIQUES

Flashback Notice how the writer takes you back to her school days before returning to the present. The flashback is necessary so that the reader comprehends the context of the article.

ASSIGNMENTS

1. Read the short story "Chickens for Christmas" (p. 63) and the article "Growing Up on Grace" (p. 250). Write an essay on immigrant adaptation of a new culture. Discuss what type of adjustments immigrants must make.
2. Write about a holiday. Discuss what it means to you or how the holiday has been adapted for life in Canada.
3. Zakiuddin states: "This [Canada] is the only country in the world where you can be everything you are and want to be" (p. 361). Is this true of Canada's history? Research the history of immigration and multiculturalism in Canada.
4. Note the number of holidays in Canada. How many of them have a religious context? Is Sunday a religious holiday? Do you consider Thanksgiving to be a religious holiday or just a long weekend?

Research the background of these holidays and show why Canadians celebrate them.
5. Should Canadians add legal holidays from other religious faiths?

PART THREE
WRITING ESSAYS

Chapter 1
THE WRITING PROCESS

Writing begins with an idea or a thought. You have an opinion you want to express. You have a thought you wish to share. In short, writing starts when you have something to say and you want to say it.

Articulating what you feel and what you know requires deep thinking on the subject. After all, you are communicating a thought, an idea, or a piece of information to someone else. You must understand what your readers want and need to know. You must understand how much background information is necessary. On the other hand, you don't want to bore your readers by including too much unnecessary detail.

Writing is expressing ideas clearly, concisely, and coherently. Clarity in thought and expression is essential. It saves readers effort in trying to decipher your thoughts on the subject. Concise writing saves the readers time. Nothing is more exasperating than having to wade through long, windy prose. Coherence is the logically organized sequence of information or arguments. Your readers must be able to see the relationship between one idea and the next.

Writing is based on reading, the act of accumulating and synthesizing knowledge. Personal experience and contemplation can only go so far. Generating ideas requires background information. The wider your general knowledge, the better you will be in drawing ideas together, coming up with your own opinions, and expressing them. You can read more about the nature of thinking in two of the articles in Part II: "What Is an Idea?" (p. 283) and "Don't You Think It's Time to Start Thinking?" (p. 268).

In addition, reading other people's writing will help you appreciate different styles of expression. Why do some writers prefer long, complex sentences? Why do some writers prefer a folksy way of addressing the reader? Why do some break the rules of grammar in their prose? Your analysis of the way others write will further your own style.

Reading also shows you how written English is different from spoken English. Spoken language tends to be less formal and less precise. Speakers rely on visual cues and other feedback from their audience. Listeners can ask questions or show by their facial expression that they do not understand, and the speaker can adjust by adding more information. Speakers also use gestures and tone of voice to help get their meaning across.

Writers have a more difficult job than speakers: They have to anticipate what their readers will think. In addition, they will have to address what questions their readers might have and what they want to know. Sometimes, they have to make sure that their humorous comments come across as humour. They have to prevent misunderstanding by using the correct words. However, writers also have the luxury of reflecting on their words and revising them, whereas speakers have less time to think and consider what they say. The written word is also subject to more analysis than the spoken word.

Finally, writing is hard work. You begin with a thought and a blank page. Now you must fill the pages with ideas. You must do it all with words, sentences, and paragraphs.

STEPS IN THE PROCESS

People handle the writing process differently. Some plan their work meticulously with detailed outlines. Others just slap some words into the document file and keep on adding, deleting, and changing until they shape their writing into a coherent structure. If you are getting satisfactory results with your writing methods, feel free to carry on. However, if your essays receive poor marks, then you should consider changing the way you work.

Essentially, writing can be broken down into three stages. In the pre-writing stage, you think through your ideas, decide what you want to say, and organize your points. Second comes the actual writing of a draft where you flesh your ideas into sentences and paragraphs. The third stage is revising and editing.

Writers who write directly on a computer often find these writing stages less distinct. They may start with a few guideline words, type in a few points, flesh out a couple of sentences, and then gradually add more while constantly revising. They may not make an outline as a separate document; instead, their outline gets absorbed into their draft.

BRAINSTORMING

The first step in the planning phase is coming up with ideas for your writing; this is sometimes called brainstorming. The more ideas you generate for a subject, the better your essay will be. Brainstorming can help you avoid writer's block—the state where you just stare at the page and can't think of what to put on it. You don't have to use every point you come up with, but having more to work with allows you to zero in on the best points. Thinking about the opposing side of an argument allows you to make your own argument stronger. For example, if you are writing an essay on the drawbacks of living in residence, it is wise to compare them with the drawbacks of living in an apartment, even if you do not put points of comparison in your essay.

Writers have different ways of dealing with the thinking stage. Some draw bubble diagrams, some create charts, some just list point-form ideas, and some do freewriting. If you've found a way that works for you, keep working with it. Otherwise, try different ways to brainstorm. Your teachers have probably shown you the various techniques. If not, ask your instructor for help.

Suppose you are asked the question "Who should bear most of the costs of postsecondary education—the government or the student?" Here's what you might come up with when you brainstorm on the topic:

The government
- the government already pays for most education (elementary and secondary)
- the government cannot afford the cost of education—schools suffering
- society requires more education: postsecondary education is now a requirement for good jobs
- the country benefits from an educated citizenry (greater productivity, lower health costs, more participation in civic life)
- more highly educated people get better paying jobs, thus paying higher taxes
- education is a good investment for the government
- all people benefit from an educated citizenry (not just the graduates themselves)

The students
- students receive the most benefit from their education
- students are legal adults, not children who have to be taken care of
- students can get loans, jobs
- other taxpayers should not pay for students' benefit
- but some students cannot afford to pay, therefore higher education will only be for the upper classes

- students cannot handle the demands of schoolwork and working at the same time
- students cannot make enough money to pay for tuition in their summer jobs
- students should not be saddled with large debts just as they're starting their careers

ORGANIZING IDEAS AND OUTLINING

An outline is a map for you to follow. It keeps you on track. It can be as simple as deciding you want to explain what causes a problem before you discuss the various solutions. The longer your piece of writing, the more you will find an outline helpful.

An outline is a list of the ideas that you want to develop, organized in paragraphs. You want to have one main idea expressed in each paragraph. If you are writing a five-paragraph essay, you have to organize your ideas so that you can cover a lot in the three body paragraphs without repeating yourself.

Your instructor may ask you to show or submit an essay outline before you submit your final draft. An outline can be in point form or in full sentences. Here is an example:

Thesis: It is the responsibility of the government to bear most of the cost of postsecondary education.

A) cost is prohibitive for most students
- they can't do well at their studies if they work part-time
- working all summer does not earn enough for tuition
- high costs limit education to the rich

B) education is a financial investment for government
- higher-educated people get better jobs, paying more tax
- fewer unemployed on welfare
- employers need educated workforce
- education employs people
- educated people contribute to GNP

C) the country needs educated citizens
- educated people become workers, producing goods and services for the country
- educated people tend to be healthier, thus reducing health care costs

- government provides basic education (elementary and secondary), but today a postsecondary education can be considered basic

WRITING A DRAFT

Once you have an idea of what you want to say, you can write your first draft. Don't worry about getting your wording perfect. You don't even have to worry about your spelling and grammar being correct at this stage — as long as you correct the mistakes before you hand in your work. An example of a first draft follows:

> The costs of tuition has been steadily rising in Ontario. Whereas students used to pay about just a fraction of the cost of their postsecondary education, now they pay almost half. Schools need more money. There is over-crowding in classrooms. Buildings have not been properly maintained. And new computer and lab equipment is desperately needed. But who should bear the responsibility of most of the cost? The government.
>
> First, it's too expensive. In the old days, students could work during the summer and earn enough to pay for most of their university year. No longer. Minimum wage jobs won't even bring in enough to pay the tuition alone never mind residence and books. Some students work long hours at part-time jobs while they are in school, thus not being able to spend as much time on their studies as they should be in order to get good grades and graduate with a degree. And they are poor and live on Kraft dinner which isn't very nutritious and doesn't help students who are starving and need good food to have the energy to work hard and succeed at their schoolwork. The parents can't afford to pay all the university costs. Some have more than one child in university or college. Even loans don't help. Some students are graduating with $20 000 and $30 000 debts. This cripples them financially for many years to come — the very years they want to get set up in life when they are not making much money but need to pay for housing, a car, and a work wardrobe. Many students decide college or university is financially out of reach. Only the rich can afford it.
>
> The government, on the other hand, needs to realize that funding postsecondary education is a good investment. Highly educated people get good jobs and pay lots of taxes. They contribute to the GNP. A well-educated workforce means fewer people on welfare. When someone from a poor family goes to university, they can help their whole family when they gets a good job. Employers need an educated workforce, so businesses are attracted to the country. Finally, the education industry also needs employees, and that

makes more of a country's citizens gainfully employed and contributing to the economy.

The best investment is in its people. The government needs educated people. Educated people make better choices. Their jobs are better. Educated people tend to be healthier, thus reducing health care costs. The government acknowledges its need to pay for basic education (elementary and secondary school), but today people need a postsecondary as a minimum.

The government should bear most of the cost of postsecondary education leaving students to pay less. It is what we need government to do.

REVISING AND EDITING

Revising and editing is a crucial stage. It doesn't mean simply fixing up some of the grammar and spelling. It means taking a careful look at what you have written. Revision, after all, means "seeing again." Professional writers often spend more time on this phase than on any other.

It is always better to let your writing sit for a day or two before you revise it. This way you will be seeing it with fresh eyes and you are more likely to find weak areas.

Make sure your writing is concise. Get rid of needless repetition. Edit out unnecessary words. Be ruthless: No matter how beautifully written your sentence is, if it doesn't fit the paragraph, delete it.

On the other hand, make sure that you have said enough to make your points clear. Back up your general statements with explanation or specific examples.

Compare this revised essay with the first draft above:

> The cost of tuition has been steadily rising in Ontario. Whereas students used to pay less than a quarter of the cost of their postsecondary education, now they pay more than a third, and in some cases close to a half. However, higher tuition has not met the financial needs of schools, which are suffering from overcrowding, inadequate and poorly maintained facilities, lack of staff, and outdated equipment. Cash-strapped institutions need more money. It is up to the government to step up and fund institutions properly and reduce tuition fees for students.
>
> University tuition fees are too high for students to handle. Before fees were raised so precipitously, students could work during the summer and earn enough to pay for most of their university year. Minimum-wage summer jobs won't even earn students enough to make a dent in tuition. Some

work long hours at part-time jobs while they are in school, decreasing the amount of time they can spend on their studies. Loans are not helping. Some students are graduating crippled financially with $20 000 and $30 000 debts. Therefore, many students decide college or university is financially out of reach. Only the rich can afford it.

The government, on the other hand, needs to realize that funding postsecondary education is a good investment. Highly educated people get better jobs, paying more income tax in the end. They contribute to the GNP. A well-educated workforce means fewer people on welfare. In poor families especially, having someone graduate from university can benefit the whole family. Furthermore, employers need an educated workforce so businesses are attracted to the country. Finally, the education industry also needs employees, so a thriving industry means that teachers and support staff are also gainfully employed and contributing to the economy.

The best investment a government can make is in its people. The government needs an educated citizenry. Educated people participate more in society. They are more informed about social and political issues. Their jobs are better. Educated people tend to be healthier, thus reducing health care costs. Even areas that are not generally seen as practical, such as a liberal arts education, are valued by employers because this type of education produces creative thinkers. Strong universities participate in research and development, fuelling more advances in science and technology. The government acknowledges its responsibility to pay for basic education (elementary and secondary school), but today postsecondary education can be considered basic because it is hard to get a decent job without a college or university degree.

The government should bear most of the cost of postsecondary education, leaving students to pay no more than 20 percent. Money spent on education benefits the whole society and is a worthwhile investment. This benefit is so obvious that it should be made clear even to those who grumble about high taxes and the childless who protest against paying for the schooling of "other people's children."

CHECKING THE ESSAY

After your revisions are done, it is time to check and double-check for the little things. Look at your assignment sheet again and make sure you have done everything the instructor asked of you. For instance, check that your cover page has the title of your essay, your name, the course code, the date, and the instructor's name. If you are supposed to hand in an outline, make sure that it is attached.

Know your weaknesses. Write them down on a checklist. If you have trouble with run-on sentences, for example, screen your essay carefully for run-ons. If your particular weakness is spelling, check any word that you are unsure of. Use the grammar and spellcheck functions in your word processing software, but don't count on them to find all your mistakes. Proofread your work carefully.

You can get someone to read over your work. This person should not do the corrections for you, but should point out problem areas. A second reader can be particularly helpful for spotting lack of clarity. A tutor at your school's writing centre can help you polish your work.

To check your essay, use the principles of good writing explained in Chapter 2.

Chapter 2

THE PRINCIPLES OF GOOD WRITING

Writing has different purposes and is designed for different audiences. You write to explain, inform, reflect, entertain, and persuade. Whether you are writing an e-mail message or an essay, the same principles of good writing apply. You have to express your ideas in a way that makes communication successful. In other words, your message must be clear to your readers. Good writing is also succinct and to the point.

This chapter presents necessary elements that you have to keep in mind while you write. You have to consider your audience and purpose, you must strive for clarity and conciseness, and you have to be aware of your use of language.

AUDIENCE AND PURPOSE

Writing is communication. In order to communicate well you must consider why you are writing something and who will read it. Your audience and purpose determine the content, organization of ideas, vocabulary, and writing style (formal or conversational). For instance, you would write a letter to a friend in a much more conversational style than you would to your supervisor. Moreover, a reader who is knowledgeable in the subject area will need less background information than a layperson. The expert can understand technical vocabulary, whereas the layperson cannot. For example, doctors would understand "cardiac infarction," whereas laypeople would prefer the term "heart attack."

The audience for your essay is your instructor, but academic writing is not like other forms of writing. Instead of writing to communicate new information, you are writing to show your instructor how you think, how well you have learned the material, and how well you communicate. Although in most pieces of writing, you try to avoid telling your readers too much of what they already know, in academic writing, you are not giving the instructor new information. Instead, you are telling your instructor what you have learned.

The purpose encompasses the thesis, since the thesis is the main idea you want to communicate to your audience. For instance, if you are writing an essay arguing that all students should study history, your purpose is to make a sound argument for that idea.

For any piece of writing, success is determined by whether it fulfills the writer's purpose and suits the intended audience.

CLARITY

Writing must communicate your message, and therefore it must be clear. When you talk to people, you can check whether they understand you by just looking at them or asking them, but you can't follow your writing around to make sure all readers understand it. Therefore, clarity in writing is vital. What seems clear to you may not be clear to your readers, so it is wise to get a second opinion on what you say. Perhaps you can get a friend or tutor to read over your work.

You achieve clarity in writing by knowing exactly what you want to say. Define your purpose. Organize your points so that you deal with them one by one. Skipping around from idea to idea simply confuses readers. Each paragraph should have one main idea. General statements have to be supported by specific ones, giving details, explanations, or examples. Sufficient explanation and examples are vital to clarity. Transition signals, such as "for example," "first," and "therefore," are essential to show the relationship between ideas.

Proper vocabulary is essential. If you use jargon or technical language, you should be sure your audience will understand it. If you are unsure whether you are using a word correctly, check a dictionary. Use precise words, not vague ones. Writing must be more precise than speaking. For example, you can't get away with writing such phrases as "that thing over there."

Gauging your readers' knowledge is difficult but necessary. In order to be clear, you have to know how much background knowledge is necessary. For example, in an essay about the Internet, you can assume that your audience knows what it is, but you may wish to give some historical background to show its development.

CONCISENESS

Good writing is short and to the point. Conciseness is hard to achieve, but essential. No reader wants to waste time ploughing through extraneous words and ideas to find the point of a document. Eliminate unnecessary repetition. You have to give enough information to make the ideas clear, but avoid padding your article just to reach the prescribed word limit.

You can achieve conciseness by reducing the number of non-essential words in your sentences. For instance, "now" is more concise than "at this point in time." Consider each word and phrase as you do your revision. The question you should ask is "Can I reduce this without changing the meaning?" Then cut to the bone.

Keep your purpose in mind. If an idea does not relate directly to your thesis, then it is irrelevant and can be cut.

COHERENCE

Coherence refers to sticking together. Your sentences should follow logically and should relate to each other. For instance, if you make a general statement, you could follow it with a specific example, introducing that sentence with transitions such as "for instance."

Your writing must be drawn together in some pattern. Often this requires organizing ideas for the reader. If your ideas are too scattered, they tend to confuse the reader. Some of the basic patterns are as follows:

- chronological (time sequence)
- climactic (from least to most important)
- logical (appropriate sequence or grouping of ideas)
- listing or anticlimactic (from most to least important)
- spatial (in one direction such as top to bottom, left to right, or clockwise)

Using transition markers is vital. Phrases such as "in addition" and "however" help your readers follow the relationship between ideas. You can find a list of such markers on page 442.

GRAMMAR

Good writing is grammatically correct. While some grammatical errors do not really hinder understanding, mistakes make your work look less professional. In addition, too many errors may distract the reader from the purpose of your piece. Then your reader may lose confidence in your argument. Serious grammatical errors include the misuse of clauses and incorrect verb tenses. ESL students have trouble with prepositions and articles, but these mistakes can generally be considered minor because they do not cause as many comprehension problems. Keep in mind, however, that writing at the college or university level is supposed to be free of grammatical mistakes.

If you use a usage guide to improve your command of grammar, you may have to learn some terminology to understand the advice. For example, you should know the basic terms for parts of speech: noun, verb, adjective, adverb, conjunction, preposition. You should know what "present tense" and "subordinate clause" mean. These terms are defined in dictionaries and grammar books. Learn the ones you need, but don't worry about mastering all the terminology. If you rarely make grammatical errors, then you don't need to become a grammar expert.

Grammar checkers are packaged with most word processing software, but they are difficult to use effectively. Because computers cannot understand language, the program often makes mistakes in parsing the sentence (dividing the sentence into grammatical units). Grammar checkers are useful for catching slips, but if your knowledge of grammar and sentence structure is not sound, the software may be more harmful than helpful. If you find your computer's grammar checker to be helpful, use it. However, be alert to the fact that the advice it gives may be just plain wrong.

Our advice on grammar is that if you are making mistakes and don't understand them, learn the formal grammar rules so that you can correct them. If your essays come back relatively unscathed by your instructor's marking pencil, then don't worry about stocking up on grammar books. Native speakers of English, especially those who read a lot, can develop a good sense of grammar without formal study. For instance, while someone may not know what "subjunctive" means, she may be able to write a grammatical sentence using it. Conversely, it is possible to find ESL students who can rhyme off the most subtle of grammar rules but who cannot apply them to their own writing.

Specific grammar problems are discussed in Chapter 8.

SENTENCE STRUCTURE

It's not enough to write grammatical sentences; you need to use appropriate sentence structure. Too many short, simple sentences, for example, can make your writing sound choppy or even juvenile. Complex sentences are especially important because they can express more complex ideas. For instance, you can put the less important information in a sentence by using a subordinate clause. To keep a reader's interest, you should use a variety of sentence structures. It's tiring to read a succession of long, involved sentences. Conversely, too many short sentences mean that your writing does not flow well.

SPELLING

Writing that is riddled with spelling errors creates a bad impression, even if the reader can figure out what you mean. It is up to you to improve your spelling. Use tools such as dictionaries and computer spellcheckers. If your work contains spelling mistakes, make a list of these misspelled words. Write the correct form of those words dozens of times so that you will remember the proper spelling. Most English spelling is regular. Learn the rules, such as "*i* before *e* except after *c*." Spelling mistakes are relatively easy to fix, so not fixing them shows carelessness.

Use dictionaries and your computer's spellchecker to help you correct your spelling. It is easier to find the correct word if you have spelled the beginning of the word correctly. English spelling is not phonetic; it does not follow pronunciation as does spelling in languages such as Italian and Polish. However, you can learn the different ways common sounds are spelled. For instance, an "s" sound could be spelled with an *s, c,* or *sc.*

Remember that a spellchecker is a flawed tool. It cannot do your work for you. It will not pick up on spelling mistakes if you have just used the wrong word, for example, if you have typed "there" instead of "their." However, it is important to run your document through the spellchecker because it can find those hard-to-see typographical errors. Just remember not to blindly accept the software's suggestions. Check the meaning of the alternatives in the dictionary if you are not sure. Be sure to proofread the document yourself to catch errors the computer missed.

Your spellchecker may use a British or an American word list. However, Canadian spelling is different. In some cases, it uses the British style, preferring "centre" over "center," for example. In other cases, Canadian spelling uses American style, such as "organize" instead of "organise." You will also see variations within Canadian spelling. Different publishers may follow different style guides. In many cases, the two spellings are both accepted. Use a Canadian dictionary, and try to remain consistent. For instance, if you use *-our* endings, make sure you spell both "neighbour" and "colour" with the same ending.

VOCABULARY

English offers the writer a huge number of words from which to choose. The English language has absorbed words from many different languages. The Norman invasion of 1066 brought Norman French to England, and as a result, Old English words acquired synonyms (words that have the same meaning) from French. For instance, you can describe something as "big" using an Old English word, or "large" using a word from French. Technical words, such as "television" and "psychosomatic," are from Latin and Greek. Many of the inconsistencies in the spelling and pronunciation system of English can be traced to imported words. For instance, the *ph* spelling of an "f" sound (as in "telephone") is from the Greek, which uses the letter phi.

It is important to use a variety of words in your writing and to use them appropriately. The larger your vocabulary, the more easily you will find the proper word. The best way to improve your vocabulary is to read a lot. Written language uses a wider range of words and expressions than does spoken language. Avid readers usually have a good vocabulary. Knowledge of Greek and Latin roots can help you build your vocabulary. For example, "autobiographical" is a simple word if you know that *auto-* means "self," *bio-* means "life," *graph* refers to writing, and *-ical* is an adjective ending. These same roots are found in such words as "autograph," "biology," "graphology," and "telegraph." You can look up the meaning of such common roots in the dictionary.

A dictionary is an essential tool, but don't reach for one every time you come across an unfamiliar word in your reading. You don't want to interrupt the flow of ideas. Moreover, constant use of a dictionary can become a chore. So try to guess the meaning of the word from the context. If you can't, and if the word seems important to what you are reading, then obviously you should look it up.

Another useful tool is a thesaurus, a book of synonyms (words with similar meanings) and antonyms (words with opposite meanings). A thesaurus can jog your memory about words with which you may be familiar but do not generally use. However, you should not use unfamiliar words from a thesaurus because you might use them incorrectly. Just because words are synonyms does not mean they are always interchangeable.

In addition to knowing the denotation (meaning) of words, you must know the connotation (emotional value). For instance, "kill" and "murder" mean essentially the same thing, but "murder" is a much stronger word and has more of a negative connotation.

STYLE

Your writing should be in an appropriate style. Essays and business reports should be written in formal English, while personal letters can be written in a conversational style. Business communication today is much less formal than in the past, just like business dress is more casual, and there are different levels of formality. However, if you write in too conversational a style for academic and business writing, you risk giving the wrong impression. It's much like showing up in shorts and a t-shirt for a job interview — it's inappropriate.

In addition, written English is more formal and precise than spoken English. In speech, we rely on visual cues and context to understand what someone is saying. A piece of paper cannot carry those clues, nor can it carry gestures or tone of voice. You can simply point to something when you speak to someone; in writing you need the precise word to make sure your audience understands your meaning.

The more formal the writing, the less personal it is. Formality is always marked by distance. That does not mean you have to avoid using "I" completely, but you should realize that the "I" is often unnecessary. Your statements express your opinions (unless you say it is someone else's opinion), so you don't need phrases such as "I think" and "in my opinion." Using "you" in an essay also gives it a more conversational tone (see p. 448).

Writing that is too formal can also be a problem because it can be stilted and difficult to understand. However, this problem is more common among bureaucrats and academics than students. Students generally need to learn to write in a less personal, more formal style, suitable for school and work purposes. Examples of informal and formal style can be found on pages 438–439.

CHECKLIST

Unlike some disciplines where an answer is either right or wrong, English courses offer many challenges for evaluation. Instructors have many factors to consider when they assign marks. Some instructors break up the marks so that they give some for content, some for mechanics, and some for vocabulary. Others grade holistically, balancing good and bad points in their head, before assigning a mark. The instructors will consider the principles of good writing explained in this chapter.

Here are some questions you can ask yourself before you hand in your essay:

- Is the main idea (the thesis) of the essay clear? Is it a supportable idea, appropriate for a thesis?

- Does the assignment meet the set criteria? For example, do you answer the question posed? Is the essay too short or too long?
- Does the essay follow proper organization? Is there an adequate introduction and conclusion?
- Does each paragraph have one main idea, clearly expressed in the topic sentence?
- Are the points supported with specific explanations and examples?
- Are the arguments logical? Are they consistent (no contradiction)? Are they presented in a logical order, with clear transitions showing the relationship between ideas?
- Are your expressions clear? Is it easy to understand what you are trying to say? Are words misused? Is the vocabulary appropriate for college-level writing?
- Is the essay in an appropriate style — not too conversational?
- Are there many grammatical mistakes? Are they major or minor errors? (Minor errors would not cause a comprehension problem, but too many of them would create a bad impression.)
- Is there variety in sentence structure? Are there enough complex sentences? Does the writing flow from sentence to sentence?
- Is spelling correct? Are there serious errors or minor slips?
- Are punctuation and spacing correct?
- Did you follow formatting guidelines set out in the assignment? For example, is the print readable? Is the essay double-spaced? Are margins wide enough?
- Have you proofread your paper carefully?

Chapter 3
THE ESSAY

The essay is a means by which teachers can evaluate your skills in writing and communication and your ability to think an idea through. Derived from the French word *essayer* (meaning "to attempt"), the modern "essay" is an attempt to explain. The essay then is an academic exercise in which you learn to express ideas and support your opinion. For reflections on the thinking process and how it relates to writing essays, read two of the non-fiction selections in this book: "What Is an Idea?" (p. 283) and "Don't You Think It's Time to Start Thinking?" (p. 268).

Use of essays is not limited to school. You read essays in newspapers and magazines in columns and on the opinion and editorial pages. These essays tend to be more loosely structured than academic ones. Many of the non-fiction selections in this book are such works.

Your instructor may lay out the structure you are to follow. The basic structure is a five-paragraph essay. Mastering this form allows you to move to more ambitious essays. As you practise essay writing, you learn how to organize a piece of writing, how to support ideas and explain them clearly, and how to introduce and conclude your work. These skills are transferable; whether you are writing a business report or a letter, essay-writing skills can help you.

The essay has three parts: beginning, middle, and end. The beginning is the introduction. It gets the reader's attention, gives the reader background information, and prepares the way for the meat of the essay. The middle paragraphs are also called the body of the essay. These paragraphs are developed paragraphs with a topic sentence introducing the main point and one to three minor points with supporting ideas. The last paragraph or section is the conclusion. In a long essay, the conclusion might contain a summary; in a short essay, the only summary is the restatement of the thesis. The introduction leads the reader into the essay; the conclusion leads the reader out.

PARAGRAPHS

The paragraph is a building block for essays. A paragraph expresses one main idea and is usually composed of several sentences. It has unity, coherence, and sufficient development. It is signalled by an indent. If block paragraphing is used, a blank line separates paragraphs. Whatever method is used, it is important for the reader to be able to clearly distinguish the beginning and end of each paragraph.

Paragraphs have shrunk. Nineteenth-century literature is full of examples of paragraphs that go on and on, sometimes for pages. Today, brief paragraphs reflect our shorter attention spans and general impatience. Short paragraphs are essential in newspaper and magazine articles, where text is broken up into one or two sentences to make it more readable in column format. Modern fiction tends to have a lot of dialogue—requiring a new paragraph for each new speaker.

In academic writing, however, paragraphs tend to be longer. A one- or two-sentence paragraph will not suffice for an essay. Generally, paragraphs in essays are four to eight sentences long. You need to be able to fully explain an idea in each paragraph.

DEVELOPED PARAGRAPHS

Independent, developed paragraphs are, in a sense, mini-essays. They have a topic sentence, ideas supported and explained, and a concluding statement. Body paragraphs in an essay are developed paragraphs, while introductions and conclusions do not have the same structure.

In the following independent paragraph, you can see the structure and development:

> University tuition fees are currently too high. Before fees were raised so precipitously, students could work during the summer and earn enough to pay for most of their university year. Today, a student working a minimum-wage summer job will earn less than $5000. This may cover tuition, but won't stretch to cover books, residence, and incidental fees. Some students work long hours at part-time jobs while they are in school, decreasing the amount of time they can spend on their studies. They are thus defeating the purpose of their education if they are not learning all they should. Loans are not a solution. Some students are graduating with $20 000 and $30 000 debts, which cripple them financially just as they are starting on their careers. Therefore, many students decide college or university is financially out of reach.

You can see how this paragraph would work in an essay on pages 372–373.

TOPIC SENTENCES

Each developed paragraph should have a topic sentence to state your main idea. It should be specific enough for the reader to know what you are talking about, and it should begin your paragraph. You will note in the above example that the paragraph begins with a clear topic sentence. A topic sentence can appear anywhere in the paragraph, or in some cases it may not appear at all. However, the most advantageous position is at the beginning. Thus, the topic sentence sets forth the idea in the form of a brief introductory statement.

Topic sentences are similar to thesis statements. While thesis statements express the controlling idea of the essay, topic sentences give the controlling idea of the paragraph. It is important that the topic sentence be a point that can be covered in the one paragraph. Each sentence in the paragraph should relate to the topic sentence. The paragraph must be unified, organized, and clear.

In "The Patterns of Eating," you can see topic sentences at work. Paragraph 5 begins with "Once carving was no longer considered a necessary skill among the well-bred, changes inevitably took place in the use of the knife, unquestionably the earliest utensil used for manipulating food" (p. 264). The first part of the sentence is a subordinate clause and thus is not the main idea; the reference to carving is a transition from the previous paragraph where carving was discussed. The main clause, "changes inevitably took place in the use of the knife," is the main idea. The whole paragraph talks about knives at the dinner table. Mention of the fork or spoon in this paragraph would be off topic. Paragraph 6 talks about the development of the fork, and it starts with this topic sentence: "The fork in particular enabled Europeans to separate themselves from the eating process, even avoiding manual contact with their food" (p. 264).

THE SHORT ESSAY

In college or university, the length of a short essay ranges from 300 to 1000 words. You are expected to have something to say on the topic you have selected. In a literature paper, you can write about characters, plot twists, and themes among other topics. In a response essay on an article or essay, you can argue the writer's stand on the particular subject.

One of the most common formats in essay writing in school is the five-paragraph essay. It has a one-paragraph introduction, three body paragraphs, and a one-paragraph conclusion. The essay in Chapter 1 (pp. 372–373) follows this format. This structure is a useful training ground—it teaches students writing skills. It is similar to learning computer programming with languages like Turing or Pascal, which are not used in "the real world" but which are good vehicles for learning the principles of programming. You probably won't have to write this kind of paper once you graduate from school, but you will learn useful skills, such as organizing ideas, supporting statements, and writing concisely. The five-paragraph essay structure is easily adapted to other pieces of writing. Business reports, for example, also have introductions, bodies, and conclusions.

THE THESIS STATEMENT

Like a topic sentence, the thesis statement gives the main idea. It tells your reader what you seek to prove in your essay.

A thesis statement that is too narrow, such as a fact that cannot be debated, is unworkable:

> Microsoft is the largest software company in the world.

A statement that is too broad does not tell the reader exactly what your topic is:

> Computers are very helpful.

A thesis should not be an announcement:

> In this essay, I will explain how people use computers.

A thesis statement is one sentence. Here is an example of an incorrect multisentence thesis:

> In "The Monkey's Paw," W.W. Jacobs uses four methods to sustain the horror for the reader. First, he creates suspense by having a mysterious stranger with an equally mysterious object. Second, he describes the monkey's paw in cryptic language. Third, he recounts the horrific death of the son. And finally, he suggests worse to come if the mother lets the corpse into the house.

The following example is an improvement. The thesis statement (underlined) is the last sentence of the introductory paragraph:

In "The Monkey's Paw," W.W. Jacobs has written a classic horror story. To create such creepy terror in the reader, he relies on proven methods, and these are worth exploring. <u>The four elements of a successful horror story are the mysterious stranger, the cryptic language, a horrific death, and the suggestion of worse to come.</u>

The introduction leads the reader to the thesis statement.

INTRODUCTION

The introduction is usually one paragraph in a short essay, but it can be more. An introductory paragraph is different from a developed paragraph because it does not start with a topic sentence. Instead, it leads the reader to the thesis statement (the main idea of the essay), which is usually at the end of the introduction. The introduction starts with a broad statement and gradually narrows down to the point of the thesis.

An introduction draws the readers' attention and prepares them for the essay. It gives them the necessary background information. It can be an anecdotal opening, telling a story from the writer's experience. It can start with a brief quotation from a well-known authority. Or, it can give historical information. For argument essays, it can explain popular opinions on the other side of the argument. The introduction should not, however, contain any points that support the thesis—those belong in the essay itself.

Here are some examples of introductions with different perspectives on the same topic:

> Owning a private vehicle seems to be essential for getting to work. We do not always live close to work, especially with the demands of the modern workplace. We change jobs frequently, work short-term contracts, and have to visit different work sites, so we cannot change our home every time we change work locations. Moreover, we may not be travelling in the direction of most public transit—into the downtown core. The car then solves the immediate problem of moving from home to work in the shortest time. However, the price of the commute is too high, encompassing financial cost, time, and stress.

> What teenager has not dreamed about owning his own wheels at age 16, the moment he receives his driver's licence? The car, whatever size, shape, or age, is the ultimate status symbol—instant respect and admiration from friends, freedom to go anywhere and everywhere. The car has

been romanticized by young people since the songs of the Beach Boys. However, teenagers must consider the cost, the responsibility, and the frustration of owning a car.

The family car has become a fixture in our society. In our grandfathers' time, owning a vehicle seemed shameless excess; by our parents' generation, one car in the driveway was normal; for our generation, owning two cars is not keeping up with the Joneses anymore, but essential to daily routine. Having two cars in a family is no longer a luxury but a necessity because of the demands of working parents, children's activities, and the modern lifestyle.

CONCLUSION

The conclusion finishes the essay and leads the readers back to your topic. It gives you a chance to explain the "so what?" of your topic and to suggest some future direction. Start with a restatement of the thesis statement and move on. Don't summarize in a short essay because it is too repetitive.

Too often essays peter out to an unsatisfactory conclusion. Students seem to run out of steam or ideas. It is important not to just repeat ideas at the end to fill up space. Additional points that support the thesis also do not belong in the conclusion. Like the introduction, the conclusion should have ideas that are not expressed in the body of the essay. The conclusion is the last chance to impress the reader.

Here are some examples of concluding paragraphs:

> With all these disadvantages, it is clear to see that the daily commute is a high price to pay. It is not always possible to live near our work, especially when other family members have to be considered. The only solution is public transit. We must make the message clear to our governments, that the development of commuter transportation is essential for all of us.

> Owning a car then has inherent responsibilities and obligations. Teenagers should balance their dream of "wheels" with reality. If they don't, they may be in for a surprise—there is no such thing as a free ride.

> Love or hate it, the car dominates all facets of our hectic lifestyles. Without the automobile, we are not longer mobile and autonomous, no longer free but captive by suburban distance, no longer living contented but disgruntled. That box of gears and gadgets has not made us independent but dependent on it.

Chapter 4

TYPES OF ESSAYS

This chapter expands on the information about essay writing by showing the different kinds of writing you may do. Most essays are essentially an argument because you are setting forth a point of view and supporting it. However, essays that focus on comparison differ slightly from essays that explain causes. Your purpose determines what kind of essay you are writing. For instance, if your goal is to explain how something is done, you are writing a process essay. In a longer essay or report, you may have more than one mode. For instance, you may include a paragraph of definition or description as background information. The different purposes are explained below and can also be seen in the reading selections.

NARRATION

Narration is essentially storytelling. Short stories and novels are narratives. In essay writing, you may use narration to tell of an experience you or someone else had to illustrate a point.

It is important that your storytelling is clear. Give as much detail as is necessary. Short-story writers give a lot of detail because their goal is to involve the reader in the action. In an essay, however, narration tends to be less detailed and includes less dialogue. To see this difference in action, compare the narration in the essay "Growing Up on Grace" (p. 250) and the short story "Chickens for Christmas" (p. 63).

Newspaper and magazine articles often start with an anecdote (narration) before going into the main argument. Essay writers also use narration as an effective technique. Notice how Kurt Preinsperg starts with a narrative (the story of a particular date he had), followed by a list of his anti-car arguments in "Have Wheels, Will Go A-Wooing" (p. 322).

In everyday life, you might have to use narration to explain how an accident happened or to describe the history of something. In your academic essays, you may use narration to explain your experience with something. Good storytelling requires that the information be presented clearly so that readers can follow the action. Generally, chronological order is preferred. How much detail you give depends on the situation, the audience, and the purpose.

DESCRIPTION

Description goes hand in hand with narration. It fleshes out the skeletal form of the telling by adding details. It shapes the reader's imagination. For example, in "Am I Blue?" Alice Walker uses description effectively to allow the reader to see, and almost feel, the horse: "I remained as thrilled as a child by his flexible dark lips, huge, cubelike teeth that crunched the apples, core and all, with such finality, and his high, broad-breasted *enormity*; beside which, I felt small indeed" (p. 349).

Description is not restricted to narrative. In business, job descriptions outline requirements and tasks to be done by the employees. In science, researchers describe the changes of states or conditions of chemicals, cells, or atoms. A photograph can only reveal the visual aspects of its subject, but a description can invoke other senses for the reader.

Describing is not a matter of tossing in adjectives, adverbs, or modifiers to fill out a sentence or a paragraph. Your description should be organized logically. For instance, if you are describing a scene, you might want to go from near to far, or from right to left. Your description should be selective; the details you give should be important. You must be sure of the words you are using.

In your essays, you might need to use description to give details to the reader, as in this example:

> While the trend toward more casual dress in the workplace can liberate employees, it can also go too far and be disrespectful. Last week, one of my co-workers showed up for Casual Friday in ragged blue jeans that looked as if they would not survive another wash. The seams were frayed and the material looked almost transparent in places. His t-shirt used to be white, but it had greyed with ineffective washing. The worst offence was the saying on the t-shirt, which hinted at sexual harassment. Even though this employee is not within public view, his appearance was an insult to his co-workers.

ILLUSTRATION

To make points clear, writers use illustration and give examples to add detailed information. Illustration is part of every essay, but some essays function as illustrative essays, simply explaining a situation to the reader without much argument. You might use definition, description, and comparison as part of your illustration.

In "Toothpaste," David Bodanis gives us a good example of illustration as he methodically explains one of the ingredients in toothpaste:

> The individual chalk particles—the size of the smallest mud particles in your garden—have kept their toughness over the eons, and now on the toothbrush they'll need it. The enamel outer coating of the tooth they'll have to face is the hardest substance in the body—tougher than skull, or bone, or nail. Only the chalk particles in toothpaste can successfully grind into the teeth during brushing, ripping off the surface layers like an abrading wheel grinding down a boulder in a quarry. (p. 241)

When you give an example to illustrate something, you usually signal the reader that it is an example and not the whole situation. To do this, you use expressions such as "for example" and "for instance" to introduce sentences, "such as" for phrases, and verbs such as "include." Do not use "e.g." and "etc." in your essays; these Latin abbreviations are fine in your notes, but not in academic prose.

ARGUMENT

In everyday speech, we generally use the word "argument" to refer to a fight, a quarrel, or a disagreement. However, an argument can simply be a reason for something. For example, the high cost of owning a vehicle is an argument for using public transit. An argument essay can also be persuasive: you try to make your reader accept your point of view. Argument can be like a formal debate, in which you take one point of view and support it. It does not have to be what you personally believe; indeed, you should be able to argue both sides of an issue as an intellectual exercise. In marking an argument essay, your instructor is not looking to see whether you agree with her, but whether you can present logical reasoning.

The sample essay in Chapter 1 is an argument essay (pp. 372–373). You can read two sides of an argument in the essays by Keith Knight and Raheel Raza on "Our Father Who Art in Classrooms..." (pp. 294 and 296). Kurt Preinsperg explains the reasons he does not drive in "Have Wheels, Will Go A-Wooing" (p. 322), and Shinan Govani lays forth his argument on the negative aspects of photography (p. 276).

In an argument or persuasive paper, it is important to have a clear position in your thesis statement. This stand must be firm, unequivocal, and clear. Don't sit on the fence. Depending on the topic, you may need to give some background so that the reader has some grounding. Then you proceed to argue your case. You present your evidence in the form of facts and statistics, testimony of experts, logic, and reasons. Your organization must be logical, giving an item-by-item account of your evidence.

Argument requires you to address the views of the opposition. Unlike a debate, an essay does not give you a chance to deliver a rebuttal. You must anticipate the objections your readers will have and deal with them. One way to do this is concession. Conceding a point is a way of saying "Yes, but," as in this example:

> Although the cost of postsecondary education represents a huge chunk of the government's budget, the money can be seen as a good investment, especially when the financial burden is shared among all citizens, all of whom benefit from an educated citizenry.

Weak arguments are referred to as "logical fallacies." Here are some common logical fallacies to avoid:

- Don't argue against the person. Argue against his or her opinions or ideas.
- Don't use hasty generalizations, such as drawing conclusions from little evidence.
- Don't use unfounded cause/effect, saying that because something occurred it caused something else to happen.
- Don't give circular reasoning, as in "He is a good person because he is good."
- Don't appeal to popular prejudices, such as racist arguments.

COMPARE/CONTRAST

In a comparison paper, you draw similarities between two items. In a contrast essay, you show differences between two items. However, we use the term "comparison" to refer to essays where either similarities or differences are discussed.

Your comparison has to be justified. You wouldn't write an essay comparing a horse and a desk because there is no reason to compare those two things. Generally, you would choose to show similarities between things that seem different or differences between things that seem similar. For instance, if you were writing about computer engineering and computer science programs at a university, it would be more logical to show how they are different rather than how they are similar. An essay could show how job hunting and fishing are similar activities.

In any comparison, you must have areas in common in order to compare or contrast. For example, to compare two schools, you might talk about location, courses offered, and staff. It is important that you do the work for the reader. It is not enough to describe one thing and then the other, and then conclude "As you can see, they are very different."

There are two main methods used for comparison essays. In point-by-point organization, you go back and forth, dealing with one point of comparison for each item you are comparing and then move on to a second point. In the block method, you deal with one item fully before you go on to the next. The topic sentence of the paragraph should mention both.

Point-by-point organization:
    Point 1: Item A
                Item B
    Point 2: Item A
                Item B
    Point 3: Item A
                Item B

Block organization:
    Item A: Point 1
               Point 2
               Point 3
    Item B: Point 1
               Point 2
               Point 3

Here is an example of a point-by-point comparison paragraph:

> Isaac Asimov's vision of a mechanical teacher in his 1957 short story "The Fun They Had" is quite different from modern computers. Asimov's machine is very mechanical. The County Inspector fixes the machine with "a whole box of tools with dials and wires." A modern computer technician would be more inclined to use software to fix problems. If there were faulty components in the hardware, a technician would simply slot in a new component. The inspector says the machine is "geared a little too quick." This kind of problem would not happen in a modern computer because the software would be able to offer the appropriate level. Another difference is the

interface. Margie has to do her work on punch cards and insert her homework in a slot for the machine to read. A modern student uses a keyboard and a mouse. What is typed appears directly on the computer screen. Asimov's short story shows us how computers have evolved over the last 50 years.

Here is the same comparison, presented in a block paragraph:

> Isaac Asimov's vision of a mechanical teacher in his 1957 short story "The Fun They Had" is quite different from modern computers. Asimov's machine is very mechanical. The County Inspector fixes the machine with "a whole box of tools with dials and wires" because the machine is "geared a little too quick." Margie has to do her work on punch cards and insert her homework in a slot for the machine to read. A modern computer technician would be more inclined to use software to fix problems. If there were faulty components in the hardware, a technician would simply slot in a new component. The problem of an appropriate level would be dealt with in the software. As for the interface, a modern student uses a keyboard and a mouse. What is typed appears directly on the computer screen. Asimov's short story shows us how computers have evolved over the last 50 years.

Analogy is a specific kind of comparison used to clarify a point. Generally, in analogy, you reduce a complicated or complex idea to something simpler that the reader can understand. Alice Walker makes an analogy in "Am I Blue?" (p. 349) when she compares the horse's existence to slavery. In "Don't Say Cheese!" Shinan Govani uses an analogy when he talks about taking pictures on a vacation and says, "It's all a bit like being at a sumptuous feast and being too worried about having some stuff for leftovers than actually taking the time to relish the spread itself" (p. 277).

CAUSE/EFFECT

Cause is the reason for an action. Effect is the result of the action. You can approach a cause/effect paper in three ways. First, you can show reasons why such an incident occurred. For example, you may want to explain why the North West Mounted Police were needed in the territories that now form the Prairie provinces. Second, you can explain the result of something that has happened or will happen. For example, due to the establishment of law and order by the North West Mounted Police, the Canadian government did not have to face the Indian wars that marked the American western expansion in the mid-1800s. Third, you can write about the reasons for and results of an incident. Sometimes you will describe a chain reaction, with one thing leading to another and then to another.

In "Shooting an Elephant" (p. 314), George Orwell demonstrates how the mechanism of cause and effect works. The cause of the rampage is a rogue elephant that is in an uncontrollable frenzy; the effect is that Orwell as a policeman must go investigate. Although Orwell is reluctant to shoot the elephant, he is goaded on by the native spectators (cause). He kills the elephant, in his words, "to avoid looking a fool" (effect).

When you want to describe the causes or reasons for an event, keep in mind the questions "Why did this happen?" and "What led to this?" Effects are the results and your essay should explain "What happened then?"

DEFINITION AND CLASSIFICATION

Definition is essential to comprehension and clarity. Sometimes you will have to define a term in your essay. For instance, if you are writing about how to be successful, you may have to give your definition of success. You could, on the other hand, write a whole essay defining success. A dictionary can give a short definition of a word, but it may not be enough to explain the nuances of the term. You may need to describe current usage, explain where the word came from and how it changed over time, or compare the word with similar concepts.

In "What Is an Idea?", Gregory and Booth use analogy to define the term "idea":

> Ideas are to writing as strength and agility are to athletic prowess: They do not in themselves guarantee quality, but they are the muscle in all good writing prowess. Not all strong and agile athletes are champions, but all champion athletes are strong and agile. Not everyone who has powerful ideas is a great writer, but it is impossible for any writer even to be effective, much less achieve greatness, without them. (p. 286)

Sometimes definition includes classification. For instance, Lynn Van der Water describes three kinds of people who frequent garage sales in "Possessed by Stuff" (p. 345). Pico Iyer compares weirdos and eccentrics (p. 289).

Methods used in extended definitions include:

- explaining the history of the word or idea, or its root (etymology)
- comparing or contrasting it with something else
- describing its features
- using illustrations, examples, or analogies
- showing how it is used or showing its relationship to another thing
- negating what it is not (unlike a quarrel, argument is a debate)
- isolating unique features that separate it from something else

PROCESS DESCRIPTION

Process description or analysis explains what happens and how something occurs. It is different from instruction, which is a set of steps you follow to accomplish something. For example, you may write a process description of an earthquake happening, but you cannot write a set of instructions to make an earthquake. Instructions are written in the second person ("you") and have command sentences ("do this"). They are often written in numbered lists. Recipes are an example of instructions. In technical writing courses, you may have to write instructions. In general English courses, you may be asked to write process description.

In "The Story of Service," Jessica Mitford details the procedure for embalming and preparing a body for a funeral service. Here is one paragraph:

> The next step is to have at Mr. Jones with a thing called a trocar. This is a long, hollow needle attached to a tube. It is jabbed into the abdomen and poked around the entrails and chest cavity, the contents of which are pumped out and replaced with "cavity fluid." This done, and the holFe in the abdomen having been sewn up, Mr. Jones's face is heavily creamed (to protect the skin from burns which may be caused by leakage of the chemicals), and he is covered with a sheet and left unmolested for a while. (p. 306)

Notice the use of the passive voice, which is common in process description. The receiver of the action is more important than the doer, so the receiver becomes the subject of the sentence. In short, it is a matter of focus. While active voice is generally preferred because it is easier to follow, the passive does have a place, especially in process writing.

Sometimes you find a mix of process and instruction in one piece of writing, especially with the move toward less-formal writing. Because "you" is used as a pronoun meaning both the reader and people in general, it may be difficult to tell the difference. Instruction, however, is generally written in a list of steps rather than in a prose paragraph.

In order to describe procedures, it is important to know your audience and purpose. For example, you should know if your readers are comfortable with technical jargon or if they are already familiar with similar processes. You should decide whether you are simply describing the process or whether you are giving instructions that will have to be followed. Both types of writing involve breaking down the action into a series of small steps, in proper order. Clarity is, of course, essential.

ANSWERING EXAM ESSAY QUESTIONS

Writing an essay in an exam is like writing one as an assignment. The differences lie in the time constraint and the lack of outside resources. Otherwise, it is the same, and so you can use any of the above essay types that fit the essay question.

The following list offers guidelines for answering essay questions on an examination:

- Make sure you understand what your instructor wants. Read the question carefully. Don't jump into writing answers without properly understanding the demands of the question or the instructions.
- Budget your time. Choose your topic quickly. You can use your gut feeling as to which topic will work best for you.
- Jot down a few notes and make a rough outline to keep your writing on topic.
- Give details and specific information. Avoid giving vague ideas, general information, and irrelevant facts. Details show that you know the material and that you can write about it adequately.
- Stay within the limits set for the number of words or pages. Too short means you don't have enough information; too long means you can't organize it. Do not pad your answer.
- Take the time to proofread your draft. It is best to double-space your essay and leave gaps and margins so you have room for changes or additions. Second, pay attention to the principles of good writing: grammar, punctuation, spelling, expression, and content.

- Have a checklist of common mistakes in grammar, punctuation, and spelling that you make in your other assignments. Under pressure, you are likely to make the same kinds of mistakes. With a checklist, you have a better chance of remedying errors before you hand in the exam.
- Write legibly. Your instructor must be able to read your handwriting.

Chapter 5

RESEARCH

In a research paper, you use information from other sources to support your ideas. Within your essay, you paraphrase and quote what you have read. However, the essay should still have your ideas and not just repeat what others say. It's not a cut-and-paste exercise.

Generally, research essays are longer than the five-paragraph essay common in writing classes, and you are given several weeks to complete the assignment. Don't leave the project until the last minute. Research essays require more time than other expository essays, especially for finding source materials. You don't want to run the risk of not being able to find material on your topic the night before the paper is due. The book you want could be checked out, your Internet service could be down, or you might have to make a trip to another library.

Be sure to keep all your notes and drafts at least until the course is finished and you have received your final mark. You may be called on to support the statements in your essay. Also keep a backup copy of your paper. Keep a copy on disk in addition to the one on your computer's hard drive or your school's server.

In your research, you need to distinguish between primary and secondary source materials. The primary source is the play, poem, short story, novel, or article you are interpreting or analyzing. For example, on the topic of "Ritual sacrifice in Shirley Jackson's 'The Lottery,' " your primary source is, of course, the short story itself. The secondary source is anything that is written about the primary source. That is, any introduction to the story, editor's notes, literary analyses (other than yours), interpretations, lecture notes from your instructor, or anything written about the story is considered a secondary source. In other words, a secondary source is anything but the primary source.

All sources, whether primary or secondary, must be referenced and documented. You must give credit where credit is due. In short, if you use someone else's material, either exact words or an idea (not a fact), you need to acknowledge your indebtedness. The information must be complete and accurate so that your readers can go to the sources you used. Incorrect use of sources or incorrect documentation can lead to charges of plagiarism or cheating, a serious offence (see pp. 437–438).

BEFORE STARTING THE RESEARCH

Your instructor will probably give you a choice of topics. These might be very specific, or they might be broad topics that you have to narrow down to something manageable within the word limit. You may be able to suggest your own topic in consultation with your instructor. Make sure you understand the demands of the topic. Read the question carefully. Discuss the topic with your instructor. You may wish to check how much information is available on a topic before you choose.

Before you head off to the library or log onto the Internet, jot down your own ideas and questions about the topic. This brainstorming session will help you distinguish your own ideas from someone else's and recognize what is general knowledge. Then it will be easier to know what to reference.

Plan your research. Make a list of questions. Be prepared to return to some information sources if you find something that changes your view or even your search terms. Schedule your work so that you don't have to do it all in one day. You might have to take some time to track down a book, for example.

Read more than what is needed. You have to accumulate general information and background knowledge on your subject—even though you may not put all that information in the body of your essay.

FINDING, CHOOSING, AND EVALUATING INFORMATION

You should consult a variety of sources for your research. Don't limit your research to just books or just Web pages. Even if you have a recent current events topic, you don't have to limit yourself to the Internet; you can get general background information from a book. You can start with an encyclopedia article for a general summary and move to magazine and journal articles. With a variety of sources, you can make sure your information is accurate.

You have to judge the reliability of your sources. What credentials does the author have? Is the publication reputable? What kind of evidence does the author present? Is the evidence well-documented, with references you can check? Is the information up-to-date?

You should be aware of bias in your research materials. For example, if you use a company's Web page or promotional literature as your only source of information on that company, you are getting only one side of the picture — the positive spin.

Check the date of the sources you are using. Even Internet information can be out of date. Look for the publication date of books on the copyright page (the back of the title page) and check whether the book has been revised since then, or just reprinted.

If you are working on a specific Canadian topic, make sure you use Canadian reference materials such as *The Canadian Encyclopedia*. American books and reference sources dominate the market, but their coverage of Canadian topics is notoriously weak.

Be prepared to go back to sources again if you find out new information that would help your search. For example, let's say you were researching the koi fish. You don't find very much at first, but then you find an article that mentions that koi is a kind of carp. Then you would try the search again with the term "carp."

Get to know your school library and your public library, the central branch as well as the local one. Try out the catalogue, and find out what periodicals are available and in what format. Look at the indexes and the CD-ROM databases. Talk to the librarians when you need help.

SEARCH TERMS

Library catalogues, CD-ROM encyclopedias, and Internet search engines generally use similar keyword searches. Become familiar with the way the particular search engine works.

Boolean operators — "and," "or," and "but" — are used to combine search terms. "Or" broadens the search because it takes into account both search terms. If the search engine does not recognize "or," you have to redo the search for each alternate term.

"And" limits a search because you are asking the program for documents that contain both terms. Most search terms assume you mean "and" when you put more than one word in. If you want the words to be treated as a unit, you can put quotation marks around it in some Internet search engines. For example, if you are looking for a person's name, putting quotation marks around the first and last names ensures that the search engine will look for the two names together and not as two separate words. This feature is particularly useful if you are looking for a phrase that has common words, such as the title of the Shakespeare play *As You Like It*.

The third Boolean operator, "not," is used to exclude items from your search. Some Internet search engines use the minus sign to show "not." Suppose you want to find more works by the author Wayne Grady. In your first set of results, you find that there is also a professional golfer named Wayne Grady. Therefore, you could enter: "Wayne Grady" – golf – PGA.

It is important to use keywords properly to get accurate results. Use correct spelling. Don't use words that are too common. Try synonyms. Look for the help feature or the hints offered by the program.

ENCYCLOPEDIAS

In the past, a row of weighty volumes of an encyclopedia was a mainstay in libraries and many homes. Today, however, most encyclopedias are on CD-ROM or on-line because print versions are too expensive to produce and update.

An encyclopedia is useful for a brief summary of your subject. You can get details such as the dates of historical events or biographical details of an author's life. In short, it is a good starting point.

BOOKS

Although proponents of electronic information sources have declared the book to be dead, it is too early to write an obituary. Books are important for a thorough treatment of a subject.

Books are generally catalogued by one of two systems. Elementary schools, secondary schools, and public libraries use the Dewey decimal system. This system uses a numerical base, dividing knowledge into sections from 001 to 999. For example, books on applied sciences are catalogued in the 600s. The other system is the Library of Congress (LC), which is used in college and university libraries. You can recognize these codes because they start with two letters of the alphabet. If you look at the copyright page (the other side of the title page) of this book, you can see the suggested cataloguing numbers: The Dewey decimal call number for this book is 808.0427, and the LC call number is PE1417.E53 2001.

Don't be put off from using books because of their length. You don't have to read the whole book. Skim and scan the contents to get the general idea. Use the table of contents and index to find specific information. If you are not doing in-depth research, you can also try the children's section for simple introductory books on various subjects.

PERIODICALS

Magazines and journals are called periodicals. They are published periodically — once a week or several times a year. For example, *Maclean's* magazine is a weekly news magazine. Periodicals can vary from scholarly academic journals to sensationalist tabloids. Some are devoted to a particular subject, such as home offices or snowboarding.

Periodicals are valuable sources of information. They offer more up-to-date information than books and can focus on narrow, specific topics. Academic journals offer the results of in-depth research.

The problem is finding what you need. You can access material from periodicals in various ways. Clippings on various subjects may be kept in a vertical file. Your library may have back copies of various periodicals. You may have to use print indexes such as the *Reader's Guide to Periodical Literature*. You may have to scroll through microfilm of old newspapers.

However, these are all old methods, which are gradually being phased out. Today, most of the information from periodicals is stored electronically. You can consult current issues in print, but back copies are put on CD-ROM and in on-line systems.

Your library probably has indexes and full-text databases available for searching. A full-text database has the text of the entire article. Other databases may only have the title of the article, where and when it appeared, and a brief abstract or summary of the contents. Searches can be done for particular authors or titles or, more commonly, for key words. For each database, you have to learn the search engines used, but they generally have the same features.

It is important that you become familiar with the resources of your own library. See what databases are offered and what the coverage is. Older material may not have been converted to electronic format. Some of the databases found in the library may be accessible to you from the computers in the lab or your own computer at home through the Internet. Some databases are subscriptions, so the library limits access because of the licencing agreement. Ask the librarians for help if you are unable to figure out which database to use or how to access it.

NEWSPAPERS

The daily newspaper is a cornucopia of up-to-date information. Besides giving you current events, articles in the dailies inform you of the latest happenings in such areas as science, business, and entertainment. In-depth news items often include sidebars of quick information, facts and statistics, and quotations from experts. For example, in stories about an outbreak of *E. coli* at Walkerton, Ontario, newspaper articles carried information about strains of bacteria, the political controversy, sewage management, sociological and medical implications, and human-interest pieces.

You can access old newspapers from several sources. First, many main branches of libraries retain recent copies of newspapers in their archives. Second, past editions are put on microfilm, microfiche, or CD-ROM. Third, you may be able to access articles over the Internet.

THE INTERNET

Unlike publishing houses, newspapers, and magazines, which have the reputation of their institution to uphold, the Internet is a publishing free-for-all. Anyone can put up a Web page and say anything he likes — he doesn't have to be an expert in the field. There is no system of reviewers and editors approving the work. That makes the information unreliable. Therefore, you must approach Internet information cautiously.

One way to verify the information is to check it against other sources. If you find the information in more than one place, it is more likely to be correct. However, even this is not foolproof. Newspapers have been known to publish the urban legends that circulate on the Net, and misinformation can be repeated in other sources.

When you use a Web site, check out the source of the information. If the site is hosted by a reputable organization, such as a university, it is more likely to have been verified. However, some organizations have misleading names. For instance, the Canadian Outdoor Heritage Alliance is not an environmental group, but an organization of trappers, anglers, and hunters. Be wary of pages that don't include names of authors and organizations and a way of contacting them.

The Internet has a reputation for offering the latest information, but every researcher has come across pages that should have been deleted from the system, such as those announcing events that are long past.

Another way to get information is from newsgroups and chat rooms. Again, however, you have to be careful. Many people spout off opinions in newsgroups without real knowledge of the topic. These postings have to be documented just as other references do.

TAKING NOTES

Taking notes is not just getting photocopies and printouts of every article relevant to your topic. It means carefully reading the material and choosing what you can use in your essay. It means summarizing, paraphrasing, and choosing relevant quotation.

Some people use index cards for their notes, some use a notebook, and some type their notes right into their computer. Whichever method you choose, make sure that what you are writing down is clear. A direct quotation should be shown by quotation marks. Otherwise, your notes should be paraphrases of what you read. Include source notes for every piece of information.

If you use index cards or small pieces of paper, you can use referencing methods as you would in your essay. For instance, a quotation from a book by Asimov can be referenced as "(Asimov 58)," where "58" refers to the page number on which the quotation appears. However, make sure you have already written down the full reference information.

Be sure to get accurate source information for all your notes. (See sample notes on pp. 420–422.) Copy down the book title, full names of the author(s), publisher, publication date, and page references. If you have photocopied pages, make sure the page number shows on the pages. For printouts of Web pages, make sure the Web address and the current date appear on the page. On your notes, write down the complete URL, which generally appears in your browser window, not just the general Web page address. The Web address should get you back to exactly the same site where you found the information. For articles and stories, you should include the source information, the name of the book or newspaper where they appeared.

Keep in mind that the Internet is unreliable. You may have trouble finding a site again, so bookmark it. Web pages are frequently altered, so get printouts of very important sites.

Don't throw out the notes once you've finished the paper. You may be called on to support something in your paper, or, if disaster strikes and you lose the essay itself, you may have to redo it.

WRITING AND EDITING THE DRAFTS

Once you have completed your research, sit back and think about your essay. What points do you want to make? What is your thesis? How do you want to organize your essay?

Write an outline. Go back through your notes and highlight information that you should use to support your points. Choose a few relevant quotations.

As you write the first draft, incorporate the information you found in your research. Use it to support your ideas. Don't just summarize everything you have read.

As you put your research information in the draft, be sure to include references for both quotations and paraphrases from other sources. Document everything except general knowledge (such as the fact that the War of 1812 was between the Americans and the British) and your own opinions. Refer to your brainstorming to help you see what you knew about the topic before you started your research.

Chapter 6 details how to cite references and prepare a bibliography. Refer to the research essay (pp. 426–429) to see an example.

After you have finished your first draft, put it aside for a day or two. You'll have a fresher view of it as you do the revisions. Look at your content first. Are there any other points you need to make? Is the essay well organized? Have you supported your ideas with examples and explanations? Have you used transition markers to show the relationship between ideas? Is everything clear? Once you are sure your essay says what you want it to say, look critically at the language. Are there unnecessary words and sentences that you can cut? Are your vocabulary choices the best you can make? Do any necessary revising and editing. (See the checklist on pp. 381–382).

Make sure you have fulfilled the requirements of the assignment— from answering the question posed to submitting a cover page or outline as requested.

The final step is to proofread your paper thoroughly and carefully, perhaps several times. Remember that running a spelling and grammar checker is not enough. Look for errors you have made before. If your weakness is spelling, check every word. If you have a problem with sentence fragments, go through every sentence to make sure each is complete.

PARAPHRASING

As you incorporate the information from your research into your essay, you will be paraphrasing, putting an author's ideas into your own words. You still need to reference the information as it is not your own. You must also be accurate in relating the content. You must understand the subject matter well enough so that you can rephrase it for your reader. Do not twist the author's meaning to fit your argument.

Paraphrasing involves more than simply slotting in synonyms. In most cases, your paraphrase will also be a summary, as it will be shorter than the original text. As an example, here is a paraphrase of the conclusion of "Grey Owl's Magnificent Masquerade":

> John Barber insists that despite Grey Owl's deception, he is a true hero because he showed Canadians the value of their wilderness, something worth safeguarding by the environmental movement. (233)

CHOOSING QUOTATIONS

In your notes, you may choose to highlight sentences that could make useful quotations. Quotations should be short and relevant. Don't just quote statements of fact that can be easily paraphrased. Quote when the author's wording is particularly apt or expressive, as in these examples:

> As Grady explains the cyclical nature of the exchange of Canadian Tire money, he calls it a "metaphysical construct." (280)

> Mr. Truepenny is described as a man who "had a Don Quixote air about him, a sense that he was forever tilting at windmills." (De Lint 55)

Copy the passage accurately, word for word, punctuation marks and all. If there is a mistake in the passage, you are expected to copy it and put "[*sic*]" after it. "*Sic*" is the Latin for "thus"; it means that you have discovered a mistake and it is not yours, but the author's.

You can see examples of quoting in the sample research essay on pages 426–429.

SUMMARIZING

Summarizing is an important skill to develop, both for academic and nonacademic purposes. For example, summarizing a chapter of your textbook is an excellent way to learn the material and to make notes you can use for studying. If you just read the chapter, you wouldn't retain as much of the material as you would if you were to write a summary for it.

If you are writing about a story or article that you know your readers have not read, you might have to summarize the action of a story or recount the main points of an article.

For secondary sources, summarizing becomes much more important. Instead of merely outlining one source, you will be gathering information from many sources. Moreover, you will discover that all these sources have a common denominator. For example, in researching the Shirley Jackson story, you will come across several articles that focus on the use of stones and the symbolic nature of stoning. Instead of listing them all, you can assemble the common elements in these sources and make your statement:

> From the earliest critical review of "The Lottery" to the most recent, many literary scholars, folklorists, and anthropologists have drawn attention to stoning the victim. Accordingly, stoning is a ritual practised in many societies, and is done as a communal effort. It not only expresses the collective scorn of the villagers but also releases the blood lust repressed in every individual in that community. It is catharsis, a purging in the participants.

Immediately afterwards, reference the main sources you have found that drew you to the collective viewpoint.

WRITING A SUMMARY

In addition to summarizing for your own notes, you may be asked to write a summary of an article. Summaries tend to be about a tenth of the original length of the article. Thus, a 1000-word article can be summarized in a 100-word paragraph. The first sentence of the summary should identify the article (author, title, and, if necessary, the source information) and give a general idea of the article's content.

Sometimes you may be called on to write summary statements. These are one-sentence summaries that give the main idea of the article. If you are asked to do an annotated bibliography, your instructor may ask for a summary statement on each item. Here are two examples:

> Mitford, Jessica. "The Story of Service." Fiction/Non-Fiction: A Reader and Rhetoric. Ed. Garry Engkent and Lucia Engkent. Toronto: Harcourt Canada, 2001, 301. Mitford explains the process of embalming a Mr. Jones from the moment he enters the funeral home to the display of his body before funeral services and interment.

> Singer, Ellen (pseudonym). "Exiled in Paradise." The Globe and Mail. 10 Jan. 2000: R1. Singer describes her harrowing experiences with a vindictive ex-husband and with the judicial system.

Conciseness is vital in summaries. Cut out excess words. Consider these examples:

In the article "Junk Food Heaven," the author Bill Bryson talks about his experience buying and eating American junk food to explain its qualities to his British audience. (28 words)

In "Junk Food Heaven," Bill Bryson explains American junk food for his British audience. (14 words)

To write a summary of a story or article, follow these guidelines:

1. Read the article or story completely so that you understand the main ideas.
2. Write down the main ideas in your own words.
3. Follow the organization of the original piece.
4. Leave out illustrations, examples, explanations, and non-essential details. Avoid adding your own commentary.
5. Use your own words rather than copy phrases from the original. Be brief.
6. Compose a paragraph from your notes. Write complete sentences; join ideas with transition markers.
7. Identify the article and give the reader some idea of the topic.
8. Make sure that your reader will understand the summary without going to the original piece.
9. Revise your draft by checking for slips in grammar, spelling, and punctuation.
10. Proofread your final, clean copy carefully before submitting it.

Here is an example of a summary:

Margaret Wente's "The End of Manual Labour" is a lament for the skills we have lost in the modern world. Wente's only manual skills are remnants of her summer jobs as a waitress. She doubts her ability to survive without her technological tools. A few generations ago, people were entirely self-sufficient, preparing their own food, making their own clothes, and building and maintaining their homes. Some people are going back to the countryside, rediscovering these skills. However, most people today can't even cook without a microwave. Moreover, new ways of deskilling our jobs and our everyday lives are being developed. (100 words)

Chapter 6

DOCUMENTATION

Once you have done your research, you must write your essay, incorporating the information you have found. In the body of your essay, you might quote from other works or you might just refer to them. In both cases, show the reader the author's name and a page reference if necessary. The full citation information is found in your bibliography at the end of the essay. This chapter goes over the basic rules of referencing; an example of a research essay with citations is found at the end of the chapter.

Currently, the preferred method of documentation is to incorporate references or acknowledgements briefly in parentheses right after the citation. The two most popular methods are the MLA style and the APA style. The Modern Languages Association (MLA) format is endorsed by writers in the arts and humanities; the American Psychology Association (APA) style is used by those in the sciences and social sciences. While they both reference research material after the quoted passage, they differ slightly in format. Our focus is on the MLA style because that is the one favoured in English courses in college and university.

Footnotes and endnotes are also used to document writing. Superscript numbers appear after a direct quotation, paraphrase, or acknowledgement of an idea, and then the source information for that number is given at the foot of the page, or at end of the document. This method, mostly commonly based on the *Chicago Manual of Style,* is used in high-school writing and in some nonacademic books. Even though references in parentheses are more common in academic articles and essays, you may find that some instructors still use the words "footnotes" and "footnoting" as generic terms for referencing in a research paper, even if the information does not appear at the bottom of a page in an actual footnote.

Your instructor or your school will tell you which style to use in your essays. Usually, handouts are available with details. Check at the library or on your school's Web site.

The different methods of citation have more similarities than differences, however. They all have some way of signalling the reference within the body of the text and a page at the end giving the full source information. For each citation, you must give the following information in the order shown:

- author(s) name(s)
- title of the book or article
- (name of journal or periodical)
- place of publication
- publisher
- date of publication

Because the Internet is a relatively new source of information, the style for citing Web pages and newsgroups is still evolving and being standardized. Check with the most recent information to which you have access and consult your instructor or librarian if you run into problems. The essential information is the same as for any source: you must cite the author, the title, and the location (the full URL, or address). Because Web sites change frequently, give the date on which you accessed the site as well as the date the site was created. Some of this information may not appear on the Web page, but record as much as is available. Check the referring home page; sometimes you can find the author or host institution named there.

Referencing can be a finicky business, and we cannot cover all possible situations in this book. If you do not know how to reference a source, you can try the following:

- Look for a similar example in this text.
- Check the documentation handout from your college library or writing centre.
- Consult English handbooks and textbooks that deal with essay writing and referencing.
- Look on the Internet for more style guidelines.
- Consult the *MLA Handbook,* which should be in the reference section of the library.
- Ask a librarian for help.
- Ask your instructor for help or clarification.

QUOTING (MLA STYLE)

When you use the exact words from a source, you are quoting. You signal to the reader that these are not your words by using quotation marks. Quotations can be full sentences or parts of a sentence that are incorporated in your paragraph.

Note this example of a quotation after the colon:

A level of civility or good manners begins at the dinner table. According to Peter Farb and George Armelagos, the humanist Eramus offered this piece of advice for good etiquette: "Do not poke around in your dish, but take the first piece you touch. Do not put chewed food from the mouth back on your plate; instead, throw it under the table or behind your chair." (262) Today, we do not play with our food, and we no longer spit out gristle with abandon. Rather, we swallow it or discreetly wrap it in a napkin.

In this example, a shorter quotation is included in the sentence:

Accordingly, the hero may not always be able to accomplish his task by himself, and often an older or more experienced person "provides the adventurer with amulets against the dragon forces he is about to pass." (Campbell 69)

If you are quoting a longer passage (more than three lines), set it off from the main text of your essay without quotation marks. The passage is indented and single-spaced, as in the following example:

The dinner knife has an interesting evolution. The sharp, pointed cutting blade changed to the dull, rounded utensil:

> The knife served as a utensil, but it offered a potential threat because it was also a weapon. Thus taboos were increasingly placed upon its use: It was to be held by the point with the blunt handle presented; it was not to be placed anywhere near the face; and most important, the uses to which it was put were sharply restricted. It was not to be used for cutting soft foods such as boiled eggs or fish, or round ones such as potatoes, or to be lifted from the table for courses that did not need it. In short, good table manners in Europe gradually removed the threatening aspect of the knife from social occasions. (Farb and Armelagos 264)

The dinner table knife today is no more than a butter knife and its presence is at times decorative rather than practical. So, when we need to cut into a steak, we are given a different knife with a serrated blade.

In either case, make sure you copy the passage accurately, even if there are errors in the original. Do not correct the mistake; instead, note the error by putting the Latin word "*sic*," which means "thus," in square brackets [*sic*] after the mistake.

Unless you can skillfully integrate your words with phrases from a source, you should avoid quoting snippets or short phrases and stringing them in your sentences. This creates a choppy sentence, as in this example:

> According to Farb and Armelagos, as "spontaneous, direct, and informal" meals gave way to propriety, the people of the Middle Ages "began to feel shame." No longer did people blow their noses with fingers but "handkerchiefs came into use" and "napkins were in common use" at the dinner table. (262-263)

More examples of quoting can be seen in the sample essay (pp. 426–429).

REFERENCING (MLA STYLE)

Whether you use a quotation or paraphrase information from a source, you have to show your reader the source of the information. This is done by referring to the author and giving a page reference in parenthesis. This is a short-form reference; the full source information is given in the "Works Cited" page (or bibliography) at the end of the essay.

Note that the parentheses (also called round brackets) contain the author's family name and the page reference with no comma separating them:

> A hero cannot always perform the task alone. "For those who have not refused the call, the first encounter of the hero journey is with a protective figure (often a little old crone or old man) who provides the adventurer with amulets against the dragon forces he is about to pass." (Campbell 69)

If you mention the author's name in the text close to the quote, you can just give the page number:

> According to Joseph Campbell, a hero cannot always perform the task alone. "For those who have not refused the call, the first encounter of the

hero journey is with a protective figure (often a little old crone or old man) who provides the adventurer with amulets against the dragon forces he is about to pass." (69)

The same type of referencing is used for paraphrasing. However, you do not use quotation marks:

Accordingly, the hero may not always be able to accomplish his task by himself, and often an older or more experienced person gives the hero some magic token to ward off enemies and monsters. (Campbell 69)

[Campbell, Joseph. <u>The Hero with a Thousand Faces.</u> New York: Meridian Books, 1949]

You can see more examples of referencing in the sample research essay at the end of this chapter.

BIBLIOGRAPHY (MLA STYLE)

The research essay should have a bibliography page at the end. It lists all the sources you have referred to in your essay and is titled "Works Cited." You may be called on to list all the resources you looked at, and not just the ones you referred to; in this case, the page would be called "Works Consulted."

Your list of sources should be in alphabetical order by author's family name. If there is no known author, then you should use the title of the article or story. Do not include "A," "An," or "The" in the title.

A distinction is made for the titles of shorter works (stories, articles, poems) that appear in larger works (books, newspapers, magazines). Story and article titles appear within quotation marks. The names of books and newspapers are underlined.

Italics and underlining are equivalent. Underlining was originally used in manuscripts because typewriters did not have italic keys. Typesetters would replace the underlining with italics before the book was published. Now that computers are used, it is easy to use italics instead of underlining in your essays. However, MLA prefers underlining for book titles in essays.

The list is double-spaced, with run-on lines indented five spaces.

BOOKS

[Family name, first name. Title of book underlined. Place of publication: Publisher, date of publication.]

> Campbell, Joseph. <u>Hero with a Thousand Faces.</u> New York: Meridian Books, 1949.
> Farb, Peter, and George Armelagos. <u>Consuming Passions: The Anthropology of Eating.</u> New York: Houghton Mifflin, 1980.
> Frye, Northrop. <u>Fables of Identity. Studies in Poetic Mythology.</u> New York: Harcourt Brace & World, 1963.

ARTICLES

[Family name, first name. Title of article in quotation marks. Title of periodical or magazine underlined. Date of the periodical: pages.]

> Bethune, Brian. "Truth and Consequences." <u>Maclean's.</u> 4 Oct. 1999: 58-59.
> Smith, Donald B. "Belaney, Archibald Stansfeld." <u>Canadian Encyclopedia.</u> 2nd Edition. Volume I: A-Edu. Edmonton: Hurtig Publishers, 1988: 198-199.
> Zakiuddin, Almas. "Rediscovering Christmas." <u>The Globe and Mail.</u> 23 Dec. 1999: A24.

INTERNET

[Family name, first name of author (if available). Title of article in quotation marks. Title of periodical or magazine underlined. Date: paging (if available). Access date. <Web address>.]

> "Katherine Govier." <u>Writers in Electronic Residence (WIER).</u> York University. June 18, 2000. <http://www.edu.yorku.ca/~WIER/kgovier.html>.
> Roberts, Taylor. "Canadian Raising and Other Oddities." June 16, 2000. <http://www.yorku.ca/twainweb/troberts/raising.html>.

ELECTRONIC SOURCES

[Author or editor (if given). Title of article in quotation marks. Name of database underlined. Edition, release, or version. Name of Publisher, publication date.]

"Margaret Atwood." <u>Discovering Authors: Canadian Edition.</u> CD-ROM. Gale Canada, 1996.

VIDEO

[Title of the film or video underlined. Name of director. Names of performers. Film company name, copyright date.]

<u>Shakespeare in Love.</u> Dir. John Madden. Perf. Gwyneth Paltrow, Joseph Fiennes, Geoffrey Rush, and Colin Firth. Miramax, 1998.
<u>Star Wars.</u> Dir. George Lucas. Perf. Mark Hamill, Harrison Ford, and Carrie Fisher. Twentieth Century Fox, 1977.

APA STYLE

APA style is used in the sciences and social sciences. Here are some examples that show how APA differs from MLA.

When you reference material within the body of the essay, APA includes the year of publication and uses commas:

A hero cannot always perform the task alone. "For those who have not refused the call, the first encounter of the hero journey is with a protective figure (often a little old crone or old man) who provides the adventurer with amulets against the dragon forces he is about to pass." (Campbell, 1949, p. 69)

The bibliography page in the APA style is called "References." The formatting is different in that the first line is indented. Only the first word in titles is capitalized. Authors' first names are represented only by the initials. The year of publication comes after the author's name.

Bethune, B. (1999, Oct. 4). Truth and consequences. <u>Maclean's,</u> 58-59.
Campbell, J. (1949). <u>Hero with a thousand faces.</u> New York: Meridian Books.
Farb, P., and G. Armelagos. (1980). <u>Consuming passions: the anthropology of eating.</u> New York: Houghton Mifflin.
Gale Canada. (1996). Margaret Atwood. <u>Discovering authors: Canadian edition.</u> [CD-ROM].

Katherine Govier. <u>Writers in electronic residence (WIER).</u> York University. Retrieved June 18, 2000 from the World Wide Web: http://www.edu.yorku.ca/~WIER/kgovier.html.

Madden, J. (Director). (1998). <u>Shakespeare in love</u> [Film]. Hollywood, Miramax.

Roberts, T. Canadian raising and other oddities. Retrieved June 16, 2000 from the World Wide Web: http://www.yorku.ca/twainweb/troberts/raising.html.

CHICAGO MANUAL OF STYLE

This method is also referred to as Turabian style because of the manual written by Kate Turabian. This system of citation and documentation — or a variation of it — is commonly used in high school. Its distinguishing feature is that it uses footnotes or endnotes instead of putting the reference in parentheses within the essay. Superscript numbers are used to show the order of notes. Here is an example:

> A level of civility or good manners begins at the dinner table. According to Farb and Armelagos, the humanist Eramus offered this piece of advice for good etiquette: "Do not poke around in your dish, but take the first piece you touch. Do not put chewed food from the mouth back on your place; instead, throw it under the table or behind your chair."[1] Moreover, "an upperclass diner was distinguished by putting only three fingers of one hand into the bowl, instead of the entire hand in the manner of the lower class."[2] Today, we do not play with our food, and we no longer spit out gristle with abandon. Rather, we swallow it or discreetly wrap it in a napkin. We are certainly more hygienic with the use of stainless steel tongs.
>
> ---
>
> 1. Peter Farb and George Armelagos, *Consuming Passions: The Anthropology of Eating* (New York: Houghton Mifflin, 1980), 168.
> 2. Farb and Armelagos, *Consuming Passions,* 168.

For the most part, the bibliography follows the MLA style, and it is called "Works Cited." Note that the titles of books and periodicals are italicized:

Campbell, Joseph. *Hero with a Thousand Faces.* New York: Meridian Books, 1949.

Farb, Peter, and George Armelagos. *Consuming Passions: The Anthropology of Eating.* New York: Houghton Mifflin, 1980.

"Margaret Atwood." Discovering Authors: Canadian Edition. CD-ROM. Gale Canada, 1996.

Roberts, Taylor. "Canadian Raising and Other Oddities." June 16, 2000. <http:// www.yorku.ca/twainweb/troberts/ raising.html>

Shakespeare in Love. Dir. John Madden. Perf. Gwyneth Paltrow, Joseph Fiennes, Geoffrey Rush, and Colin Firth. Miramax, 1998.

Zakiuddin, Almas. "Rediscovering Christmas." *The Globe and Mail.* December 23, 1999: A24.

A SAMPLE RESEARCH ESSAY

In this section we show some of the steps involved in writing a research essay, from the assignment topic to the finished product.

ASSIGNMENT TOPIC

Here is a question that might be asked for a research paper: "Show how sacrifice is important in Jackson's 'The Lottery.' Research the concept of sacrifice." Consider the topic carefully before you begin. Make sure you choose a topic on a story that you like and understand.

BRAINSTORMING

After choosing the topic, think about the story and about the question posed. Read the story over several times to make sure you've caught all the nuances. From the story itself, you draw out the related episodes and details. You might take notes like the following:

- stones, piles made by school kids in the opening
- stoning Tessie Hutchinson, own child does so
- drawing lots, use of black box and chits, less interest as time goes by
- ceremony in town square
- Old Man Warner, 77 years, escaped being sacrificed
- ritual of choosing
- related to farming, vegetation, fertility
- rhyme about June and corn soon
- ritual killing, no guilt?

Before looking at secondary sources, establish a list of ideas to consider:

- define sacrifice, scapegoating (see dictionary)
- symbolism of stones and stoning (martyrs in Christian terms)
- Bible stories about sacrifice: Jesus, Abraham and Isaac
- anthropology theories, fertility rituals
- symbolic action: Freud? Jung? (see Joseph Campbell, James Frazer)
- why need to sacrifice? religion, fear, superstition, nature
- what has been written on this topic, especially regarding Jackson's story?

Write down your own ideas before you do research so that you know which ideas belong to you alone and which you have researched.

WORKING BIBLIOGRAPHY

It is a good idea to have a working bibliography to keep track of your references. This may be incorporated within your notes or kept separate. If you have a full citation written down, you can use quick references to your bibliography in the notes themselves.

Works Consulted

Campbell, Joseph. <u>The Masks of God: Occidental Mythology.</u> New York: The Viking Press, 1964.

Chetwynd, Tom. <u>A Dictionary of Symbols.</u> London: A Paladin Book, 1982.

Doane, T.W. <u>Bible Myths and Their Parallels in Other Religions.</u> 4th edition. New York: University Books, 1971.

Eliade, Mircea. <u>Cosmos and History: The Myth of the Eternal Return.</u> Trans. by Willard R. Trask. New York: Harper and Row, 1959.

Frye, Northrop. <u>Anatomy of Criticism: Four Essays.</u> Princeton, NJ: Princeton University Press, 1957.

<u>Holy Bible.</u> The King James I, Authorized Version, 1611.

"Human sacrifice." <u>Encyclopaedia Britannica. 1999-2000. Online.</u> 16 Aug. 2000. <http://www.britannica.com/bcom/eb/article/6/0,5716,42396 +1,00.html>.

Jackson, Shirley. "The Lottery." <u>Fiction/Non-Fiction: A Reader and Rhetoric.</u> Ed. Garry Engkent and Lucia Engkent. Toronto: Harcourt Canada, 2001: 105-115.

Slochower, Harry. <u>Mythopoesis: Mythic Patterns in the Literary Classics.</u>
Detroit: Wayne State University Press, 1970.

Walker, Barbara G. <u>The Woman's Dictionary of Symbols and Sacred Objects.</u>
San Francisco: HarperSanFrancisco, 1988.

NOTE-TAKING

As you research your topic, you can take notes by writing down relevant quotes or paraphrasing information. You can use full sentences in your paraphrase or just take point-form notes. Make sure that you know where each piece of information originated, including the page number.

Slochower, p. 333
"Primitive man depended for his existence on the elements and the seasonal changes. He felt them to be divine powers that spelled drought or deluge, an arid or fertile soil — that is, death or life. They were not regarded as automatic events, but had to be adjured by elaborate ceremonies. The seasonal rituals were at once commemorations of what had happened and incantations that they happen again. The succession of the seasons represented a *crisis* and the entire community was engaged to meet this crisis by rituals of propitiation."

Eliade, p. 35
"A sacrifice, for example, not only exactly reproduces the initial sacrifice revealed by a god *ab origine*, at the beginning of time, it also takes place at that same primordial mythical moment; in other words, every sacrifice repeats the initial sacrifice and coincides with it. All sacrifices are performed at the same mythical instant of the beginning; through the paradox of rite, profane time and duration are suspended. And the same holds true for all repetitions."

Chetwynd, p. 345
- conscious life sacrificed by one generation (the dead) in order to be bestowed on the next (the living)

Chetwynd, p. 345
"Animals were substitutes for man in the ritual sacrifice, possibly chosen unconsciously for their symbolic significance: the bull for the physical side of procreation, the dove for the transmission of the powers of the feminine soul..."

Walker, p. 177
"the sacrifice most acceptable to the gods was man"; then, in later ages "for the man a horse was substituted, then an ox, then a sheep, then a goat, until at length it was found that the gods were most pleased with offerings of rice and barley."

Doane, p. 40
"Human offerings to the gods were at one time almost universal. In the earliest ages the offerings were simple, and such as shepherds and rustics could present. They loaded the altars of the gods with the first fruits of their crops, and the choicest products of the earth. Afterwards they sacrificed animals. When they had once laid it down as a principle that the effusion of the blood of these animals appeased the anger of the gods, and that their justice turned aside upon the victims those strokes which were destined for men, their great care was for nothing more than to conciliate their favour by so easy a method. It is the nature of violent desires and excessive fear to know no bounds, and therefore, when they would ask for any favour which they ardently wished for, or would deprecate some public calamity which they feared, the blood of animals was not deemed a price sufficient, but they began to shed that of men."

Frye, p. 106
"Ritual is not only a recurrent act, but an act expressive of a dialectic of desire and repugnance: desire for fertility or victory, repugnance to drought or to enemies."

Frye, p. 106
- pharmakos or sacrificed victim, who has to be killed to strengthen the others

http:// www. britannica.com/bcom/eb/article/6/0,5716,42396+1,00.html
- human sacrifice: the offering of the life of a human being to a deity
- related to blood as sacred life-force
- bloodless forms of killing (strangulation, drowning) used in some cultures
- killing a communion with a god
- offering of human life, as most valuable material for sacrifice, is also attempt at expiation
- sacrifices offered in return for victory in war
- killing of prisoners of war once common
- sacrifice for earth's fertility explains why most adopted by agricultural (not hunting) peoples

OUTLINING

When you have completed the research, you should make a reasonably detailed outline. This outline becomes the skeleton of your paper. It gives you an idea of how your ideas will be organized. Note that the example below lies somewhere between a scratch outline and a very developed outline. Your instructor may ask you to hand in an outline as partial fulfillment of the research project.

> Concept of sacrifice in Jackson's "The Lottery"
> Introduction
> Working thesis: examine nature and history of sacrifice and how it changes in The Lottery.
>
> Topic 1: Use dictionary definition of word sacrifice
> Bible episode: Abraham & Isaac
> Change from human to animal or vegetable: use Walker's passage
> Topic 2: What sacrifice entails
> Concept in the past: why important
> Use Slochower, to show man's need to sacrifice
>
> Topic 3: Sacrifice as ritual action
> Fertility and vegetation
> See quotes from Britannica and Chetwynd
> Relate this idea to "The Lottery": Old Man Warner & Tessie
>
> Topic 4: Degeneration of the concept of lottery/sacrifice
> Civilization changes rituals
> People impatient
> Use Frye about sacrifice
> Change purposes: violence and bloodlust in "The Lottery"
>
> Conclusion
> Ending in "The Lottery"
> How nature of sacrifice changed in the story.

PREPARING A DRAFT

In your first draft, you gather the information from your outline and write the essay. This version may be quite rough, lacking polished sentence structure. The main goal is to put the information down on paper to show the development of ideas.

> At the end of "The Lottery," Shirley Jackson has the townsfolk all throw stones at one of their neighbours, Tessie Hutchinson. Even her own young child, Davey, cast a pebble at his mom. They all do this to kill her and by stoning her to death they make a sacrifice of her to get harvest in the fall. This sacrifice seems important for the welfare of the community. However, Shirley Jackson makes a difference between the ritual and what the ritual has become. So, in order to understand the story and the ideas therein, we must look at the nature of human sacrifice, history of sacrifice and the changes in sacrifice in "The Lottery."
>
> Sacrifice is a religious act because from the dictionary the term comes from the Latin meaning holy and making, therefore holy action. In this case, human beings are killed for some purpose. We have the Bible story of Abraham and Isaac. In this story, God wanted to test Abraham's faith so God asked that Abraham sacrifice Isaac. But at the last minute, God told Abraham he could use an animal instead. What this story shows is that human beings were sacrificed and practised since Biblical times and longer ago. *In The Woman's Dictionary of Symbols and Sacred Objects*, B. Walker says: (see p. 177)
>
>> Sacrifice is something that a community must give up, even though it can't afford it, but must in order to survive. Sacrifice is absolutely necessary. In primitive days, all members of that tribe or community is important and useful; to lose one may lose the life of the community. From child to elders, all have something to contribute. However, these primitives see that there are many powerful and unfriendly forces about and they need to be appeased or else.
>
> Slowchower says: (see p. 333) By offering up one of their own, the community is saying that they mean business, and the gods might look kindly on that group.
>
> Sacrifice then is also related to vegetation and fertility. (Use Britannica quote). This concept is relevant in "The Lottery" in which Tessie Hutchinson is stoned to death. Old Man Warner repeats the saying about Lottery in June, corn be heavy soon. So Tessie must die in order that the others might live. (paraphrase from Chetwynd, 345). Without a sacrifice of blood and life, man's connection with nature and harvest is cut. Without food, every man, woman and child may die from starvation.

However, this concept of sacrifice gets lost as societies become more sophisticated and civilized. Shirley Jackson shows that the lottery ritual has transformed, even degenerated over the years until all the symbols of sacrifice—the box and the chits—lose significance. The long ceremony before the sacrifice is lost and becomes short. The townsfolk are impatient to end the ceremony so that they can start stoning the loser of the lottery, in this case, Tessie Hutchinson. According to Frye (148), the sacrificed victim has to be killed to strengthen the others, but Jackson says the only reinforcement in this situation is blood lust.

The people in "The Lottery" retain human sacrifice. But it is not to appease the gods of harvest and fertility. Sacrifice is not a serious business, at least not religious, anyway. They don't care about losing a valued member of society. They just want to have a chance to express their dark side—the desire to maim, hurt, and kill Tessie Hutchinson.

REVISING AND EDITING

After completing the first draft, you should leave it for a day or two that you will have a fresh eye when you revise it. Rushing too quickly into a second draft may cause you to lose objectivity.

We suggest that you consult the checklist in The Principles of Good Writing (pp. 381–382). In some cases, be prepared to revise several times to get the research paper right. Be critical with your work. Pay some attention to your quotations. Are they copied accurately? Do your citations follow the proper style? Proofread carefully.

THE FINAL DRAFT

The final essay with documentation follows. It is 810 words long. Although MLA style does not ask for a cover page, many professors prefer one. The format may vary slightly.

Sacrifice and Shirley Jackson's "The Lottery"
by
Joanna Lesage
90008765

for Prof. Engkent
EAC 150 TJ
October 6, 2002

In Shirley Jackson's classic story, "The Lottery," the neighbours, friends, and family of Tessie Hutchinson hurl stones and kill her without a qualm and without hesitation. The moment she draws the lot that would condemn her to death Tessie becomes a victim of an ancient ritual. She is the blood offering to appease the deities of the natural order and to bring about propitious harvest for the community. Like countless others before her, Tessie is the unwilling sacrifice. Jackson brings to the foreground the features of sacrifice, nature of sacrifice, and its relevance to the short story.

According to etymology, sacrifice comes from two Latin words *sacer* and *facere:* "holy" and "to make." In this sense, it is a religious ceremony in which human beings are offered up to the gods for some specific purpose. We find this in the Biblical story of "Abraham and Isaac" in which the patriarch is asked to give up his only male child on an altar as proof of his faith. Fortunately, this allegory ends happily: God changes his mind and is willing to accept an animal as burnt offering instead of Isaac. Nonetheless, what the story shows is that the slaughter of human life is acceptable and has been practised from the dawn of civilization. Barbara Walker makes this point: "the sacrifice most acceptable to the gods was man"; then, in later ages "for the man a horse was substituted, then an ox, then a sheep, then a goat, until at length it was found that the gods were most pleased with offerings of rice and barley." (177)

Sacrifice involves the giving up of something that a person or the community can ill-afford to lose. In short, sacrifice hurts, costs, and is necessarily given. In primitive society, every member of a village or tribe has a meaningful role to play. For example, young children can forage the surrounding areas for firewood or berries. Women can bear children so the village can grow and propagate. Men protect the village from other tribes and dangerous beasts, and more often hunt for food. And the old can dispense wisdom and the history of the tribe. To lose one productive member means reducing the chances of surviving the often harsh and capricious seasons of nature. Yet there are dangerous, powerful, and unfriendly forces surrounding primitive man that require appeasing. To him, they are gods. Slochower explains:

> Primitive man depended for his existence on the elements and the seasonal changes. He felt them to be divine powers which spelled drought or deluge, an arid or fertile soil—that is, death or life. They were not regarded as automatic events, but had to be adjured by elaborate ceremonies. (333)

By giving the gods something of great value, man impresses upon them his sincerity in the sacrifice. Then they just might let man survive another cycle of the seasons.

As a ritual, sacrifice has strong ties to vegetation and fertility especially among agricultural societies. "The relation of human sacrifice to the promotion of the earth's fertility may explain why the phenomenon has been most widely adopted by agricultural rather than by hunting or pastoral peoples." (Britannica) This explanation seems relevant in the light of Tessie Hutchinson's death in "The Lottery." Old Man Warner repeats the ritualistic axiom: "Used to be a saying about 'Lottery in June, corn be heavy soon.'" (Jackson 109). Accordingly then, one person must be sacrificed so that the whole community and the next generation may survive. (Chetwynd 345) Without this sacrifice of life and blood, man's link with nature and thus with harvest is severed. And without a bountiful harvest, every man, woman, and child would probably starve and die.

Unfortunately, as societies become more civilized and sophisticated, the meaning of the sacrifice becomes blurred, even forgotten. In "The Lottery," Jackson explains how the ritual has transformed, even degenerated over the years, when the concrete symbols—the black box and the chits—lose proper significance. Instead of long ceremonies with solemnity and fanfare, the ritual of sacrifice becomes brief. The meaning of sacrifice gives way to blood sport, communal purging of primitive savagery. This is evident from the innocent looking piles of stones the youngsters gathered together to the setting upon Tessie Hutchinson with stones for the ritualistic kill. Accordingly, the sacrificed victim has to be killed to strengthen the others. (Frye 148) Jackson says, however, the only strengthening here is bloodlust.

Unlike people in other places, the villagers in "The Lottery" never abandoned human sacrifice. To them, sacrifice is no longer to appease harsh gods for a better yield in the fields. To them, sacrifice is not a sacred, solemn act; it is not about losing a valued member. They forget its true purpose but retain its most basic impulse—the desire to hurt, maim, and kill.

Works Cited

Chetwynd, Tom. <u>A Dictionary of Symbols.</u> London: A Paladin Book, 1982.

Frye, Northrop. <u>Anatomy of Criticism: Four Essays.</u> Princeton, NJ: Princeton University Press, 1957.

<u>Holy Bible.</u> The King James I, Authorized Version, 1611.

"Human Sacrifice." <u>Encyclopaedia Britannica.</u> <u>1999-2000.</u> <u>Online.</u> 16 Aug. 2000. <http://www.britannica.com/bcom/eb/article/6/0,5716,42396+1,00.html>.

Jackson, Shirley. "The Lottery." <u>Fiction/Non-Fiction: A Reader and Rhetoric.</u> Ed. Garry Engkent and Lucia Engkent. Toronto: Harcourt Canada, 2001: 105-115.

Slochower, Harry. <u>Mythopoesis: Mythic Patterns in the Literary Classics.</u> Detroit: Wayne State University Press, 1970.

Walker, Barbara G. <u>The Woman's Dictionary of Symbols and Sacred Objects.</u> San Francisco: HarperSanFrancisco, 1988.

Chapter 7

TROUBLE SPOTS

This chapter reviews some common problems in essay writing and literature analysis. Some are minor (referring to the author by first name), and others are major (plagiarism). Students can refer to the topics that pose a problem for them.

CONFUSING NARRATOR AND AUTHOR

Do not assume that because the writer does not identify the narrator of the short story by a specific name, the narrator is the writer. For example, in "Greasy Lake" (p. 35), T. Coraghessan Boyle does not give a name to the "I" narrator, but Boyle is not talking about himself. He has created a character, speaking in the first-person point of view. You must distinguish between character/narrator and author.

In some stories, the dialogue will reveal the narrator's name. If not, you can call that character "the narrator," "the speaker," or "the unnamed character." Sometimes you can use other identifying characteristics. For example, you could refer to the narrator of "The Use of Force" (p. 216) as "the doctor," and the narrator of "Chickens for Christmas" (p. 63) as "the son."

Stories with first-person narration, and the narrator named, include: "The Cask of Amontillado" (p. 177), "Chickens for Christmas" (p. 63), "Greasy Lake" (p. 35), "The Loons" (p. 128), and "Mr. Truepenny's Book Emporium and Gallery" (p. 54). Stories with first-person narration, and the narrator unnamed, include: "My Financial Career" (p. 145), "An Ounce of Cure" (p. 153), "The Use of Force" (p. 216), and "We So Seldom Look on Love" (p. 86).

In articles and non-fiction prose, you can usually assume that the author is writing in his or her own voice.

REFERRING TO THE AUTHOR BY FIRST NAME

In essay writing, the accepted practice is to refer to writers by their family names rather than their given names. Using authors' first names gives your writing undue familiarity because you imply that you know the writers personally.

The first time you mention the author, give the whole name, such as "Katherine Govier." Afterwards, you can refer to her as "Govier" or use the pronoun "she." You can also refer to "the writer" or "the author," but don't use such terms too often because this usage can make your writing awkward.

Most of the time you can tell whether to use "he" or "she" by the author's first name. This is not foolproof, however, since some authors use initials, some first names can be either male or female (such as "Robin" or "Chris"), and some first names can be surprising. For instance, names such as "Evelyn," "Beverly," or "Ashley" used to be boys' names, but today they are generally given to girls. Moreover, if English is your second language, you may have trouble telling the gender implied by a name. If you are not sure of the author's gender, try to avoid using "he" or "she."

INADEQUATE DEVELOPMENT OF IDEAS

Writing essays involves making statements and supporting them. A general statement needs to be supported with explanation or specific examples. Always try to answer the implied question "Why?" or "How?"

The following example shows unexplained ideas:

> It is hard to believe that Grey Owl's masquerade was so successful, given that his writing and his appearance revealed his British origins. However, at that time Canadians were duped because of their lack of knowledge and their willingness to be misled. Thus, the masquerade was effective and was not publicly revealed until after Belaney's death.

In the following revision, the points are supported by specific information and explanation:

> It is hard to believe that Grey Owl's masquerade was so successful, given that his writing and his appearance revealed his British origins. However, at that time Canadians were duped because of their lack of knowledge and their willingness to be misled. First, even though Grey Owl did not look anything like an "Indian," the image most Canadians had of Native people was provided by Hollywood. They were used to non-Native actors portraying Indians and therefore accepted Grey Owl's appearance. Second, Canadians needed an international champion of nature and Aboriginals, and Grey Owl was their articulate "noble savage." After all, he made the

lecture circuit and he journeyed all the way to England to meet the King. Therefore, the masquerade was effective and was not publicly revealed until after Belaney's death.

In essays, paragraphs should be fully developed. One-sentence paragraphs are inadequate as part of the body of the essay. For an average expository paper, each paragraph should have at least 100–150 words or 4–10 sentences. Shorter paragraphs are sometimes used as transitions, but generally you should avoid writing one- or two-sentence paragraphs.

INADEQUATE INTRODUCTIONS AND CONCLUSIONS

Students often find the introduction and the conclusion paragraphs difficult to write. They have the body of the essay all laid out but don't know what to say at the beginning and the end. The introduction and conclusion should not contain points that belong in the body — statements that support the thesis. Introductions and conclusions are discussed in Chapter 3. If this area is still your weakness, here are some tips and examples.

If you are stuck on the introduction, write the body of the essay first, and come back to the introduction. Then you may have a better idea of what you need to include in or exclude from the opening paragraph.

Make sure you put your thesis statement at the end of your introduction. If you start with it, you will have nothing else to say in your introduction. However, your conclusion should start with your thesis statement — but expressed differently from its wording in the introduction.

Think of the introduction as a funnel, narrowing down from broad statements to your specific thesis. The conclusion is the opposite, starting with the narrow restatement of the thesis and leading to broader statements.

Here is an inadequate introduction, followed by an improved version:

> In both the article and short story, the two authors show that Christmas is a good idea even for non-Christians and that it is worth celebrating because it promotes goodwill and gets people together and makes them happy. Therefore, Christmas is good even if you are not Christian.

> Christmas has evolved from a religious holiday to a national one. Time off school and work is supplemented by parties and various festivities. While some Christians bemoan the secular nature of Christmas, non-

Christians criticize so much effort put into a holiday that is not theirs. However, other non-Christian viewpoints are shown in "Rediscovering Christmas" and "Chickens for Christmas," where both Almas Zakiuddin and Garry Engkent focus on the positive aspects of Christmas.

Here is an inadequate conclusion, followed by an improved version:

> Schoemperlen and Singer have shown that ex-lovers can be violent. This is an important issue.

> Both the fictional character in Schoemperlen's story and Singer are met with murderous rage from ex-lovers dedicated to killing them. Hell hath no fury like a man spurned. Women must be protected from the men whom they once loved and whose love has turned not only to hatred but also to violence. These stories help bring the issue into the public eye, and this is an important step toward some solutions.

SUMMARIZING THE PLOT

Writing literary essays involves analysis of the story. Sometimes students just retell the story and think they are analyzing it. The action of the story can be recounted, but this information should be given as supporting information. In other words, you should make a point and then show that something in the story supports the point.

You can avoid the problem by opening your paragraph with a topic sentence that reflects an opinion and makes a point. Second, select only the items or episodes that support the topic sentence. Third, reorder these supporting items in a logical or climactic sequence rather than in the same order as they appear in the article or story.

Here are illustrations using T. Coraghessan Boyle's "Greasy Lake" (p. 35). The assignment topic is "Show how the boys are immature in 'Greasy Lake.'"

Plot summary, which does not answer the question:

> When the three boys got bored of cruising the streets, they got drunk and drove to Greasy Lake. There they spotted a car parked near the lake and assumed that a friend was in it making out with a girl. They disturbed the

two people in the car, and one angry stranger then came out and started beating up on them. They thought they could handle one greasy guy. They were wrong. The narrator had to take a tire iron to the stranger's head, and he thought he had killed the guy. Anyway, the half-naked girl started screaming bloody murder, and the boys attempted to molest her. Suddenly, another car came by and the three boys scattered into the woods and the muddy lake. Luckily, the stranger came to, so the boys didn't kill anybody. Then the stranger and the others took out their anger on the car, which was actually the narrator's mother's Bel Air. In the morning, the strangers left Greasy Lake. The three boys returned to the car, which was seriously damaged: smashed windows, grill, headlights, ripped seats and everything. However, it was still drivable. Now the boys had to drive home and explain why the wagon was so damaged.

Analysis, answering the question:

The three 19-year-olds — Digby, Jeff, and the narrator — show their immaturity or lack of good judgment in three ways. First, they get drunk and start to look for trouble at Greasy Lake. Second, they take on a tough guy in a brawl because they mistakenly believe that three against one is excellent odds. Third, when the narrator almost kill the tough guy with a tire iron to the head, he should have immediately sobered up and realized his action was serious and criminal. Instead, the three boys try to rape the unconscious man's half-naked girlfriend. At each step the three 19-year-olds could have stopped themselves, but because they let their drunken bravado loose, they get deeper into trouble.

 In a literary essay, it is unnecessary to recap the story before you begin your analysis. You assume your reader — basically, your instructor — knows the plot or the particular episode. What that person does not know is your perspective, opinion, or interpretation of the story. Moreover, the instructor needs to know whether you have answered the assignment question. To this end, you explain how you "see" the narrative.
 Now, this rule is not carved in stone. In some cases, if you are writing to a larger audience who may not have read the story, you may wish to give a plot summary. Other times, your instructor may ask you to recap the story to show your understanding of it. In general, though, summarizing the plot does not answer the question in an essay or test.

OVER-QUOTING

Including a lot of quotations in your essay does not make the paper better; it merely makes it longer. It shows your instructor that you do not yet have the skill to select relevant information. Like your own writing, quoting must be concise and appropriate. This is true for both primary and secondary sources (the story itself and the research materials). Generally, students over-quote because they believe that the author's wording is preferable to their own, because they are padding their essay, or because they do not know how to paraphrase or summarize someone else's words.

Keep the length and number of quotations from the story or article to a minimum. Be judicious and select only the appropriate statements needed to illustrate or support your point. For example, a statement of fact rarely has to be quoted.

Rosie DiManno describes her background: "My parents are Italian immigrants and I was born in Toronto, grew up on Grace St. downtown, but didn't learn English until I started school" (p. 250). These facts are easily paraphrased:

> As the daughter of Italian immigrants, Rosie DiManno grew up in Toronto and learned English in school.

An explanation of summary and paraphrase can be found in Chapter 5.

PADDING

Padding a paper generally occurs when you don't have enough content in your essay. To meet the suggested word count, you may repeat points or stretch out ideas. This problem is similar to over-quoting, in which the writer extends a point or a comment for no practical purpose other than to fill up space.

Some telltale signs of padding include: wordiness, retelling the story, repeating ideas in different words, and going off topic entirely.

Here is an example of padding with unnecessary words:

> In the story "All the Years of Her Life," the character Alfred Higgins does not come to the realization that his mother, who has come to save him once

again from juvenile mistakes of his own making, is a woman frightened for her own future and for her family's and that she is tired of it all and getting old until he sees her alone in the kitchen trying to steady herself with a cup of tea. (77 words)

To improve this, cut unnecessary words:

In "All the Years of Her Life," Alfred Higgins does not realize that his mother is frightened, tired, and old until he sees her in the kitchen with an unsteady hand holding a cup of tea. (36 words)

To fix the problem of going off topic, be critical of your writing. An outline can help you stay focused. Here is an example of what happens when a writer drifts into something else:

In "The Story of Service," Jessica Mitford gives a very detailed procedure of how the human body is prepared for a funeral. With blood being sucked out and chemicals pumped into the arteries, even a living body would become a corpse. You stay dead. Yet, in the many horror movies, such embalmed corpses come to life: talk, walk, stalk, and think. In the movie *The Night of the Living Dead*, interred bodies in graves six feet deep easily open their locked coffins, rise out of the graves, and stalk helpless girls. Moreover, once killed, these newly made corpses also get up and go after other living people. How can you do that if your body is messed up from the inside?

Your instructor may give you guidelines for the length of your paper. You should try to meet the guidelines but not at the expense of handing in a poorly written paper. A word count is an approximation. Quality is always better than quantity.

To make sure your essay is as lean as it should be, ask yourself these questions:

- Can I say the same thing in fewer words? What is irrelevant information?
- Am I merely retelling the plot and not explaining my point? What is my point?
- Am I on topic? Is this example or illustration appropriate for the topic?
- Am I going in circles, saying the same thing?

FAILING TO MAKE YOUR POSITION CLEAR

The essays you write in college or university are expository papers; that is, you are explaining or commenting on a given topic and making your ideas clear to your instructor. In most cases, you are presenting an argument—a point of view that you take. Sitting on the fence does not make for an effective paper. You need to take a stand. Even if you are presenting the advantages and disadvantages of something, you should take a position that one outweighs the other.

While creating interest is acceptable, dramatizing your essay is not. Don't confuse analytical with creative (imaginative) writing. An analytical paper is not like a mystery novel where the detective reveals all at the end. Withholding essential information in the introduction until the conclusion is an improper strategy in an essay.

Here is an example of an improper thesis statement:

> Whether John Barber's "Grey Owl's Magnificent Masquerade" or Colin Ross's "The Story of Grey Owl" is closer to the truth about Archie Belaney (Grey Owl) is debatable. So I propose that we weigh both articles in the balance, and then I will tell you which side I am on.

In this introduction, the thesis is clear:

> Both John Barber in "Grey Owl's Magnificent Masquerade" and Colin Ross in "The Story of Grey Owl" explore the deception that Archie Belaney (Grey Owl) perpetrated on the Canadian people. Barber praises Belaney's efforts; Ross mocks the man. Ross makes a better case.

You must state your thesis, opinion, or idea in the beginning of your paper. Sitting on the fence on an issue in an expository paper is bad strategy. See the two pro and con essays by Raheel Raza and Keith Knight on religion in the classroom (pp. 296 and 294).

PLAGIARIZING AND CHEATING

Plagiarism is the act of deliberately using someone else's words or ideas in part or in total without proper acknowledgement and calling that work your own. The plagiarism could involve as little as one sentence copied from another writer or a whole essay downloaded from the Internet. Cheating is handing in someone else's work and claiming it to be your own. This includes getting a paper from another student or from an essay-writing service.

Sometimes students inadvertently cross the line between doing research and plagiarizing, between getting help and cheating. In some education systems, for example, students may copy authors' words as a model for their writing. Students who get help from tutors and friends may hand in work that has been so rewritten that it is no longer the student's own writing.

English instructors are knowledgeable about writing style and can identify work that has not been done by their students. The penalties can vary from getting zero on that assignment to being expelled from school.

It is important that your assignments be your own work, in your own words. In research papers, be sure to properly document and reference your sources. (See Chapters 5 and 6 for more information on using research.) When using the school's writing centre, be sure your tutor is not over-zealous in correcting your words.

USING CONVERSATIONAL STYLE

Although North American society has moved toward less formality in all spheres, it is important to be able to write in more formal styles when the occasion demands it. Just as you would not wear your blue jeans to a job interview, you should not use overly conversational style in academic, business, and technical writing.

Students who do not read much generally have more difficulty writing formal prose. They are used to speech, which is generally less formal than writing, and are unaware of the conventions of prose. They may pepper their essays with expressions like "Well, let's see" or use slang words like "jerk" and "ten bucks."

Below are some examples of conversational style followed by more formal styles:

Slang, idioms, and informal expressions:

> The kids were blown away that it only cost 12 bucks.
> The children were surprised that it only cost 12 dollars.

Conversational expressions:

> Well, let's see, it's unlikely to happen.
> It is unlikely to happen.

They're gonna put that in the new law.
They are going to put that in the new law.

Personal pronouns "I" and "you":

In my opinion, I think that school uniforms are good for high-school students.
School uniforms are good for high-school students.

When you read about all the stuff in toothpaste, you wonder why you ever put it in your mouth and grind it into your teeth.
Knowing all the ingredients in toothpaste, consumers may wonder why they ever brush with toothpaste.

Contractions:

He should've been paying more attention.
He should have been paying more attention.

Phrasal verbs:

He will check out the new proposal.
He will examine the new proposal.

Starting sentences with coordinate conjunctions ("and," "but," "for," "or," "so," "yet"):

And then she hired a new manager.
Then she hired a new manager.

But the initiative was underfunded.
However, the initiative was underfunded.

It is important to remember that informal expressions have a cumulative effect. Using idioms once or twice in your essay does not make it completely informal, but the more of these characteristics your essay has, the less formal your writing will tend to be.

Chapter 8
COMMON GRAMMAR PROBLEMS

This chapter provides a quick overview of some grammatical mistakes common in student writing. The problems are explained briefly and illustrated by correct and incorrect sentences. Incorrect sentences are marked with an asterisk (*).

This chapter is not meant to be a comprehensive explanation of grammar. We offer brief explanations, grouping some points together. We have also tried to simplify our use of grammar terminology, but some terms are unavoidable. For example, to understand why "but" and "however" cannot be used in the same way, students must understand that "but" is a conjunction and "however" is an adverb. If you need more detailed explanation for a particular grammar point, ask your teacher or consult a grammar book or usage guide.

MISUSE OF CONJUNCTIONS AND ADVERBS

A conjunction joins two sentences or parts of sentences. Adverbs modify a sentence or part of a sentence. In the following examples, conjunctions are in boldface, and adverbs are underlined:

> **If** I pick up the report before the meeting, <u>then</u> I'll have the time I need.
> **Although** we hired more staff, we could not complete the project by the deadline.
> We hired more staff, **but** we could not complete the project by deadline.
> <u>Unfortunately,</u> we had to re-enter the figures.
> I was summoned to his office <u>immediately,</u> **and** he read me the riot act.

Some adverbs are called conjunctive adverbs because they act almost like conjunctions:

> We hired more staff. <u>However,</u> we could not complete the project by deadline.
> We needed to get clearance, **so** we contacted him at home.
> We needed to get clearance. <u>Therefore,</u> we contacted him at home.

One of the easiest ways to tell these two parts of speech apart is to recognize that while conjunctions can only appear between the clauses or phrases they join, conjunctive adverbs can appear in different spots in a sentence, as in the following:

<u>However,</u> the students could not raise the money for their trip.
The students, <u>however,</u> could not raise the money for their trip.
The students could not raise the money for their trip, <u>however.</u>

"But" is a conjunction with the same meaning as "however," yet it could not be substituted for "however" in the second and third sentences above.

*The students, **but**, could not raise the money for their trip.
*The students could not raise the money for their trip, **but**.

Coordinate conjunctions are used to join two sentences or parts of sentences:

and, but, for, nor, or, so, yet

Examples:

I talked to Anne yesterday, **and** she explained the situation in detail.
We had to work with inadequate data, **yet** we managed to make a scenario.
You have to be tough **but** compassionate.

In formal English, coordinate conjunctions are not supposed to begin sentences. However, this rule is relaxed in less formal styles. The following sentences would be considered unacceptable in academic writing:

So I asked him to return the file.
But he said he didn't have it.
And he directed me to the other department.

Subordinate conjunctions can also be used to join sentences, but the subordinate conjunction begins a subordinate clause that is less important than the main clause:

after, although, as, because, even though, if, since, when, whereas, while

Examples:

While we were discussing his inability to focus, his cell phone rang.
Because we had so many problems on this project, we made a new plan of action.
We will establish new criteria **after** we have finished our post-mortem.

Conjunctive adverbs can be grouped according to their meaning:

Addition	also, finally, first, furthermore, in addition, moreover, next, second
Cause and effect	accordingly, as a result, consequently, therefore, thus
Comparison	likewise, similarly
Contrast	however, in contrast, instead, nevertheless, on the contrary, on the other hand, otherwise
Emphasis or clarity	in fact, indeed, in other words, of course, that is
Special features or examples	for example, for instance, in particular, mainly, specifically
Summary	in brief, in closing, in conclusion, in short, on the whole, to conclude, to summarize
Time relations	afterwards, at that time, earlier, in the meantime, lately, later, meanwhile, now, then

Incorrect use of conjunctions and conjunctive adverbs can lead to sentence fragments and run-ons (see below).

SENTENCE FRAGMENTS

Sentence fragments are incomplete sentences or non-sentences. A sentence requires a subject and a complete verb. An *-ing* verb form, for instance, is not a complete verb. A sentence starting with a subordinate conjunction (see above) must have a main clause. Here are some examples of sentence fragments followed by corrections.

*Being a sore loser.
Being a sore loser, she objected to Khaled's interpretation of the rules.

*Because it is due at the printer's tomorrow.
We must finish editing this report now because it is due at the printer's tomorrow.

*Although they would rather take the train.
Although they would rather take the train, they agreed to fly.

*The managers at the proposal meeting.
The managers are at the proposal meeting.
The managers at the proposal meeting could not agree on the next step.

*The report commissioned last year.
The report was commissioned last year.
The report commissioned last year is still not complete.

*Reason being he hadn't prepared for the exam.
He did not pass because he hadn't prepared for the exam.

*For example, people who talk all the time in class especially when something is being explained.
One example is people who talk all the time in class especially when something is being explained.
For example, some people talk all the time in class especially when something is being explained.

*After they completed the report and presented it to the vice-president, who was relieved that it didn't have any negative repercussions on his department, despite the fact that he had to shoulder some of the blame, because the debacle definitely started with faulty orders issued by his most trusted manager, who had been suffering from family problems at the time and could be excused for his lapse.

After they completed the report, they presented it to the vice-president, who was relieved that it didn't have any negative repercussions on his department, despite the fact that he had to shoulder some of the blame, because the debacle definitely started with faulty orders issued by his most trusted manager, who had been suffering from family problems at the time and could be excused for his lapse. *(Note that this sentence is still not well written, but it is now a grammatical sentence.)*

It should be noted that sentence fragments are often found in less formal kinds of writing, such as novels and magazine articles. However, you should avoid writing sentence fragments in essays.

RUN-ON SENTENCES

Run-on sentences are sentences that should be divided into more than one sentence, either for grammatical or stylistic reasons. While grammarians tend to distinguish between run-on sentences and comma splices (two sentences incorrectly connected with a comma), we will deal with both errors together.

A grammatical sentence contains a subject and a verb in the main clause. If the sentence has more than one clause, a conjunction is necessary.

> *I had to translate the document they had trouble with the technical language.
> *I had to translate the document, they had trouble with the technical language.
> I had to translate the document. They had trouble with the technical language.
> I had to translate the document because they had trouble with the technical language.

> *The music teacher was a skilled musician she lacked people skills.
> *The music teacher was a skilled musician however she lacked people skills.

The music teacher was a skilled musician; however, she lacked people skills.
The music teacher was a skilled musician, but she lacked people skills.
Although the music teacher was a skilled musician, she lacked people skills.

*Archie Belaney was not a real Aboriginal he took on the name of Grey Owl.
*Archie Belaney was not a real Aboriginal, he took on the name of Grey Owl.
Archie Belaney was not a real Aboriginal; he took on the name of Grey Owl.
Archie Belaney was not a real Aboriginal. He took on the name of Grey Owl.

To fix run-on sentences, make two separate sentences, use a semicolon, or add a conjunction.

VERB TENSES

Sometimes students get tangled up with verb tenses in their writing. While it is easy to say use the present for the present, the past for the past, and the future for the future, not all cases are that simple. However, the following pointers can help.

Use the simple present tense to describe facts and general situations:

The earth is round. The sky is blue. I love you.
Spider Robinson buys a new coffee maker every year.
Garage sales are popular in Canada.

Sometimes students use a continuous form or a simple future when a simple present tense would be more appropriate and concise:

The author is saying that we need technology to simplify our lives.
The author says that we need technology to simplify our lives. *(better)*

Students will often doze during lectures.
Students often doze during lectures.

Literature is often discussed in the present tense, even though the writer may be long dead:

Shakespeare tells the story of mad ambition in *Macbeth*.

Use the past tenses to describe past events with a definite past time:

The author grew up in an Italian neighbourhood of Toronto.
I bought a coffee maker at a garage sale.

The present perfect is a tense that straddles the past and present. It is used to describe past situations and experiences that are still true.

I have lived in Montreal for five years. *(I still live in Montreal.)*
I lived in Montreal for five years. *(I no longer live in Montreal.)*
I have never been skydiving. *(In the past, and still true now.)*
He has recently taken up skydiving.

In essays, it is important to avoid switching tenses unnecessarily:

*Professors are careful to avoid situations that may be perceived as favouritism or harassment. For this reason, they suggested students see counsellors instead of telling their professors about personal problems. They are not wanting to get too close to students. Male professors will try to avoid seeing female students alone.

Professors are careful to avoid situations that may be perceived as favouritism or harassment. For this reason, they suggest students see counsellors instead of telling their professors about personal problems. They do not want to get too close to students. Male professors try to avoid seeing female students alone.

PRONOUNS

A pronoun refers to a noun. It must agree with the noun in person and number (singular, plural).

The author discusses common problems with technology. **He** says **they** are due to poor design. *("He" refers to the author, and "they" refers to problems.)*

When you are referring to a company or an institution, it is tempting to use the pronoun "they" to refer to the people in the company. While this usage is accepted in less formal writing, it is grammatically incorrect.

*Harcourt Canada publishes a variety of college textbooks. They are always looking for new writers and new ideas.

Harcourt Canada publishes a variety of college textbooks. It is always looking for new writers and new ideas.

SPECIFIC PRONOUNS
its/it's

"It's" is a contraction of "it is" or "it has." Its is the possessive pronoun, meaning "belonging to it." If you can replace "it's" with "it is" or "it has," then you need the form with an apostrophe. If a word like "his" makes more sense as a replacement, you need the possessive form ("its"). You would not put an apostrophe in "his," so don't put one in "its."

It's time to take the dog for its shots.
It's been nice seeing you again.

whose/who's

"Who's" is a contraction of "who is" or "who has." "Whose" is the possessive pronoun, meaning "belonging to whom." This distinction is similar to "its/it's."

Whose coat is this?
Who's going to replace Hasim as vice-president?

their

"Their" is often misspelled or misused as "there" or "they're." "Their" is the possessive pronoun, showing that something belongs to "them."

Jane and Kyoko should pay attention to their own work.

Another error is using "their" for singular subjects. However, this grammatical error is commonly found and is somewhat controversial. Some writers accept this usage because it is widespread in speech, it can be found in the works of famous writers such as Jane Austen and Charles Dickens, and it solves the "he/she" problem in pronoun reference. In essay writing, however, you should try to avoid this usage.

*Each student must bring their own sleeping bag.
Each student must bring his own sleeping bag. *(Grammatically correct, but might be considered sexist.)*

Each student must bring his or her own sleeping bag. *(Works for a single use, but it can be tedious saying "his or her" repeatedly.)*
*Each student must bring his/her own sleeping bag. *(Slashed words are not acceptable in essays.)*
All students must bring their own sleeping bags. *(The use of the plural avoids the problem.)*

Some writers solve the problem by alternating between male and female pronouns in their prose, but this should not be done within a single paragraph.

you
The pronoun "you" has two meanings in English. It can refer to the audience (the reader, the listener) directly, or it can refer to people in general.

As you can see in Singer's article, battered wives have a hard time escaping the wrath of determined ex-husbands and lovers.

When you are young, you think you know everything about the world, and then as you mature you realize how little you know.

In essay writing, avoid using "you." It makes your essay to conversational. Use the third person.

As is evident in Singer's article, battered wives have a hard time escaping the wrath of determined ex-husbands and lovers.

When people are young, they think they know everything about the world, and then as they mature they realize how little they know.

MISPLACED MODIFIERS

One kind of misplaced modifier is the dangling participle, an adjective form of the verb that is modifying the wrong noun.

*Breathing heavily, the race was stopped finally.
Breathing heavily, we stopped running the race.

In the above example, the participle "breathing" is describing the race in the first sentence. It should, of course, describe the people. Relative clauses (beginning with "who," "which," "that") should be as close as possible to the noun they modify.

> *He wanted to eliminate the identification test from the final grade, which the students found too difficult.
> He wanted to eliminate the identification test, which the students found too difficult, from the final grade.

MIXED CONSTRUCTION

When your sentence unnecessarily switches from active to passive voice, you have made a grammatical error.

> *John read the novel and this response was written by him.
> John read the novel and wrote this response.

Strive to write in the active voice. It is more clear and concise.

PARALLEL STRUCTURE

When parts of the sentence are joined by "and," they should have the same grammatical structure.

> *Her goals were to head the task force, eliminate unnecessary steps in the process, and proving her worth to the company.
> Her goals were to head the task force, eliminate unnecessary steps in the process, and prove her worth to the company.

> *Robin likes reading philosophy, attending art exhibitions, and chess.
> Robin likes reading philosophy, attending art exhibitions, and playing chess.

PUNCTUATION

APOSTROPHES

Incorrect apostrophes are epidemic in written English. You can see incorrect usage in signage and publications. Apostrophes are used to indicate possession, contractions, and rare plural forms in which the *-s* alone would be difficult to read. They are not used for regular plurals or verb forms.

*The Johnson's are hosting a reception for the newcomer's.
The Johnsons are hosting a reception for the newcomers.
The Johnsons' party was meticulously planned.

COMMAS

The comma has specific uses in writing: it separates items in a series, it sets off interjections and words in apposition, and in a periodic sentence, it distinguishes the dependent clause from the independent.

The comma, however, should never be used to separate subject and verb:

*George Orwell, was badgered into shooting the elephant by the crowd of spectators.
George Orwell was badgered into shooting the elephant by the crowd of spectators.

The comma should never be a breath stop:

*I think, I can go to, the store once I, catch my, breath.
I think I can go to the store once I catch my breath.

The comma should not be used to join two complete sentences:

*The students were asking for a public debate, the principal did not allow it
The students were asking for a public debate; the principal did not allow it.

SEMICOLONS AND COLONS

The semicolon acts like the coordinate conjunction "and" in most cases. It separates two complete sentences.

The students enjoyed the field trip; however, they did not learn much about mushrooms.

Do not confuse the semicolon with the colon. The colon sets up an example or a list.

Everything we have for the party is here: salads, cold cuts, rolls, butter, casserole, plastic forks, and paper plates.

These are the books you must read this semester: *Lord of the Rings, The Magic Mountain, Finnigan's Wake,* and *War and Peace.*

HYPHENS AND DASHES

The hyphen is used within a word. It is used for compound words (such as *Indo-Canadian, best-kept secret, co-author*) and to break a word into syllables if it does not fit on a line. The hyphen is a character on the standard keyboard.

The dash, a longer stroke than a hyphen, is not on the regular keyboard; however, it can be represented by two hyphens or with an em-dash, which is available as a special character in word-processing software. (Em-dashes are the width of a the letter *m*. The en-dash is width of the letter *n* and is used with numbers, as in "1998–1999.") The em-dash is also referred to as a parenthetical dash. It is used to emphasize something or to allow the writer to go off topic for a moment before returning to the topic.

When we were kids, George and I—we know better now—used to put our ears to the railway tracks to listen for an approaching train.

SUBJECT–VERB AGREEMENT

Students sometimes make errors in verb forms when they do not pay attention to the grammatical subject of the sentence. In the following examples, the grammatical subject is in boldface and the verb is underlined:

*One of the students are missing.
One of the students is missing.

*The class that sold the most pizzas are going to get a bonus.
The **class** that sold the most pizzas is going to get a bonus.

*The plumbers in the organization that was formed by the previous head of the union is left out of the loop.
The **plumbers** in the organization that was formed by the previous head of the union are left out of the loop.

WRONG WORDS

Many errors in writing are the result of confusion between words that sound the same or are otherwise similar. Here is a list of some commonly confused words. If you are not sure of the difference, check your dictionary.

accept, except
advice, advise
affect, effect
a lot, allot
are, our, hour
assure, insure, ensure
choose, choice, chose
complement, compliment
cite, sight, site
does, dose
hear, here
hole, whole
its, it's
knew, new
know, no, now
loose, lose
passed, past
plain, plane
quiet, quite
right, write, rite
scene, seen
stationary, stationery
than, then
their, there, they're
though, thought
to, too, two
threw, through
weak, week
wear, were, where, we're
weather, whether
which, witch
who's, whose
you're, your

Credits

David Arnason, "A Girl's Story," from *The Happiest Man in the World and Other Stories* (Vancouver: Talonbooks, 1989), pp. 157–164.

Isaac Asimov, "They Fun They Had," from *Earth Is Room Enough: Science Fiction Tales of Our Own Planet,* (London: Abelard, 1957), pp. 146–148. Reprinted by permission of the Estate of Isaac Asimov c/o Ralph M. Vicinanza, Ltd.

John Barber, "Grey Owl's Magnificent Masquerade," *The Globe and Mail,* September 30, 1999, p. A17. Reprinted with permission of *The Globe and Mail.*

Brian Bethune, "Truth and Consequences," *Maclean's,* October 4, 1999, pp. 58–59.

David Bodanis, "Toothpaste," from *The Secret House: 24 Hours in the Strange and Unexpected World in Which We Spend Our Nights and Days* (New York: Simon & Schuster, 1986), pp. 17–19.

T. Coraghessan Boyle, "Greasy Lake," from *Greasy Lake and Other Stories.* Copyright © 1979, 1981, 1982, 1983, 1984, 1985 by T. Coraghessan Boyle. Used by permission of Viking Penguin, a division of Penguin Books USA Inc.

Bill Bryson, "Junk Food Heaven," from *Notes from a Big Country* (Toronto: Doubleday Canada Limited, 1998), pp. 71–74.

Morley Callaghan, "All the Years of Her Life," from *Morley Callaghan's Stories* (Toronto: Macmillan of Canada, 1959), pp. 1–6.

Charles De Lint, "Mr. Truepenny's Book Emporium and Gallery," from *The Ivory and the Horn,* by Charles De Lint (New York: Tom Doherty Associates, 1995), pp. 46–52.

Rosie DiManno, "Growing Up on Grace," *The Toronto Star,* June 28, 1997, pp. C1, C4. Reprinted with permission — The Toronto Star Syndicate.

Fred Donnelly, "The Golden Years of Electronic Helps," *The Globe and Mail*, February 23, 1998, p. A18.

Garry Engkent, "Chickens for Christmas," *Storyteller*, Summer 2000, pp. 21–24. Reprinted by permission of the author.

Peter Farb and George Armelagos, "The Patterns of Eating," from *Consuming Passions: The Anthropology of Eating*. Copyright © 1980 by The Estate of Peter Farb. Reprinted by permission of Houghton Mifflin Company. All rights reserved.

Northrop Frye, "Don't You Think It's Time to Start Thinking?" from *Reading Writing*, 2nd ed. Edited by Geri Dasgupta and Jon Redfern (Toronto: Nelson, 1998), pp. 251–252. Originally published in *The Toronto Star*, January 25, 1986. Used by permission of the Estate of Northrop Frye.

Charles Gordon, "The Joys of Keeping in Touch, Virtually," *Maclean's*, December 15, 1997, p. 9.

Shinan Govani, "Don't Say Cheese!" *The Globe and Mail*, September 15, 1999, p. A22. Reprinted by permission of the author.

Katherine Govier, "The Immaculate Conception Photography Gallery," from *The Immaculate Conception Photography Gallery (Stories)* by Katherine Govier, Vintage Canada, 2000.

Barbara Gowdy, "We So Seldom Look on Love," from *We So Seldom Look on Love* (Toronto: Somerville House Books Ltd., 1992). Copyright © 1992 Barbara Gowdy. With permission of the author.

Wayne Grady, "Canadian Tire Money," *Saturday Night*, July/August 1999, p. 22.

Marshall W. Gregory and Wayne C. Booth, "What Is an Idea?" from *The Harper and Row Reader: Liberal Education Through Reading and Writing*, 3rd ed. (Toronto: HarperCollins Publishers, 1992), pp. 15–18.

Lawrence Hill, "So What Are You, Anyway?" from *Fiery Spirits & Voices*. Published by Harper*Perennial* Canada. © 1992 by Lawrence Hill.

Pico Iyer, "Of Weirdos and Eccentrics," *Time,* January 18, 1988. Copyright © 1988 Time Inc. Reprinted with permission.

Shirley Jackson, "The Lottery," from *The Lottery.* Copyright © 1948, 1949 by Shirley Jackson, and copyright renewed © 1976, 1977 by Lawrence Hyman, Barry Hyman, Mrs. Sarah Webster, and Mrs. Joanne Schnurer. Reprinted by permission of Farrar, Straus & Giroux, LLC.

Keith Knight, "Our Father Who Art in Classrooms: No," *The Toronto Star,* September 18, 1999, p. L14. Reprinted by permission of the author.

Margaret Laurence, "The Loons," from *A Bird in the House* (Toronto: McClelland & Stewart Limited, 1974), pp. 114–127. Used by permission, McClelland & Stewart, Inc. *The Canadian Publishers.*

Stephen Leacock, "How We Kept Mother's Day," from *The Leacock Roundabout: A Treasury of the Best Works by Stephen Leacock* (New York: Dodd, Mead & Company, 1972), pp. 32–35. "My Financial Career" from *The Leacock Roundabout: A Treasury of the Best Works by Stephen Leacock* (New York: Dodd, Mead & Company, 1972), pp. 11–13.

Jessica Mitford, "The Story of Service," from *The American Way of Death Revisited* (New York: Alfred A. Knopf, 1998), pp. 41–53. Copyright © 1998 by the Estate of Jessica Mitford. Reprinted by permission of Alfred A. Knopf, a Division of Random House Inc.

Alice Munro, "An Ounce of Cure," from *Dance of the Happy Shades and Other Stories* (Toronto: McGraw-Hill, 1968), pp. 75–88. Reprinted by permission of The Writers Shop. All rights reserved.

Patricia Nurse, "One Rejection Too Many." © 1978 by Davis Publications, Inc.; first published in *Isaac Asimov's Science Fiction Magazine,* July/August 1978.

Tim O'Brien, "The Man I Killed," from *The Things They Carried: Haunting Stories of the Vietnam War.* Copyright © 1990 by Tim O'Brien. Reprinted by permission of Houghton Mifflin Co./Seymour Lawrence. All rights reserved.

"Shooting an Elephant" by George Orwell (Copyright © 1936 by George Orwell) by permission of Bill Hamilton as the Literary Executor of the Estate of the Late Sonia Brownell Orwell and Secker & Warburg Ltd.

Kurt Preinsperg, "Have Wheels, Will Go A-Wooing," *The Globe and Mail,* April 1, 1997, p. A14. Reprinted by permission of the author.

Raheel Raza, "Our Father Who Art in Classrooms: Yes," *The Toronto Star,* September 18, 1999, p. L14. Reprinted by permission of *The Toronto Star.*

Spider Robinson, "I'll Decide What's Broken," *The Globe and Mail,* August 26, 1999, pp. T1, T3. © 1999 by Spider Robinson. All rights reserved.

Colin Ross, "The Story of Grey Owl," *The Compass* 5 (1979): 79–83.

Diane Schoemperlen, "Red Plaid Shirt," from *The Man of My Dreams* (Toronto: Macmillan of Canada, 1990), pp. 178–192. Reprinted by permission of the Bella Pomer Agency Inc.

Sam Selvon, "Ralphie at the Races" from *West of Fiction.* Edited by Leah Flater, Aritha van Herk, and Rudy Wiebe (Edmonton: NeWest Press, 1983), pp. 204–213.

Ellen Singer, "Exiled in Paradise," *The Globe and Mail,* January 10, 2000, p. R1.

Lynn Van der Water, "Possessed by Stuff" *The Globe and Mail,* August 13, 1999, p. A18. Reprinted by permission of the author.

Alice Walker, "Am I Blue?" from *Living by the Word: Selected Writings, 1973–1987* copyright © 1986 by Alice Walker, reprinted by permission of Harcourt, Inc.

Margaret Wente, "The End of Manual Labour," *The Globe and Mail,* September 4, 1999, p. D11. Reprinted with permission from *The Globe and Mail.*

William Carlos Williams, "The Use of Force," from *The Doctor Stories* (New York: New Directions Publishing, 1938).

Almas Zakiuddin, "Rediscovering Christmas," *The Globe and Mail,* December 23, 1999, p. A24. Reprinted by permission of the author.

Author and Title Index

Aesop, 19
All the Years of Her Life, 47
Am I Blue?, 349
Armelagos, George, 262
Arnason, David, 22

Barber, John, 232
Bethune, Brian, 236
Bodanis, David, 241
Booth, Wayne C., 283
Boyle, T. Coraghessan, 35
Bryson, Bill, 245

Callaghan, Morley, 47
Canadian Tire Money, 280
Cask of Amontillado, The, 177
Chickens for Christmas, 63
Cowherd, The, 73

De Lint, Charles, 54
DiManno, Rosie, 250
Donnelly, Fred, 258
Don't Say Cheese!, 276
Don't You Think It's Time to Start Thinking?, 268

End of Manual Labour, The, 355
Engkent, Garry, 63, 73
Exiled in Paradise, 337

Farb, Peter, 262
Fox and the Grapes, The, 19
Frye, Northrop, 268
Fun They Had, The, 30

Girl's Story, A, 22
Golden Years of Electronic Helps, The, 258
Gordon, Charles, 272
Govani, Shinan, 276
Govier, Katherine, 76
Gowdy, Barbara, 86
Grady, Wayne, 280
Greasy Lake, 35
Gregory, Marshall W., 283
Grey Owl's Magnificent Masquerade, 232
Growing Up on Grace, 250

Have Wheels, Will Go A-Wooing, 322
Hill, Lawrence, 99
How We Kept Mother's Day, 140

I'll Decide What's Broken, 326
Immaculate Conception Photography Gallery, The, 76
Iyer, Pico, 289

Jackson, Shirley, 105
Jacobs, W.W., 116
Joys of Keeping in Touch, Virtually, The, 272
Junk Food Heaven, 245

Knight, Keith, 294

Laurence, Margaret, 128
Leacock, Stephen, 140, 145

Loons, The, 128
Lottery, The, 105
Luke 15:11–32, 150

Man I Killed, The, 170
Mitford, Jessica, 301
Monkey's Paw, The, 116
Mr. Truepenny's Book Emporium and Gallery, 54
Munro, Alice, 153
Munro, H.H., 186
My Financial Career, 145

Nurse, Patricia, 165

O'Brien, Tim, 170
Of Weirdos and Eccentrics, 289
One Rejection Too Many, 165
Open Window, The, 186
Orwell, George, 314
Ounce of Cure, An, 153
Our Father Who Art in Classrooms: No, 294
Our Father Who Art in Classrooms: Yes, 296

Patterns of Eating, The, 262
Poe, Edgar Allan, 177
Possessed by Stuff, 345
Preinsperg, Kurt, 322
Prodigal Son, The, 150

Ralphie at the Races, 205
Raza, Raheel, 296
Red Plaid Shirt, 191
Rediscovering Christmas, 359
Robinson, Spider, 326
Ross, Colin, 330

Saki, 186
Schoemperlen, Diane, 191
Selvon, Sam, 205
Shooting an Elephant, 314
Singer, Ellen, 337
So What Are You, Anyway?, 99
Story of Grey Owl, The, 330
Story of Service, The, 301

Toothpaste, 241
Truth and Consequences, 236

Use of Force, The, 216

Van der Water, Lynn, 345

Walker, Alice, 349
We So Seldom Look on Love, 86
Wente, Margaret, 355
What Is an Idea?, 283
Williams, William Carlos, 216

Zakiuddin, Almas, 359

Subject Index

Active voice, 396, 449
Adverbs, 440–43
American Psychology Association (APA) style, 411, 417–18
Analysis, 396–97
Apostrophes, 449–50
Articles, citing in bibliography, 416
Audience, 375–76, 397
Author
    references to, 430–31
    distinguishing from narrator, 430

Bibliographies, 411, 415–17, 420
Books
    citing in bibliography, 416
    source materials, 402
Brainstorming, 368–70
Business writing, 380–81

Canadian reference materials, 401
Canadian spelling, 379
Cheating, 438
Checklist, essay, 381–82
Chicago Manual of Style, 411, 418–19
Citations, 411–12
Clarity, 372, 376, 395, 397, 437
Coherence, 377
Colons, 450–51
Commas, 450
Conciseness, 372, 376–77
Conclusions, 388, 432–33
Conjunctions, 440–43
Conversational style, 380–81, 438–39

Dangling participles, 448–49
Dashes, 451
Defining terms, 395
Definition and classification, 395–96
Dictionaries, 379, 380

Editing, 372–73, 405–406
Electronic sources
    citing in bibliography, 416–17
    keyword search techniques, 401–402
Encyclopedias, 402
Endnotes, 411
Essay types, 389–98
    argument, 391–92
    cause/effect, 394–95
    compare/contrast, 392–94
    description, 390
    illustration, 390–91
    narration, 389
Essay writing, 383–98
    five-paragraph essay structure, 385–88
    paragraphs, 383–85
    topic sentences, 385
Exam essay questions, guidelines, 397–98

Films, citing in bibliography, 417
First drafts, 371–72
First-person narration, 430
Footnotes, 411
Formal vs. informal writing styles, 380–81, 438–39

SUBJECT INDEX

Grammar
   common problems, 440–52
   importance of, 377–78
Grammar checkers (computer software), 378

Hyphens, 451

Instructional writing, 396–97
Internet
   citing in bibliography, 416
   searching techniques, 401–402
   source materials, 404
Introductions, 387–88, 432–33

Journals, 403

Libraries, 401

Magazines, 403
Modern Languages Association (MLA) style, 411
   bibliographies, 415–17
   quotations, 412–14
   references, 414–15
Modifiers, 448–49

Newspapers, 403–404
Note-taking, 405, 421–22

Outlines, 370–71, 423

Padding, 435–36
Paragraphs, 383–85, 432
Parallel sentence structure, 449
Paraphrasing, 406–407
Passive voice, 396, 449
Periodicals, 403
Plagiarism, 437–38
Planning research, 400

Plot summaries, 433–35
Primary source materials, 399
Process descriptions, 396–97
Pronouns, 446–48
Proofreading, 373–74
Punctuation, 449–51
Purpose, 375–76

Quotations, 407, 412–14, 435

Reference information, 401, 405
References, 411, 414–15
Research, 399–410
Revising, 372–73, 405–406
Run-on sentences, 444–45

Sample essay, 419–29
Search terms, 401–402
Secondary source materials, 399
Semicolons, 450–51
Sentence fragments, 443–44
Sentence structure, 378, 449
Source materials, 400–404
Spell checkers (computer software), 379
Spelling, 379
Subject-verb agreement, 451
Summarizing, 407–10

Thesaurus, 380
Thesis statements, 386–87, 437
Topic selection, 400
Topic sentences, 285
Transition markers, 377, 442

Verbs
   active, 396, 449
   passive, 396, 449
   subject-verb agreement, 451
   tenses, 445–46

Videos, citing in bibliography, 417
Vocabulary, 379–80

Words
    commonly confused words, 452
    connotation and denotation of, 380
    non-essential, 377, 435–36
    transition markers, 377, 442
    vocabulary, 379–80
"writer's block," 368
Writing principles, 375–82
Writing process, 367–74
Writing style, 380–81, 438–39